History of Puerto Rico

A Panorama of Its People

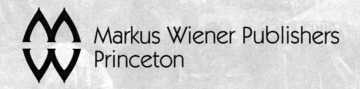

Markus Wiener Publishers
Princeton

History of Puerto Rico

FERNANDO PICÓ

For information write to:
Markus Wiener Publishers
231 Nassau Street, Princeton, NJ 08542
www.markuswiener.com

Library of Congress Cataloging-in-Publication Data
Picó, Fernando.
  [Historia general de Puerto Rico. English]
  History of Puerto Rico : a panorama of its people / Fernando Picó.
  Includes bibliographical references.
  ISBN-13: 978-1-55876-371-5 paperback
  ISBN-10: 1-55876-371-6 paperback
  ISBN-13: 978-1-55876-370-8 hardcover
  ISBN-10: 1-55876-370-8 hardcover
     1. Puerto Rico—History. I. Title.
  F1971.P5313 2005
  972.95—dc22   2005045511

Markus Wiener Publishers books are printed in the United States of America
on acid-free paper, and meet the guidelines for permanence and durability
of the Committee on Production Guidelines for Book Longevity of the
Council on Library Resources.

Contents

List of maps vi

Weights and Measures vi

Preface to the English Edition vii

Preface to the First Spanish Edition ix

1. The Formation of the Land of Puerto Rico 1

2. Amerindian Societies 9

3. Backgrounds of the New Settlers of Puerto Rico 19

4. The Conquest of Boriquén 29

5. Agriculture and Cattle Raising in the Sixteenth and
Seventeenth Centuries 51

6. Puerto Rico in the Struggle for Commercial Hegemony
in the Sixteenth- and Seventeenth-Century Caribbean 67

7. Corsairs and Settlers, 1700–1765 95

8. Political Transformations, 1765–1823 113

9. Faces New and Old: The Population, 1765–1823 137

10. The Transition to Monoculture, 1765–1823 153

11. A Slaveholding Society, 1824–1868 171

12. The Hour of the Mountains, 1868–1898 199

13. Puerto Rico Becomes a Vast Sugar Plantation 231

14. The New Industrial and Urban Order, 1940–1980 265

15. Changes in Perceptions and Values from the 1960s to 2005 293

16. From Alternation in Power to Shared
Government, 1980–2005 305

Notes 315

Selected Bibliography 347

Maps

Map 1: The Caribbean in the Sixteenth Century xiv
Map 2: Europe during the Spanish conquest of America 28
Map 3: Africa in the Fifteenth Century:
    main ecological zones and important cities of the west 170
Map 4: Puerto Rico: Major Towns and Cities 264

Weights and Measures

1 arroba = 25 pounds
1 quintal = 100 pounds
1 ton = 80 arrobas or 20 quintales = 2000 pounds
1 caballería = 200 cuerdas
1 cuerda = 0.97 of an acre
1 cuadro = 1/4 cord

16th Century Currency:

A maravedí is the smallest denomination. Ruth Pike estimates that it was equivalent to 1/6 of a U.S. cent in 1980

1 cuarto = 4 maravedís
1 real = 34 maravedís
1 ducado = 375 maravedís (before 1537)
1 peso = 450 maravedís
1 doblón = 2,720 maravedís (80 reals)

19th Century Currency:

1 real = 34 maravedís
1 peso = 8 reals
1 escudo = 1/2 peso

Preface to the English Edition

Over the last hundred years historians have written four different types of histories of Puerto Rico. Some, like Salvador Brau, Cayetano Coll y Toste, and Lidio Cruz Monclova, came to the writing of history from different professional backgrounds. They wanted Puerto Ricans to feel proud of themselves, and in their work chose to focus on famous people and the key moments which they believe to have shaped the identity of Puerto Ricans. Their narratives have been punctuated by moral reflections and grave warnings. Their efforts to enlighten us led them to construct an island where, more often than not, disastrous events were seen as the result of decisions made in North Atlantic capitals.

The second kind of history is that written by professional historians who trained at universities abroad and who teach in Puerto Rico or elsewhere. They have sought to understand how the island's institutions and political processes were part of the overall pattern of the Western Hemisphere. Their usual point of departure has been a particular institution or a period which has been well-researched elsewhere, but that is little understood from the perspective of our own historiography. The island has therefore been represented as being in continual interaction with the prevailing norms, transactions and forces of the Western world. Central to these endeavors is the conviction that history can provide rational explanations and analogies for what we have experienced as a society.

A third type of Puerto Rican history has emphasized the economic and social processes which have helped to shape us a people. It is characterized by careful research into local sources, a sharp eye for discerning the conflicts and cracks in our social fabric, and a keen desire to illustrate the interaction between external influences and local responses to these. This history has mistrusted institutional historians' certainty that the laws, regulations, and directives from abroad were continuously in operation in our country, but it has been aware of the enormous effect that the global market economy has had on our daily lives.

A fourth kind of history chooses to examine the historians' own ambivalent practices, their hidden political and social agendas, and their efforts to construct imaginary entities which become actors in their narratives. It insists that history is a literary genre that uses the tools and approaches of the literary workshop in unacknowledged ways. There is an urgent need to write a history of these practices and of the succession of discourses which have produced the history of Puerto Rico, so as to understand the ways in which we have come to view our past.

Writing Puerto Rican history today requires us to address the claims made by all four currents of our historiography. It seemed simpler a generation ago, when I first taught Puerto Rican history at Fordham as a visiting instructor. The fact that the perspectives of our historiography have changed is an indication of the energy and dedication which our historians, both in Puerto Rico and abroad, have applied to the study of our common discipline. My hope is that translating and updating this book will make the ongoing research by our scholars available to the English-speaking public and enable us to participate in the wider debates on Caribbean and Latin American History.

I thank Markus Wiener for his interest in making this work available in English, and I am grateful to Christine Ayorinde and Susan Lorand for their editorial work on this edition. I also would like to express my gratitude to my editor, Carmen Rivera Izcoa of Ediciones Huracán, who published the text in Spanish.

Preface to the First Spanish Edition

One afternoon in September, 1970, while I was cataloguing thirteenth-century French cathedral canons in New York City, I received a phone call from Joseph Fitzpatrick, the Jesuit sociologist at Fordham University. He wanted to ask me a favor. The previous April a group of Puerto Rican students at Fordham had occupied the University President's office to press their request for a Puerto Rican History course at the Rose Hill campus. In keeping with its liberal reputation, the university had promised them a course for the following September. Now, two days before classes were due to start, the professor they had hired for the course informed them he was going to work in another part of the state. Would I teach a course on Puerto Rican History?

With all the modesty and scruples appropriate to a medievalist who had recently received his doctorate, I accepted. The following day the committee of students who had requested the course interviewed me, and explained what they wanted. I went to "La Librería" in Manhattan, the only place in New York at the time where one could find a variety of Puerto Rican books. I bought a whole shelf. And putting aside the contentious thirteenth-century canons, I began to read.

I had never taken a university course on the History of Puerto Rico. In high school, a North American recently arrived to Puerto Rico, Tom Hanrahan, had given the class and as course requirement he had each one of us make a presentation on some topic and write a paper on it. Mine was on the assigned subject of Spanish explorers in the southwestern United States. It seemed incredible that, with such a shaky background, I would be teaching a Puerto Rican History course at Fordham.

Ignorance, as they say, is *atrevida* (bold). But sometimes it is something more. It is curious. I was coming to Puerto Rican History with many questions; those of my prospective students as well as my own. But I did not always find the answers to my questions in books. The books would detail Columbus' journeys; they would give day-by-day accounts of what happened during the English attacks on Puerto Rico; they would describe the institutional mechanisms designed to regulate Puerto Rican life in centuries past. But neither I nor my students were interested in these things. Although most of them did not read Spanish, they felt themselves to be Puerto Rican. The country which most of them had only visited at Christmas time gave them their identity.

I have learned from all my students, but I learned more from these than from any others. I learned that in the process of getting to know the past, the most important thing is asking good questions. They were so keen to learn about the history of Puerto Rico that they constantly challenged me. For them the course was not a three-credit class to fill an academic record. it represented the fundamental university experience. In their classes on Shakespeare and Ancient Philosophy they learned what they needed in order to pass examinations, but in Puerto Rican history they came in order to find out who they were. I had to show them on the map where Moca was, but for a particular student, Moca was the place of origin, their grandfather's town, the place where their cousins lived, where, at a time when there may have been pirates and princesses, coffee was harvested and the Magi were awaited.

With those students I came to know Moca in that way, as a marvelous, legendary place. Books used to specify how many inhabitants, which dates, or the amount of votes counted in Moca, Ceiba, Salinas, and Barceloneta on this or that statistical column. And I, who, like Sancho Panza, had been there, did not know that those towns were more than just administrative units and electoral precincts. But I learned from the students who came, worn out from traveling by subway or on the Bronx and Manhattan buses, that these were enchanted places. In a white-haired and infirm old lady on the sidewalk I was able to recognize an exiled *cacica* from Guamaní and in a rock musician, the heir to enchanted palaces in Camuy. It was a necessary stage of falling in love with my country's history.

Too many years have passed since then. I kept my faith with the thirteenth-century canons. Utuado took hold of me, I came to know Caimito. And one fine day, like that on which Alonso Quijano or perhaps Ignatius of Loyola set out in search of giants and lofty deeds, I decided to write a history of Puerto Rico.

I have sought to write a history of Puerto Rico in which the fundamental processes are those of the people itself, and to show that these processes are more important than the decisions made by the ruling figures of the North Atlantic. We are all tired of histories written from above and from outside. We acknowledge that whatever happens over the long term is an essential part of our historical process while whatever is episodic can only capture the trends of a particular era. We want a history that explains rather preaches. This all calls for a great deal of knowledge and not a little patience. I do not claim to have much of either, but I acknowledge a desire to acquire them.

This book is the sum of the research of many individuals, whose work is acknowledged in the footnotes. As it is normal in this kind of a book, one cannot hope to include everything that has been published about our history. In this sense, the footnotes serve as a starting point for more specialized and detailed reading.

Current conceptions about history tend to limit the historian's role to the compilation of facts. But a good history is not one that burdens the reader with a lot of information, but one that presents the most significant problems of a period in a coherent way. In history, a good question is worth more than a thousand names and dates. A discussion of the big issues is more important than remembering arcane details. In our discipline there has been a lively and continuous debate about the historical processes in Puerto Rico. What this book owes to that discussion is not as easily documented as the sources for a particular fact. That is why, in expressing my gratitude to my university colleagues with whom I have shared concerns and pointers, I am also highlighting the context within which this historical reflection has been conducted.

The knowledge and patience in the study of Puerto Rican history that I may have acquired I owe to my colleagues at the University of

Puerto Rico in Río Piedras and at other universities. These include: Gervasio García, Andrés Ramos Mattei, Angel Quintero Rivera, Blanca Silvestrini, Juan José Baldrich, María de los Angeles Castro, Lydia Milagros González, Guillermo Baralt, María Barceló Miller, María Dolores Luque, Manuel Alvarado, Carmen Raffucci, Jorge Iván Rosa Silva, Luis Agrait, Julio Damiani, Milton Pabón, Héctor Feliciano, Juan González Mendoza, Luis González Vales, José Curet, Francisco Scarano, Laird Bergad, Kenneth Lugo, Carlos Buitrago, Rubén Dávila, Jorge Rodríguez Beruff, Arnaldo Licier, Gilberto Aponte, Luis Martínez Fernández, Peter Katsilis, Carmen Campos, Carlos Casanova, Pedro Juan Hernández, Félix Matos, Pedro San Miguel, Ricardo Otero, Carlos Rodríguez Villanueva, Gregorio Villegas, Roberto Alejandro Rivera, Carlos Pabón, Astrid Cubano, Luis Figueroa, and Antonio Gaztambide.

It also gives me great pleasure to acknowledge my debt to those who have assisted me in archives, research centers, and libraries. In particular, Luis de la Rosa, Eduardo León, José Flores, Milagros Pepín, and Gustavo Santiago Rivera, in the General Archives of Puerto Rico (the AGPR of so many footnotes); Nelly Vázquez, José Cruz Arrigoitia, and Sylvia Alvarez, in the Historical Research Center at the University of Puerto Rico; and Annie Guiven, at the Río Piedras parish records office.

For the writing and revision of this work I have had the encouragement, advice and wisdom of Carmen Rivera Izcoa. I offer her and her colleagues at Ediciones Huracán my gratitude and love.

My mother, Matilde Bauermeister de Picó, and my sisters and brothers, Alvilda, Matilde, Carmen, Jorge, and José, have lent encouragement at every stage of this book. My fellow Jesuits, especially Orlando Torres, Maximino Rodríguez, Robert White, David Ungerleider, Ramón Ruiz, Guillermo Arias, José Angel Borges, and Jorge Ferrer have cheered me on to completion, so that at last they can have some peace.

No one, in the foregoing Deuteronomical list, is to blame for my mistakes, although I believe they all did everything within their power to keep the errors to a minimum.

This book is dedicated to the memory of my brother-in-law

Enrique Bird Piñero, sociologist, public official, lawyer, teacher, writer, humanist, and dreamer, who died in 1985, after having taught me many things in an ongoing conversation which lasted for too few years.

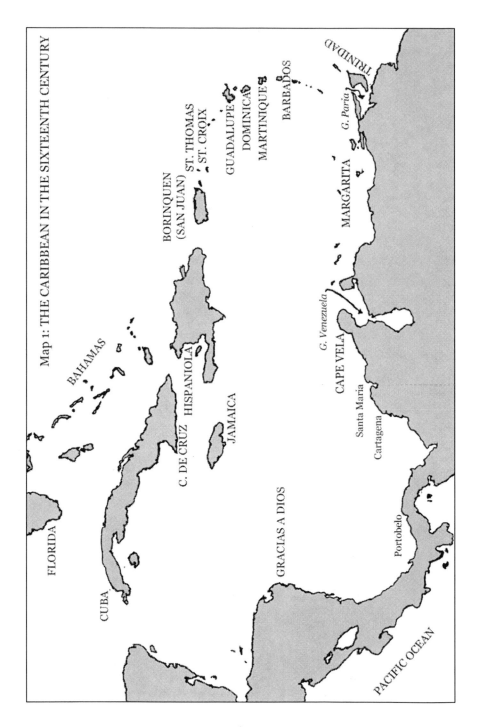

Map 1: THE CARIBBEAN IN THE SIXTEENTH CENTURY

TRINIDAD

BORINQUEN
(SAN JUAN)

ST. THOMAS
ST. CROIX

GUADALUPE
DOMINICA
MARTINIQUE

BARBADOS

G. Paria

MARGARITA

BAHAMAS

HISPANIOLA

C. DE CRUZ

JAMAICA

FLORIDA

CUBA

GRACIAS A DIOS

G. Venezuela

CAPE VELA

Santa Maria

Cartagena

Portobelo

PACIFIC OCEAN

CHAPTER

1

The Formation
of the Land
# of Puerto Rico

The Caribbean is much more than the sea represented on maps.[1] The word Caribbean conjures up a cluster of islands, languages, and peoples. It brings to mind colors, aromas, intonations, rhythms, and rituals. We expect to find hidden treasures and fantasies that disregard scientific facts and logical evaluation. For many of us who live on its shores, the Caribbean is a construct of the imagination rather than a geographical area. For the inhabitants of the North Atlantic, the Caribbean is a word that encodes a motley collection of myths, bundled together into a fascination with the exotic: pirates, secluded beaches, international intrigue, exuberant religious practices, luxury hotels, menacing masses, ancestral dances, and exquisite cocktails.

Travel brochures and the stereotypical action films portray the Caribbean as one and the same. But for those of us who live in the region, it is also a plural entity. It includes the Hispanic, the English-speaking, the French *créole* and the Dutch Caribbeans; the Leeward and Windward Islands, the Greater and Lesser Antilles. It is populated by Afro-Caribbeans, East Indians, Euro-Caribbeans, Amerindians, and Chinese. Versions of orthodox Christianity exist alongside African religious syncretism as do different phases of the market economy, different aspirations towards socialism, different remnants of pre-capitalist institutions; wealth and poverty, luxury and misery, modernity, post-modernity and primitivism, too many or too few paved roads. There too, laser surgery and herbal healers coexist as well as different orders of rationality and different definitions of happiness. In sum, it is a spread of illusions.

That diversity within unity is already apparent in the geological formation of the islands.[2] The natural shifts that raised and lowered the Caribbean landmass at different periods formed a long chain of mountains reaching from the entrance of the Gulf of Mexico down to the coast of Venezuela. Islands and peninsulas emerged from these telluric movements. The remnants of an imposing range of mountains formed in the Tertiary period provide evidence of the volcanic origins of that phase of Caribbean history. The ocean kept open some gaps between the towering peaks. Those trenches and passages prevented the Caribbean from becoming an enclosed sea, though this has not prevented observers from comparing it to the Mediterranean.[3]

However, unlike the Mediterranean, the Caribbean has been defined less by the continents on its shores than by the series of islands separating it from the Atlantic Ocean. The larger islands of the Mediterranean—Cyprus, Crete, Corsica, Sardinia, Sicily, Malta, the Balearic and the Aegean islands—were centers of power and wealth which easily fell prey to the power-hungry societies of neighboring continents. Over time, most of those islands became territorial annexes of European states. But in the Caribbean, it was from the islands that the European powers launched their military, religious, and economic conquest of the Americas. It was from the Caribbean that America came to be defined. In spite of repeated attempts by the American continent to define the Caribbean world on its terms, it has never managed to gain its revenge.

The Geological Formation of Puerto Rico

As with its political shifts, the Caribbean's geological formation has also passed through a number of stages. The formation of what we know today as Puerto Rico and its neighboring islands is relatively recent.

The geological history of the Greater Antilles, and specifically that of Puerto Rico, can only be traced back over the last 135 million years.[4] If the Earth has been in existence for more than three billion years, this means that the Antilles have not been present for more than 95% of that time. That is not necessarily a significant detail, since it was only 135 million years ago that the Earth began to acquire its distinctive contours. The movement of the tectonic plates resulted in earthquakes and volcanoes. Some of the undersea volcanoes erupted, hurling out huge quantities of rock, which piled up and protruded above the surface of the sea. There are areas of Puerto Rico, like the district of San Lorenzo, where rocks from that remote age have been found. That kind of rock is called serpentinite.

Some 70 million years ago, the formation of mountains and valleys was under way. Earth movements spewed out huge quantities of rock. At that time what would eventually become Puerto Rico was linked by land to neighboring islands, including Saint Croix. But that which had been raised by earthquakes and volcanoes was eroded by wind and water. The volcanoes became dormant. Then, some 45 million years ago, the sea, aided by erosion, began to reclaim the spaces occupied by the rocks. The sea deposited calcareous sediment over these rocks. Any peak standing above the water was subjected to erosion by the wind and the rain. The eroded material in turn formed a new layer of sedimentation.

The most recent stage of Puerto Rico's formation began some 17 million years ago, when telluric movements once again threw up the mass of rocks that became Puerto Rico. As in previous eras, erosion softened the sharp edges of the mountaintops, covering the coasts with sand to create dunes. Water sought out its course and formed basins. Marshes appeared. Some twelve thousand years ago the surface of the island was fairly similar to that of today. If we regard the time that has elapsed since the beginnings of planet Earth as being equivalent to twenty-four hours, Puerto Rico emerged in its current form at fifteen seconds to midnight.

The Formation of Ecosystems

Nevertheless those fifteen seconds were marvelous. The island became the habitat of many forms of animal and plant life. There are more than two hundred varieties of fern,[5] sixteen kinds of *coquí*, more than ninety different types of orchid, immense trees like the *ceiba* and hard wood like the *ausubo*. Also found were *jutía, carrao,* and other birds and animals which barely survive today on other Caribbean islands; the manatee which played in the river estuaries; the huge flocks of parrots and parakeets which filled the dense canopy of treetops with their chatter; many species of fish in the streams and rivers; iguanas and lizards, swarms of gaudy insects, throngs of turtles and crabs. It took thousands of years to enrich the island with so much life and it has taken less than five hundred years to squander this enormous natural wealth. Nevertheless, Puerto Rico has retained much more of its original flora and fauna than most of the islands in the Eastern Caribbean.[6]

The complex living world that was being formed in Puerto Rico gave rise to three ecological systems which have over time enriched the collective experience but which now are under threat.

The Mangrove Swamp

It is hard to imagine the history of the coastal urban areas without the mangrove swamps.[7] The organic decomposition evident in the perennial putrid smell of the mangrove swamp is a sign of the ongoing life cycles harbored by the swamp. Fish spawn and small crustaceans feed off microorganisms and algae. They in turn become the prey of larger fish and birds. The biological cycle includes the tides, which renew and revitalize the site. There are also the annual cycles of birds which migrate from the continent as well as the cycle of human life.

Urban people regard the mangrove swamp as an unhealthy place. But for those who in past centuries lived outside the city walls, the mangrove swamp offered freedom and an abode. It was a center of danger and lawlessness, but it was also a provider. The nineteenth-century *hacendado* found wood for his sugar mill furnaces there. Runaway slaves, deserting soldiers, and outlaws, but also charcoal-makers, fishermen, and hunters fled to the swamp in search of a source of income. The sailing boats that patrolled the channels under the hanging mangrove branches might bring the authorities or smugglers, but it also carried crabs, turtles, ducks, and fish for the San Juan market.

Home-distilled rum and shantytowns characterized the suburban mangrove swamp of the twentieth century. The state only managed to tame the mangrove swamp when it cut down the trees, filled in the channels, and paved the resulting land. But it lived on. The telltale smoke which might betray the liquor still also indicated the charcoal pit or the kitchen of a family that subsisted among the stumps and fishing nets. The helicopter, symbol of the authorities' suspicion, would fly over the isolated homesteads and the houses built on stilts. Both sailboats and helicopters fought for dominion over that which the city wanted to eradicate and which ecologists defended as essential breeding grounds for fish and birds. By the beginning of the twenty-first century, some areas of mangrove in the San Juan estuary which had been cut down were allowed to grow back. It has become possible to visit the lagoons and channels by boat and to appreciate the exuberant life of this surviving ecosystem.

The *Mogote* (Karst Landscape)

The northern coastal plain, between Aguadilla and Canóvanas, is dotted with densely wooded hillocks which are covered in creepers.[8] The bulldozers tearing down these hillocks have allowed passers-by to see the stones and soil exposed to the sun. It is calcareous terrain, easily penetrated by rainwater and prone to the formation of caves.

The popular imagination has attempted to locate Indian dwellings in many of those caves. It is much more likely that the animal fossils and human remains found in the caves belong to runaway slaves or other fugitives from the authorities.

With the expansion of sugarcane in the first decades of the nineteenth century, some of these karst hillocks provided a place for workers to build their houses. The greedy *hacienda* owners only granted them these poor lots, where their dwellings, perched almost one on top of the other, assured them a roof between labor during the harvest.

The *mogote* also provided fuel for cooking, a refuge for the species displaced by the onset of commercial agriculture, and a playground for children. Victims of the ongoing urbanization of the northern coastal plain, the karst formations have disappeared before the leveling obsession of builders. The *mogote*'s fragments are transferred to parks to hinder illegal parking. Its wild rock orchids have survived through the efforts of amateur botanists, and the caves live on in the folktales of the elderly.

At the beginning of the twenty-first century, thanks to a combined effort of the federal and island authorities and in response to civic efforts, a karst reservation area has been set up in the area of Barceloneta and the surrounding district.

The Coral Reef

Thousands of years of organic deposits formed the coral reefs which are characteristic of the Caribbean islands.[9] A long coral reef shelters part of Puerto Rico's northern coast, from Fajardo to San Juan from the onslaught of the Atlantic Ocean. This has created the quiet, sandy beaches that tourists have come to appreciate. The coral reef supports and nurtures a community of many different sea creatures, which find shelter and security within the recesses of the reef. It is a breeding ground for fish, for crustaceans, for different kinds of maritime vegetation, and it presents an ever-changing spectacle of color and beauty to the onlooker. Reefs are now protected by laws that prohibit pilfering and destroying the sites, but the public needs to become more aware of the fragility of this ecosystem and its many functions

The Political Formation of Puerto Rico

The ongoing processes which created Puerto Rico's geological and ecological forms are not the only ones that have defined its fundamental traits. There are islands, like the neighboring Hispaniola, that harbor more than one nation. There are also nations, like Indonesia and the Philippines, that inhabit a multitude of islands. One should not take the process by which Puerto Ricans have acquired a political identity for granted. Especially when one considers that the territorial extent of Puerto Rico includes not only what those from Vieques call the Isla Grande (Big Island, i.e. San Juan), but also Vieques, Culebra, Mona, Desecheo, and many other neighboring small islands and keys.

When Ferdinand of Aragon, the regent of Castile, wrote to his officials in 1511 that he wanted the island of Mona "to go with that of San Juan,"[10] he set in motion the process by which Mona would eventually gravitate within the orbit of Puerto Rico. In the case of Vieques, as late as the eighteenth century there were attempts to colonize it—thus free it from the jurisdiction of Puerto Rico—by the Scottish, the Danish, and the English. It was not until the nineteenth century that the links between Vieques and the Isla Grande were institutionalized. The prolonged occupation of two-thirds of the island of Vieques by the U.S. Navy, from World War II up until 2003, threatened the peace and security of its population and prevented effective development of its tourist potential. The settlement of Culebra began in 1879, and in the twentieth century there was even a moment when its depopulation seemed imminent.

The political processes which created the Puerto Rican jurisdiction have been open-ended ones. It has taken the five hundred years since the Spaniards arrived in the Caribbean for a clear and precise judicial definition of the territories and waters embraced by the government of Puerto Rico to emerge. Defining the extent of that hegemony within the territorial limits of Puerto Rico has been regarded as an ongoing process by the three main political movements on the island.

CHAPTER 2 ‖ Amerindian Societies

One of the favorite subjects of those interested in the Puerto Rican past is the human settlement of the island prior to the Spanish incursions and colonization.[1] As with any stimulating topic, the subject has provoked serious and prolonged academic debate. It has also set fire to the imagination of many who, lacking an academic background or archeological and documentary evidence, have tended to project their dreams of a happy isle into the past.

In spite of the fact that some textbooks authoritatively describe the sequence and duration of the periods of human habitation in Puerto Rico, the fact is that the stages that are so neatly traced in those schoolbooks are only the hypotheses of scholars. A hypothesis is a tentative explanation for a given problem. Based on the evidence of the diversity of *cultural* forms which has been found at the different strata of archeological sites, scholars have offered hypothetical explanations that attempt to describe, in a coherent and consistent way, the various stages of the human occupation of Puerto Rico.

Archeologists generally consider whatever is found at the deepest level of an excavation to be oldest. At this level in the Amerindian sites in Puerto Rico the remains of a simple culture of fisherfolk who lived near the coast and lived on crabmeat have been found. It is generally believed that these were the first inhabitants of Puerto Rico. Since similar sites have been found in the arc of islands that stretches all the way down to Venezuela, it has been suggested that there were migrations of Amerindians from the estuary of the Orinoco river. Moving from island to island, over a considerable period of time, these migrants came to occupy the Caribbean archipelago. It has been estimated that these earliest inhabitants of this part of the world may have begun their migration from the coast of Venezuela around 2300 B.C.E.

Judging from the remains found thus far, this first group of Amerindians in Puerto Rico had a fairly simple culture.[2] Their settlements were located near mangrove swamps and beaches protected by rocks and reefs. Their centers of activity appear to have been more numerous on the southern than the northern coast. According to the archeological finds, the occupations of these early inhabitants may have been fishing, hunting, and gathering wild fruits. No pottery remains have been found. Some scholars call this culture *archaic.* Others have called it pre-ceramic, and still others have called it the culture of the crab. The settlement of Puerto Rico by this group in the centuries preceding 200 B.C.E. does not appear to have been intensive. The sites studied appear to have been inhabited by groups of around 25, a number of adults and children which can be fed on a daily basis by hunting, fishing, and gathering fruit.

From 200 B.C.E. until around 600 C.E. the inhabitants of Puerto Rico were engaged in farming. They also developed the arts of pottery, stone carving, and fashioning items out of seashells. Archeological excavations in different sites, especially in the area known as Hacienda Grande, near Loiza, have yielded the remains of vessels used for storing grain and eating and drinking. The techniques of making incisions on the clay and coloring the vessels red and white reveal a level of technical development and artistic sensibility which suggest a more complex social organization than their "archaic" predecessors.[3]

Most scholars consider that these and other features found in the archeological remains are best explained by the theory of a second wave of Amerindian immigration from the northern coast of South America, most probably the region of the lower Orinoco River and the Guyanas. Movement into the area would have been a gradual process and would not necessarily have resulted in the extermination of the previous inhabitants. The name *igneri* or *saladoid* has been given to this group of settlements in Puerto Rico.

A recurring problem for the study of these Amerindians is the question of why, in later periods, the ceramic vessels do not display the same technical and artistic capacity of the earlier period. A study of the sites of Tecla in Guayanilla and Hueca and Sorcé in Vieques has further complicated the theories about Amerindian cultures in Puerto Rico. These settlements show skill in their decorating of stones and shells, and original bird and animal designs which distinguish their culture from that of the *igneri*.

Since 1981, a group of archeologists, and in particular Luis Chanlatte, director of the Center for Archeological Research at the University of Puerto Rico at Río Piedras, have explained the periods of the post-archaic phases of Puerto Rican history in order to illustrate more precisely the different and changing patterns of culture found in the excavations.[4] For the period since 200 B.C.E., Chanlatte has suggested the presence in Puerto Rico of a number of different cultures which he defines as Agro-Ceramic I, II, III, and IV. Those called I and II correspond to two Amerindian migratory waves which did not necessarily originate in the lower Orinoco river. The Agro-Ceramic II culture, which corresponds to findings at sites in Tecla, Hueca, and Sorcé, would have been assimilated in the short term. The transformation of the archaic culture through the influence of the immigrants is called Agro-Ceramic III. The next stage of development of Agro-Ceramic is called IV. According to Chanlatte's scheme, this Agro-Ceramic IV culture encompasses all the Amerindian culture in the period immediately prior to the Spanish Conquest. This is often known as the Taíno period.

The advantage of Chanlatte's scheme is that the development of new technologies and skills by the Amerindians is not solely attributed to immigration. Furthermore, it accommodates the hypothesis that relations between the early and later inhabitants were more complex and enduring than that implied in sudden conquest by a group with better weaponry and organizational skills.

Taíno Culture

The best-known phase of the pre-Columbian human settlement of Puerto Rico is the final one, usually called the Taíno phase. This is partly due to the greater number of archeological remains, but also to the existence of Spanish documentary sources.[5]

For the history of the neighboring island of Hispaniola these sources include administrative correspondence, legal files, capitular acts, and narrative testimonies called chronicles or memoirs. There are also other written sources, such as private letters, poetry, and apologias. These sources often refer to the Amerindians of Puerto Rico but the references are not based on the authors' direct observation.

Even those sixteenth-century Spanish authors who specifically write about the Amerindians of Puerto Rico rely in most cases on secondhand reports. Thus Gonzalo Fernández de Oviedo, Bartolomé de las Casas, and Juan de Castellanos, when they turn their attention to Puerto Rican affairs, must resort to the accounts and observations of the few Spaniards who remained on the island after the Conquest. This is because, when the chroniclers had occasion to live on or visit the island, those Amerindians who remained were forced under the *encomienda* system to work for the Spaniards in the gold mines or in farming. The majority died.

Although these narrative sources are partial and incomplete, scholars have been able to identify the main features of Taíno culture in Boriquén, the name given to the island by its inhabitants, according to the chroniclers. They have done so by noting the similarities between the forms of social organization in Puerto Rico and Hispaniola as well as the relative abundance of archeological remains and also references in Spanish fiscal documents.

Taíno Economy and the Ecology

At each stage in history the various inhabitants of the country have used the natural resources of the Puerto Rican islands to satisfy their needs for food, housing and collective needs. Nevertheless, their use of these resources has sometimes failed to preserve the necessary balance for their renewal.

The early Amerindians barely modified the insular ecology. Their settlements near the mangrove swamps made little impact on the surrounding land. Since they were few in number, they did not threaten the fauna and flora.

It is likely that the Amerindians of the agro-ceramic cultures began cultivation by using the technique known as slash-and-burn. They set fire to a piece of land to clear the undergrowth and then to take advantage of the initial fertility provided by the ashes. This practice, although it damaged the soil which was then exposed to erosion by wind and rain, did not affect the fertility of the land when the number of people who lived on it was relatively low, between 25 and 100. Nine or ten years was long enough for the abandoned terrain to recover its residual topsoil and develop new tree canopies.[6]

The population growth which resulted from the introduction of agriculture and pottery to the island, as evidenced by the many sites, was accompanied by the settlement of the interior valleys and the development of agricultural techniques. In its Taíno phase, Boriquén's Amerindian society practiced a more structured form of agriculture, known as planting on *montones* or heaps. Frank Moya Pons graphically describes the planting of cassava during the analogous Taíno phase on Hispaniola:

> Cultivation was started by setting fire to the area of forest which was to be cleared. Then the soil was heaped into mounds on top

of which stalks were planted. These heaps measured some nine to twelve feet across, and were two or three feet apart. This arrangement of the soil favored its aeration, and at the same time allowed the roots to grow more easily. The mounds were in rows, several thousand across and lengthwise, and they covered extensive areas of land.[7]

The Amerindians also cultivated corn, *achiote* trees, tobacco plants, and chili. Many fruits and medicinal herbs also grew, but apparently were not systematically cultivated. They had pots in which to store food and ferment beverages. Having an organized system of cultivation ensured their subsistence and made it possible for several members of the group to devote themselves to specific tasks in agriculture, hunting, handicrafts, and other occupations. It is likely that women carried out basic agricultural roles and made articles from cotton as well as hammocks, while the men devoted themselves to hunting and fishing. Stonecarving, which required great patience and skill, and other handicrafts are likely to have occupied many hours of labor. Little is known about their goldsmithing, since their gold objects were melted down by the Spaniards at the time of the Conquest, but one can imagine that metalworking must have called for specialized skills.

The productive capacity of the Taínos has led some researchers to attempt to estimate the size of the Amerindian population of the Greater Antilles before 1492.[8] There is no doubt that the extensive plantations of cassava and corn could feed many people, but we also know that the Amerindians lived in densely forested islands. Under the tree canopies they could also hunt for indigenous rodents, reptiles, and birds, which, along with the fish, provided the necessary protein for their diet. Although there were many Amerindian settlements in Puerto Rico at the time of the Conquest, very few could have exceeded 500 inhabitants, and most may not have exceeded 50 persons.

There is a strong tendency for Puerto Ricans to idealize the life of the pre-Conquest Amerindians. The benign climate, the fertility of the soil, and the abundance of fauna are cited in support of this. Francisco Moscoso's studies of the Amerindian economy, however, have underscored the laborious nature of the daily tasks carried out by Amerindian workers and the degree of social organization that was required for these tasks.[9] As regards their integration into the surrounding natural world, while it is true their occupations and world-view resembled plants and animals in that they followed the rhythm of the moon, the tides, the rain, and the wind, their existence was constantly threatened by disaster and illness. They did not always have adequate defenses against these calamities, as we can deduce from the young age of many of the skeletal remains.

The Taínos went about naked, but they anointed their skins with natural oils that protected them from insect bites. Older women wore a cotton skirt. Necklaces made of seashells were commonly worn, and people often complemented their attire with bird feathers of brilliant colors. Persons of high rank wore gold ornaments; that most frequently mentioned by chroniclers is the *guanín*, a gold medallion which hung from their necks.

Sociopolitical Organization

The division of labor among the members of a Taíno community was allocated according to hierarchy. The *naborías* were free workers subject to service obligations who carried out the more onerous and repetitive tasks. Chanlatte has speculated that they may have been descendants of early Amerindians, whose numbers would increase during the Agro-Ceramic III phase.[10] Under the Spaniards, the services formerly performed by the *naborias* for the *caciques* were transferred to the holders of the *encomienda*. The pre-Conquest organization of the *naborías'* labor made it easier to introduce the eventual distribution of the workers.[11]

In Amerindian society the *nitainos* were the ruling class which headed war expeditions and influenced collective decisionmaking. Spanish chroniclers, who compared them with their own institutions, attributed to them aristocratic qualities which perhaps did not correspond to the size and level of complexity of the Amerindian communities.

The Taíno period is often seen as marking a transition from tribal organization to one headed by *caciques,* a more structured form in political terms. The members of one or more communities recognized the authority of a chieftain or *cacique,* who stood out from the others on account of the style of his residence, his demeanor and air of command, and his personal ornamentation. The *cacique* could dispose of the communities' resources and exercise his discretion on behalf of all. In practice a *cacique*'s power depended on the recognition of his authority. Although there is not enough information to write a political history of the Taínos, the events of the Spanish Conquest showed a notable variety in the levels of power held by the *caciques.* In any case, they exercised authority over people rather than land. The maps that sometimes are drawn to show the political divisions of Boriquén are anachronistic. Although according to the chroniclers one of the *caciques* in Boriquén enjoyed greater authority than the others, the island was not constituted as a political entity in the territorial sense of today.

Jalil Sued Badillo has compiled a series of testimonies in support of his theory that women frequently exercised power in Taíno society. In the documentary sources of the sixteenth century more than fifteen women in Boriquén are called *cacicas.* Some scholars argue that it was only an honorific title given to the mothers, sisters, or daughters of a *cacique.* Sued maintains that the roles assumed by women in the Amerindian economy and the weight of matrilineal descent are sufficient reason to grant the full meaning to the term *cacica.*[12]

The family constituted the basic unit of Taíno society. The Amerindians were exogamous, that is, they married those who were not their relatives. That may explain the frequent integration of settlements in a region on account of the kinship ties resulting from marriage. For example, unions linking residents of the settlements on the western coast of Boriquén with persons from the eastern part of Hispaniola were not uncommon. There are documents that mention the frequent relations between the two islands.[13]

Belief Systems

Archeological remains indicate that the Amerindians were very religious, in the animist sense. The supernatural forces to which they attributed climatological events and recurring unusual phenomena were represented in figurines of clay and stone with animal and human features. According to some of the chroniclers, particularly Pané and Las Casas, the Amerindians from Hispaniola recognized the existence of an eminently benevolent being. His name has been spelled in different ways, but in Puerto Rico it is commonly written as Yuquiyú.[14] There was also a furious and malevolent being known as Juracán, from whose name the word hurricane is derived, which denotes the Caribbean's extraordinarily destructive storms. Some have attempted to use the references to these two deities as evidence of a dualist religious system, in which the forces of good and evil battle perpetually, affecting the destinies of humans. However, one must remember that chroniclers, to whom we owe these and other references, attempted to explain Amerindian religious practices by comparing them with Christian religious elements, in order that their sixteenth-century readers could understand them. One must be particularly aware of the desire of Las Casas and other religious to demonstrate a convergence between indigenous and Christian beliefs. By doing so, they hoped to reveal the Amerindians' natural disposition to the Christian life, which made subjugating them to the holders of *encomiendas* an injustice.

There are descriptions of Amerindian religious ceremonies, in particular the *cojoba* ritual, which involved the inhalation of dust extracted from the bud of the *cojoba* tree. This was done to receive divine revelations. There has also been much emphasis on the figure of the *bohique*, who combined cultic and medicinal roles.[15]

Amerindians liked to work and celebrate as a community. The *areyto* seems to have been the most solemn celebration. It reportedly combined communal dancing and recitations. Participants chanted their memories of great battles and the legends of the origins of deities and human beings. In this way, the collective memory reinforced solidarity and roused the spirit of the warriors. Apparently, on occasion what was recited was spoken in a tongue not known by all.[16]

By the time the Spaniards arrived in the Caribbean, the Taínos of Boriquén were fighting the inhabitants of the islands to their east. That is why some Spanish observers saw them as being more warlike than Taínos in other parts of the Greater Antilles.[17]

Many of the Taíno institutions have parallels in those of the South American Amerindian tribes described by twentieth-century anthropologists. These studies make possible a greater understanding of the narratives of the early chroniclers of the Indies. They also help us to visualize their use of implements and the role of religious elements in the collective life of the Taínos. Much research still needs to be done to understand this phase, the earliest in Puerto Rican history.

There has been speculation as to how the culture of the Taínos of Boriquén and the rest of the Caribbean might have developed if the Spaniards had not arrived at the end of the fifteenth century. But there were not many options remaining for the Caribbean Amerindians by then. The development of other societies with expansionist tendencies would, in a relatively short space of time, lead to the intrusion of foreign elements into the insular world of the Caribbean.

Backgrounds of the New Settlers of Puerto Rico

The Spaniards

In the time of Christopher Columbus, Hispania (Spain) was a geographical concept rather than a political entity. Since the beginning of the eighth century, when Syrian, Arab, and Moorish troops had overthrown the kingdom of the Visigoths, the peninsula that the Romans had called Hispania had not experienced political unity. The emirate, later caliphate, which had its capital in Córdoba, was a strong and flourishing state up until the first half of the eleventh century. Its political priorities did not lie in integrating within its domain the few mountainous areas of Asturias and the Pyrenees where herdsmen, shepherds, and peasants lived on the margins of the political and cultural institutions of the rest of the peninsula. Córdoba's rulers found it more convenient to maintain the small northern Christian states as tributary states. The fear that the kingdom of the Franks had designs on the peninsula diminished after Charlemagne's death in 814. Thus, only the Catalan fiefdoms, which were theoretically incorporated into the Carolingian state, stood as reminders of the Christian Europe beyond the Pyrenees.[1]

In the eleventh century, however, the crisis that ended the Córdoba caliphate, and resulted in its dismantling into weak successor states in 1037, favored the expansion of the old Christian tributary states. These had growing populations, and were inspired by the new religious zeal of the eleventh century, which brought many adventurers with visions of holy wars to the peninsula. They were able to occupy the desirable plateaus, which were suitable for sheepfarming. First they settled the area north of the River Duero, and having crossed it, occupied the territory north of the River Tagus. Between 1037 and 1085 the peninsula's political geography was fundamentally altered. The capture of Toledo by King Alfonso VI of Castile and León and the southwards expansion of the new kingdom of Aragon, which included the county of Barcelona, placed peninsular Christians in a powerful position.[2]

This phase of expansion, however, reached the limit of its possibility of populating and settling the occupied areas. Islamic forces, backed by the new Almoravid state in Morocco, were able to reorganize their territories and halt the advance of the new northern states. In the middle of the twelfth century a new phase of expansion was once more contained by the intervention of the Almohads, a fundamentalist Moorish movement. Finally, between 1212 and 1266, the Spanish Muslim kingdoms collapsed. Alfonso VIII of Castile, with an army recruited throughout the entire peninsula, repelled an Almohad offensive at Las Navas de Tolosa in 1212. His grandson, Fernando III of Castile and León, captured Jaén, Córdoba, and Seville. Fernando's son, Alfonso X, captured the kingdom of Murcia. Meanwhile James I of Aragon conquered the Balearic Islands and the kingdom of Valencia. The kingdom of Portugal advanced southwards. Out of this catastrophe, the Islamic forces were only able to salvage the kingdom of Granada, which declared itself a vassal of Castile.[3]

The dramatic expansion of Christian Spain in the thirteenth century had a significant impact on the formation of peninsular society. In order to guarantee the stability of the newly conquered lands, the kings of Castile encouraged the settlement of Andalusian towns. They granted vast lordships to the military orders and northern nobles who had fought in the wars of conquest. The creation of the Andalusian estate facilitated the development of socioeconomic structures that would maintain the peasant population of old Moorish stock in a state of close dependency. At the same time, the inducements offered to the northern Christians who occupied Andalusia resulted in a sharp fall in population on the Castilian plateau. As a result, the devalued lands in Castile were acquired cheaply by wool producers who formed themselves into an association called the Mesta. The Castilian plateau was taken over by huge sheep farms and its wool became highly prized in Italian and Flemish markets.[4]

Castile's wealth, increased by sheep farming and the fertility of its new dominions, became concentrated in the hands of a hereditary nobility which was jealous of its privileges and therefore keen to thwart political centralization. Moreover, Castile's newly acquired power, enhanced by its permanent union with the kingdom of León, loomed as a threat over its neighbors, Portugal and Aragon. For the greater part of the fourteenth and fifteenth centuries, peninsular energies and resources were consumed by Castile's internal conflicts and by dynastic and imperial wars against its neighboring states. Portugal and Aragon eventually gave up attempting to invade Castile and found alternative routes for expansion. From the 1280s onward the Aragonese, spurred on by Catalan merchants and mercenaries known as *almogávares*, established a maritime Mediterranean empire. The *almogávares* even ruled part of the Greek peninsula in the fourteenth century. Meanwhile the Portuguese were engaged in exploring the western coast of Africa. They established commercial posts in the most important regions of West Africa and developed the trade in gold, precious stones, and eventually slaves. They also sought navigation routes to India via the southern tip of Africa.

In the latter half of the fifteenth century the dynastic marriage between the heir to the crown of Aragon and the heiress to the throne of Castile resulted in the union of the two kingdoms. Ferdinand II of Aragon and Isabella I of Castile exploited the favorable conjuncture of peace and the availability of resources to launch the reconquest of the kingdom of Granada. Following their success in this venture, they pursued Ferdinand's dynastic claim to the throne of Naples in Italy and established a network of matrimonial alliances between their children and the heirs to the thrones of Portugal, Flanders, and England.[5]

However, the dynastic alliance of Ferdinand and Isabella did not necessarily guarantee the continued union of Castile and Aragon. Both states retained separate political structures. After Isabella's death in 1504 the throne of Castile passed to her eldest daughter Juana, who was married to the Hapsburg archduke Philip. Ferdinand contracted a second marriage with Germaine of Foix and successfully upheld her rights to the throne of Navarre in the Pyrenees. If this marriage had resulted in a male heir the dynastic union of Castile and Aragon would not have continued.

But beyond the historical accident of the monarchs' dynastic policies was the force of Spanish woollen and commercial interests. Castile recognized that Aragon's naval and commercial resources were important for ensuring Castile's access to wool markets in Italy. The matrimonial alliance with the Hapsburgs guaranteed Castilian access to the other key wool market: Flanders. Thus Catalan commercial and Castilian sheep-farming interests coincided. Although the peninsular manufacturing industry undoubtedly suffered from policies favoring the export of their primary resource, the discovery and conquest of America would provide Castilians with an outlet for their manufactured goods as well as the possibility of emigration for their unemployed population.

In the sixteenth century the vast quantities of gold and silver brought into Europe by the Spaniards launched an economic revolution which displaced those who depended on fixed incomes from inherited agricultural holdings. Artisans were also affected because they were unable to compete against the cheaper merchandise brought in from other parts of Europe. The New World offered both of these sectors an outlet for their energies.

The kingdoms of Castile and Aragon, however, became involved in long and costly European wars to defend the dynastic interests of the new Hapsburg ruling house. Under Charles I of Castile (Charles V of the Holy Roman Empire), Italy, Flanders, imperial Burgundy, and Germany became a theater of war for Spanish troops paid for with the gold of the Indies. The huge cost of these military operations determined Spain's colonization priorities in America and delayed urban and manufacturing development in the New World. The Hapsburgs' enemies also went to sack the Caribbean territories, using their loot to finance wars against Spain.

The need to settle their debts diverted the Spanish monarchs' attention from the long-term problems that the exhaustion of the goldmines would pose for the development of the Caribbean islands. It was left to the islands to explore solutions. For a long time, the need to maintain Spanish rule in Flanders, a market for Castilian wool, was regarded as more important than Antillean affairs. It was not until the eighteenth century, following the loss of their domains in Flanders and Italy, that the Spanish kings began to pay more attention to their American territories.

The Africans

The history of Puerto Rico has tended to take Africa too much for granted. From the sixteenth century on, it was the place of origin of many of the island's new inhabitants. But if Spain, whence came Ponce de León's companions, was a complex and diverse entity, Africa, a continent three times bigger than Europe and the site of human habitation since the dawn of mankind, was even more so.

The vast majority of the Africans who arrived in Puerto Rico came from West Africa, from the area that is present-day Mali down as far as Angola. In the sixteenth century, the catchment area became smaller, from Mali to present-day Nigeria. In the centuries that followed it expanded southwards to include Angola.

By 1500, West Africa was a vast and complex ecological, economic, political, and cultural mosaic. Coastal mangroves, savannas, forests, and deserts offered very different environments for human activity. Rivers, especially that known as the Niger by Europeans, were reduced to a trickle in the dry months, and then would flood the valleys in the rainy season. The shifting deltas were the habitat of dense labyrinths of mangrove trees, which made the area unattractive for establishing towns and trade.

The dense tropical forest also held little attraction for hunters and farmers. It was the savanna that attracted the bulk of the population. In those areas where there was abundant game people planted millet, yams, and a type of rice, and raised livestock like donkeys and guinea fowl. Groups that had little political cohesion and limited economic development were forced to relinquish space in the savanna to the more powerful, and were driven towards the mangroves, forests, or desert. On the other hand, when a group from among those peripheral sectors acquired sufficient power, it was not unusual for it to attempt to settle in some area of the savanna and to subjugate or expel the existing inhabitants.[6]

The West African savanna could not, however, provide sufficient food over prolonged periods of time for the larger population centers which created stability and a steady supply of goods for the state. Once the savanna was cleared for the intensive agriculture required to feed a large city, the wind and the rain tended to denude the soil of its thin top layer. In this way, the establishment of large-scale farming led to the impoverishment of the soil. The recurring annual droughts encouraged the planting of fast-growing vegetables. Only a few domestic animals were kept. Thus the environmental realities discouraged large concentrations of population and facilitated political fragmentation.[7]

The desertification of vast tracts of the Sahara in the Neolithic era had greatly reduced population density in that region. Many inhabitants from that area had moved southwards to the savanna, forcing the Pygmies and other groups to seek refuge in the dense forests of central Africa. At the time when the Roman Empire was flourishing on the shores of the Mediterranean, trans-Saharan routes, which largely followed the reservoirs of underground water left over from the era when the area had lakes, linked West Africa with Egypt and the cities of North Africa. It is likely that, through the indirect influence of the Romans, knowledge of ironworking was extended to Western Africa.[8] The spread of Islam in the seventh century separated West Africa from Christian Europe. It was not until the fifteenth century that contact was re-established. Nevertheless, their relations with the Islamic states of northern Africa enabled sub-Saharan Africans to retain profitable commercial, cultural, and religious links with the Islamic Mediterranean.

The ecological diversity and the multiplicity of ethnic, linguistic, and cultural groups in West Africa was not necessarily an obstacle to the development of great empires at given moments. Three of these left a permanent mark on the collective memory of Africans: Ghana, Mali, and Songhai. Ghana, whose territory only partly corresponded to that of the African country that now bears its name, flourished between the tenth and the middle of the eleventh centuries C.E. Mali emerged towards the end of the thirteenth century and reached its peak in the fourteenth. Songhai flourished in the fourteenth and fifteenth centuries.[9]

One particular resource served as the nucleus around which the trade of these empires hinged and also provided their rulers with remarkable power: gold. The abundance of gold deposits in the rivers and the constant demand for it in the Islamic centers of the Mediterranean gave rise to the intensive and constant exploitation of these deposits. At the same time, the desire to discover and control new sources of gold dust and nuggets led each of the three states to attempt to expand eastward. The control of these gold deposits and of the resulting trade gave the kings of Ghana, Mali, and Songhai access to other minerals, such as iron, copper, and tin. This helped to guarantee their superiority in weaponry and technology, as well as the display of the pomp and power needed to ensure the prestige of their states. The income from his gold mines enabled the king of Mali to make Timbuktu a center of Islamic studies and a magnificent city which became the destination of the main trans-Saharan caravan routes.[10]

According to the testimony of the Arab writer Al-Umari, a king of Mali called Abu Bakr was so powerful that towards 1310 he sent two hundred boats westward to search for the limits of the Atlantic Ocean. Only one of them returned. The king then led an expedition of two thousand boats to discover what was on the other side of the ocean. He never returned.[11]

The three empires collapsed in turn on account of the contradictions inherent in the extension of their realms and the environmental limits for the development of their urban centers. But other states, more compact and less dependent on the trade in gold, had become notably prosperous by the fourteenth and fifteenth centuries C.E. In the eleventh century, the Yorubas founded a kingdom which had its capital at Oyo. Their king, called the Alafin ("master of the house"), received the sacred sword that symbolized his office from the hands of the Oni, the religious head of the Yorubas who lived in Ifé. It was from Ifé that the techniques for the working with bronze spread to other areas.[12]

Among the lands that were culturally influenced by Ifé, from the thirteenth century on, Benin, which was closer to the coast, stands out. One of its kings, Obvola, had a master foundryman come from Ifé to teach his subjects the art of making bronze masks. In the fourteenth and fifteenth centuries Benin not only gained great fame for its bronzes, which were produced by the "lost wax" method, but also showed great virtuosity in the carving of wood and ivory.[13]

Other peoples formed stable and powerful states: the Hausa, who from the tenth century on founded city-states that are still flourishing, such as Kano. There was also the kingdom of the Jolofs, in the Senegal River delta. The kingdom of Nupe, south of Hausaland, was famous for its guilds of artisans and for the tribal settlements that merged with the powerful kingdom of Dahomey at the end of the seventeenth century.[14]

Some writers have insisted on discerning the influence of Islam on the development of West African states before the sixteenth century. That influence was not uniform and it is much more evident in Mali and Songhai than in the other states mentioned above. Sources from Arabic-speaking writers document in greater detail life in those cities where there were permanent quarters of Arab traders and the rise of the kings who accepted the Koran. But if Islam gained easy acceptance at the court of Mali and had one of its important centers of study in Timbuktu, the conversion of the Hausa was a much slower process and it did not have much success among the Yoruba until the nineteenth century.[15]

The slow advance of Islam among these other ethnic groups is partly related to the hostile relations with the Islamic Tuareg tribesmen, who made advances into the savanna from the desert. Another delaying factor was the friction caused by the commercial relationship which began to direct the slaving caravans towards the Mediterranean.[16]

The type of slavery that was common in West Africa before Islamic and Christian slave traders turned it to their own ends revolved around the requirements of the palace and the domestic sphere. In some cases captives from wars of expansion became conquering soldiers in the service of their new masters. Moreover, domestic African slavery incorporated individuals into the household routine. The tasks of hauling wood and water, artisan and agricultural labor, and animal husbandry rarely reached the level of intensity, exploitation, and inhumanity which eventually characterized European plantations in the Caribbean.[17]

Long before Portuguese slavers began the massive trade in captured Africans, the caravans heading for Morocco and Tunis already carried tens of thousands of slaves towards the workshops, fields, and construction sites of North Africa. Plunder by both European and North African slavers weakened West Africa. The demand for captives increased the frequency of armed conflicts and extended the area from which people were taken. The savanna became dangerous. Many towns fortified themselves, while some people retreated into the forested areas. Some, sure of their weaponry, settled near the river estuaries to trade with the Europeans. Thus the sixteenth century launched an era of violence in West Africa whose effects, primarily in terms of interethnic rivalry, are still felt today.

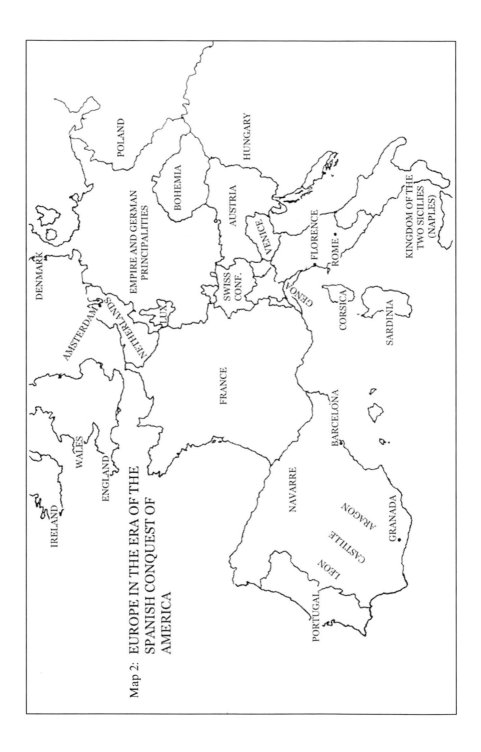

Map 2: EUROPE IN THE ERA OF THE SPANISH CONQUEST OF AMERICA

IRELAND

WALES

ENGLAND

DENMARK

AMSTERDAM

NETHERLANDS

LUX.

EMPIRE AND GERMAN PRINCIPALITIES

POLAND

BOHEMIA

AUSTRIA

HUNGARY

SWISS CONF.

VENICE

GENOA

FLORENCE

ROME •

KINGDOM OF THE TWO SICILIES (NAPLES)

CORSICA

SARDINIA

FRANCE

BARCELONA

NAVARRE

ARAGON

CASTILE

LEÓN

PORTUGAL

GRANADA

CHAPTER 4

The Conquest of Boriquén

The European Background

At the beginning of the fourteenth century, after two centuries of creativity and expansion, the vigorous medieval European civilization had entered a phase of structural contradiction. The aristocracy had become sedentary and lived off their rents. The peasantry, which profited from the rising agricultural prices of the thirteenth century, was affected by the rising cost of renting land. The credit system, instead of stimulating manufacture and commerce, had become a pawn of the kings' aggressive policies. A series of natural disasters revealed the precarious nature of the balance between life and death in a relatively overpopulated Europe. Existing agrarian techniques no longer sufficed to meet the demand for foodstuffs. Towns had exceeded their capacity to handle concentrations of population. The epidemics which plagued Western Europe from the 1340s until the 1660s took hold in the crowded neighborhoods behind the city walls that had been made necessary by the constant wars. The main Florentine banks, financiers of kings and popes, went into bankruptcy between 1347 and 1355. Economic crises had an impact on social order. The second half of the fourteenth century witnessed numerous peasant and urban uprisings in France, England, the Spanish kingdoms, Italy, and Germany.[1]

The neighboring peoples exploited the manifest vulnerability of the Europeans. In Russia the Tartars maintained their hegemony until the second half of the fourteenth century. The Turks garnered the remains of the Byzantine Empire and began to expel the Genovese and the Venetians from their commercial centers in the islands of the Aegean Sea. Commercial routes to China and India began to be blocked when the territories conquered in the thirteenth century by Genghis Khan were parceled out among successor states that erected tariff barriers along the way. Trading directly with the Far East, source of the exotic spices which were in high demand in Western Europe, became more expensive and more insecure. At the time, the generic name of "spice" was applied to more than a hundred items, including sugar, porcelain, cloves, and cinnamon. In Europe the main suppliers were Italian merchants.[2]

By the beginning of the fifteenth century there was a marked Italian withdrawal from long-distance trade. Not only had the costs and risks of such trade risen, but investors also had more attractive opportunities at home than those offered by commerce and manufacturing. As a result of the dismemberment of the Visconti Milanese state in 1402, Venice had acquired ample territories in its own periphery. Many Venetian businessmen began to systematically exploit the agricultural potential of the Po valley. They introduced a new and profitable type of agriculture which turned the territories of Padua and Verona into an area of agricultural experimentation. The Florentine *popolani grassi* discovered that investing in their state was more secure and profitable than manufacturing. They lived off the income from a state which moved more rapidly towards oligarchy with the accession of Cosimo de Medici and his entourage in 1434.[3] The Genoese, hampered in establishing a strong and independent state by the continuing rivalry among its aristocratic families, made the Bank of Saint George the main focus of unity for their city-state. In that way the citizens of Genoa, lacking a stable state, supported their aspirations for collective endeavors by the consolidation of their public debt.[4] But they too tended to become *rentiers*.

Lacking the support of the state, those Italians who were interested in exploring new commercial routes looked for finance and political backing for their ventures from the established monarchies of Western Europe. Of these, Portugal offered the best prospects of supporting exploration to find a new route to India. The Portuguese objective was to bypass the costly Asiatic caravans, whose trade was practically monopolized by the Italians. It was the trade barriers that increased the cost of the merchandise carried by camel and mule, especially the tariffs imposed by the Ottoman Turks, who had conquered Constantinople in 1453 and ruled over the Levant.

In Portugal, Prince Henry the Navigator (1394–1460) had encouraged attempts to find a route to India by circumnavigating Africa.[5] The first major obstacle to this objective was to get beyond Cape Bojador. A Portuguese captain named Gil Eanes was able to sail beyond it in 1434. Between then and 1460 the Portuguese reached Sierra Leone. It seemed only a matter of time before they would round the southern tip of Africa and reach India.

Each significant advance by the Portuguese was marked by the establishment of a center for trade and storage. These trading posts were called *factorías*, in the commercial language of the Italians who often accompanied the expeditions. The Portuguese objective was not to occupy Africa, but to obtain gold dust, exotic merchandise, and slaves, which were in demand in Europe, at the coastal trading posts. In exchange, the Portuguese carried textiles, glass objects, and iron tools. The presence of the Portuguese *factorías* provided economic and political incentives for the neighboring African states, which became intermediaries in this trade.

Christopher Columbus

One of the many Italian seamen who participated in Portuguese commercial enterprises was the Genoese Cristoforo Colombo (whose name was later anglicized to Christopher Columbus). He advanced the theory that the difficulties of sailing around Africa could be bypassed by sailing due west.

European academic circles were familiar with the theory of the second century C.E. Greek geographer Ptolemy that the Earth was round. More recently, the Florentine Toscanelli had issued a description of the world based on the same premise. The difficulty in exploring this alternate route to the Far East lay in the size of the Earth's circumference which Ptolemy had calculated. It would take too long to reach India; one would have to ship a considerable amount of provisions and water, and there was no sign of favorable winds for making the return trip.[6]

Columbus believed that the globe was smaller than Ptolemy had calculated. On that mistaken premise he based his plan to reach the Orient in around seven weeks. The Portuguese crown considered Columbus' proposal and rejected it. This was because it preferred to continue the plan of sailing around Africa. That is why Columbus decided to seek the backing of England, France, or Castile, monarchies which had some interest in Atlantic navigation.

After prolonged negotiations, which were delayed because the main concern of the Castilian court at the time was the conquest of Granada in 1492, Columbus was successful in reaching an agreement with the Castilian crown. This agreement is known as the Capitulations of Granada. Its terms were much more generous than those the king of Portugal would have granted, because the Portuguese had sufficient experience from its trading posts in Africa to be able to measure the benefits of such an undertaking. Columbus would be given the titles of admiral, viceroy, and governor-general in all the islands and mainland which might be discovered and that were obtained through his efforts and labor. Columbus would receive one-tenth of all the gold, silver, pearls, gems, and other merchandise obtained through exchange or from mining. He would have the power of adjudication of all the cases involving the said merchandise or products, and the option of investing up to an eighth of this in the ships which were sent to the new possessions.[7]

But the splendid terms of the Capitulations were not in proportion to the actual resources provided by the crown to Columbus in 1492. The port of Palos, near Cadiz, had been compelled, for some misdemeanors, to provide the crown with two equipped caravelles for the term of a year. On April 30 the Crown ordered that these two caravelles, which came to be know as the *Niña* and the *Pinta*, be handed over to Columbus. He also leased a third ship, the *Santa María*.[8]

On August 3, 1492, the expedition set off from Palos. Columbus made a stop at La Gomera, one of the Canary Islands. Although the Romans had known the Canaries, these islands had not been in contact with Western Europe for many centuries. Their inhabitants, called *Guanches*, seem to have lost the art of open-sea navigation. In the fourteenth century the Normans and the Italians visited the islands, and some of them settled there. The Betancourts who later migrated to Puerto Rico from the Canaries, for instance, were descendants of those Normans. The Portuguese established *factorías* in the Canary Islands, but eventually the Castilians displaced them and occupied the islands. The Castilian colonization of the Canaries is interesting as it offers many similarities with the later experience in the Antilles.[9] Columbus himself had lived in the Canaries, where he had the chance to study the prevailing winds in the different seasons.

Columbus set off from the Canaries on September 6. He headed southwest and arrived in the Bahamas 36 days later. Although he was glad to arrive, it was not what he expected. According to his theory, the island of Cipango (Japan) should not be too far away, and beyond it, the continent of Asia. Thus he continued on in search of the continent or mainland, the discovery of which would demonstrate the correctness of his hypothesis. On October 28 he landed in Cuba and on December 6 he discovered the island of Hispaniola. An accident suffered by the flagship, the Santa María, forced him to leave some of his men in Fort Natividad, built with the wood from the wrecked ship, and he returned to Europe on the Niña. Martín Alonso Pinzón preceded him on the Pinta with the news of the discovery.[10]

In March 1493, Columbus presented the proof of his discoveries to the monarchs, Isabella and Ferdinand, who at the time were residing in Barcelona. Although the profits from the trip were meager, the novelty of the discovery and the palpable evidence of the exotic products of those lands encouraged the Queen to organize a second expedition. Since Columbus was a partner of the Crown in the enterprise, as established by the terms of the Capitulations, the Queen named Juan de Fonseca, archdeacon of Seville, as her representative for the second trip. The cleric Fonseca would be a zealous upholder of the rights of the Castilian crown in the lands discovered over the next thirty years.[11]

The expedition of seventeen caravelles that set off for Hispaniola on September 25, 1493, was much better equipped than the first one. It carried between 1,200 and 1,500 men (still no women) and a quantity of supplies which would support colonization as well as trade. These preparations showed the diverse criteria for the mission that was being undertaken. According to the Dominican historian Frank Moya Pons, Columbus still had in mind the Portuguese model of *factoría* on the African coast, while the Castilians favored the model of occupation developed during the conquest of the Canaries. For the time being both models coincided, since the priority was to develop settlements from which to supervise the extraction of gold.[12]

On November 3 the armada sighted a small island, which Columbus named Santa María la Galante. In the following days the armada, proceeding with favorable winds from the East, sailed past other islands, to which Columbus gave names recalling his religious devotion and his friends. The thickly grouped islands near the Anegada passage he called the Virgin Islands, because it seemed to him that there were as many of them as the legendary companions of St. Ursula, who numbered eleven thousand. To Vieques he gave the name Graciosa, in honor of the mother of an Italian friend, Alessandro Geraldini.[13] Finally he reached the island which some Amerindian women he had shipped on board at Guadeloupe recognized as their native island and which they called Boriquén. To this island Columbus gave the name of San Juan Bautista.[14]

Historians have debated about which of Puerto Rico's coasts

Columbus sailed past— the southern or the northern—and about the exact day when the sailors went ashore to collect water for the ships, and at which precise point on the Boriquén coast Columbus took possession of the island in the name of the Queen of Castile and León. But does this really matter? It makes no difference whether Columbus landed on this or that place, and it is an enormous waste of time to speculate about something which did not substantially alter the process that had already begun when the Spaniards sailed into the waters of Boriquén. What all the contemporary testimonies underscore is that Columbus was in a hurry to reach Fort Natividad, where he had left some of his shipmates the previous year. Boriquén did not detain him.

Although Columbus made two other voyages of discovery, he does not seem to have returned to the island of San Juan Bautista, that is, Boriquén. His eagerness to reach the continent of Asia, which he believed lay beyond the islands, made him lose interest in the multitude of islands which he discovered east of Hispaniola. The Spaniards would only be interested in these islands to the extent that they could meet their needs.

Columbus' shipmates noticed the abundance of gold that was to be found in Hispaniola and forced the inhabitants to work for them extracting the mineral from the riverbeds. Using the old tributary customs of the natives, they incorporated into a workforce those whom they called Indians because they thought they were inhabitants of Asia. Thus they ensured the Spanish population was fed. Although the Amerindians were not slow to rebel, their lack of resistance to the viruses brought by the Europeans, as well as the superiority of Spanish weaponry and military organization, soon resulted in the subjugation of the indigenous population.

It is likely that the Taínos of Boriquén, who were in close contact with their counterparts in eastern Hispaniola, received news of the events in the land of their kinsmen. However, the Spaniards hardly set foot on the island of Boriquén for a number of years. The Capitulations of Granada ensured that no one could undertake the conquest of the island without the consent of Columbus, as he claimed these rights as the discoverer. After Columbus' capture and return to Spain, his rights were questioned by the Crown, which contracted the terms of a possible conquest with Vicente Yañez Pinzón. Pinzón did not assert his questionable rights beyond releasing goats and pigs on the western coast of the island in order to prepare the future colony.[15]

Finally in 1507 a nobleman from the kingdom of León, who was based at Higuey in the eastern part of Hispaniola, asked Nicolás de Ovando, who then ruled the island on behalf of the Castilian crown, for authorization to make an expedition to Boriquén. In 1508 Juan Ponce de León departed in a small vessel from Higuey and landed at a beach on Boriquén. With his compatriot Juan González acting as interpreter, he succeeded in making a pact with an important *cacique*, whose name has been transcribed as Agueybana or Guaybana. Following his directions, Ponce de León sailed along the northern coast of Boriquén. The first settlement he made may have been near the mouth of the river Manatí, which also seems to be confirmed by archeological findings.[16]

For reasons unknown, the original settlement did not meet the needs of the members of the expedition. Ponce de León returned to Hispaniola, where he negotiated the terms of colonization with Ovando in order to safeguard both his and the Crown's rights. Afterwards, Ferdinand, who was then regent of Castile, would consider those terms too advantageous for Ponce.[17]

The Golden Hour

The conquerors soon found rich gold desposits in Boriquén. Following the model of Hispaniola, they forced the Amerindians to work for them. The *naborias* of each *cacique* were granted in *encomienda* to different Spanish settlers, both to work in the mines and to perform agricultural tasks to provide food for the whole community. Ponce de León established a settlement on the land neighboring some of the gold mines and cassava plantations of the Toa valley, not too far from the sea. He called it Caparra, name of a place in León with which he had some connection.[18]

The news of the settlement of Boriquén pleased Ferdinand of Aragon, who needed gold to further his aggressive diplomacy in the Pyrenees and Italy. Although Ponce de León's rights were not clear, since the crown was then in litigation with Columbus' heirs over his rights to the islands he had discovered, Ferdinand of Aragon did not hesitate in backing the colonizing effort. The crown decreed incentives for Seville traders to visit the useful port that had been identified near the town of Caparra, so that Spaniards could be provided with all necessary materials. He also authorized Ponce de Leon to obtain supplies at the city of Santo Domingo, on Hispaniola.[19]

Between 1508 and 1512, the island of San Juan Bautista provided the Spanish Crown with an abundant income from its gold.[20] News about the island's wealth encouraged other Spaniards to join in the colonization. Some royal officials were successful in obtaining from Ferdinand of Aragon grants of *naborias* to work in the gold mines.

The accelerated pace of work in the mines of Boriquén took its toll on the Amerindian population. Contact with the Spaniards exposed them to diseases they had never before experienced and for which they lacked immunity. Their health was threatened by the new work regime, so different from their usual occupations. Possibly they were also affected by changes in their diet, since they could no longer engage in fishing and hunting.

The Rebellion of 1511

Amerindians were used to living in small population units, perhaps no bigger than three or four hundred people. Joint military action was uncommon, although the frequent raids on Boriquén's coasts by inhabitants of the eastern Caribbean had accustomed them to war. But the new situation in which they found themselves called for a coordination of effort.

The Amerindians' collective resentment was fueled by the frequent assemblies and *areytos* which were held in the spring of 1511, especially in the southwest of Boriquén. As the Spaniards spread throughout the island, according to the locations of the Amerindians subordinated to them and of the gold mines, it was easy to take them by surprise at the beginning of the rebellion. The Amerindians destroyed the town founded by the nobleman Cristóbal de Sotomayor, killing between 150 and 200 Spaniards throughout the island. The surviving Spaniards retreated to Caparra, where there were some veteran soldiers and weapons.[21]

Ponce de León and his followers were able to save Caparra and take the offensive. They burned down Amerindian villages, took many prisoners and branded their foreheads with the "F" of the regent Ferdinand of Aragon, thus reducing them to slaves. Defeat in open battle and the death and dispersal of the principal *caciques*, including another Guaybaná, ended the rebellion. But the Spanish victory was precarious on account of the pockets of resistance that appeared, especially on the eastern side of the island. The Amerindians opted to join forces with their former enemies from the eastern Caribbean and launched many joint expeditions that blocked the settlement of the east. They also compelled the Spaniards to reinforce their defenses in the bay of Puerto Rico (eventually called San Juan), at the mouth of the Loiza river, and in the mining and agricultural outposts in the west. As late as the 1580s, the subjects of the king of Spain in Puerto Rico were constantly on the alert for Amerindian attacks.[22]

With the suppression of the rebellion, the indigenous depopulation of Boriquén accelerated. Many Amerindians took refuge in the islands east of Boriquén and many more perished under the harsh servitude, which was now even more severe with the legal pretext of slavery. As in Santo Domingo, a smallpox epidemic took a terrible toll. Some inhabitants from other islands, like the Bahamas and Trinidad, were brought to Puerto Rico to meet the pressing demand for labor. But by the 1520s it was evident that the population the Spaniards had tried to conquer had disappeared.[23]

Officials and Offices

In 1511 Diego Colón, son of Cristóbal, had attempted to install Juan Cerón and Miguel Díaz as his delegates for the governorship of

Puerto Rico. Ponce de León did not recognize their legal authority to substitute for him as the representative of royal authority and sent both of them back to Spain. But in Castile, the royal council finally decided the case of the rights of discoverer in favor of Diego Colón. Accordingly the authorities designated by Diego Colón returned to the island in 1512 and, with royal approval, took control of the government.[24]

The Crown rewarded Ponce de León's endeavors in a number of ways. It allowed him to undertake the conquest of the island of Bimini, where, according to Amerindian oral tradition, there was untold wealth and marvels. Ponce de León set sail and discovered Florida in 1513.

Diego Colón's delegates continued the labor on the mines and in agriculture. Seville's traders, attracted by the abundance of gold, provided the necessary supplies for the townships of Caparra and the newly founded San Germán. Seville's notarized records from that time convey the feverish activity. Here are some examples: On June 14, 1512, Benito de Guadalcanal, resident of Seville, promises to serve Pedro Ruiz de Barrasa, citizen of the island of San Juan of the Indies. On January 30, 1514, Inés de Orvaneja, a widow from Seville, pledges to work for four years with the *alguacil mayor* of the island of San Juan, Miguel Díaz. On October 10, 1515, Andrés de Vega, a merchant from Burgos who was resident in Seville, empowers Andrés de Haro, treasurer of the island of San Juan, and Martín de Arvide, a citizen of Bilbao, to collect from Juan Sánchez, a merchant, and from Pedro Moreno, a citizen of Puerto Rico, that which is owed to him. On October 30, 1520, Ana de Segura, "who is going to the island of San Juan, to the city of Puerto Rico of the Indies, with Alonso López, acknowledges that, besides the merchandise valued at the sum of 6 thousand *maravedís* owed to Juan López, they carry their own, which is valued at 6,000 *maravedís*, the profit from which should be shared."[25] These and other synopses of notarized acts of the time evidence the fever which overtook Spaniards seeking their fortunes in the recently conquered island.

The gold was sent to Seville cast into bars. Several officials presided over the accounting of the royal mining rights: a treasurer, an auditor, and accountant and an overseer (*veedor*). The legal wrangling among these officials filled many files over the following twenty years. The reason behind their disputes was competition for the control of the declining Amerindian workforce.[26] Struggles for jurisdiction and for precedence meant a greater or lesser number of Amerindians who could be effectively dedicated to the search for gold in the rivers and streams.[27]

The Crown, protective of its rights even though its power was curtailed by that of Diego Colón, found new ways of ensuring the profitability of its remaining rights. It demanded fees for minting the gold and for trading rights, in particular a duty called *almojarizfazgo*, which taxed trade between Seville and the island of San Juan. It also conferred the status of towns on the settlements at Caparra and San Germán, with their respective districts bounded by the Camuy River to the north and the Jacaguas River to the south. The petitions and the appeals made by the town councils increased the crown's influence on the important affairs on the island. Finally, with the installation of Alonso Manso as first bishop of Puerto Rico and General Inquisitor, the powers of the governors nominated by Diego Colón were limited by the power of the Church.

The Institutionalization of
the Catholic Church

In the thirteenth century, bishops in most western European churches were elected by the cathedral chapters, that is, the councils of canons who conducted and supervised worship in the cathedrals. The pope intervened in the selection of bishops only when there was a dispute about the validity of an election and the case was sent for appeal to the papal court.[28]

When the crown of Castile conquered Andalusia in the thirteenth century, King Ferdinand III asked the papacy for the right to nominate bishops for the reconstituted dioceses in the conquered territories.[29] Since the dioceses of Jaén, Córdoba, Seville, and other Andalusian sees did not have cathedral chapters at the time of their restoration or creation and the churches lacked the necessary income to support the clergy or worship, the King of Castile was granted permission to nominate the bishops in exchange for his patronage of the dioceses and endowing them with an income. The king's rights over these dioceses as their patron was called the royal *patronato*.

In 1504, the crown of Castile suggested to Pope Julius II that three dioceses be created on the recently-conquered island of Hispaniola.[30] The crown would endow them with an income and would obtain from them the *patronato*, with the consequent right to nominate bishops. Pope Julius II approved the proposal and the nomination of three Spanish clergymen to occupy these sees, but none of them set out to fill the episcopal chairs.

With the depopulation of Hispaniola as a result of the extinction of the Amerindians, the crown sought permission from Julius II to move one of the sees that had been created to the island of San Juan. Alonso Manso, the canon of Salamanca, was then tranferred to this see in August 1511. The first bishop to arrive in the New World, Manso traveled to the island in 1513. He soon realized that the crown had not made the necessary preparations to establish and maintain the ecclesiastical institutions. After instituting religious worship, he returned to Spain with the intention of resolving the legal and economic problems that hindered the development of the diocese. He would return several years later.[31]

The Dominicans, Champions of the Amerindians

Even under the contradictory conditions in which the evangelization of the Amerindians was carried out, it resulted in the christianization of most of the *encomendados* and enslaved Indians. This shook the conscience of the Dominican friars, who, in Hispaniola as well as in San Juan, began to reflect on the contradictory nature of the Christian message of salvation presented to the Amerindians, since it represented the creed of the very people who enslaved and ill-treated them. In a Sunday sermon delivered in December 1511, Antonio de

Montesinos presented his congregation with the issue of the injustice of exploiting the Amerindians. That sermon, the first in a series, caused an uproar in the city of Santo Domingo:

> . . . you are all in a state of mortal sin and in it you live and die, on account of the cruelty and the tyranny which you use on this innocent people. Tell me, with what right and with what justice do you hold these Indians in such cruel and horrible serf-dom? . . . Are not they men? Do they not have rational souls? Are you not obliged to love them as yourselves? Do you not understand this, do you not feel? How have you sunk to such depths, sleep in such a lethargic slumber? Be assured that in the state in which you find yourselves, you cannot be saved, any more than the Moors or the Turks who lack and do not desire to have faith in Jesus Christ.[32]

The following Sunday Montesinos warned the *encomienda* holders and Hispaniola's officials that they would not be granted absolution at confession unless they freed the Amerindians. As a result of this sermon, Dominican friars in Hispaniola were not allowed to preach.

The Dominican friars continued their offensive against the exploitation of the Amerindians. Montesinos traveled to Spain and had the opportunity to present his cause to Ferdinand, the King Regent and to the principal officials of the Castilian crown. His efforts resulted in the Laws of Burgos of 1512, which were modified by the Ordinances of Valladolid in 1513. This piece of legislation reiterated previous royal orders requiring the correct treatment of the Amerindians and added new clauses protecting those born in the Indies.[33]

Like so many other inspired texts, the laws and ordinances did not go beyond an expression of good will. They did not have a major impact on the actual treatment of Amerindians in the Antilles. The fundamental question was avoided: the dubious right of the Spaniards to exploit other human beings. It is true that the legislation stated that, before conquering the Amerindians, they should be required to accept the Christian faith, but this obviously turned into a farce. Bartolomé de las Casas later summed up the situation when he wrote:

. . . we have usurped all the kingdoms and lordships of the Indies . . . the natives of whatsoever regions we have entered in the Indies have an acquired right to wage most just war against us and to erase us from the face of the earth, and this right will be theirs until the Day of Judgment.[34]

The Dominican friars' courageous stance in defense of the rights of Amerindians is the first chapter of a long history of intervention by Christian churches in the Americas on behalf of those being subjected to abuse and injustice.[35]

The Relocation of Caparra

Since 1511 some settlers had been proposing to move the town founded by Ponce de León three miles from the bay to the actual islet that stood at the entrance to the bay. This question was debated heatedly throughout the following decade. Finally, after inquiries made by the Hieronymite Friars and Rodrigo de Figueroa, the issue was settled in 1521, when the town was moved to the site of what is today San Juan de Puerto Rico.

The debate about the move showed two divergent views of what the principal city of Puerto Rico should be. Those who favored moving it to the bay pointed out not only the health problems represented by the swamps and wetlands near Caparra, but also the convenience of having the city next to the port. This would help avoid transporting goods along muddy trails and would facilitate communications with the harbor. For Ponce de León, who had built his stone house in Caparra, it was more important that the city be near the gold mines, the farms on the banks of the Toa River, and the meadows where cattle grazed. He envisaged the citizens of Caparra as people who were busy producing and who should not live far from their places of work.[36]

But for those in favor of the move, the important issue was not the site of production, but the port which gave access to trade. In opting for the move, the city was cutting itself off from direct production. In the sixteenth and seventeenth centuries San Juan scarcely produced anything; food had to be brought to it. The city assumed a parasitic relationship with the rest of the island. Its links to the outside world came to be more important than its relationship with "the Island." That was evident, for example, from the description written by López de Haro in 1644.[37]

In this sense, the history of San Juan in the pre-industrial era is substantially different from that of San Germán, Coamo, or Arecibo, places which were tightly linked to production and more attentive to the demands of producers. The reasons presented by Ponce de León to Rodrigo de Figueroa in 1519, when he asserted that one should give greater consideration to the residents than to the sailors and merchants, reflected a different vision of the life of the city. Puerto Ricans cannot claim Ponce de León as the founder of San Juan, but we pay hardly any attention to Pedro de Cárdenas, who represented those favoring the move, or to any other of the early residents of San Juan. While other cities in America point to this or that figurehead as the prime mover behind its foundation, conservative San Juan only wants to refer to some anonymous collective interests which provided it with its commercial vocation.

There is a certain poetic justice in the notion that a city which has gone out of its way to revere powerful figures does not owe its foundation to any notable personage. The city of San Juan, as if wishing to make amends to the founder of Caparra—who died from an arrow wound received during the second expedition to Florida in the year of the city's move—eventually erected a statue to Ponce de León in the square known today as San José. But as all Sanjuaneros know, the statue faces the other side of the bay, towards Caparra.

The Peregrinations of San Germán

But if the town of Caparra was moved to the bay of Puerto Rico because it lay inland, San Germán tried out several possibilities before it moved inland to its final location. Since the settlement which Diego Colón had ordered built had been destroyed by the Amerindians on February 23, 1512, the regent king Ferdinand ordered Cerón and Díaz to have it rebuilt, with the same name of San Germán. He added the clause, however, that if the location was not suitable either for navigation or for access to the gold mines, it should be built in another place.[38] The mouth of the Guaorabo (Añasco) river was chosen, which met both conditions. In the 1520s, there was an attempt to move it to Aguada, but the settlers on the River Guaorabo opposed this. In a 1526 file on the stone repair of bridges, one of the questions asked of witnesses was:

> 6. Also if they know etc. that this town favors much the service of His Majesty and the pacification and security of this Island, because it is peopled, and if it became depopulated would there be much harm done to the Island, both on account of the runaway blacks and Indians, and because ships which do trade among the islands would not find a secure harbor in it, and if it is not peopled His Majesty would receive much harm and damage to his rents and lose the service he receives from it, etc.[39]

In 1528, some sixty French corsairs, the first to pillage the waters of Puerto Rico, sacked and burned the settlement of San Germán. When the invaders arrived, the inhabitants, along with their families, fled, abandoning farms and mines. From that day on, the need to provide San Germán with sufficient defenses was underlined. In the 1530s, Fernández de Oviedo proposed that San Germán and the island of Mona be fortified to prevent corsairs from establishing bases there from which to plunder Spanish trade.[40]

The circumstances could hardly have been less favorable to the Sangermeños. Gold was becoming scarce in the neighboring mines, while the entire continent was being opened up to Spanish exploration. The Spanish crown, involved in grueling wars against France for the control of Italy, did not pay sufficient attention to its first settlements in the New World.

In the 1530s, repeated attacks, both by corsairs and by Carib Indians, resulted in the dispersal of the town's inhabitants. As long as merchants still frequented the port, there was an incentive to keep the town at the river's mouth. But once the fleet system was established, as explained in a later chapter, the port lost interest for the major traders. Pierre and Huguette Chaunu have identified the ships that set out from San Germán to Nombre de Dios on the Panama isthmus in 1544, 1547, and 1551. After those dates the name of San Germán does not reappear in commercial registers.[41]

In 1543 bishop Bastidas informed Charles V that owing to the lack of fortifications, the citizens of San Germán were abandoning the town and were taking their families to the hills. As the request for a fort was not granted, some thirty-odd heads of family who remained moved a mile and a half away, where they were found by Bastidas in 1548. But that place also became insecure. Finally, in the 1570s, the remaining residents of San Germán moved to the hills of Santa Marta, at sufficient distance from the coast and at a height which allowed them to keep an eye on the possible access routes to the town.[42]

Although the population of San Germán grew dramatically over the following two centuries, most of its inhabitants lived on the land. Only on important occasions would they come into town. Eventually some groups of inhabitants who lived in the extensive hinterland founded a number of other towns.

The Crisis of the 1530s

The changing circumstances of the San Germeños mirrored the crisis facing the Spanish conquerors of Boriquén. Since the 1520s, the experiences of the neighboring island of Hispaniola had foreshadowed this crisis. The demographic catastrophe that virtually wiped out the Amerindian population and the falling production of the gold mines both pointed to the imminent depletion of this mineral resource. Although the introduction of African slaves seemed to deal with the problem of the lack of a workforce, only an increase in the mines' profitability would justify the necessary investment.

Agriculture was the obvious alternative for the islands. But the resounding success of the conquerors of Mexico and Peru encouraged many of the settlers to set off for the mainland, lured by the possibility of instant wealth. In fact, the island served as the base for an attempt to conquer Trinidad, and the horses for Peru's conquerors were raised in the meadows of Puerto Rico.

The census taken by Governor Francisco de Lando[43] in 1531 still showed the island of San Juan, which by identifying itself with its main town and port would end up being called Puerto Rico, as having a sizeable Spanish population and a declining, but still considerable, Amerindian population. The African inhabitants, however, constituted the majority: 2,264 persons, of which 1,931 (85.2%) were within the jurisdiction of San Juan de Puerto Rico.[44]

Both Spaniards and Africans would leave the island for the mainland in the following years, despite the prohibitions and punishments that governor Lando tried to impose on the residents. In 1546 the treasurer Juan de Castellanos figured that only 80 heads of household remained on the island and he proposed that the introduction of African slaves be allowed so as to provide a workforce.[45]

Eventually agriculture and cattleraising replaced mining as the main source of income. But the crisis of the mining period would leave its mark on the minds of the people. In future the island would no longer be at the center of Spain's colonizing efforts nor would it receive as much attention as in the initial period. Shunted aside by the very dynamics of the conquest of the New World, from which they were excluded, the remaining inhabitants of Puerto Rico would end up dissociating themselves from the great world of empires and would turn their backs on the sea. Inland there was a world of possibilities, although not all of them would meet the criteria of the Council of the Indies.

The Political Regime

After careful negotiation, the crown and Columbus' heirs agreed that, from January 1537 onward, the crown would have direct jurisdiction over the islands settled under the terms of the Capitulations of Granada and its revisions.[46] Thus the inhabitants of Puerto Rico became subjects of the crown in terms analogous to those of the inhabitants of the kingdoms of the Iberian Peninsula.

In the initial phase of this new political regime the *alcaldes* of the city acted as governors, with the same powers as those previously held by representatives of the Columbus family. But the fact that the *alcaldes* were also residents whose interests in cattle raising and agriculture frequently placed them in competition with other inhabitants of the district, prompted some to ask the crown to send outside governors who were not implicated in local interests.[47]

Although initially the crown did not pay much attention to these petitions, the recurrence of the pleas and the complexity of the island's problems resulted in the sending of "lettered governors," that is, delegates of the crown with a legal background.

The pressing needs of defense, however, resulted in a short duration for the "lettered governors." The appointment of Francisco de Bahamonde in 1564 began the era of military governors. Except for a brief interruption at the beginning of the 1820s, this era would last to the very end of Spanish rule in Puerto Rico. Having a person from a military background responsible for the immediate supervision of military affairs as well as civil government led to a militarization of the political system. Many governors were not able to distinguish between military discipline and the requirements of civilian jurisdiction. At the beginning of the eighteenth century, there was even one governor who, after a summary military trial, hanged a mulatto mason from the Canary Islands who had accused him in verse of misappropriating funds for a building.[48]

We learn about the misdeeds of each governor from the *Juicio de Residencia*, a notarized record of all complaints about a governor presented at the end of his term.[49] The governor was able to answer the complaints and present his own witnesses, but ultimately a judge decided on the merits of the accusations and fined the outgoing governor if this seemed to be justified.

The *Audiencia*

The *audiencia* provided the institutional counterweight to the governor. It was an appeals court composed of various career judges, and often it received complaints about the arbitrary behavior of governors and tried to provide solutions for this. Puerto Rico fell within the jurisdiction of the Audiencia of Santo Domingo following its foundation in 1511 until the end of the eighteenth century.[50] Although slow to act and at times erratic, the Audiencia prevented the institutional regime from being wholly arbitrary. Its interventions helped to shape the notions of legality which nurtured the development of a sector of Puerto Rican society.

Emancipation of Sixty Indians

In 1543 the Council of the Indies decreed the freedom of the Amerindians in Hispaniola and Puerto Rico. In January 1544, Bishop Bastidas noted that the decree had been observed, and freedom had been granted to sixty Amerindians, young and old. It was later discovered that there were more, whom the *encomienda* holders had tried to withhold from the emancipation decree.[51]

Although the intention had been that the freed Amerindians should live near San Juan and San Germán, they preferred to live in the mountains. What eventually became the site of San Germán turned out to be closer to the place of their settlement. The post–sixteenth century Amerindian presence in Puerto Rico can be ascertained from the eighteenth-century censuses, and they usually appear listed within the municipal limits of San Germán. The last time they were listed separately was in 1802, when their number totaled 2,300. Thereafter they were included in the numbers of the free *pardos*.[52]

It is possible that some of the so-called *indio* population in the eighteenth century included Amerindians brought to Puerto Rico from other parts of the Caribbean in the sixteenth, seventeenth, and eighteenth centuries for different reasons. Eighteenth-century parish registers occasionally refer to an individual as an *indio*.

Although *indios* made up only 1.4% of Puerto Rico's population in the 1802 census, one should bear in mind that the number of their descendants is potentially higher than that of non-Spanish European immigrants of the nineteenth century. One should also point out that part of the population then called *pardo* had Amerindian blood.

All in all, it is important to remember that the process of mythologizing the Amerindian past, begun in the 1530s, has not yet ended. Although the Amerindian legacy is important in the formation of Puerto Rico's agrarian culture, one should not use this to diminish another, much more important one, that of the African population. Since the sixteenth century, as one can see from Lando's census, the percentage of the population of African origin has been larger than the Amerindian.

Agriculture and Cattle Raising in the Sixteenth and Seventeenth Centuries

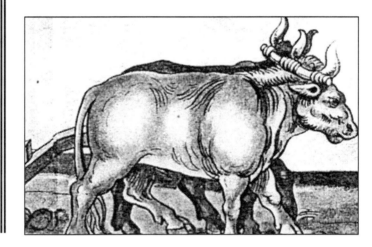

The first sugar era

From the perspective of the Spanish crown, once the export of gold from Puerto Rico declined in the 1520s, the island became less productive. Like their peers in Santo Domingo, the settlers who had opted to live on the island explored alternatives to mining. In Santo Domingo, sugar mills had been successful. Since 1510 the European demand for sugar had stimulated the establishment of sugar mills near the city of Santo Domingo, as proximity to the city made financing and transportation easier.[1]

Before sugar became popular, the Europeans would sweeten their dishes with honey, or in the case of the well-to-do, with cloves and cinnamon. Sugar had been introduced into Europe by Arab trade in the Mediterranean. Venetians, sizing up the possibility of cornering the market in what they considered another spice, planted cane fields in the Greek islands they had held since the Fourth Crusade of 1204, particularly Crete. Apparently it was the Genoese who introduced its cultivation into Sicily and the Canary Islands, and it was the Portuguese who perfected and disseminated the manufacturing techniques.[2]

The acquired taste for sweeteners brought hefty profits to the growers and the merchants from the Canaries. Since the first experiments in the cultivation of sugarcane and the manufacture of sugar were so successful in Santo Domingo, competition soon broke out to obtain the necessary workforce and finance for the sugar industry in the Antilles.

According to the Dominican historian Frank Moya Pons, by 1527 in Hispaniola there were nineteen mills operated by waterpower and six by animal traction. One acre of land planted with cane would produce twenty hundredweight, that is a ton, of sugar.[3] This average productivity may help us calculate the area of land devoted to sugar in the sixteenth and seventeenth centuries.

Planting sugarcane and manufacturing sugar required many resources and skills: the clearing and the preparation of the soil, planting, harvesting, and transporting the cane, the grinding, boiling and separation of the juices, the packing, storage, and shipping. Of all these operations, the most specialized was heating the sugarcane juice for just the right amount of time to achieve the crystallization of sugar. The office of "master sugar maker," initially held by Genoese, Canary Islanders, or Portuguese, came to be dominated by Africans, who became the key to the manufacturing success on account of their knowledge of the art of making sugar.[4]

On account of the many different operations involved in the production and export of sugar, this branch of the agrarian economy needed adequate financing from the start. As the sugar industry came to depend on a slave workforce, the question of the capital investment represented by the slaves was added to the problem of finance.

In the 1530s there was an early attempt to develop the sugar industry in Puerto Rico. Tomás de Castellón, a Genoese who, together with his son-in-law, had powerful economic and political contacts, attempted to set up a sugar mill in the vicinity of the former site of San Germán, now within the jurisdiction of Añasco. The location was probably linked to the possibility of obtaining Amerindian workers, who were still available in that area. But the success of this mill was short-lived. The failure was not due to its profitability, but to the fact that the mill became entangled in the lawsuits for debts to the crown left by Castellón on his death.[5]

From the 1530s on, the *cabildo* of the city of San Juan de Puerto Rico stressed the benefits of promoting sugar mills as a replacement for the mining economy. In 1538, the *cabildo* asked the Crown for more financing and a permit to introduce African slaves. The Crown was more ready to grant the first petition than the second. In 1546, the treasurer Juan de Castellanos wrote to Charles V informing him that he had lent six thousand gold pesos from the royal treasury for the development of two sugar mills. In 1548, Bishop Bastidas asked Charles V to endorse the two parishes founded by the bishop in the sugar mills of Gregorio de Santolaya, in the jurisdiction of San Juan. One of the mills is powered by water, the other by horses. The following year it is the San Juan *cabildo* that asks the monarch to extend the term of the loan of 1500 pesos made to Alonso Pérez Martell, owner of a water-powered mill nine miles from San Juan.[6]

By 1582 there are eleven sugar mills producing 187.5 tons of sugar. This figure represents an estimated average production of 17 tons per mill. In Santo Domingo a large mill could produce 125 tons. Informants in 1582 explained the modest production in Puerto Rico by citing the lack of workers. They said production would be tripled if each sugar mill had one hundred slaves. However, the available data shows that sugar production in Puerto Rico had already reached the limits of its first peak in production.

This is based on the known number of boxes of sugar sent to Seville from Puerto Rico between 1568 and 1594. According to the Spanish researcher Lorenzo Sanz, the amount of sugar in each box averaged between 23 and 30 *arrobas*.[7] Taking 30 *arrobas* per box as the average, the data gathered by the Chaunu and by Lorenzo Sanz would yield the following approximate amounts of Puerto Rican sugar exported to Seville:

TABLE 5.1

Boxes of sugar from Puerto Rico imported to Seville, 1568–1594

Year	Number of Boxes	*Arrobas*
1568	740	22,200
1569	379	11,370
1570	267	8,010
1571	284	8,520
1583	79	2,370
1584	186	5,580
1589	—	1,170
1593	—	5,640
1594		9,105

Sources: Chaunu, *Seville et l'Atlantique* VI, 2, 1994, table 750
Lorenzo Sanz, *Comercio,* 1, 615, table 72.

A fall in productivity may be in part attributed to the difficulties in marketing discussed in the next chapter. But Elsa Gelpí has argued that there was a second peak in production in the final decades of the sixteenth century.[8] In 1598 the Earl of Cumberland took more than a thousand boxes of sugar from Puerto Rico,[9] that is to say, some 30,000 *arrobas*. This quantity is vastly superior to that registered at Seville as having been imported from Puerto Rico in the preceding years. But is likely that difficulty of financing and the lack of workers also hindered the development of sugar production.

In Seville the price of sugar coming from the islands in the 1590s was lower than those reached in 1570, but it was still high. Throughout the period 1550–1650, sugar provided the highest source of income for Puerto Rico in the official trade with Seville and Cádiz.[10]

It is interesting to note the location of the existing sugar mills. Given the difficulties and costs of transportation, proximity to the official port explains why production at the time was concentrated in the northern region. River currents powered the mills and also the canoes loaded with boxes of sugar carried to the city. According to Melgarejo's report, there were four mills powered by animals in the

Bayamón valley, two powered by animals and one by water in the Toa valley, two by animals and one by water ("Canobana") in the Loiza valley, and one powered by animals about three miles from the depopulated site of Caparra. According to the authors of that report, settlements in the Loiza valley suffered frequent attacks from the Carib Indians:

> a mill . . . that is near the river mouth of said Loiza has been burnt and robbed three times by Caribs who enter with their pirogues upriver from the said mill and in the three times they have carried off many Africans, for in one time they carried off twenty-five and they killed off the master sugar maker. It has not been abandoned because it is one of the good *haciendas* of this island and of the best equipped, and because certain repairs have been made to fortify it at the expense of the owner.[11]

There is evidence, however, that by mid-sixteenth century there were *haciendas* and sugar mills in other parts of Puerto Rico. Jalil Sued Badillo has identified several *haciendas* in the area of Guayama for that period, and the Melgarejo Report itself mentions *haciendas* and places abandoned on account of attacks by Carib Indians.[12]

In the centers of sugar production the living quarters were centered round the big house and the mill. This pattern was partly for reasons of security and partly to control the enslaved workers. The layout leads the authors of a 1582 report to compare the sugar mills to Spanish villages "because the slaves and the agents, outside of the big house, have each got their house in the vicinity, so that they resemble a Spanish *alcaria*, and they have a church and in some mills there are chaplains, when they are to be found . . ."[13]

In the seventeenth century Puerto Rican sugar production fell. Demand at the beginning of that century in Amsterdam led to a rapid expansion of plantations in Brazil, Madeira, the Canary Islands, Andalusia, and Sicily, and, after the 1640s, in the British West Indies. Puerto Rican producers, chronically lacking access to markets and without the capital or sufficient credit to acquire the workforce and the necessary imported materials to improve production, were not able to profit from sugar's popularity in European daily life. By the

1640s, only seven of the mills mentioned in 1582 remained: four in Bayamón, two in the Toa valley, and the "Canobana" in Loiza, "the other four that existed, two in the Loiza valley, one in the Pueblo Viejo (Caparra), and the other one on the upper Toa valley, have been demolished either by the attacks of enemies or for the greater convenience of the owners."[14] The same source notes that there were mills producing molasses in San Germán and the Coamo valley.

The Spanish historian García Fuentes has retrieved the statistics on Puerto Rico sugar received in Seville for a selection of years between 1650 and 1670.

TABLE 5.2

Sugar from Puerto Rico imported to Seville, 1650–1670

Year	Number of *Arrobas*
1650	333
1651	534
1652	230
1654	308
1660	1,100
1663	216
1670	132

Source: García Fuentes, *Comercio*, Appendixes 522–24.

Although the amounts are well below those available for the end of the sixteenth century, in this period Puerto Rico still contributed 5% of the sugar imported from the Indies. In comparison, Cuba supplied 63%, Tierra Firme (the South American mainland) 29%, New Spain 1.3%, and Santo Domingo 0.8%.[15] By the second half of the seventeenth century, however, the British islands had become the main sugar producers in the Caribbean.

Cattle

Although it was the most profitable item in the economy in the second half of the sixteenth century, sugar provided an income for only a minority of the population. For many residents, cattle provided the source of income which complemented their subsistence crops.

As in Santo Domingo, the initial phase of Spanish colonization included the introduction from the Iberian Peninsula of domestic animals which were not a part of the indigenous fauna. The abundance of unused land and the favorable climate supported the breeding of cows, horses, goats, pigs, dogs, and sheep. In 1542, one of the criteria cited for consideration before imposing Spanish models of land distribution on the island implied that cattle ranchers allowed their animals to roam freely in the wasteland, without branding them, and would only occasionally herd together the heads of cattle they required.[16]

It was not long before the usefulness of this livestock was recalled. Hispaniola and Puerto Rico provided the horses for the conquistadors of New Spain and Tierra Firme. The expeditions that sailed from Puerto Rico, as well as those that set off from Trinidad, carried animals such as goats and pigs that had been raised on the island.[17]

Nevertheless, it was cattle that brought the island a steady income. In the second half of the sixteenth century, the frequent European wars prompted a heavy demand for leather, which was used to make boots, cuirasses, harnesses, belts, and crossbow strings. Moya Pons, who has studied that aspect of Dominican history, points out that leather also had multiple civilian uses, among which he lists shoes, hats, pants, jackets, cords, pulleys, and also its use as covers for furniture, doors, books, beds, and even walls.[18]

Apparently the price of leather depended on the skill with which it had been cured. Leather from the Antilles received a lower price than that from New Spain, where the herds of cattle had multiplied in the closing decades of the sixteenth century. The Chaunu have collected the figures for the traffic in Puerto Rican leather arriving in Spain, and Lorenzo Sanz has added to these numbers:

TABLE 5.3

Leather from Puerto Rico Imported into Seville, 1569–1594

Years	Units	Total Value (in *maravedís*)	Average price (in *maravedís*)
1568	6,638	4,513,840	680
1569	4,348	2,956,640	680
1570	6,321	4,298,280	680
1571	2,631	1,789,080	680
1577	11,636	—	
1583	967	386,800	400
1584	2,875	1,096,375	381
1585	4,705	2,352,500	500
1589	5,191	3,114,600	600
1593	4,731	3,075,150	650
1594	8,536	5,548,400	650

Sources: Chaunu, *Seville et l'Atlantique* VI, 2, 1017; Lorenzo Sanz, *Comercio* I, 620–21

Layfield, the chaplain of the invading Earl of Cumberland in 1598, tells of a resident named Chereno, who had twelve thousand heads of cattle near Aguada. Since Layfield considered the western coast to be one of the least propitious places for cattle raising, he assumed that there was a great abundance of cattle throughout the island.[19]

Both Puerto Rican and Dominican cattle lent themselves to smuggling, an activity whose main perpetrators in the first decades of the seventeenth century were the Dutch. The sheer amount of smuggling in Hispaniola prompted the crown to authorize the depopulation of the Atlantic and western coasts of the island. This had huge consequences for the course of Dominican history.[20] In Puerto Rico the government seat and official port was on the north coast, while the western coast received occasional visits from the fleets that stopped for provisions in Aguada. Thus the southern and eastern coasts would have been the most affected if there had been an order to remove the inhabitants on account of cattle smuggling. However, such a regrouping of population had been already carried out in San Germán and in the Coamo valley as a measure of protection against the corsairs and for religious purposes.[21] For the greater part of the seventeenth and the eighteenth centuries, the southern coastal plains, settled only thinly by farmers, were given over to grazing for the herds of the co-owners of the *hatos*. The cattlemen were often tempted to trade with the Dutch and the English, who needed draft animals, salted meat, and leather.

Although Torres Vargas states in 1647 between eight and ten thousand pieces of hides were sent to Spain annually,[22] the figures that have been obtained for the subsequent decades only occasionally match his optimistic claim:

TABLE 5.4
Leather from Puerto Rico Imported into Spain, 1650–1696

Year	Number of Units
1650	170
1651	1,207
1652	4,009
1654	859
1660	1,500
1663	158
1670	339
1696	1,180

Source: García Fuentes, *Comercio,* 519–21.

García Fuentes estimates that, in the second half of the seventeenth century, Puerto Rico's share of the amount of leather imported to Spain was 2.4%. Other suppliers were Santo Domingo (31%), Venezuela (25.3 %), Buenos Aires (15.8%), Cuba (11.8%), New Spain (6.3%), Tierra Firme (5.3%), and Honduras (2%). The modest amount of leather sent by Puerto Rico to Spanish markets in this period probably does not reflect a fall in production, but rather a loss of interest in official trade.[23]

Ginger

Between 1580 and 1650 the third most important item for export production in Puerto Rico was ginger. This plant, relatively simple to cultivate, was not native. It was introduced into America, either from Asia by way of New Spain or from Africa by way of Brazil.[24] This highly prized root was used in Europe both as a seasoning for food and for infusion to make beverages.

From the 1570s on, Hispaniola was the principal Antillean producer of ginger destined for the Seville market. The authors of the Melgarejo Report say in 1582 that the planting of ginger had been started in Puerto Rico: "it grows well and some people in Spain consider it finer than the one from Hispaniola."[25] In fact, competition between the two islands for the ginger market in Seville intensified in the 1590s. Hispaniola's authorities even asked the crown to prohibit the cultivation of ginger on the other islands. These are the figures collected by the Chaunu for Puerto Rican ginger imports to Seville:

TABLE 5.5
Puerto Rican Ginger Exports Received in Seville, 1583–1594

Year	Hundredweight	Price per hundredweight (in *maravedís*)
1583	33	4,500
1584	214	4,300
1589	403	4,080
1593	2,089	5,000
1594	3,168	5,100

Source: Chaunu, *Seville et l'Atlantique* VI, 2, 1031.

The registry books inform joint numbers for Hispaniola and Puerto Rico in 1596 and 1597. In 1598, the Earl of Cumberland took home two thousand hundredweights of ginger from Puerto Rico.[26]

One of the advantages of ginger was that its cultivation was accessible to many people: "ginger plantings do not need choice soils, so that the poor can easily have them and they do not need great resources to start its cultivation."[27] According to the Melgarejo Report, the main area for ginger growing was the Toa valley.

In the seventeenth century, either on account of the efforts to regulate the trade in ginger so as to benefit Hispaniola, or because of the difficulties in marketing the product after the fall in prices brought about by Brazilian production, Puerto Rican ginger had few outlets. Although Torres Vargas is probably exaggerating when he claims that production reached 14,000 hundredweight a year, and had dropped to 4,000 by 1646, the fact is that by the mid-seventeenth century ginger had disappeared as a major item in official exports. López de Haro laments that "all the traffic of this island and its crop is ginger, and it has fallen down so low that no one buys it nor do they take it to Spain."[28] In García Fuentes' figures for ginger imports to Seville, in the 1650s the Puerto Rican figures total only 4,675 hundredweight for the decade. Hispaniola too greatly reduced its ginger exports after prices fell in 1654.[29]

Although it never regained its importance to our economy, ginger was an established item in the Puerto Rican diet, in medicinal infusions, refreshments, and desserts. It was used to make a hot beverage drunk at wakes and nighttime family and religious gatherings. It was not until the eighteenth century that it was displaced by coffee.

Other Products

Besides sugar, leather, and ginger, the remaining production for official export between 1550 and 1700 was modest. No item appeared regularly on the Seville registers. In the sixteenth century the fruit of the *cañafístola* tree was exported, because its pulp was used to prepare laxatives. Although it was sold at 6,000 *maravedís* a hundredweight in 1529, going against the inflationary tendency of the period, the item became cheaper and was priced at between 2,200 and 3,000 *maravedís* by the late 1580s and early 1590s. Eighty hundredweight arrived in Seville from Puerto Rico in 1589. In 1593 this had dropped to ten hundredweight. In subsequent years unknown quantities were received in joint shipments from Cartagena and Santo Domingo.³⁰ At the beginning of the nineteenth century, Puerto Rico still exported some *cañafístola* to Spain.

There were other trees with medicinal uses, such as the *guayacán* and the *palo santo,* whose resins were considered useful for the cure of syphilis. In 1581 Seville received 2,530 hundredweight of *guayacán* from Hispaniola and Puerto Rico, and in 1585, 190 hundredweight from Puerto Rico. In 1594, there was a shipment of 80 hundred-weight of *palo brasil,* valued at 80,000 *maravedís.*

Although they may never have been sent to Seville, the products of several trees were considered useful in 1582. Torches for processions were made from the *tabonuco.* Its resin was used to tar the planks of ships. The *úcar's* wood was employed for presses, gun carriages, and axles for the sugar mills. The *capá* provided wood for the construction of houses and ships. The wood from the *maga* tree, "of very good color, tending to ebony, lasting . . . very good for carving," was used for furniture.³¹

Two other crops tried commercially without much success in the seventeenth century were tobacco and cacao. Tobacco became popular in Europe from 1610 onward, to the extent that Pope Urban VIII had to forbid smoking in churches. In Puerto Rico, although tobacco had been harvested by the Amerindians, it was not cultivated on a commercial scale until the 1620s. The 1630s, as in St. Christopher and Barbados, showed the crop's cultivation possibilities and it rendered 4,500 pesos in taxes in 1638 and 1639. But the year 1638 was fatal for Caribbean tobacco, on account of the fall in European prices due to the abundance of tobacco leaf from Virginia. From one year to the next, exports from Barbados, where a boycott of planting was begun, dropped from 2,050 to 280 hundredweight. For the remainder of the seventeenth century, European markets did not recover from the glut of Virginia leaf. Data gathered by García Fuentes shows Puerto Rico exporting 800 pounds of tobacco to Seville in 1651, 625 in 1654, and 50 in 1670. While between 1650 and 1699, Cuba supplied Spain with 57.3% of its imported tobacco and Venezuela with 32%, Puerto Rico supplied only 0.1%.³²

Torres Vargas reports on cocoa plantations on the island towards

1647, but he estimates that it would take four years to harvest. There are doubts as to whether the amounts of cacao sent from Puerto Rico to Seville between 1651 and 1670 was actually Venezuelan production re-exported from Puerto Rico. For those years Esquemeling (aka Exquemelin) reports that the pirate L'Olonais captured a ship in transit from Puerto Rico to New Spain carrying 120 hundredweight of cacao.[33]

That same ship carried a cargo of coconuts. That is the only known mention of this type of export in the seventeenth century, probably because it was expensive and slow to ship coconuts to Spain. One has to imagine that in an age when transportation was much slower, the goods exported to New Spain or Tierra Firme would be items that complemented the consumption patterns of those American lands, such as molasses, salt, and tortoise shells.

As well as the production for trade with Spain and Spanish America, agriculture, hunting and fishing supplied the island's basic necessities, although local trade sometimes resembled barter rather than sales. Cassava and plantain were the staples of the daily diet, but already in 1644 Bishop López de Haro pointed out that rice had captivated local tastes: "ordinarily there is rice on the table, produced in this land." On this bishop's table, when there was no beef, there was turtle meat. The people from Cangrejos were not yet able to ensure a regular supply of fish to the city, although already by 1598 there is mention of a fisherman near the point where the British disembarked. Oranges, limes, and lemons were common in the city both at the end of the sixteenth century and in the middle of the seventeenth. Towards the middle of the sixteenth century, Canon Diego Lorenzo introduced the coconut palm and the guinea fowl, which have given rise to several Puerto Rican culinary traditions.[34]

The System of Land Tenure

It is important to point out that all of this production for the local and international markets was unequally distributed over the surface of the island. From the end of the sixteenth century to the middle of the seventeenth, sugar production was concentrated between the Loíza and Toa river valleys. Wild cattle were found all over the island, but Aguada and San Juan on the north and northwest coasts were the official ports for export. Of course, goods were also exported illegally from everywhere else. The remaining production for official export was also concentrated in the zones near the official ports.

This distribution helps to explain why there was so much land available for a population which, in the seventeenth century, does not seem to have exceeded ten thousand inhabitants. Access to land near the capital was limited. Coastal valley lands had been granted in enormous concessions of *hatos*. There were no title deeds, but their possession was hereditary. Most of their surface was covered by extensive forests where cattle grazed. Cattle would have needed less land for grazing if the forest had not limited the extent of the pastures. But in the treeless areas near the capital, guava shrubs proliferated and defied efforts to create natural pastures.

While the population was low and the workforce scarce, the *hato* was the most productive type of land tenure. The inhabitants of the many *estancias* lived beside *hatos* which belonged to the families of important officials and old Puerto Rican families. These consisted of small lots of land with a house. The inhabitants' use of the land was the result of the tolerance of the *hato* owners, or their own spontaneous occupation of the land. These *estancias* were often established on the banks of rivers or on hillsides. During its boom period ginger was grown there. But the reason behind the *estancias'* existence was the need to provide for their inhabitants' subsistence, which they complemented with hunting and fishing. In the northern region they also supplied the San Juan market with plantains, bananas, cassava, and some other products for daily consumption. Typical of *estancieros* were the inhabitants of Cangrejos, an area which in the second half of the seventeenth century occasionally received fugitive slaves from the British islands.[35]

At that time the *hacienda* was the third and the least common form of land tenure in Puerto Rican agriculture. It was different from its contemporary, the original Mexican *hacienda*, which had large areas of land and where springs were valued for watering the cattle or irrigating wheat and corn.[36] In comparison, the Puerto Rican *hacienda* at the end of the sixteenth century was a modest area of land, generally situated on the banks of a river, and destined for sugarcane cultivation and the necessary food supplies for its workers. It generally included meadows for oxen and other domestic beasts of burden, and it also had woods to provide timber and charcoal for domestic and industrial use. At that time the hacienda usually had a mill. By the middle of the seventeenth century there probably remained only a dozen of these units of production throughout the island.

The few slaves left on the island by the end of the sixteenth century were concentrated on the *haciendas*. The *estancia*'s workforce was its household. Depending on the resources of the *hato's* owners, it could accommodate kinsmen, slaves, servants, or any others who, in one way or another, found in it a means of subsistence.

If sizeable investments in capital and a slave workforce had been made, and if there had been adequate access to European markets, Puerto Rican land tenure and the economy would have undergone the radical transformation that shook Jamaica after British conquest in 1655.[37] Puerto Rico did not pay the enormous human cost of promoting production on the island to satisfy the interests of several hundred absent planters and merchants.

The lack of capital and systematic access to the markets instead resulted in the formation of a society of farmers who went into the mountains in search of wild cattle and freedom from supervision by the authorities.[38] It was the *estancia* dwellers, and not the *hato* or *hacienda* owners, who began to define the features of our society. As a result, the emergence of an explicitly Creole consciousness was delayed until such time as the population began to make common cause for its needs and affirmed a common identity. The low population density of the seventeenth century did not inspire a greater identity consciousness than that evidenced by the laborious boasts of Canon Torres Vargas. In order to demonstrate the worth of his country, he had to proclaim how productive it was for the Crown and how prodigal it was in producing soldiers and clerics who distinguished themselves serving other Spanish dependencies.[39]

CHAPTER 6

Puerto Rico in the Struggle for Commercial Hegemony in the Sixteenth- and Seventeenth-Century Caribbean

The profitability of agricultural and cattle production in the sixteenth and seventeenth centuries rested on the commercial opportunities within the Spanish monopolistic mercantile system. Storing leather, boxes of sugar, and hundredweights of ginger was not worth the time and effort if there was no chance of selling them. As the second half of the sixteenth century progressed, such opportunities became more limited for several reasons, particularly the Andalusian monopoly system of trade, the changes in navigation routes, and the fleet system. On the other hand, the incursions of other Europeans in the Caribbean induced both the Spanish crown and the inhabitants of Puerto Rico to explore options for the island's role as one of Seville's trade partners.

The Andalusian Commercial Monopoly

The economic views that prevailed in Europe at the time suggested that the Castilian crown would obtain maximum profit from its New World possessions if it strictly controlled transoceanic trade. In England, for instance, the crown had received a profitable and effective income from the wool trade and from the textile products it traded with Flanders after establishing the Staple at Calais, a French town that belonged to the English crown until 1553. Any merchandise destined for the Flemish textile market had to pass through Calais. This trade was controlled by a guild or company of English merchants, most of them from London, who paid hefty sums to the English monarch for the privileges represented by the Staple.[1]

After Columbus' first voyage, the commercial possibilities offered by the New World awakened the interest of the Castilian crown. Out of this interest appeared, in 1503, the *Casa de Contratación*, a body designed to regulate all the aspects of trade with Hispaniola, up to then the only island on which the Castilians had founded settlements.[2]

Under the norms of the *Casa de Contratación* and of the Council of the Indies, a body which from 1523 on coordinated all communications with the New World, commercial traffic with the so-called West Indies was restricted to Seville, and in a lesser proportion to Cádiz. This was a logical option. Andalusia provided the shortest, most convenient, and safest point of departure for sailing routes between Spain and the Indies. Seville had access to sufficient resources to provision expeditions. It would not be until the eighteenth century, when the difficulty of navigating the Guadalquivir River increased, that the American traffic would be routed through Cádiz.[3]

The choice of Seville as the main port for the American trade transformed the city into a great metropolis. While other regions of Spain lost population, Seville grew in inhabitants and in wealth to become one of the principal European cities. From the great bankers and Italian merchants to the adventurers and fortune-seekers from all over Europe, all made Seville their meeting place, endeavoring to make quick fortunes with the gold, silver, pearls, and other merchandise from the New World. Seville became an exotic and violent city, opulent and gaudy, in whose streets notaries, soldiers, sailors, stevedores, artisans, students, clerics, musicians, acrobats, mimes, and missionaries mingled. Monkeys and parrots, scarlet cloth and tinsel, anything that was prized or had a price was exchanged in Seville.[4]

The merchants of Seville presided over all this confusion. Following prolonged negotiations with the Crown, which wanted to finance the defense of its interests in the New World, the merchants were granted the privilege of incorporating themselves in a guild, the *Consulado* of Seville. Only *Consulado* members would have the privilege of participating in the lucrative trade with the New World, which soon produced enormous dividends. All of Europe competed to fill the caravels sailing from Seville, which could only receive shipments from the *Consulado* members, and to a lesser extent, their counterparts from Cádiz.[5]

But the very success of Sevillian trade had a damaging effect on Spanish manufacturing, with fatal consequences for the future industrial development of Spain and of Spanish America. Why did the development of trade between Seville and the West Indies, which should have stimulated production in Spain, have such a negative effect? This paradox is largely explained by the inflation which affected sixteenth-century prices.[6]

The influx of substantial quantities of gold and silver triggered a demand for goods in Spain, which in turn increased their price. Other parts of Europe, like Flanders, France, and Italy, took advantage of the rise in prices to flood the Spanish market with goods which ended up being cheaper, even allowing for the tariffs. Seville merchants bought French, Flemish, and Italian cloth to send to the New World, because this was more profitable than buying Castilian cloth. This competition eventually ruined many textile centers in Castile, like those of Segovia. To supply its internal market and that of the Indies, Spain would become an importer of many commodities that had previously been made in its workshops. At the same time, no longer able to keep up with the foreign competition, the Spanish factories stopped buying raw materials from the New World, such as cochineal and indigo dyes and leather. Instead, Spain supplied American raw materials to the rest of Europe while at the same time importing goods, many of them manufactured using these same raw materials. In short, the fact that it was cheaper to buy foreign commodities than to manufacture them in Spain created a dependent economy.

Why did the Castilian crown allow this dangerous trend to develop in the sixteenth century? To some extent it was the crown's hereditary interests in other parts of Europe, such as Flanders, the Franche-Comté de Bourgogne, Milan, and the kingdom of Naples. Charles V and Philip II ruled over all these dominions. To reinforce their domain in those hereditary territories, the kings allowed their subjects preferential access to Castilian trade. It was a way to provide them with a market for their manufactures and to guarantee a supply of the raw materials to manufacture them, especially Castilian wool and the dyes that came from the Indies.[7]

In this way, although the Andalusian commercial monopoly apparently only favored Seville and Cádiz, in fact it also guaranteed the interests of other European economic sectors which, through their contacts with the Seville *Consulado*, benefited from the privileges the crown had granted to Sevillian trade. But at the same time the interests, not only of Spanish artisans, but also of the agrarian and cattle interests of the New World, were affected, especially in the areas far from the principal trade routes, which did not have regular access to the official trade.

Above all, the Andalusian monopoly eventually resulted in a profound change in the royal policies for the development of the New World settlements. In the early phase of colonization, the crown encouraged the opening of workshops and the cultivation of European crops in the New World. But in the second half of the reign of Philip II, the interests that converged on Seville obtained the royal implementation of a policy designed to restrict manufacturing in America. Philip II tried to stamp out wine production in the viceroyalty of Lima and textile manufacture in New Spain.[8]

Throughout the seventeenth century, traders in Seville kept watch for signs that the New World was trying to manufacture or become self-sufficient in the commodities that came from that city. For them, the main role of the Indies was to supply the gold, silver, pearls, and raw materials which were in great demand in Europe. Since Puerto Rico was not a constant supplier of those goods by the seventeenth century, the island lacked importance for Seville's traders. Few ships came to trade. Puerto Rico was poor in the seventeenth century, not because it lacked productive capacity, but because it barely featured in the economic strategy of Sevillian traders, who ultimately controlled and profited from the official trade of the West Indies.

Changes in Navigation Routes

The Andalusian trade monopoly was not the only factor that explains Puerto Rico's limited participation in the Atlantic economy in the centuries following the Spanish conquest. Another factor was the navigational routes of the sailing ships. Sailors seeking the shortest possible crossing of the Atlantic soon identified the prevailing winds in each area as well as the most favorable months to benefit from the winds and currents which assisted navigation.

From the Canary Islands—the last port for taking on water and provisions en route to the New World—one reached the Caribbean by means of the northeasterly winds.[9] When there was no wind there were anxious becalmed days at sea and the crossing was prolonged. Food ran out and water had to be rationed, with the result that some members of the crew and passengers sickened and died.[10]

In the first half of the sixteenth century, many Spanish ships took advantage of the favorable northeasterly trade winds to make one of the coves on Puerto Rico's western coast their first stop in the New World. There they took on water and provisions for their journey to Santo Domingo, Veracruz, the Panama coast, or some other Spanish port. These stops at the watering places on the western coast stimulated the early development of that part of the island.[11]

However, the proportion of ships sailing to the New World which stopped on the western coast of Puerto Rico declined after 1550. The Mona Passage was difficult for ships sailing to the Isthmus of Panama, and these difficulties increased as the ships became bigger. The growing Spanish trade with the New World and the need for security made it advisable to reduce the number of ships that had to be escorted, and bigger galleons were built. The large ships with rounded prows were difficult to maneuver and to steer southwards against the rapid currents of the Mona Passage.[12]

Spanish sailors preferred to dock at Dominica, Martinique, or Guadeloupe. It was easier to reach their destination points from these islands, using the easterly winds. According to the historians Pierre and Huguette Chaunu, between 1550 and 1650 only 19% of the ships coming from Seville made a stop for water on the island of Puerto Rico.[13] Although this was a small percentage, it represented a small-scale trade that benefited the development of Aguada and San Germán, which supplied fresh meat, vegetables, and fruits to the fleets that docked.

For the return trip to Spain, the winds and the Gulf Stream dictated that ships sailing from Veracruz or Nombre de Dios should proceed through the Florida straits towards Havana. This port became the meeting place and the point of embarkation, with the corresponding advantages for the economic development of its hinterland. Naturally, the return route via Havana reduced the opportunities for Puerto Rico and Santo Domingo to sell their products to the traders.[14]

The importance for Caribbean navigation of the leeward or east wind had some advantages for Puerto Rico, the easternmost of the Greater Antilles. From there, news and requests for help reached the other islands more rapidly than from any of the other settlements because it was easier to sail from east to west than vice versa.[15] For that reason there were several attempts to make San Juan de Puerto Rico the base for the Spanish fleet in the Caribbean.[16] Nevertheless, the lack of supplies and of skilled workers frustrated such attempts to give Puerto Rico a more prominent role in the defense of Spanish commercial interests in the Caribbean.

The System of Fleets

Implicit in this discussion about navigation routes is the fact that Spain, like Venice at the height of its commercial power,[17] had coordinated commercial navigation by means of a system of fleets. The advisability of this decision became evident from the 1530s onward, when a great many French and English corsairs began coming to the Caribbean. Between 1535 and 1547, 66 ships were captured by corsairs, 41 of them near to Spain. The most dangerous places in the Antilles were the Mona Channel, the approach to Havana, and the north coast of Puerto Rico.[18] It was safer to sail in convoy, with the heavier cargo ships escorted by armed ships ready to pursue any suspicious vessel.

From the 1540s on, the Council of the Indies arranged that two fleets would set off each year from Seville: one for New Spain (present-day Mexico) and the other for the Isthmus of Panama, where the traders from the viceroyalty of Lima gathered. These dispositions became enshrined in decrees of Philip II in the 1560s. It was left to the Council of the Indies to set the dates for the fleets' departure each year for the New World. Once it was decided to send a fleet, an announcement was made. The *Consulado de Cargadores de Indias* of Seville, to give it its full title, informed the *Casa de Contratación* of the volume of freight it believed could be marketed. A third of the load was reserved for the merchants and producers of Cadiz, and the rest was distributed among the merchants and producers of Seville.[19]

At times the Consulado opposed the sending of a fleet because it deemed there was insufficient demand for European goods in the New World. On other occasions the merchants of the Consulado sought to delay the departures from Seville as a way of increasing the demand for its goods in the New World and thus raise the prices.[20]

The system of fleets ensured the flow of merchandise between Andalusia and the American ports of Veracruz and Nombre de Dios. Corsairs were not able to prevent the system from working, and had to limit their raids to ships which lagged behind or were separated by hurricanes. They concentrated their activities in the waters of the Bahamas and in the area between the Azores Islands and the Cape of

Saint Vincent, the last stage of the return trip. It was not until 1628 that a large Dutch fleet was able to capture, in Cuban waters, the greater part of a fleet that was returning to Spain.[21]

The very success of the fleet system as a guarantee for the safety of Spanish commercial traffic had an enormous effect on the possibilities for production and trade in those areas on the margins of the return route to Spain. The Dominican historian Frank Moya Pons has described the effects of the system of fleets on supplies in Hispaniola:

> The system of fleets profoundly altered the rhythm and flow of navigation in the Caribbean and it set the seal on the growing isolation of Santo Domingo. . . . Now the ships that wanted to go to Santo Domingo had to set off every six months from Spain and sail along with the fleet. Upon arriving in the Caribbean Sea, they had to follow their own route, alone and unprotected. . . . Thus, little by little the navigation to Hispaniola became more expensive, since the costs of freight increased . . . on account of the higher costs of marine insurance, which was much lower for Mexico than for Santo Domingo.[22]

The Puerto Rican situation was similar, but the docking of the Seville fleets in Aguada supplied the need for some commodities. From Aguada, ships had to sail against the wind along the dangerous north coast to reach the capital.

Although in 1565 the government of Puerto Rico requested that each fleet be accompanied by a ship carrying goods for the island, that minimum was not achieved.[23] Pierre and Huguette Chaunu have counted the number of ships that came to Puerto Rico from Seville up to the middle of the seventeenth century and those that left the island for Seville. The Spanish historian García Fuentes did the same for voyages made between 1650 and 1699. A summary of their data shows that, after 1625, Puerto Rico was progressively marginalized from commercial traffic between the New World and Seville (see table 6.1).

In the seventeenth century this limited commercial traffic with Andalusia affected Puerto Rican agricultural interests by limiting the marketing of the production. In addition there was the threat to life and property represented by the growing numbers of corsairs.

TABLE 6.1

Commercial Traffic between Puerto Rico and Seville, 1512–1699, by number of ships and known tonnage

Period	Departures for Puerto Rico		Arrivals from Puerto Rico	
	Number of Ships	Total Tonnage	Number of Ships	Total Tonnage
to 1525	18	1,710	9	930
1526–1550	17[a]	2,100	28	3,440
1551–1575	19[b]	2,230	105	13,190
1576–1600	35	3,645	105	13,605
1601–1625	50[c]	5,715	136[d]	16,363
1626–1650	18[e]	2,462	25	2,965
1651–1675	8	Not indicated	15	Not indicated
1676–1699	8	Not indicated	4	Not indicated

a. Includes one ship for Puerto Real and 1 with Puerto Rico as final destination
b. Includes 1 ship for Puerto Plata via Puerto Rico
c. Includes 13 ships en route to Havana with a tonnage of 1020
d. Includes 1 ship from the Orinoco via Puerto Rico
e. Includes one ship en route to St. Martin

Sources: Chaunu, *Seville et l'Atlantique* VI, 2, 488–90, tables 231–33; García Fuentes, *Comercio*, 417–20 and 421–24, Appendixes, tables 1 and 2.

The Alternatives: Ships with Special Permits, Trade with the Canaries, and Forced Arrivals

The authorities in Spain offered only a few alternatives to the services rendered by the fleet to the trade of Puerto Rico and other equally marginalized zones. Ever since the system of fleets had been established, Santo Domingo and Puerto Rico had tried to have an annual visit paid by the *navíos de permisión*, the ships licensed to separate from the fleet and sail towards determined ports in order to supply them with commodities, as well as to take on local products. Unfortunately, the Sevillian merchants had little interest in promoting that type of trade, which they considered to be of limited potential volume. Only when the Antilles offered products not readily available in

New Spain and Tierra Firme was there any possibility that the Sevillians would be tempted to face the risks and additional costs entailed by a *navío de permisión*. As has been shown above, there was little seventeenth-century shipping from Seville.

Ships from the Canary Islands offered another possibility. Since the early period of colonization, Canary Island traders had received licenses from the Crown to supply the Antilles. Although the triumph of the Andalusian monopoly seemed to have excluded them from the New World, the particular needs of the Greater Antilles offered an opening for trade with the Canaries. As the official trade dwindled, the more frequent became the requests from Santo Domingo, Cuba, Puerto Rico, and Tierra Firme and the easier it was to present the Canaries' offer to attend to their needs to the Crown. The course of the negotiations is interesting. The Sevillians' tenacious opposition achieved the limitation of the term of the licenses, the number of permitted ships, the volume and type of the cargo, and the places of origin of the merchants involved.[24] In short, Seville did everything to defend its privileges, and little to serve the needs of the Antilles.

The Canary Islanders, on the other hand, made maximum use of the opportunity that the licenses gave them. They were accused of shipping more merchandise than was allowed, and of stopping in unauthorized ports. There was an effort to require, as a condition of granting licenses, the taking on board of specific numbers of emigrants to Santo Domingo and Puerto Rico. There were attempts to monitor their operations even more closely. All these difficulties did not succeed in cutting the commercial link between the Canaries and the Caribbean, and this persistence naturally had consequences for the cultural formation of the Spanish Antilles.[25]

Another course of action attempted by local economic interests and external elements was the expedient of forced arrivals. A ship could arrive in port without the necessary royal permit if compelling reasons made it necessary. In this way, ships damaged in storms, pursued by corsairs, needing water or provisions, or the victim of navigational errors could enter San Juan harbor in search of help, and humanitarian reasons dictated that they be received. Since the 1530s, when a Portuguese ship in distress had arrived in Puerto Rico, there had been experiences of forced arrivals. In such cases it was expected that the ship would dispose of part of its cargo to pay for the expenses incurred in repairs or taking on supplies of food.[26]

Spurred on by suspicious Sevillians, the Spanish authorities began to carefully examine the court records on forced arrivals, especially in the case of foreign ships. Legally, these had few reasons to be in these latitudes. But in the time it took for the reports to travel back and forth, the local authorities had already authorized unloading. They would then write up the most justifiable cases. Sometimes, acting via a third party, they would themselves be the main purchasers of the prized goods.

All these ships that arrived by unusual routes were not sufficient to satisfy the needs of the principal ports left on the margins of the main fleet routes. In the seventeenth century, communities like that of San Germán, far from San Juan and without easy access to that port by either land or sea, began to voice the need for increased opportunities for trade. In 1692 San Germán gained a license, which applied to all other communities outside the capital, allowing authorized ships to make stops in their harbors and trade with the people. The license was extended for four years. According to López Cantos, the only registered ship that came to Puerto Rico during those four years did not make use of the license.[27] The license was useless since ships did not even attempt to reach San Juan.

The Corsairs

Spain's wars in Europe, first with France, then with England, and finally with the rebellious United Provinces of the Netherlands, also had a devastating effect on trade.[28] Corsairs from rival nations sacked cities and attacked shipping in Spanish America. In a similar fashion, Basque corsairs from the Iberian Peninsula attacked European cities and ships belonging to the nations which were at war with Spain, especially Holland.[29] They were perhaps not so frequently romanticized by the authors of children's novels and cinema scripts, but were nonetheless fierce and aggressive.

The New World was more vulnerable to attack by corsairs on account of the enormous distances, the relative isolation, and the rudimentary systems of defense that were initially in place. Although their prime targets in America were the merchandise and the shipments of precious minerals and gems carried by the galleons, the success of the fleet system forced the corsairs to attack the ports and the production centers near the coasts.[30]

As previously noted, San Germán, which was located near the mouth of the Guaorabo River, had been attacked by French corsairs in the 1520s.[31] Since the rivers in the western part of the island had abundant gold, that region was settled early on by Spaniards and Africans. When gold became scarce, the free inhabitants developed *hatos* and plantations. As they sailed through the Mona Passage, ships coming from Spain brought them wine, oil, textiles, and tools, and the settlers in turn supplied them with fresh provisions.[32]

On May 15, 1538, some French corsairs sacked and destroyed this site of San Germán. In 1543, Bishop Bastidas informed Charles V that, fearing another attack, the residents wanted to fortify the town. Meanwhile, they had settled inland with their families and possessions.[33]

The fortification of the settlement at San Germán, however, relied on the strategic priorities of the crown. Spain did not feel there was enough justification for the implied costs of the construction project, as well as the cost of the armaments, garrison, and maintenance required by a fortress. Such works would, in effect, only safeguard the interests of the thirty-odd inhabitants whom Bastidas said were residing in San Germán in 1548.[34] Residents then chose to rebuild their town on another site, initially half a league away and then eventually on the hills of Santa Marta. The raids by corsairs and the Crown's reluctance to finance the fortification of San Germán explain why the seat of the island's western jurisdiction finally came to be located in a place far away from the coast.[35] The people of San Germán learned early on that they had to fend for themselves. Corsairs also impeded the potential development of the areas where Guayama and Ponce are now located.[36]

Selective Fortification

Instead of expending resources on attempting to fortify all the New World Spanish settlements against corsairs, the Spanish crown opted for a policy of the selective fortification of those points considered to be of key importance for the defense of the main commercial routes. As on so many other occasions, the interests of the Seville traders prevailed over those of the New World colonizers. It was not the production but the circulation of goods that was protected. This seemed a logical option in view of the large areas required for production, as, for example, in the case of cattle raising, which took up a huge amount of land.

The impressive fortifications in the Caribbean which are the result of this defensive strategy inspire admiration in the thousands of visitors to Cartagena, Havana, and San Juan today. But far from being symbols of Spanish power, they represent instead Spain's vulnerability in the New World. They are like the houses with iron bars in contemporary urban areas, symbols of their residents' fears. There are no comparable fortifications from that era in the British and Dutch settlements, although some of them, like Barbados, at the time had larger populations than Puerto Rico. The strength of those European settlements lay in their respective fleets.[37]

The fortification of the bay of San Juan began to be planned in the first decade after the original town of Caparra was moved to the site. Initially it offered protection against the intrepid flotillas of the Carib Indians. But in the 1530s the residents began to suffer attacks by French corsairs. The first place to be fortified was the seat of government itself, which today is called La Fortaleza. Between the 1530s and the 1570s, a castle was built on that site for defensive purposes and the crown's income and the city's strategic supplies were deposited there. Its personnel consisted of a provisional garrison of fewer than ten persons, including the warder, an artilleryman, and some servants. The residents' militia was still the main defender of the city.[38]

The strategic value of the mound or *morro* which towers above the entrance to the bay was obvious from very early on, since it presented an obstacle for those attempting to enter the bay. Ships attempting to force their way into the bay could only enter the channel if those who protected that promontory allowed it.

When the crown began laying out the first system of fortifications in the New World, it accepted the repeated suggestions that the promontory at the entrance of the bay of San Juan should be fortified.[39] The original tower was soon reinforced with walls and gun emplacements. Eventually its guarding was entrusted to soldiers who were considered professionals.[40]

In other parts of Spanish America a similar transition was taking place from reliance on local militia to the establishment of garrisons with professional soldiers, paid out of crown funds. For inhabitants occupied in their various private enterprises, many of them working in the fields, it was increasingly difficult to comply with their guard duties during the period of the corsairs' forays, or to maintain the necessary training regime. In any case, the number of men in the age range most suitable for combat was limited in the Spanish Caribbean. It is calculated that in sixteenth-century San Juan there were never more than 200 militiamen available for its defense.[41]

Not all the Spanish American towns were fortified or received permanent garrisons. Once soldiers were garrisoned in El Morro and as its military construction progressed, the differences between the histories of San Juan and San Germán became more evident. In San Juan, military considerations would eclipse the inhabitants' activities to the point that even today what most *sanjuaneros* know about the first three centuries of their history is the military aspect. But those from San Germán, thwarted in their petitions for a fort at the mouth of the river, finally opted to settle far from the coast, in an elevated position which allowed them to watch over their interests. While San Juan saw the inevitable military angle in every consideration of their institutional problems, the residents of San Germán realized their economic projects through relying in great measure on their own resources. That is why historians like Aida Caro have emphasized the need to study more closely the documents produced by the *cabildo* of San Germán for its petitions to the Audiencia of Santo Domingo or to the Council of the Indies.[42]

The establishment of a permanent garrison in San Juan in 1582 also entailed the allocation of funds for its upkeep. The fundamental value of this garrison for the Spanish Empire was seen as protecting one of the key ports for the fleets which supplied the Indies. For that reason, a permanent sum was set aside from the revenues generated by the mines of New Spain for the garrison's salaries and other related services. That amount was known as the *situado* or subsidy.[43]

The *situado* assigned to Puerto Rico, as well as that for the other Spanish garrisons in the Caribbean and the Gulf of Mexico, passed through several stages. By the eighteenth century it was common to charge to the *situado* some expenses less directly related to defense, such as widows' pensions and grants for pious works. This practice made other sectors outside the strictly military sphere dependent for their economic security on the remittances of the *situado*. But it would be a mistake to describe this economic aid as some sort of "welfare" on which the whole of the Puerto Rican economy came to depend. It is true that when the *situado* was late, many soldiers took goods on credit from San Juan merchants. If the delays went on for a long time, as was the case in the seventeenth century, a great many people fell into debt. A whole chain of debt resulted which involved the whole city, from the very rich to the poor. But that situation actually reflected the shortage of the coinage needed to meet the requirements of trade and the hardship experienced by producers who lacked sufficient external markets. When Spanish merchants arrived they tended to collect the circulating money from the *situado* in exchange for wine, cloth, tools, flour, oil, and other peninsular and European goods. The money that came from Mexico went on its way to the Iberian Peninsula. Thus, in its original as well as in its acquired functions, the *situado* was yet another prop for the Andalusian trade.[44]

English Attacks on San Juan

In April of 1595 a damaged galleon carrying part of the treasure of the Spanish fleet took refuge in the harbor of San Juan. While it was being repaired and its escort prepared, its cargo was deposited in La Fortaleza. Rumors of the presence of so much wealth in the bay of San

Juan reached the ears of one of the most famous corsairs of all times, the Englishman Francis Drake.

A sailor since his adolescence, Drake had a checkered career.[45] His raids covered the Caribbean and Europe. In one of his voyages he circumnavigated the globe and attacked Spanish settlements in the Pacific Ocean. In 1588 he was one of the architects of the naval victory over the so-called Invincible Armada of Spain in the English Channel. His reputation inspired awe and terror throughout Europe. Elizabeth, the queen of England who also shared in the profits from Drake's plunder, had made him a knight.

With so many exploits to his name it was not surprising that the English corsair should make a daring attempt to obtain the treasure stored in La Fortaleza. On November 22, 1595, Drake arrived with a flotilla of ships at the entrance to the bay of San Juan. But El Morro's fortifications had been sufficiently strengthened to prevent Drake from forcing his way into the bay. The well-aimed shot of a Spanish artilleryman that night succeeded in shattering the lighted chamber where Drake ate with several of his officers, leaving two of them dead.

On the night of the 23rd, Drake tried to set fire to some Spanish ships anchored in the bay. He entered the harbor with launches and succeeded in setting fire to one of them, but the resulting glow allowed El Morro's battery guns to make easy targets of the English launches. On the 24th, Drake appears to have tried to enter the bay with his entire flotilla. The Spaniards, however, sank three of their own ships to close the channel and Drake gave up the enterprise. This successful defense was celebrated in Puerto Rico for a long time.[46]

The attack by an armed expedition led by George Clifford, the earl of Cumberland, three years later would prove more dangerous. This impetuous young man wished to imitate and outdo Drake's feats. He equipped seventeen ships in England, most of them with his own resources, and set out in November 1597 to attack the Portuguese fleet as it departed for India from the mouth of the River Tagus. While he waited, he captured several Catalan and Flemish ships. The Portuguese became aware of his presence and Cumberland gave up the plan of capturing the fleet. With his fleet reinforced by the ships he had captured and with 2,200 men he set sail for the Canary

Islands, but he did not capture any substantial booty in Lanzarote and had to give up the idea of attacking Palma. Cumberland then thought of raiding the Portuguese settlement of Pernambuco in Brazil, but his captains and pilots showed him that he did not have enough water and was too far off course to take that risk. He then decided to head for the Spanish Antilles.[47]

The English squadron reached "Labonica" (Dominica?), where they took on water, and then sailed between the Virgin Islands using a less well-known route. Cumberland reviewed his troops on one of the islands, and found that only 1,400 men remained. Since the Canaries he had been losing men in combat and especially from disease.

Once in Puerto Rican waters, and against the advice of veteran sailors from Drake's expeditions, Cumberland decided to lay anchor and disembark in the cove of Cangrejos in the early morning and to march from there to take the city. They began walking along the beach. Finally a captured guide reluctantly took them through the dense woods and thickets of Cangrejos to where the Dos Hermanos Bridge is now located, at the mouth of the Condado.

Meanwhile, a fisherman had raised the alarm. The population of San Juan crossed the bay to seek shelter in the Toa valley and in the mountains. From the forts defending the eastern entrance to the island of San Juan the Governor tried to block the English advance. This forced them to make a laborious detour around the lagoon, through its adjoining mangroves, until they reached the sandy trail leading to the San Antonio bridge between what is now Miramar and the island. But the bridge had been destroyed. On the following day, wading, they attacked the emplacements where the defenders who impeded their crossing were posted, but they had no better luck. In that action the English lost sixty men.[48]

Cumberland, who had ordered that the ships remain in a convoy by sailing close to the shore, re-embarked many of his troops to then disembark them at the Escambrón beach, behind the first Spanish lines of defense. The Spaniards had anticipated the strategy and after attempting to block the landing, causing the English some losses, they fell back to El Morro.

Unfortunately the castle was not well provisioned. Cumberland succeeded in obtaining the Governor's surrender and quartered his troops in the city. According to his chaplain, John Layfield, who wrote the best-known account of the English occupation of 1598, Cumberland ensured that no atrocities were committed against the *sanjuaneros*. This care did not prevent the English from eventually carrying off the cathedral's organ, the bells from all the churches, a thousand boxes of sugar, and two thousand hundredweight of ginger.

While the English were occupying the city, a ship arrived in the bay with the slaves that San Juan residents had so insistently requested from the Spanish crown. Without suspecting that the English were running the city, the ship entered the bay, and the cargo was impounded and seized. Two other ships arrived, one with a cargo of pearls from Margarita, and fell in the same trap.

An epidemic, apparently of gastroenteritis, spread rapidly among the English garrison, which had already become ill in the Canaries. The number of dead rose, and when Cumberland saw that only seven hundred men remained, he feared he did not have enough troops to hold San Juan and also send part of the fleet to England to ask for reinforcements. Above all, he feared San Juan residents, seeing the English sick and dead, might try to attack the English from their hiding places on the island. Thus he decided to leave San Juan at the end of August of 1598. Soon afterwards, a fleet from Spain arrived to recapture San Juan.[49]

After Cumberland's success in occupying San Juan in 1598, successive governors paid greater attention to the need to keep el Morro well-manned and equipped with weapons and provisions. This was not easily ensured on account of the delays in the arrival of military supplies from Spain. Another factor was that military service in San Juan de Puerto Rico held little attraction for Spanish soldiers, because it offered few possibilities of seeing action or winning honor, wealth, pleasure, and the guarantee of a prompt return to the homeland. Captain Alonso de Contreras, a contemporary soldier of fortune, tells in his picaresque memoirs of the mission given to him around 1618 to go and supply Puerto Rico with powder, rope, lead and firearms. Governor Beaumont asked him to leave behind forty soldiers to reinforce the garrison. Nobody wanted to volunteer:

. . . never before in my life did I see greater confusion, because no one wanted to stay and they almost wept at the thought of remaining there, and they were right, because it was to remain in eternal slavery. . . . I told them, "My sons, it is necessary to leave forty soldiers here, but you yourselves will be the instruments of your damnation, because I am not going to point out anyone, not even one of my servants, that if it is his lot, he must stay." I made as many tickets as soldiers, and among them forty black ones, and put them in a pitcher, and mixed them up, and then I called them by list and would say: "Your worship put your hand in and if you draw a black one, you will stay." They did it that way, and it was a sight to see how they reacted when they drew black. But finally, seeing that it was necessary and that there was no other way, they consoled themselves, especially when they saw that my servant, who was my barber, was the first one to draw a lot to stay.[50]

In fact the chances of returning to Spain after having served the twenty years of the term of enlistment were, for most soldiers, slight. Military regulations also forbade them to marry, although that did not prevent them forming families in the vicinity of the forts.

The Dutch

In 1621, at the end of a twelve-year truce agreed between Spain and the United Provinces (the Netherlands), the possibilities of seeing military action in Puerto Rico rose considerably. In the same year a great commercial company was formed in Amsterdam to exploit all the opportunities for profit created from the Dutch involvement in the trade routes and salt mines of the West Indies. The company, which had a projected capital of seven million florins contributed by its members, called itself the West India Company. Very soon some of the most skilful and famous seamen entered its service.[51]

Salt was prized by the Dutch, who used it to preserve the large quantities of herring and other fish supplied each year by their fishing fleets in the North Sea. The Netherlands exported vast quantities of salted herring to Northern European countries. For a long time the

Dutch relied on the saltworks in Spain and Portugal to supply their needs. Later the dispute with the Spanish crown intensified, culminating in the detention of hundreds of Dutch ships in the Iberian Peninsula in 1585, 1595, and 1598. This forced them to seek alternate sources for the extraction of salt in the New World.[52]

Their ships soon anchored near the fabulous salt flats of Araya, on the Venezuelan coast. They also approached other salt deposits in the Caribbean, including Bonaire, Saint Martin, and the southern coast of Puerto Rico. From the final years of the sixteenth century onward, Dutch fleets were extracting salt from different salt pans in the Caribbean. The Spaniards made repeated efforts to discourage this by means of decrees issued by Philip II and Philip III, but they were not successful. The number of Dutch ships involved in the salt trade was enormous, and the salt beds generally lay in areas not frequented by Spanish shipping.

The operations of the salt trade familiarized the Dutch with the Caribbean world and its economic possibilities. At the same time the relative vulnerability of Spain in this still uncolonized area became evident. The Dutch also noted the enormous potential of the Brazilian coast, whose exploitation was reserved for the Portuguese, who at the time were subjects of the Spanish crown.[53]

The Dutch West India Company coordinated a series of naval expeditions aimed at exploiting the opportunities presented by the European war begun in 1618, to attack and loot the Spanish crown's possessions in the Caribbean and Brazil. Thus Puerto Rico became part of the setting of one of the most destructive conflicts of all time, the so-called Thirty Years' War (1618–1648).[54]

In 1624 the Dutch occupied San Salvador de Bahia in Brazil. The Spanish crown sent a squadron under the command of Fadrique de Toledo to recover that vital portion of its dominions. Attempting to defend their conquest, the Dutch in turn sent a squadron under the command of General Boudewijn Hendriksz. When the Dutch squadron arrived near Bahia it learned that the Spaniards had recaptured it. After having explored the possibilities for inflicting harm on the Spanish and the Portuguese along the Brazilian coast, Hendriksz decided to attack the Spanish islands in the Caribbean.[55]

On September 25, 1635, taking advantage of the element of surprise and a favorable breeze, Hendriksz entered the bay of San Juan:

> . . . with the aplomb with which he carried himself, he entered it as safely and securely as if he were coming in by one of the channels of Holland or Zealand, on account of the little or no skill of the artillerymen, who were few and the artillery so ill-prepared, that on their first shot many of the weapons misfired because the gun carriages were old and some of the guns had been loaded for four years.[56]

The unexpected attack by the Dutchmen caused a huge commotion among the residents of San Juan. Many took refuge on the other side of the bay or in El Morro, and most resigned themselves to the loss of their belongings. Hendriksz occupied La Fortaleza and proceeded to systematically loot the city. He centered his attention on the churches, which, on account of the religious sentiments of the times, constituted suitable targets for the Dutch to spoil and vandalize. From the cathedral of San Juan they took "even the deeds."[57]

The attackers, however, lacked siege engines to capture El Morro. They were not able to overcome the Spanish garrison in battles on the esplanade in front of the fort, nor could they induce Governor Juan de Haro to surrender by threatening to set fire to the city.[58] Hendriksz loaded his ships with the spoils, set fire to a considerable number of houses, and then set out from the bay with his flotilla. However, the departure was costly. El Morro's batteries fired steadily on the ships and the Dutch lost the Medenblick, which became stranded trying to avoid Spanish artillery fire.[59]

San Juan was in ruins as a result of the Dutch attack, the worst disaster in the history of the city. This catastrophe of 1625 intensified calls to provide the city with walls to protect it against surprise attacks.[60] As the European war dragged on, the authorities in Puerto Rico endeavored to have the funds needed to begin building walls around San Juan allocated from those destined for military purposes.

In 1628 the Dutch captured almost all of the Spanish fleet on its return journey to the Iberian Peninsula, together with the huge treasure it carried, valued at eleven and a half million florins.[61] The

Spanish crown was obliged to take more decisive measures to defend its interests in the New World. The possible alternatives were to develop an armada to pursue and harass the Dutch or to build fortifications to provide the fleets with better bases and places of refuge. Spain had a long military tradition and solid experience of the type of combat carried out against or from castles and walled emplacements. The crown opted to make a long-term investment in the fortification of its key places in the Americas. This decision resulted in the series of walls that came to characterize San Juan de Puerto Rico. Work began in 1630 and was completed in the 1780s. The castle of San Cristobal was built to guard the entrance to the city by land. La Fortaleza was integrated into the defense system and the only points of habitual contact between the city and the external world were the four city gates, which were closed at night.[62]

This defensive system based on fortifications drained most of the Spanish crown's available resources. By the second quarter of the seventeenth century, merchants continued to suffer losses at the hands of corsairs and insistently requested that a more aggressive policy be adopted against the plunder of trade. The greatest insistence came from Mexico's merchants, because they found that the imposing fortifications of San Juan de Ulua in Veracruz were not sufficient to guarantee the protection of their interests.[63]

The formation of an armada to protect the security of the routes and the coasts, and which could when necessary attack the operational bases of the corsairs in the Caribbean, had been under consideration since the reign of Philip II. Various experiments had been made with some degree of success, but there always came the moment when the merchants could not keep up with the costs of maintaining a squadron in operation. On the other hand, the increasing rivalry between Andalusian traders and those of New Spain posed serious problems for royal officials. Andalusians attempted to limit the trade carried out by the Mexicans in the Pacific through the annual voyage of the Manila galleon. That trade brought merchandise from the East which was then re-exported to Peru and other points in the West Indies, and this led to competition with the textiles exported from Seville. In this cunning interplay of interests, the

Mexicans conceived of a formula to underwrite the greater part of the costs for an armada in the Caribbean in exchange for various financial privileges. These concessions acted as incentives to their commercial operations and at the same time reaffirmed the authority and prestige of the *cabildo* of Mexico.[64]

An economic recession in the mid-seventeenth century, however, reduced the funds destined by the Mexican *cabildo* for building, equipping and operating a sufficiently powerful and mobile Windward Armada which could put an end to the corsairs' attacks.

In the case of Puerto Rico the delay in developing an aggressive policy against the corsairs ruined its trade. Between 1630 and 1650 the volume of trade dropped dramatically, as the Chaunus have shown in their studies of Atlantic navigation. Even the traffic between Puerto Rico and Santo Domingo became precarious in this period.[65] The Chaunus deduce that smuggling, especially the barter of ginger, supplied Puerto Rico with its basic necessities from 1628 on.[66]

When the Windward Armada attained the minimal necessary financing and began operations in the Caribbean, the situation improved temporarily. The fact that the harbor of San Juan was used on different occasions as a winter base and place where repairs were carried out by the Armada acted as a stimulus for its development. But eventually the Armada adopted Havana as its habitual base, in spite of the advantages offered by San Juan for navigation because it lay leeward of the other Greater Antilles. The move to Havana was due to the shortage of supplies in San Juan, and above all to the lack of personnel skilled in tarring prows, making new masts and sails, and preparing tackle, rigging, and cordage.[67]

In any case, after the Thirty Years War ended in 1648, the problem of the corsairs became less important as far as the authorities were concerned. For them, the vigorous smuggling trade which developed between producers in the Spanish colonies and the settlers of the English, French, and Dutch Antilles was regarded as more damaging.

Other Europeans in the Caribbean

Since the 1590s the English had been contemplating the convenience of having islands in the Caribbean to cultivate the tropical products that were beginning to be in demand in Europe. According to Layfield, Cumberland dreamed in 1598 of establishing an English settlement in San Juan. In the 1620s the initiatives of the English private sector finally resulted in the settlement of Saint Christopher and Barbados.[68]

The Spanish crown considered that the Lesser Antilles were "useless islands" for colonization because they lacked precious metals. Their forests were impenetrable and were inhabited by an Amerindian population considered to be cannibals.[69] But even though the Spanish did not colonize the eastern Caribbean, this did not mean that they ceased claiming jurisdiction over it. Dominica, Guadeloupe and Martinique were islands where the incoming Spanish fleets watered and frequently took on provisions. St. Martin, on account of its salt beds and strategic position, was fortified. Expeditions were periodically undertaken to the eastern Caribbean to reaffirm Spanish sovereignty.[70]

Nevertheless, once the English began to settle in the region, there was little that Spain could do. In fact, from the English viewpoint, it was the Caribs who presented the main obstacle to the colonization of Saint Christopher. Barbados, on the other hand, was uninhabited, and the Amerindians from the islands of Nevis, Montserrat, and Antigua, which were settled from the 1630s onward, were dispossessed with relative ease. They were replaced by numerous servants, both English and Irish, who had been indentured for a fixed term, and hundreds of African slaves. By the 1630s Barbados came to be the most densely populated place in the New World.[71]

Tobacco was first staple export from these islands. Using the open areas between the dense tropical forests, the English settlers made numerous tobacco plantations. They learned from the Dutch and the Portuguese in Brazil how to cure and store the leaves. By the end of the 1630s the English settlers in St. Christopher and Barbados were exporting considerable quantities of tobacco to London. Barbados alone sent 124,593 pounds in 1637 and 204,956 in 1638.[72] But in 1638 the price of this item plummeted because of an excess of production in relation to demand, especially in Virginia.[73] The fall provoked a crisis in the English islands. Many workers and indebted farmers abandoned the settled islands in search of better opportunities in the new colonies.

Sugar became the alternative to tobacco, since it was in demand in Amsterdam and London. Up to the 1630s the main suppliers of sugar for the European market were Sicily, the Canary Islands, Cuba, Brazil, and other territories then ruled by the Spanish crown. The Dutch, however, sought to extend the sugar plantations in the part of Brazil then under their control, in an attempt to end the domination of sugar production by the territories under the King of Spain.[74]

The rapid success of the sugar plantations in Barbados and the other English islands led to a wave of investment in land, slaves, and tools to extend the plantations and improve sugar processing. Property became concentrated in fewer hands, as small planters of tobacco, on account of debt or because they gave in to tempting offers to buy, sold their lands to the planters. The thick tropical forests were cut down, leading to the destruction of the local fauna and vegetation. And since the planting of sugarcane yielded a better income than other crops or other activities, the English began to be dependent for basic provisions on the other regions of the Caribbean.[75]

Among the things needed were meat and oxen for plowing and pulling loads. Wood became scarce and food was expensive. European indentured servants were replaced by slaves and that shift in the workforce yielded higher profits. It was calculated that in a year and a half an African slave rendered in work the equivalent of the price paid for his purchase. Everything he or she produced from then on, once one subtracted the minimum required for subsistence, was profit.[76]

The English became rich, but they needed to obtain supplies from other islands. They could offer in exchange basic European goods which the declining official trade had made scarce in Puerto Rico, Hispaniola, Venezuela, and southeastern Cuba. As a result, and despite the Spanish royal policies, the economies of both regions of the Caribbean became complementary in the second half of the seventeenth century.

The Smuggling Economy

In Puerto Rico everything was in short supply. The island was becoming depopulated because the men left to seek their fortunes in Havana and New Spain. There was the case of one Puerto Rican who even got as far as the Philippines, by adventure and misadventure.[77]

The Spanish historian Angel López Cantos has counted all the known cases of smuggling in Puerto Rico between 1650 and 1700.[78] Naturally the known cases constitute a small proportion of the whole. Sources from that period agree that the incidence of smuggling was so high that in 1699 it was stated that it was impossible to apply the existing penalties, including the death penalty, "because to put a stop to such trade by means of punishments would be for Your Majesty to be left without subjects . . . on the whole island, since there would be only a few who are not compromised."[79]

López Cantos does not claim that his sample has strict statistical accuracy, as it only includes cases which came to official notice. Even so, the sample gives a good idea of how extensive smuggling was in Puerto Rico. López Cantos' tables show 16 ships originating in the territories of the King of Spain and 65 foreign ships. Among the foreigners the Dutch predominate (29 ships, 7 of them from Curacao) and the English (15 ships, 6 of them from Jamaica), but there are also French, Portuguese, and Danish vessels. It is interesting to note which products were smuggled, according to the denunciations. For instance, there were illegal imports of clothing, wine and liquor from Spanish territories. These same goods were brought in from abroad, as well as slaves, spices, preserved foods, salt, and general merchandise. From the island the foreign traders illegally took cattle, meat, leather, wood, tobacco, cocoa, and money.

All the governors between 1650 and 1700 were accused of being implicated in the illegal trade, as were many royal officials and members of the clergy. Both the soldiers and residents from all social backgrounds bought from the smugglers. Many farmers and cattlemen from the areas furthest from the official port in San Juan had the foreign smugglers as their best customers. These, besides paying the best prices, went to buy in the areas close to the producers. In this way the seller saved the costs of transporting his goods to San Juan in order to await the arrival of an authorized ship.

However, one of the most startling facts collected by López Cantos is that the main place for smuggling in the whole island was San Juan itself. This is the case in 31 of the 81 denunciations of illegal trade. San Germán, Ponce, Aguada, Coamo's beach (today Santa Isabel), Bella Vista, and Arecibo also appear as sites for smuggling.[80]

The ubiquity of the contraband mentality in insular life nullified any efforts made by the new authorities to suppress it. The law of silence was imposed. It was impossible to obtain statements from the residents. When Francisco Sanabria, the parish priest of San Germán, observed in a letter sent to San Juan that Ponce residents distinguished themselves by their inclination for illegal trade, forty of them came to San Germán, kidnapped him, took him to the hills, and almost killed him. Ponceños presumably had received a warning from San Juan suggesting that "they knew how to slaughter cattle in the hills, but they did not know how to get rid of blabbermouths."[81]

The death penalty that Governor Arredondo imposed on some smugglers from the Cibuco area became a dead letter when they escaped into the dense forests of the mountain range. The very poverty of the inhabitants limited the effect of economic sanctions. Their main belongings were their hunting dogs and their spears for killing unbranded cattle, nothing of much value to be confiscated.

Some notorious smugglers enjoyed the support of many members of the community. Martín Calderón, owner of an *hato* in Canóvanas, strutted arrogantly about the streets and the authorities were unable to pin any illegal acts on him. In no other period of Puerto Rican history has the state shown a greater inability to establish its authority over the people effectively. Some measures taken at the time to curb the illegal trade provoked spirited resistance and resulted in unrest in San Germán, Coamo, Ponce, and Aguada.[82] The complicity of the authorities in illegal acts undermined confidence in the state as the guarantor of the public order.

The island not only came to have two economies, the official and the contraband,[83] it also developed two political faces, one which obeyed the Laws of the Indies and royal edicts, and one which operated in accordance with the agreement of the inhabitants. In an effort to overcome the obstacles posed by these mutual allegiances to the state, in 1692 Governor Arredondo installed representatives in Ponce, Arecibo, Loíza, and Aguada, which he called *tenientes a guerra*.[84] This experiment linked the residents of those areas directly to central government. But these officials, selected from among the elite of the neighborhood, soon succumbed to peer pressure.

Thus the first authorities assigned to those centers of population did not emerge out of their own local dynamics but out of the desire of central authority to extend its power at the local level. From their time of origin, the municipal institutions became tinged with autocracy. In spite of claims that Puerto Rican municipalities have a common origin with medieval Spanish urban traditions, the reality is that, while this may be true for those towns that obtained *cabildos*, it is not true for most of the municipalities which emerged from the *tenencias a guerra*.

The administrative areas created in 1692 could hardly stimulate the development of towns. Neighborhoods were basically rural, with scattered houses and low population density. As long as cattle raising and the unsystematic exploitation of natural resources prevailed, the state could barely institutionalize everyday life. Only by promoting the militias did it impinge on the lives of the men, at the annual reviews held on July 25, the Feast of St. James, or in the alarms and emergencies sparked off by the War of the Spanish Succession (1702–1713). As for the women and children who lived on the mountainsides, only the blessings of some itinerant priest or the occasional visit to the parish church could bring them in contact with a wider community than that of relatives or mountain neighbors.

CHAPTER 7 ‖ Corsairs and Settlers, 1700–1765

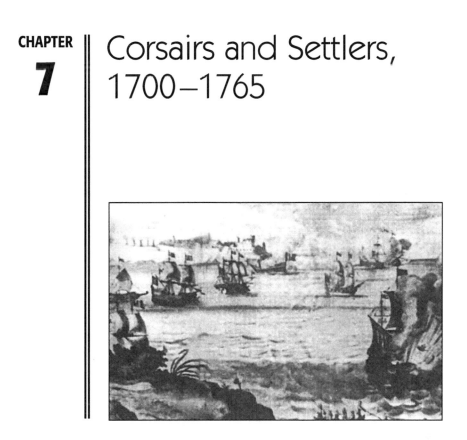

The seventeenth century was a disastrous period in the history of Puerto Rico. It was not as desperate as the previous century, which witnessed the almost total extinction of the indigenous population, but it created much anxiety in the form of recurring epidemics, natural disasters, and loss of population, in addition to the apathy of the metropolitan government.

The epidemics and emigration threatened to undo San Juan. The 1673 census shows many more women than men: 1,136 females and 627 males. The men went to Mexico or Cuba to seek their fortune. There was a shortage of skilled workers. In 1668, when it was necessary to repair the ship *Concepción* and other vessels from the Windward Armada in San Juan harbor, "there were in the city only two carpenters and four caulkers, and without the necessary tools."[1]

Even if any Sanjuaneros developed those skills, following the rec-
ommendation made by the Crown to the governor in 1670 that they
should be developed in "idle and vagrant young people,"[2] there was
a much greater demand for their services in other ports of the
Caribbean. But Caribbean migratory flows at the end of the seventeenth century also had their moments of ebb which, from time to
time, stirred the backwater that was Puerto Rico. The middle of the
seventeenth century saw the beginning of immigration by Afro-
Caribbeans who sought their freedom on the island. At first they
came from the British islands, but then from most of the Eastern
Caribbean colonies. For example, in the 1740s the Danish authorities
unsuccessfully attempted to reclaim 300 fugitive slaves.[3] In later years
Spain signed treaties with Denmark as well as other European nations
for the mutual return of runaway slaves.

Indentured servants and indebted runaways from other European
colonies also defied official regulations to seek refuge in our coasts.
The licensing of trade with the Canary Islands as a way of encourag-
ing the settlement of the Spanish Antilles also left its mark on the
composition of the population. The governorship of Puerto Rico was
even granted to an official from the Canaries, Juan Fernández Franco
de Medina, because he promised to bring twenty families to encourage the repopulation of the island.[4] In fact the governor only brought
fourteen families with a hundred members between them. Among
the surnames of these Canary Islanders are Rodríguez, Morales, Bello,
García, González, Martín, Marrero, Pérez del Castillo, Vera, Mora,
Hernández, Correa, Fernández, Andusa and Ribera.[5]

By 1700 the number of known inhabitants of the island was
around 6,000.[6] The distribution of militiamen, that is, free and able-
bodied laymen between the ages of sixteen and sixty who were
counted, reflects the areas of economic activity of the seventeenth
century and foreshadows the demographic profile of the eighteenth
century (see table 7.1).

Almost 35% of the male population was found between the Toa
and the Loiza rivers, while a little more than 33% was concentrated
in the west, in the Aguada and San Germán administrative areas. The
northeast and the west held more than two-thirds of the economic-

TABLE 7.1
Geographical Distribution of Puerto Rico's Militiamen,
According to the Place of Registration of the Companies

Place of Registration	Number of Militiamen	Percentage of total
San Juan (including Bayamon and the Toa Valley)	270	25.1
Loiza	104	9.6
Arecibo	128	11.9
Aguada	119	11.1
San Germán	238	22.1
Ponce	89	8.3
Coamo	128	11.9
Totals	**1,076**	**100.00**

Source: Brau, "Fundacion de pueblos," 88

ally active men. The east, the south, and the central mountain range were sparsely populated. Almost 24% of those counted in the census were found in two old population centers, Coamo and Arecibo. Out of these would develop important new settlements in the eighteenth century.

This population, which was geographically dispersed along two different axes of communication and where different world views developed, experienced increasing external pressures once the War of the Spanish Succession began. In none of Spain's previous wars had Puerto Rico been so isolated and militarily exposed as in the conflict that ensued because England, Austria, and the Netherlands refused to allow Philippe de Bourbon, a grandson of Louis XIV of France, to become the next king of Spain. France was an ally of Philip V of Spain in this war, which lasted from 1702 to 1713.

For Puerto Rico the conflict meant even fewer ships from Andalusia and the Canary Islands and the constant fear of English attacks. San Juan lacked adequate military protection. This situation moved Governor Gutierrez de Riva to call up in rotation militiamen from districts that were far from the capital to take turns guarding San Juan's forts. He also tried to stock the capital with provisions against a possible attack by forcing the inhabitants from the western part of the island to bring pigs and other goods to San Juan.

Francisco Lluch Mora has described the spirited resistance that these orders and the corresponding punitive measures inspired among the residents of San Germán, Ponce, Coamo, and Aguada.[7] The Sangermeños zealously guarded their town's autonomous privileges, and they always sought to prevent governors from supervising their commercial dealings. They felt that this arbitrary order from the Governor implied a modification of the political principles that sustained the autonomy of their municipal council. It was not a coincidence that a summary of the town of San Germán's privileges was drawn up at that time.[8]

If Governors Gutierrez de Riva and Danio Granados argued that the need to defend the only fortified place in the island took precedence over any other consideration, the *sangermeños* prioritized the need to protect their families and their possessions against possible English landings. The Mirabal, Gonzalez, Santiago, Colazo, Ramos, Lugo, Ortiz de la Renta, Montenegro, Martinez, Sanchez, Velazquez, Candelaria, Martin, Rosa, Velez, Ponce, Luciano, Rodriguez, Rivera, Cruz, Rosario, Feliciano, Soto, Ramirez de Arellano, Pagan, Cintron, Vega, Batista, and Gracia families were firmly united. Many of them were related by marriage. But they suffered greatly as a result of their legal battles against the Governor and the consequent resistance, evasion, prison, and exile. The Spanish crown, although it did not revoke the substance of the orders dictated by the governors, ended up reducing the penalties imposed on these combative subjects. In the end, as in a similar case from 1589, the primacy of military interests was confirmed.[9]

In the end it was by Arecibo that the English made their principal incursion during the War of the Spanish Succession. The militia from Arecibo had limited resources with which to confront the aggression of some forty Englishmen who were searching for provisions and easy spoils.[10] The military action in Arecibo and Captain Correa's role in it may have been militarily insignificant, from the point of view of world history, but it was psychologically important for Arecibo's history. The town came to be identified with Captain Correa in a way that no other municipality in Puerto Rico has been linked with its heroes. Thus, while San Germán forgot its struggles to defend its ancient municipal charter, Arecibo institutionalized the memory of its successful resistance against the English in terms increasingly linked to a discourse of loyalty to the metropolis.

Puerto Rican Corsairs

The Peace of Utrecht in 1713, which ended the oppressive war in Europe, did not bring an end to the anomie which had been unleashed on the Caribbean during those eleven lean years.[11] English, French, Dutch, and Spaniards had encouraged their respective bands of corsairs during the war so as to weaken enemy settlements and trade. For Puerto Rico the period of the war had ushered in some changes. Up until then, the corsair was the enemy who roamed around the coasts, intercepted trade, and was responsible for the scarcity of resources and the lack of trade. But in this period there appeared some corsairs who were licensed by the governors of Puerto Rico. Now the victims were the English and the Dutch—that is, it was the rich foreign colonies which became the target of raids to steal slaves who were later sold in San Juan. The Puerto Rican corsairs, and their counterparts in Santiago de Cuba, represented a creative and profitable solution to the smuggling problem for the Spanish government. Any foreign vessel that approached the coast was suspected of illicit trade and became a prey for the corsairs.[12]

The English and Dutch colonists complained to London and Amsterdam about the attacks on their trading ships. Traders from Boston, Newport, Salem and Philadelphia, whose ships, sailing along their usual routes to the Windward Islands, were exposed to these attacks demanded that England put an end to these activities which had for some time now blurred the thin line that separated the corsairs from the pirates. But the English government demurred as it had to balance the losses from corsairs in the Antillean traffic against the tidy profits it obtained by supplying slaves to the Spanish dominions in America by means of the Asiento, or monopoly, that had been granted by the Peace of Utrecht.[13]

Puerto Rican corsairs came to play a part in the hazardous power struggles in the Caribbean. Although most of these rapacious adventurers have remained in the shadows of history, at least one came to occupy center stage on account of his audacity and his successes. Miguel Enriquez, a *mestizo* corsair who amassed a fabulous fortune from capturing English cargoes and reselling them in San Juan, St. Thomas, and Curaçao,[14] had everyone, from the governor and the bishop down, owing him money and favors. When a ship was needed to repel foreign attempts to occupy Vieques, when a message had to be sent to a nearby island, when the trousseau of a daughter to be given in marriage needed to be completed, or when the finest decorations were required for a religious feast, everyone looked to Enriquez.

As happens in such cases, the extent of the dependency on Enriquez aroused jealousy, envy, and resentment. People began to murmur that he was proud, that he was a usurer, a smuggler. What better way of avoiding repayment that to have him entangled in legal proceedings? What easier way of getting rid of his competition than to accuse him of insubordination to royal authority and noncompliance with the terms of his corsair's patent? Thus declined the fortunes of Enriquez, a man who had come to be courted by those who boasted of their *hidalgo* blood.

In the 1740s there was another entrepreneur who owed his wealth to the opportunities for attacking English ships created by the European war of 1739–1748. Pedro de la Torre, a resident of San Juan, was the owner of vessels that roamed the Caribbean on the lookout for trading ships en route between New England and the British Windward Islands. Many years ago Arturo Morales Carrión drew attention to a victim's account of his treatment by some corsairs supported by De la Torre.[15] The author is an anonymous Englishman who had previously been a victim of French corsairs. In 1748 this man was an officer on a schooner captured off Tortola by two armed ships from Puerto Rico. What stands out in the story is the conscientious way in which the captors sold everything in a port in western Puerto Rico, even the clothes worn by the Englishman. The prisoner was then taken to San Juan, where he was able to meet Pedro de la Torre, who set the other captives to work on the docks, but when these protested because the Dutch received more pay than they, he personally beat them with a stick.

It is worth quoting here the impression of the island gained by the unwilling visitor:

> It might in the Hands of the English or Dutch be rendered a Paradise on Earth, but the Present Inhabitants are Mere Devils . . . . The Soil of this Island is very firtel and might produce excellent Sugar Canes, Some of which I saw while on Shore at Laguire Bay of an Uncommon Size yet as I have ben Informed they have not one Sugar Plantation Worthy to be so Call'd.[16]

It is interesting to note in the capitular acts of San Juan that Pedro de la Torre, not content with the wealth he obtained as a privateer, nor with the title of Official of the Holy Office bestowed on him by the Inquisition in Cartagena, had unsuccessfully tried to have the Cabildo recognize him as a *hidalgo*:

> A notice of nobility was presented on behalf of don Pedro Vizente de la Torre, resident of this city, with a brief in which it is asked that he be received as an *hidalgo* gentleman of known lineage and that he be allowed to set a coat of arms on the door of his house and that he be granted the honors, freedom and immunities which as such he should enjoy. . . . the proofs to be presented for examination by don Pedro de la Torre to the previous meeting of the cabildo . . . [the commissioners] state that all the necessary circumstances for declaring nobility are lacking and that the said don Pedro is not a legitimate descendant of don Juan Bautista de la Torre, whose son he claims to be and as for doña Maria Margarita Tuller, who he says is his mother, he in no way accounts for her quality as he should by attaching her parents' marriage certificate and his own baptismal certificate

. . . in view of this, they declared that don Pedro de la Torre's request cannot be granted. . .[17]

In the foregoing passages it is worth comparing the different mentality of the corsair who wants to be treated as an aristocrat and the former captive, the calculating Englishman, who observes that Puerto Rico could prosper if the appropriate investments were made in slaves, sugar mills, and marketing. The privateer, who has already become rich by exploiting the weaknesses in other people's trade, now wants access to the symbols of gentility as a means of consolidating his social position. The Englishman, robbed by the privateer's henchmen, does not stop speculating on the potential for profit which he detects in an island still covered by its primeval forest.

But fortunately neither of these mentalities drove the transformation of Puerto Rico at the time. Aristocratic parasitism or the untrammeled exploitation of its human and natural resources would have materially and spiritually impoverished the island forever. What the anonymous English captive did not see, because his movements were restricted, and what the privateer who wanted to be a gentleman did not promote, was the slow but steady inland settlement by hundreds of farmers and small-scale cattlemen.

Population Growth

Behind this significant change to the settlement of the island was an impressive growth in population. It was the most rapid growth that had been registered in Puerto Rico since the Spanish conquest of the island. Between 1700 and 1765 the population grew sevenfold, from some 6,000 inhabitants to over 44,000. What had stimulated this growth? Immigration, forced or voluntary, does not seem to account for more than a small percentage of the population growth during this period. In Arecibo, for instance, the population grew fourfold, from some 750 persons in 1700 to 3,171 in 1765. But between 1708 and 1750 there are only 52 immigrants contracting marriage in Arecibo—little more than one a year. Of these 22 are from Spain, 11 from the Canaries, four from Spanish dominions in America, five from foreign countries, and 10 slaves born in Africa, St. Thomas, and St. Kitts. In contrast with this evidence of low immigration, Arecibo's marriage register for the same period details 101 marriages that required one or more dispensations from consanguinity, that is to say, ecclesiastical permits allowing marriages between second or third cousins. Of these dispensations, 32 are for the fourth degree of consanguinity and 18 for third with fourth degree, which suggests that the families of the couple had been already settled in the area for four generations.[18] This pattern reinforces the argument that the population growth owed more to natural increase than to forced or voluntary immigration.

The natural increase may be explained by the coincidence of low mortality and an exceptionally high birth rate. In the seventeenth century, when the Eastern Caribbean was colonized, epidemics, some brought from Europe, others from Africa, periodically ravaged the islands. Between September 1647 and April 1649 some 15,000 people died in an epidemic that raged through Barbados, Saint Christopher, Nevis, Monserrat, and Antigua. In 1647–48 the French lost a third of their insular population in an epidemic. These disasters eventually affected Puerto Rico.[19] In 1647–48 San Juan lost 800 people in an epidemic. In 1681, more than 250 died in another epidemic. A smallpox epidemic in 1689 killed 631 people in San Juan, 98 in Coamo, 106 in Ponce, 18 in San Germán, 25 in Aguada, and 40 in Arecibo.[20] By contrast, in the first half of the eighteenth century there were fewer of these disasters in both the Caribbean and Europe.

One factor which may have contributed to a reduction in mortality was a better diet, as the predominantly island-born population developed a taste for Caribbean foodstuffs and also undertook the necessary planting and raising of livestock.[21] The relatively easy access to land, as well as a more liberal attitude on the part of the government since the 1720s towards recognizing new settlements, may have acted as incentives to early marriage and a higher birth rate. Another factor behind the population growth may have been a better ratio of men to women (10,968 men and 11,497 women in 1765). This gender balance, in comparison to the ratio observed in San Juan in 1673, may have been related to a fall in the number of young males emigrating. That reduction was a likely result of the fewer opportunities now available in New Spain and the increased chances for individual betterment on the island through participation in privateer and smuggling operations. Also noteworthy in the Arecibo marriage register for this period is the fact that free women were marrying slaves. This was an interesting way to remedy the gender imbalance and it also endorsed the racial mixing which characterized the eighteenth century.[22]

One effect of the increase in population was the recognition by the government of the juridical character of the new settlements. Añasco is the precursor of this new generation of municipalities. In a file on the foundation of Añasco, discovered by Salvador Padilla in the Archivo General de Indias,[23] one can trace the vicissitudes experienced by the founding residents during the three years, from 1726 to 1729, that they needed to overcome the obstacles posed by the owners of the neighboring *hatos*.

The Foundation of Añasco

On June 21, 1726, the *sargento mayor* José de Santiago, in his own name and that of the 81 residents of Calvache, Añasco, and Piñales, presented a petition to the *cabildo* of the town of San Germán requesting permission to found a town in Upper Añasco, where there was a hermitage dedicated to Saint Anthony. The main reason for the petition was the difficulty experienced by the inhabitants of that zone, especially in the rainy season, in attending the church in Aguada.

The San Germán *cabildo* decided that the petition should be presented to Governor Mendízabal. Santiago does this on September 6, in his own name and that of 83 other residents. Mendízabal charges officials in San Germán and Aguada with verifying the advisability of the town's foundation, and they promptly do so. Nevertheless, proceedings are stalled until August 1727, when the Governor entrusts officials and clerics from San Germán and Aguada with examining the proposed site for the foundation. On December 2, these officials measure the terrain for the church and assign plots to the residents

It is then that Martín de Burgos and 47 others, joint owners of the neighboring *hatos* of Piñales, Cerezal, Sabanetas, Gaspar, Bermejales, and las Ovejas, present their opposition. The objectors argue that the town's foundation would harm their livestock and would give grounds for disputes and lawsuits each time their cows broke into the settlers' sown fields. They suggest that the town be founded at a point further upstream, where there would be no danger of floods and where it would not deprive cattle of good pasture, so that the inhabitants would be

> . . . thus free of the enemies which can come along the Guaorabo river in launches to attack, that place being as it is so near the coast, not even a quarter of a league, and if the enemies see the smoke from their burning the brush so close by, they may choose to attack because it is so near . . .[24]

The governor hands over examination of this matter to the officials of San Germán. On February 1, 1728, both sides appear to present their arguments. Burgos mentions the longstanding presence in the area of the objectors' families and the importance of their livestock, to the extent that the lamps in Aguada's parish church are lit using tallow from the smaller herds.

Santiago, as the representative of the founding settlers, answers the opposition's arguments and reiterates the need to establish a new town:

> in this time of Lent . . . many people go to Aguada to attend the Church, on foot and with great hardship, ill dressed and breastfeeding their children because many of the residents are very poor as is commonly known and notorious and they do not have sufficient doctrine nor education to fully enter into the knowledge of our holy Catholic faith . . .

He speaks eloquently of how the founders would make productive "the fine meadows by the river":

Those whom I represent would be able to work, like those in the valley and town of Arecivo, where one has seen the many supplies yielded both of livestock and crops for the fortress of His Majesty and City of Puerto Rico, and in this territory this would be achieved in greater abundance.

He says that the opponents only have a small number of cattle, "some have two heads, some three, and no one has more than eight." He argues that precisely on account of the possibility of an invasion by river there should be a town not too far from the mouth, for this would enable the residents to speedily repel the invaders.

Santiago's arguments were convincing and Mendízabal approved the foundation of the town on June 3, 1728. But the objector Burgos presented an appeal on June 14. Santiago then offered to buy Burgos' livestock. He accepted the offer on condition that all the objectors' livestock was bought. But this delaying tactic failed. Santiago apparently contacted the other owners of the *hato,* and these withdrew the powers they had given Burgos to represent them. With Burgos out of the way, the foundation proceeded. In November the Governor promised Santiago the title of *teniente a guerra* during his lifetime and for his son's lifetime. In December the residents grant a surety, by which they promise the bishop to build a church and to maintain a priest. On February 21, 1729, José de Santiago was given the title of *teniente a guerra.* With the consent of his superiors, Santiago named the other militia officials on March 18. On April 19 the Bishop gave his approval to the arrangements made to guarantee worship and on May 31 Governor Mendízabal sent the dossier of the foundation to the Crown with the request that it be approved. The approval is eventually received, drawn up in terms which encourage the foundation of other townships.[25]

Other Towns are Founded

Añasco's example inspired other founders. Between 1729 and 1732 Manatí attained its separation from Arecibo, when some residents who had already settled on the banks of the Manatí river obtained the relevant gubernatorial and ecclesiastical permits. By 1765 Manatí had 2,475 inhabitants.

Between 1733 and 1739 a number of Arecibo residents, along with some others from elsewhere who gradually joined them, bought an *hato* in the middle of the mountain range to establish a town there.[26] By 1734 these enterprising Puerto Ricans had settled in the Otoao. Many of these founders were previously linked by kinship and by becoming godfathers to each other's children. It is possible that the majority of the founders were free *pardos*. Of the residents who requested the town's foundation in 1733, only the *cabo de escuadra* Sebastián de Morfi knew how to sign his name. None of those giving him the power of representative held the rank of a militia officer. In 1733 apparently only Sebastián de Andújar owned any slaves. Although official recognition of the new jurisdiction of Utuado was granted on October 12, 1739, they had to wait for five more years before a priest arrived to minister to the parishioners, and it was not until 1746 that the parish church was built.[27]

The slowness shows that the process of founding towns was a gradual one, but it also underscores the fact that the process emerged from the initiative of the founding settlers rather than the expressed interest of those who governed.

La Tuna and Pepino seem to have followed a similar process in the 1740s. In the following years there was a veritable explosion of towns. After several attempts to build neighborhoods around hermitages, Caguas was established. Bayamón and Guaynabo emerged, which for a time were both under the same *teniente a guerra*. Río Piedras and the former neighborhood of Cangrejos are recognized as towns, although the latter did not obtain its own *teniente a guerra* until 1774. Mayaguez was founded under the patronage of the Virgin of Candlemas. Yauco received its papers. There was an attempt by veterans to found Fajardo. In the Toa valley two neighborhoods acquired legal status. Las Piedras gathered its cattlemen and farmers under the same jurisdiction. Guayama rediscovered its possibility of becoming a Caribbean metropolis.[28]

Cabo Rojo, eager to become a town, cannot yet shake off the careless guardianship of San Germán's *hato* owners.[29] In the middle of the eighteenth century, Puerto Rico is simmering with conflicts between the cattlemen, who do not want to have the movement of their wild livestock restricted, and the uncouth farmers, who insist on building fences for the animals. The foundation of each township is really a victory of the planters over cattle farmers. But the outdated world of the *hateros*, shaken by the foundation of Añasco, resists institutional changes which do nothing but officially ratify what the people have already done. Instructions to the governors cross the Atlantic, the examination and division of the *hatos* is delegated to certain persons, and slowly and painfully, starting with the meadows and wetlands surrounding San Juan, the old *hato* lands begin to be divided up and allotted.[30]

Slash-and-Burn Farming

Agriculture prevailed, but which kind of agriculture? It was not yet the commercial planting of crops, which, with the example of St. Croix in mind, some would promote in the following decades. It was rather half an acre of plantains, a quarter acre planted with yams, *demajagua* saplings, some rows of tobacco to supply the cigars which the harvester would smoke in his hammock. The vision of the country's development, as exemplified by the numerous small farms of Puerto Ricans of the period, is very different from the profitable schemes for the metropolis in which some ideologues of progress, from O'Reilly to Ramón Power, would try to interest the Spanish rulers. The irony is that historians have only focused on the "paper" planters who clamored for Puerto Rico's transformation into another St. Croix, and they have not stopped to consider the hundreds of men and women who, torch and machete in hand, prepared the land for sowing. Although some history books prefer to focus on the officials who indulged themselves in speaking out on foreign plantations and their slave workforce, the interior of Puerto Rico was opened up by these farmers.

This basic form of agriculture, which exploited the fertility of the scorched hillsides to ensure that the family had food, was also carried out with an eye on the Caribbean markets. Agricultural activities were supplemented by cattle raising and logging.

The available data on production for the end of this period are speculative, because they were based on Alejandro O'Reilly's calculation of the amount of illegal trade with foreigners.[31] Nevertheless, his figures shed light on the relative importance attributed to the different farming activities.

According to the figures, out of the five zones considered important for smuggling in 1765, the two corresponding to Coamo and Guayama contributed more than half the total value of the goods exported: all the cows, 63.5% of the tobacco, 68% of the coffee, all the pepper, and 58% of the *guayacán* wood.

In 1765, Añasco was an important point for the illegal export of plantains and other vegetables. From there too were shipped some mules and horses, a little coffee, and a substantial amount of tobacco. Ponce monopolized the export of horses, donkeys, and mules, and was also important in the sale of *palo de mora*. Coffee and tobacco, *guayacán, mora* logs, and mules were exported from the San Germán district.[32]

Marketing

The prevalence of smuggling at the time of the War of the Spanish Succession did not cease with the ending of hostilities. The official trade was now centered on Cádiz, because the difficulties of navigating the silted-up River Guadalquivir had loosened the Seville monopoly. The Andalusians now found that Spanish American markets were saturated with cheap goods supplied by the English and the French. The English ships authorized by the Asiento to introduce African slaves into the principal ports of the Spanish territories also acted as illegal suppliers of textiles, wine, and tools.[33]

Puerto Rico was caught up in the contradictions of the official monopoly. The government penalized smuggling, but was unable to satisfy basic necessities through legal trade. Smuggling was a calculated risk, which on the one hand offered an outlet for the land's products, and on the other hand guaranteed access to commodities that were considered to be essential.

Trade with the Canaries fell in volume.[34] Until the 1720s, when they were displaced by the Guipuzcoan Company, the Canary Islanders preferred to sell to the Venezuelans. Seeking to extricate Puerto Rican trade from its gridlock, the Crown finally licensed the trade of the Royal Barcelona Company, a Catalan association which was expected to relaunch local production.[35]

Like all the other official solutions devised in the metropolis, the Barcelona Company fulfilled only a few of the expectations raised by its franchise. The basic problem was still access to San Juan, the only authorized port for transatlantic trade, which was difficult for western and southern producers. These, however, generated the greater proportion of the island's wealth. English merchants, seeking cattle, wood, and provisions for Barbados, Antigua, Nevis, and the other eastern Caribbean islands, paid more and brought cheaper and more varied goods to the inlets of the southern coast.[36]

Thus Puerto Rico, theoretically poor on account of the low income raised from customs duties, was producing goods according to the requirements of the neighboring islands that were better integrated into the market economy. From them it received the leftovers from the vigorous European trade with the West Indies.

The Family and Officialdom

While urban life in San Juan was carried on within the official framework of relations between La Fortaleza, the *cabildo*, the fortifications, the port, the bishop's palace, and the cathedral,[37] the rest of island society organized itself according to its own occupations. Almost nobody lived in towns. The farmers and the *hato* owners went there on Sundays and high holidays, but promptly returned to their huts or wooden houses in the countryside. Some well-to-do families, like those of San Germán, had houses in town and in the countryside and spent time in one or the other.

The family, which included relatives by marriage, was the best defense against hardship. In time of crisis, the older men who head-ed veritable clans assumed their corresponding responsibilites. But in emergencies, the mettle of the women was also evident.[38]

Although the sources may not discuss such matters, it is not sur-prising that, even given the limitations of the roles assigned to them by men, women had a say in the disposal of what they produced and exerted influence on the proposed marriages of their children and on family priorities.

The state, which was omnipotent according to the compilations of statutes, rarely intervened in private life. City life was totally regulat-ed.[39] But outside of San Juan and San Germán, each person lived on his land, without public schooling, effective control of his move-ments, accountability for his activities, or hindrance to his undertak-ings. Occasionally the *cabildo* on some moralizing campaign, or the bishop during one of his pastoral visits to his episcopate, came for-ward to promote marriage, the separation of the races, work, public order, respect for authority, orthodoxy, and a degree of moderation in ritual activities. Some *regidor* (councilman) would go into the coun-tryside and surprise some couple living in sin, and the priest would go to the jail to preside over a wedding of dubious canonical validi-ty.[40] Or if the bishop arrived and found that the tendency to celebrate on feastdays exceeded the decorum appropriate to the solemnities of the religious calendar, he would lay down rigorous norms,[41] and con-tinue on his way to the next municipality. And so life went on. This may explain why slave women, who, according to the articles prom-ulgated by the bishop in his pastoral visit, were protected from sexu-al harassment,[42] gave birth to children who were deprived of the rights which were only conferred by marriage. The eighteenth centu-ry was a period of both noble rhetoric and incompetent practice. Thus arose the principal contradictions in Puerto Rican society, which our public figures have been trying to solve ever since.

Puerto Rico Almost Becomes British

Spain fought on the side of France in the wars with England for the control of the centers of production and markets of the Caribbean. It had lost the stronghold of Gibraltar during the War of the Spanish Succession. The desire to regain it drove the Spanish government to repeatedly side with France, its dynastic ally. Thus, and at risk of causing serious harm to its American empire, Spain became involved in the disastrous Seven Years' War (1756–1763). The British capture of Havana threatened Puerto Rico.

On previous occasions some sectors of the English ruling class had expressed interest in annexing Puerto Rico.[43] They saw it as a possible base from which to protect their own commercial traffic and, when necessary, to harass the Spanish and French. Moreover, annexation by Britain would put an end to the Puerto Rican privateers. Under this logic, even before Havana was captured, it was proposed on several occasions that Gibraltar be exchanged for Puerto Rico. In the specific case of the negotiations of 1762–63, the British government considered returning Havana to Spain in exchange for Florida or Puerto Rico.[44]

What ultimately saved Puerto Rico from becoming a British colony as a result of eighteenth-century diplomatic dealings was the apathy of the sugar planters in the British islands. Neither they nor their agents in Parliament favored the addition to the British realm of an island whose potential for the development of sugar represented a threat to their own interests. Caribbean British sugar was protected by a tariff barrier which guaranteed the planters a favorable price. But Puerto Rico, with abundant uncultivated land and numerous timber and cattle resources, would in no time surely glut the British market with cheap sugar. Fear of Puerto Rico's sugar-producing potential made the acquisition of the island less desirable. Following the negotiations of 1762–63, Britain ended up exchanging Havana for Florida, which it kept until 1783.

CHAPTER

8

Political Transformations, 1765–1823

In the years between 1765 and 1823 Puerto Ricans began to affirm features of a nationality. Some even went as far as defining or naming the main elements of their collective identity. The change that occurred in Puerto Rico during those years is best understood by placing it within the context of the economic developments and political and social conflicts taking place in the Atlantic World.

The Atlantic Revolution

The population of Europe and the Americas increased rapidly during the course of the eighteenth century, especially between 1730 and 1780. For Europe it was the period of greatest population growth since the Middle Ages.[1] Although demographic historians still argue about the cause of this dramatic surge in European population, no one questions the huge stimulus that this demographic growth gave to agricultural production, manufacturing, and trade. In order to feed, clothe, shoe, and house the growing populations of Europe and America, producers intensified agriculture, disseminated agronomic knowledge, and developed machine workshops. The commercial traffic of the principal European powers grew apace. Some regions which until then had only been marginally involved in the European market, such as Russia and Poland in Eastern Europe,[2] the Plata River region and Venezuela in South America,[3] and the Carolinas in North America, stepped up their production for western European markets. As the demand for tropical products rose, Caribbean planters wished to enlarge their slave workforce. This led to an increase in the slave trade with the west coast of Africa, and at the same time stimulated an increase in production in the textile workshops of England, the Netherlands, and France, which supplied cloth to Africa.[4]

The huge profits produced by external trade intensified competition for markets. France and Great Britain, which by this time were the main European powers, struggled to control external markets and to supply consumers in other parts of Europe. In preceding chapters it has been shown how the wars resulting from this competition had an impact on life in the Caribbean islands. But the wars also had important repercussions in France and England themselves.

The governments of both nations had to face the fact that they could not count on having sufficient means to pay the debts resulting from these wars, and at the same time maintain a position of military readiness. In an attempt to increase their income so as to ensure financial stability, both governments tried to increase revenues from direct and indirect taxation. This led to serious confrontations in both France and England with those who opposed underwriting greater financial burdens in order to sustain traditional political institutions.

In the case of Britain, the confrontation required a re-evaluation of of its relationship with thirteen of its North American colonies.[5] In these colonies, many planters, merchants, and professionals did not want to take greater responsibility for maintaining the armies that the British kept there. Disputes over sales taxes on various items and over the billeting of the troops were soon carried over into debates about the nature of the political relationship between the British Parliament and the colonial assemblies. British attempts to subdue dissidents provoked the final break. Thus began the American War of Independence. Great Britain found itself fighting desperately to maintain control over its territories from Massachusetts to Georgia.

France attempted to take advantage of that weakness. After the American victory at Saratoga in 1778, the French had sufficient indication that it was possible to defeat the British. Spain and the Netherlands also joined the war.[6] By 1783, taking into consideration the low level of support for the war in England itself, the British government opted to recognize the independence of the thirteen colonies in the Treaty of Paris. Furthermore, it agreed to the devolution to Spain of its fourteenth colony, Florida. The only remaining territories that Britain retained in North America were what we now call Canada.[7]

France invested heavily in the American War of Independence.[8] Hopes that the independent colonies would trade with France instead of Britain soon vanished. Nor did a treaty of free commerce between France and England in 1786 have the desired effect. An economic recession was added to the enormous burden of public debt, and the Crown saw that it was necessary to carry out fiscal reforms. But, accustomed to its traditional privileges, the aristocracy was opposed to shouldering a greater proportion of the direct taxation. On the other hand, an enlightened sector of the population, which was reading and discussing works on social and political criticism, was acquiring a greater awareness of the arbitrary nature of privilege. This, along with the creditors' refusal to extend new lines of credit, led the French monarch to call a meeting of the Estates General, that is, a meeting of the representatives of the aristocracy, the clergy, and the plebeians or Third Estate. The convocation proposed an examination of the problems of the crushing public debt in order to advise to the King on possible reforms.[9]

When the representatives of the Third Estate came to dominate the Estates General, King Louis XVI tried to intimidate them. He dismissed the reformist Comptroller General Necker, who had advised the king in the period of the convocation, and ordered that troops be concentrated in the vicinity of Paris. But the people of Paris, roused by the daily political discussions and suffering from the higher prices for food, seized weapons from various arsenals and took the principal fort in the city, the Bastille. In the following days the news of the taking of the Bastille spread throughout the center and north of France. As a result, crowds of peasants, armed with their tools, attacked those buildings which symbolized absolute power and aristocratic privilege. From then on, France entered an accelerated revolutionary process which established the equality of all before the law, suppressed the privileges of the nobility, nationalized the property of the Catholic Church, and decreed a political regime based on reason and collective consent. This process culminated in 1792 with the abolition of the monarchy.[10]

The news that reached other regions of the Atlantic world from France reinforced the awareness developing in some sectors of the population of the outdated nature of their political institutions. Although the British and the Spanish governments tried to suppress popular discussion of these subjects,[11] revolutionary ideas were gaining acceptance in some circles of government officials, small tradesmen, and artisans. In Germany, Italy, and Poland, the French Revolution inspired the development of nationalist sentiments.[12] In the French colony of Saint-Domingue that same revolutionary ideology spurred on resistance to slavery, which already had a long history of struggles by runaway slaves and slave rebellions. When the colonial authorities unsuccessfully tried to prevent the abolition of slavery following the Declaration of the Rights of Man in 1789, the slaves and the free blacks launched their own revolution. Subsequent efforts by the French Army to reestablish the authority of France failed. In order to defend its sovereignty, Haiti, the Amerindian name chosen by the new nation, forced the French to leave the island. It also occupied the Spanish side of Hispaniola, which threatened to become a base of operations against the revolutionaries.[13]

The Spanish State in Puerto Rico

While the revolutionary currents inspired the Atlantic world to undertake the revision of its political structures, the Spanish state sought to safeguard its interests in Spanish America, including Puerto Rico. How to make Puerto Rico profitable for the Spanish crown was the main concern in the second half of the eighteenth century. People from such different viewpoints as Alejandro O'Reilly, Miguel de Muesas, Iñigo Abad, and James O'Daly tried to provide an answer to that question by means of different formulas for liberalizing trade and land tenure, importing slaves, and promoting agriculture.[14]

All of these options assumed that the solution would be handed down from above and from outside, that is to say, from the Council of the Indies. Puerto Rican historiography has suffered from a tendency to interpret the island's subsequent development in those same terms. If something happened, it was on account of that or this measure from above. It is worth critically reviewing the political history of that period and seriously reflecting about the role of the Spanish state in the development of Puerto Rican society in the eighteenth and nineteenth centuries is worth the effort. Obviously it was no longer the patrimonial state of the early Hapsburgs (1516–1598), but nor was it yet the bureaucratic, impersonal, and laical state of the current era. The Bourbon state of the eighteenth century, equipped with councils and committees and obsessed by the language of reform, barely managed to govern the island of Puerto Rico.

And there are other indications of this apart from smuggling. If one examines Torres Ramírez' observations on the activities of the Royal Treasury,[15] one immediately notes that the few officials nominated by Spain in the 1770s lived in San Juan and were more concerned with their private affairs than with those of the Crown. There is little coinage in circulation and it leaves the island on the slightest pretext. To facilitate trade, the government has to grasp at any possible solution, even the issue of vouchers.

The judiciary was no better than the Treasury. A superficial reading of governors' directives, such as the Directory of Governor Miguel de Muesas, or Dabán's Bando de Buen Gobierno, might lead one to believe that authorities had at hand a solution for abuses or a punishment for insubordination. One might think that the government watched everything:

> . . . That the blacks and people of color may not carry with them under any pretext cudgels, sticks or clubs on account of the bad use they have made of them . . .
>
> . . . That none either from the city or the island may move his residence without first obtaining permission from the justices of the neighborhood they are leaving, the punishment befitting the contravention remains at the discretion of his worship . . .
>
> . . . That none dare advise, protect or hide in any form whatsoever the flight or concealment of slaves, convicts, fugitives, delinquents, runaway children or married women who leave their husbands . . .
>
> . . . It is prohibited for those who carry debris and rubbish to throw them in a different place than that assigned to the public, against a fine, in case of contravention, of two pesos . . .[16]

The reality was different. When the state wanted to strike a blow against smuggling, it would request the Church to apply the penalty of excommunication to transgressors. But as the bishop himself acknowledged, not even that could stop the illicit trade.[17] When the sailors and the soldiers deserted from the fleets in Aguada they received a welcome in the homes of Creoles who lived in the hills.[18] Royal charters and royal reforms reached San Juan, and although the government might arrange for their implementation, it took decades for this to happen. For instance, anyone reading Muesas' disposition that, in each jurisdiction, "a person of good standing and reputation be dedicated to teach children" might believe that this order was sufficient to ensure that schools were found everywhere. But on his pastoral visit of 1797–98, Bishop Zengotita found that almost all towns had paid no heed to that article in the Directory.[19]

It was not merely the lack of an adequate communications network, or the scarcity of administrative personnel, or the vested interests that conspired to delay change. The daily life of the vast majority of Puerto Ricans who lived outside the walls of San Juan was organized in a different manner from that provided for in the laws and regulations. If one reads the reports of the bishops' pastoral visits or the accounts of eighteenth-century travelers, one can detect that, in the workplace and in social activities, there was no constant presence of the state or of its ideology.

At a lower level than that of the governorship, the *cabildos* of San Juan and San Germán in their respective areas of jurisdiction attended to the regulation of urban existence and reclaimed their former right to supervise the rural areas.[20] The work of the *cabildo* is a splendid exercise in clarity and method. Everything is the subject of minute discussion and arrangement: the supply of meat, fishing, river crossings, the lodgment of the victims of epidemics, the removal of stray dogs, the celebration of royal festivities, and precedence in civic processions. But although the council members meet on the Mondays appointed for the *cabildo*—unless they are on their *haciendas* in the countryside—the rest of the time they are as occupied as the others with their business and private affairs. When there is an emergency, they express their opinions in the decorous language appropriate to the meeting room. At such times, counterclaims and reconsiderations, reports and petitions, manifestations of loyalty and allegations of disinterest emerge, burnished with rhetoric. But even more interesting than what they said on those particular occasions would be to know what was the source of their income, what they bought and sold, to whom they married off their daughters, how many slaves they owned and to whom they owed money; because it is in such matters that their hearts lay.[21]

The State in the Atlantic Vortex, 1797–1823

The revolutionary era shook political institutions in Puerto Rico in a number of ways. The Haitian revolution in particular awakened a degree of interest in the great debates and conflicts of the moment. The cession of Santo Domingo to France by the Treaty of Basel in 1795 and the resulting Haitian occupation severed the centuries-old link between Puerto Rico and the Audiencia of Santo Domingo. For several decades appellants had to travel to Cuba. But what shook the government to its foundations was the British capture of Trinidad and the subsequent naval and military attack on San Juan.

Never before had so great a threat to the Spanish regime in Puerto Rico appeared. The British government wanted to penalize Spain for having taken up arms on the side of revolutionary France in 1796. In October of that year the British government organized a series of lightning attacks with the intent of breaking up the Spanish system of defense in the Caribbean, which was based around the chain of fortresses from Pensacola down to Trinidad. Ralph Abercromby, the most prestigious of the British generals of the time, received orders in November 1796 to coordinate a joint expedition to Trinidad and Puerto Rico with Admiral Henry Harvey. The intention was to strike two blows. In Trinidad the surprise tactics were effective and delivered the rule of the island to the British.[22] Puerto Rico, on the other hand, was forewarned and prepared its defense.

It was then that the enormous expense incurred since 1765 to improve the state of the fortifications[23] had the desired results. The British, knowing it was impossible to enter the bay, chose to disembark some 6,000 troops at Punta de Cangrejos, near the Torrecilla Lagoon. Four of the sixty-eight attacking ships blockaded San Juan harbor, another guarded the western approach, and two more remained by the landing place. In Punta de Cangrejos there was a light skirmish with some 100 militiamen who hindered the landing and then fell back to the isle of San Juan. The British troops went on to occupy the village of San Mateo de Cangrejos. Abercromby set up his headquarters in the house that Bishop Francisco de la Cuerda had maintained as his vacation home. They installed a powerful battery on Miraflores and from there commenced the bombardment of the fortifications on the bridge of San Antonio.[24]

The British sent provisioning parties to the haciendas of Josefa Giralt and James O'Daly in Puerto Nuevo to bring the troops fresh meat and other supplies. Governor Castro then concentrated militias in the area of Río Piedras, to block the raiding parties. The British, fearing the harassment of these militias, destroyed the bridge at Martín Peña, between Cangrejos and Río Piedras. But the people from

Loiza and Cangrejos relentlessly attacked the communications that the British had established with their beachhead. Some free black men from Loiza captured two German soldiers in the service of the British and took them to San Juan, where they were interrogated on the distribution of the invading troops.[25]

Meanwhile urban militias from the whole island were entering San Juan to take part in the defense. First to arrive, in the night of the April 17 to 18, was the cavalry company of Guaynabo and Bayamón. On the 19th, Toa Baja and Río Piedras arrived; on the 20th, Guaynabo and Caguas; on the 21st, Toa Alta, Vega Baja, and Manatí; on the 22nd, Juncos, Arecibo, and Cayey; on the 24th, Utuado; on the 25th, cavalry from Coamo and Aguada; on the 28th, 252 additional reinforcements arrived from Toa Alta; and on the 30th, the second militia company from Ponce. Militiamen went into action at the fort of San Jerónimo and on the fortified bridge of San Antonio.[26]

On April 30, after a furious exchange of fire at Martín Peña in which the British feared they would be caught between the militias there and the troops advancing from San Antonio, Abercromby called for a retreat. There was clearly no possibility of taking the island. Without siege equipment or the possibility of reinforcements they would not be able to force their way onto the islet, much less attack the forts. It was obvious that the garrison had enough provisions and armaments and that it was reinforced by island militias on a daily basis. The British position could only deteriorate. The Martín Peña action could foreshadow the moment when the besiegers of San Juan might become the besieged of Cangrejos. In Abercromby's words: "It appearing, therefore, that no act of vigour on our part, nor that any combined operation between the sea and the land service could in any manner avail, I determined to withdraw." After midnight the invaders abandoned their positions and re-embarked their troops in orderly fashion. Nevertheless, they had to leave behind "seven iron guns, four iron mortars, and two brass howitzers" and a great deal of supplies.[27]

For the British, the reversal suffered in Puerto Rico in April 1797 was simply the price of a calculated risk: some 200 dead, wounded, and prisoners. But for the Puerto Ricans, the victory assumed epic proportions. They had just defeated the principal naval power in the world. The British were not able to cross the San Antonio channel nor to shut down the San Jerónimo cannons. And in Martin Peña the attack of the island's troops had forced the British quarters to raise the alarm.

On Martín Peña's bridge
Pepe Díaz was killed,
the bravest soldier he was
of all that Spain's king had.

The *Sargento Mayor* of Toa Alta's urban militias, José Díaz, killed in action on May 30, is the hero best remembered by oral tradition. But alongside him were others; the priest of Pepino, artilleryman Ignacio Mascaró, commander Toro, militiamen Mauricio Rosario and Tomás Villanueva, who prevented grenades tossed against the battlements of San Antonio from exploding. There were many anonymous people from Cangrejos who, according to their *teniente a guerra*, would still be recounting their deeds years later for their activities in the mangroves and swamps to sabotage the British undertaking.[28] Although the British decision to withdraw was largely determined by the impenetrable aspect of San Juan's fortifications, Puerto Ricans, who had flooded in from different parts of the island to defend the capital, were convinced that the reason for their victory was simply the daring and bravery of the troops. For many Creoles, 1797 marked the crystallization of national sentiment in the heat of the victory against Great Britain.

Spanish authorities exploited the psychological moment of triumph to reinforce all the possible Creole expressions of loyalty to the Crown. San Juan obtained the title, which it still bears, of Most Noble and Most Loyal. Decorations and pensions were handed out liberally. Governor Ramón de Castro skillfully used the climate of general benevolence to push for reforms at the Madrid court and for greater discipline and collaboration on the island. The popularity of Ramón de Castro at the time, as evidenced by the children baptized with his name, would not be matched by any other Spanish governor in the century that followed.[29]

Served well by its representatives, the state gained some advantages from the military crisis of 1797. For the remainder of the Napoleonic Wars it could appeal to the heroic sentiments of 1797 to justify introducing measures of austerity and restraint. Supported by the island's need for security, the governmental dictates acquired oracular force.

Spain Occupied

The next crisis facing the Spanish state in Puerto Rico was of peninsular origin: the occupation of Spain by the French troops of Napoleon Bonaparte. Between 1792 and 1815, with brief intermissions, France was continually at war with the main European powers. At first those powers wanted to suppress the revolution in France. Against all the odds, the French revolutionary government survived the concerted attack of European armies between 1792 and 1793. The French revolutionary government was able to survive enemy attacks in part by taking severe steps to subdue counterrevolutionary opposition and internal rebellion. But much of the French success was also due to to the mobilization of all men of military age. The French revolutionary armies were the result of a system of compulsory military service, the first of its kind in Europe.[30]

In order to safeguard its revolution, the price France had to pay in the short term was the loss of the freedoms and rights consolidated in the struggle against absolute monarchy and the aristocracy. These rights were gradually rescinded, first at the hands of the politicians, and then by the military. Out of the triumphant revolutionary armies emerged a new type of military officer, promoted on account of his merits and proven skill rather than because of courtly favor and formed in the heat of the constant battles for survival. Suspicious of politicians' cliques in Paris, the new type of official, often from peasant or artisan stock, began to want to play a more important role in French society.[31]

Of all the officers who fought in the wars of the 1790s, only a handful ended up joining the intrigues of the political leaders of the National Convention (the French legislature) and the representative bodies that succeeded it. One of these officers eventually rose to power with the backing of a political faction which, at the time, saw him as a mere instrument. It was the Corsican Napoleon Bonaparte, from a large family of impoverished minor aristocrats.

Napoleon Bonaparte, with the backing of the soldiers, ambitious politicians, and businessmen who desired political stability, consolidated his control of the French government and pushed France towards the conquest of Europe.[32] In 1803 he crowned himself emperor.

In March 1808, following court intrigues at the summer residence at Aranjuez, King Charles IV abdicated the throne of Spain in favor of his son Ferdinand, Prince of Asturias. After the abdication, the plotters sought to remove Godoy, who for a long time had led the government, from the ministry. Napoleon, wishing to prevent the events at Aranjuez leading to the estrangement of his ally Spain, intervened and persuaded the new and the old kings to renounce their claims in favor of Joseph Bonaparte, his elder brother. Napoleon's troops occupied Spain and his emissaries traveled to the New World with instructions to coordinate the subordination of the Spanish territories to the new regime headed by his brother.[33]

The Spanish people had a different opinion from that of its rulers. On May 2, 1808, an uprising against the French troops broke out in Madrid. This revolt was repeated in the provincial capitals. Soon all of Spain was in flames. Many sectors of the Spanish army joined the war against Napoleonic occupation. A supreme *junta* was instituted to coordinate resistance against the French and to administrate the areas freed from them. This *junta* sent messages to the Spanish authorities in the Americas asking for their support in the struggle against Napoleon.

In Puerto Rico the governor at the time was Toribio Montes. He was the first Spanish administrator in America who had to decide to accept the authority of the rebel *Junta* and reject the government of Joseph I. Placed in this quandary, he obtained the support of all the other influential figures of the island: Bishop Juan Alejo de Arizmendi, the members of San Juan's *cabildo*, and the principal merchants and landowners, as well as the military officers. The governor announced his decision with public ceremonies.[34] Puerto Rico was joining the ranks of Napoleon's enemies.

At that time there was little risk that Napoleon would retaliate. French efforts to suppress the Spanish rebels were not having much success. Other European powers were renewing their military efforts against Napoleon and a British expeditionary force was being sent to help the Portuguese and the Spanish.

Most of the Spanish American authorities took the side of the *Junta Suprema y Gubernativa* of Spain and the Indies and sent contributions to help defray the costs of the peninsular war. The *Junta* invited the Spanish American dominions to send representatives, but several military defeats and the dissolution of the *Junta* left this invitation hanging in the air. At this point, in some parts of Spanish America resistance against Napoleonic hegemony found other outlets. In Caracas, Francisco de Miranda led a group of conspirators who proclaimed independence. In Buenos Aires independence was declared on May 25, 1810. In Dolores, a small town in central Mexico, another group of revolutionaries led by the priest Miguel Hidalgo raised the standard of rebellion on September 16 of that same year. These proclamations aroused similar passions in other parts of the vast Spanish American Empire.[35]

In Spain a Regency Council, the successor to the *Junta*, in February 1810, called a meeting of the Cortes, Spain's traditional parliament, in Cádiz, the safest city in rebel hands. The Spanish-American subjects of the captive king, Ferdinand VII, were invited by the Council to send representatives to the Cortes. By means of a procedure which fell somewhere between an election and a lottery, Ramón Power y Giralt, a naval officer and the son of Josefa Giralt, a *hacienda* owner, was chosen to go to Cádiz as Puerto Rico's deputy.[36]

The *cabildos* of San Juan, San Germán, Aguada, and Coamo wrote instructions for the deputy to present to the Cortes.[37] These instructions are an important indication of the contrasting aspirations of the ruling classes. In 1809 the San Juan *cabildo* had commissioned a report from councillor Pedro de Irizarry, a *hacendado* and a former *teniente a guerra* of Río Piedras. The *cabildo* extracted the main points of this report to draw up its instructions. These established the primary needs of the country as trade liberalization, more workers for the landowners, the elimination of squatting, and providing incentives for agriculture. The spirit behind these instructions was the idea of letting *hacendados* and merchants do whatever was profitable, and inducing others to work for them.[38]

The *cabildo* of San Germán was more interested in the political system than in economic liberalization. In its instructions the most frequently quoted phrase was one which captures the contractual nature of the political system:

> Firstly it protests that this Town recognizes and subjects itself to the said Supreme Central Junta now and for all time that it govern in the name of our beloved, august and most worthy king Ferdinand VII and his Dynasty; but if by Divine Disposition (which God forbid) this were destroyed and the Spanish Peninsula were lost, let this island remain independent and in free determination to elect the best means for the conservation and subsistence of its inhabitants in peace and in the Christian Religion.[39]

The towns of Aguada and Coamo, which along with Arecibo had had *cabildos* for less than a decade, emphasized the need to ensure the export of the island's produce and for more equitable distribution of land. There is a marked contrast between Coamo's position and that of San Juan regarding the problem of squatters on other people's lands. While the Sanjuaneros planned to make them take up paid work, the Coameños wanted to give them land: "That to the landless residents that there are on the island, from the unappropriated terrains be granted to them lands with title . . ."[40] This reflects the different stages of development of the two agrarian economies. Sanjuaneros sought maximum profits from their *hacienda* lands, while Coamo pursued the ideal of a society of self-sufficient farmers.

While the political debate in Puerto Rico revolved around the petitions made to the Spanish Cortes, a national independent government was formed in Caracas. The island's *cabildos* soon received letters from the *cabildos* of Cartagena, Coro, and Caracas seeking their solidarity. Some Puerto Ricans, including Bishop Juan Alejo de

Arizmendi, exchanged correspondence with the rebels for a time. But Puerto Rico did not throw in its lot with the insurgents. The new governor, Salvador Meléndez, watchful for any sign of sympathy, and armed with the extraordinary powers given him by the Regency Council, purged the Cabildo of San Juan of its most audacious elements in September 1810. At the same time, he tried to prevent Puerto Rican ecclesiastics from having contact with their peers in Caracas, and he exiled several personages from the island. He informed the Regency Council of his suspicions about Arizmendi, Power, and other prominent figures. He incarcerated in El Morro castle the separatists sent from Maracaibo, and arranged for troops and supplies to be sent to the royalist troops in Tierra Firme.[41]

An anonymous pasquinade shows the extent of the dissidents' discontent:

This people, which is sufficiently docile to obey recognized authorities will never allow a single American to be taken from the Island to fight against his brothers the Caraqueños.[42]

The pasquinade's resolute language did not prevent two thousand troops being sent to fight in Venezuela, nor did it prevent the financial health of the island treasury being seriously depleted after provisioning the expeditionary troops en route for Mexico. Moreover, Melendez decreed the collection of taxes destined to support the first wave of refugees from Venezuela.[43]

Those who were more open to change, not yet known as "liberals," a term which would become common usage at the Cortes of Cádiz, hesitated between their sympathies for some of the rights claimed by the insurgents of Tierra Firme and their natural reluctance to confront the established powers. The economic stability of the country was still measured by the remittals of the *situado* from New Spain. Independence already threatened to be something that might place slavery in jeopardy, and many among the ruling classes had invested a sizable portion of their capital in slaves. Also, the outbreaks of anticlericalism and secularism in Venezuela did not impress those who identified themselves as religious.

As the cabildo of San Juan made known in its reply to Cartagena, the inauguration of the Cortes of Cadiz was intended to dispel all these concerns:

> Fluctuating in this vessel of confusion and comparing those extremes to the dangers of Scylla and Charybdis, this Cabildo has maintained a profound silence. But Providence, by means of its unfathomable judgment, in the midst of these tribulations sent a north wind to dispel the clouds and a rainbow to announce peace and serenity to our spirits, so that we may walk without stumbling and danger. Yes, sirs, the happy news has arrived that the Regency, displaying its paternal solicitude and desirous of uniting us closely to the Metropolis, has hastened to hold the extraordinary general Cortes to consolidate the good and prosperity of all.[44]

The ancien regime prose of the San Juan Cabildo seemed to close the door to communication with the new political order that was dawning in Spain and in all Spanish America.

The Constitution of Cádiz in Puerto Rico

On March 19, 1812, the approval by the Cortes of the first written constitution in the history of Spain arrived to support those who promoted change.[45] On July 14 of the same year Governor Meléndez promulgated the constitution approved in Cádiz. It was celebrated with the usual festivities, and the administrative apparatus that ensured the implementation of the constitutional dispositions was set in motion. One of these dispositions was the establishment of city councils in every municipality. Members were to be elected by delegates chosen from among the white male heads of household. The constitution did not recognize the political rights of women or mixed-race and black people.[46]

Between August and October of 1812 the constitutional elections were held. In general, the elected mayors, councilmen, and procurators came from the ranks of the principal landowners and merchants from each town. It is interesting to note the disputes that arose during and after the elections among those residents who exercised their right to vote. According to Cruz Monclova, elections were most often contested in San Germán, Juncos, Humacao, Toa Baja, Moca, and Rincón.[47]

The next step was the election, again indirect, of the members of the Provincial Deputation. This was the first legislative institution, representative of the whole island, that Puerto Rico had. Although it was in session for little more than a year, the Deputation provided the best forum for the discussion of the principal problems of the country, especially those of a fiscal nature.[48]

In its initial application in Puerto Rico, the Constitution of Cadiz did not promote the launching of a vigorous independent press. Nor was there such confidence in the institutions organized under its aegis that the more prudent were roused to comment on and openly debate the public agenda of the country. But it provided town councils, in places where there had been little experience of corporate bodies, the opportunity to assume responsibilities and initiatives which up until then had been in the hands of the *tenientes a guerra*. At town council meetings and in the Provincial Deputation there was debate on issues such as the roster duties of militiamen, the establishment of cemeteries, the need to build roads and the means of doing this, the distribution of untitled lands, the lack of coinage, the benefits of founding schools, and the problems of public order. Copies of the acts of the town councils for the period between 1812 and 1814 provide evidence of the enthusiasm of the ruling sectors in towns for the opportunity to deliberate on municipal matters.

The Fiscal Crisis

But while the towns became initiated into political oratory, the government's financial crisis intensified. The Mexican *situado*, never punctual and in recent years reduced to half of what it had formerly been, ceased.[49] Hidalgo's revolution in 1810 put an end to the Mexican subsidy to the garrison and administration of Puerto Rico. Moreover, Governor Meléndez had been generous in his expenditure on the royal forces in Costa Firme and Mexico and on behalf of Venezuelan refugees. For example, he had spent the then-considerable sum of 12,000 pesos to support an expedition that was en route from Spain to Veracruz. In July 1812 Treasury officials told Meléndez that they had no cash with which to pay that month's debts.[50] The government was bankrupt.

Meléndez, who was not exactly scrupulous, found it opportune to consult the *cabildo* of San Juan, so that he could have someone to share the blame for an unpopular decision. Numbers, which were normally manipulated to justify the administrators, revealed the necessary truth this time. Even after cutting all salaries by half, the budget remained at 313,000 pesos, but income was only 214,000, more than 90,000 pesos short.

The solution was to issue paper money, something which had been done before. When the *situado* was notoriously late at the end of the eighteenth century the government had resorted to issuing vouchers with a nominal value. In 1812, 80,000 pesos were printed, 350,000 in 1813, and 500,000 in 1814. But the more money was printed, the less credibility the paper pesos had. It reached the point where one silver peso was equivalent to three hundred paper pesos.

Under these circumstances trade fell into chaos. In Saint Thomas, where importers used to supply themselves, only silver was accepted. In Puerto Rico creditors did not want to be paid in the new money. And as if that were not bad enough, it began to be forged.

The Spaniard Alejandro Ramírez, the first intendant of Puerto Rico, is generally credited with managing to alleviate these problems.[51] The intendancy was an administrative unit instituted in most of Spanish America from the 1780s onward to oversee the orderly development of fiscal operations and economic incentives.[52] In Puerto Rico it was created in 1803, but only on paper, as an office linked to that of the governorship. In November 1811, at the request of the deputy at Cortes, Ramón Power, the Regency agreed to the separation of the offices of governor and intendant of Puerto Rico. In January 1812, the Regency nominated Alejandro Ramírez, then secretary of the Intendancy of Guatemala, to the newly created office. As a result of various mishaps, Ramírez was delayed for thirteen months from reaching San Juan to assume his duties. He spent thirty-eight days waiting for a ship in Havana, and that allowed him to become familiar with the administrative procedures of that country to provide incentives for the development of sugar plantations and sugar mills.[53]

Luis González Vales' research into the measures carried out by Ramírez during his Intendancy underscores the grave nature of the problems faced by that official and the long time period needed for his measures and suggestions to bear fruit. Ramírez battled with the lack of confidence in paper money, and adopted several tactics to remove a large proportion of it from circulation. He placed a new tax on exports which was payable in paper money. He induced merchants to make a mandatory loan to the government, in paper money, guaranteeing them 6% interest. Then he burned the bills as they were handed in. One of his solutions to the monetary problem, the creation of a Lottery whose history has been traced by González Vales, had a huge impact on the popular imagination. Even the *approximación* prizes, those given for numbers closest to the winning number, of today date back to the first draw in 1814.[54]

Among the reforms instituted by Ramirez, the renovation of the customs houses was important, including the new ones he authorized in 1815. Other initiatives were the circulation of silver pesos from Venezuela, the *macuquino* or spent coin, the support given to the *Sociedad Económica de Amigos del País*, an organization which examined and discussed economic projects, and the publication of the *Diario Económico* which lasted for over a year. He also occupied himself in promoting agricultural production and exports. He developed a more rational tax system, collecting together a variety of small taxes on commercial transactions and personal property and consolidating them into a single tax on personal wealth called the *subsidio*.[55] Although the financial difficulties of the government of Puerto Rico continued throughout the nineteenth century, the state emerged stronger from the crisis of 1812–13, with fiscal structures and mechanisms which enabled it to do without the Mexican *situado*.

The *Cédula de Gracias*

For six years Spaniards fought to uphold the right of Ferdinand VII to the Spanish throne. He returned to the throne in 1814 after allied powers forced Napoleon to abdicate and retire to the island of Elba. Ferdinand VII was convinced that the Constitution of Cadiz would undermine his exercise of absolute power and for that reason he abolished it. In exchange he instituted a series of reforms, some of them in the old style, which guaranteed the interests of those economic sectors which seemed to have consolidated their hold on the restored Bourbon Spain. It is within that context that the granting of the *cédula de gracias* to Puerto Rico in 1815 should be interpreted.

The return to absolute rule was proclaimed in Puerto Rico on June 30, 1814. The governor disbanded the constitutional town councils and the provincial deputation. The few liberties enjoyed up until that moment were abolished.[56]

On October 10, 1814, the King requested a report from the *cabildo* of San Juan "on the most convenient measures for the promotion of settlement, agriculture, and commerce." On January 9, 1815, the *cabildo* named a commission for the preparation of the document. Among its members was Pedro de Irizarry, who had drawn up the initial report on Power's instructions. Although the dates of delivery and of the report's approval are not recorded, the capitular acts register that Manuel Hernaíz was commissioned to deliver the requested report to the King. On April 23 Hernaíz fulfilled his mission. Some time afterwards he wrote to the *cabildo* suggesting that a proctor or permanent agent at court be named to follow up this and other matters that were pending in the metropolis. The San Juan *cabildo* hired the services of Manuel Ledesma for two hundred pesos a year. The efforts of Ledesma and Francisco Xavier de Abadía paid off on August 10, 1815, with the royal charter that has been popularly known as the "Cédula de Gracias."[57]

This charter, most of the clauses of which remained in force until 1836, extended to Puerto Rico the license for free trade that had, on different occasions, been granted to some ports in the Indies. Besides liberalizing trade with other nations, including the United States, the charter also promoted the entry of foreign capital and technology. It created a mechanism for legalizing the residence of foreigners on the island, with the additional privilege of granting them untitled lands, especially if they brought in slaves. Moreover, the charter exempted foreign immigrants from paying taxes for five years and guaranteed them the extraction of their capital if they subsequently decided to return to their countries of origin. It also entitled them to become naturalized after five years of residence and facilitated the introduction of slaves from the neighboring islands.[58]

When one compares the Cédula de Gracias with the instructions given to Power by the *cabildos* of Coamo, San Germán, and Aguada, one perceives the gap between what Madrid in 1815 believed to be helpful for Puerto Rico and what the leaders of those *cabildos* regarded as being the island's problems in 1810. It is true that some of the measures are similar to the petitions made in San Juan, but on the whole, the charter shows a different conception of what actually were the priorities for the island. The difference is even more marked when one looks at the implementation of the charter by the governor and the intendant.[59] Since the charter considerably reduced the revenue from customs, the authorities devised a system of taxation to supplement the needs of the treasury with a direct tax, the aforementioned *subsidio*. Thus it was the producers who ultimately compensated the state for the privileges accorded to the merchants and foreign immigrants.

The work of Francisco Scarano has helped to demystify the supposedly decisive role of the 1815 Cédula de Gracias in launching the economic takeoff of the country. Scarano has placed it within the perspective of contemporary economic trends and the preceding political measures.[60] There is no doubt that the removal of trade barriers brought a greater volume of imports and exports. But the economic acceleration which became evident in Puerto Rico over the next two decades did not happen by itself nor was it simply the result of a rise in the number of foreign *hacendados*.

The Second Constitutional Period

The ending of the Napoleonic wars in Europe prompted the beginnings of a widespread economic recession that harmed agricultural interests. In different parts of Europe and America the crisis led to a greater rationalization of production costs and to a shortage of credit for manufacture and commerce. It also eased repressive government policies against social movements that protested or resisted the fiscal measures imposed to alleviate the effect of the crisis on governments.[61]

In Spanish America this was a favorable juncture for relaunching the revolutions for independence. The Spanish government was short of economic resources and it was beset by internal conflicts; both of these induced it to capitulate in America. The withdrawal of the reforms granted in the constitutional period, on the one hand, and the blood shed during the wars of independence in America, on the other, placed the regime at the limit of its political possibilities. In 1820, troops destined to fight in America rebelled and proclaimed the Constitution of Cadiz. The crown's weakness became evident and Ferdinand VII had to agree to govern according to the articles of the constitution.[62]

As a result Puerto Rico had a second constitutional period. Once more, allegiance was pledged to the constitution with festive lights, speeches, and Te Deums. Town councils, provincial deputies, and deputies to Cortes were elected again; once more there was insistence on the exercise of constitutional liberties.[63] Priests were ordered to take the time to explain the constitution to the faithful each week after Sunday mass.

One of the more interesting experiments of this constitutional period was the separation of the civil government from the military command. Since the sixteenth century the predominantly military nature of the governorship had overshadowed the development of administrative institutions. In 1822 a civil governor was installed, Francisco González de Linares, and a military one, Miguel de la Torre. The latter had fought against the victorious revolutionary leader Simón Bolivar in the battle of Carabobo.

The most telling act in the first year of the double-headed government was the repression of a slave conspiracy in Guayama,[64] and the suppression of a separatist conspiracy led from the United States by a veteran Alsatian adventurer called Ducoudray Holstein. Spanish agents in different parts of the Caribbean and the authorities on the islands of St. Bartholomew and Curaçao discovered the insurrection plans. According to the plan, several foreigners living on the eastern coast were expected to collaborate and there was to be a landing at Añasco. Mayaguez would be captured and the headquarters of the war of independence of the Boricua Republic would be established there. In the proclamation drawn up for the declaration of independence, *hacendados* were promised that slavery would not be abolished because it was considered essential for the country's prosperity.[65]

Dubois and Romano, two correspondents of Ducoudray Holstein in eastern Puerto Rico, were executed in el Morro. The Dutch government seized the boats and armaments which Ducoudray had assembled in Curaçao, but refused to hand him over. Ducoudray was eventually pardoned by the king of the Netherlands and in 1830 he wrote a book satirizing Bolivar. The so-called Ducoudray conspiracy has never been satisfactorily explained. It seems improbable that the costs of the projected expedition, estimated at 24,000 pesos, could have been met by foreigners alone. The fact that the theater of war chosen by the conspirators was western Puerto Rico might provide clues for future researchers.[66]

In 1823, following the intervention of French troops to restore Ferdinand VII to absolute monarchy, the constitutional regime was abolished in Spain. In Puerto Rico Governor De la Torre once more united in his person civil and military powers. The town councils that had, three years previously, celebrated the restored constitution, now expressed the appropriate joy at the restitution of the king's powers. The island sank into apparent political lethargy, which pleased the apologists of absolute rule. But De la Torre stepped up his vigilance. His measures secured the island for Spain, and incidentally for the slaveholding sugar-producing regime. In sixty years the state had passed from being the proponent of change to the guarantor of continuity.

The absolutist restoration in Spain, however, did not alter the course of the Spanish-American revolutions. By 1826 the crown had lost all of its American dominions except Cuba and Puerto Rico. Puerto Rico suddenly became important for Spain. But it was no longer the same Puerto Rico that O'Reilly had visited in 1765. During all those years a transformation had occurred which is the subject of the next two chapters.

CHAPTER 9

Faces New and Old: The Population, 1765–1823

Between 1765 and 1823 Puerto Rico's population increased sixfold. As in the first half of the eighteenth century, the greater proportion of this demographic growth may be attributed to high birth rates. But two trends modify this tendency. On the one hand, there are higher mortality rates, especially among those inhabitants subjected to harsh working and living conditions. On the other hand, the immigration of foreigners, both forced and voluntary, modifies the composition of the booming population.[1]

Szaszdi's studies of San Germán's parish records show high birth rates for that municipality: 35.6 per thousand in 1797 and 35.2 in 1798. In Guaynabo, Gregorio Villegas found rates that fluctuated between 36.79 in 1787 and 60.87 in 1781.[2] Río Piedras and Utuado have comparable proportions:

TABLE 9.1
Birth rates in Río Piedras and Utuado, 1765–1807

Year	Río Piedras	Utuado
1765	n.a.*	42.7
1769	n.a.	43.1
1787	43.7	n.a.
1793	63.9	57.9
1799	59.1	61.8
1807	33.4	44.5

* n.a.: data not available
Source: Baptismal Records and Yearly Population Reports

The high birth rates in this period are not necessarily an indication of stable families. The transition to sugar and coffee is marked by the breakup of the family. One indication of this is the growing percentage of children born out of wedlock in Río Piedras, one of the first centers of the sugar boom:

TABLE 9.2
**Proportion of children born out of canonical wedlock
in Río Piedras, 1772, 1788, and 1799**

Year	Percentage of Children Born Out of Wedlock
1772	13.5
1788	20.1
1799	29.8

Source: Parish of Our Lady of the Pillar, Río Piedras
Books 2, 3, and 4 of Baptisms

On the other hand, mortality rates were rising. This fact is explained by the relative aging of the population, the incidence of epidemics, and the deterioration of working conditions, especially among African slaves. It is interesting to note that the rise in mortality is more evident in the sugar-growing regions:

TABLE 9.3

Deaths per Thousand Inhabitants in Mayaguez, Río Piedras, and Utuado for one out of every five years from 1782 to 1812

Year	Mayaguez	Río Piedras	Utuado
1782	18.1	21.5	14.2
1787	15.7	23.8	15.3
1792	11.9	28.1	10.8
1797	22.2	27.8	24.1
1802	19.6	31.6	18.0
1807	n.a.*	29.2	n.a.
1812	26.2	32.7	14.8

* n.a.: data not available
Sources: Parish Burial Books of Mayaguez, Río Piedras, and Utuado;
photocopies and microfilms of censuses in the Archivo General de Indias
in the Scarano Collection and the Centro de Investigaciones Históricas
of the University of Puerto Rico at Río Piedras.

During this period a higher proportion of African slaves were dying than among the free population. Many of them died in the months following their arrival on the island. Those who survived had to work harder to make up for the loss caused to the *hacendados* by the death of their slaves.

The incidence of epidemics such as smallpox and yellow fever is characteristic of this period. The subhuman conditions in which some refugees and slaves lived led to outbreaks of disease. For example, 1804 was a particularly difficult year in the history of Mayaguez. One can see that the monthly average of thirty to forty deaths jumps in the summer months when the numbers nearly tripled.[3]

In some cases the burial entries give details of the circumstances of death. For instance, in the Third Book of Burials of Río Piedras there is a notice that on February 8, 1805, Eugenio del Valle was buried in the countryside because he died of smallpox and could not be carried to church. On March 30 of that year a slave of Lorenzo Kercadó is buried in a field outside town "because he had died eaten up by the smallpox." From time to time there is a touch of drama, as in the case of a burial entry in Mayaguez referring to Francisco Neaux, of French nationality, who was thrown off the freebooter La Fugosa in June 1804.[4]

Forced and Voluntary Immigrants

Tens of thousands of people from Africa, Europe, and America came, for various reasons, to live in Puerto Rico between 1765 and 1823.[5] Many were obliged to do so, either by force, as in the case of slaves, convicts, and refugees, or by economic circumstances or for political reasons, as in the case of servants from the Canary Islands, the Irish, or the immigrants from Costa Firme (Venezuela). For others, difficult personal circumstances combined with the attraction held by Puerto Rico in determined moments for migrants who came to the island voluntarily.

Coming to live in Puerto Rico was never free from hardships and difficulties. Parish burial records provide eloquent testimony of the failures, disillusionment, and cutting off in their prime of some immigrants. For example, these cases from the burial records of Mayaguez: "Juan Joseph, from Maracaibo, nothing else is known"; "Joseph Luis, a Basque, who died suddenly"; "Pedro, they say he is a Spaniard, died suddenly"; "María de la Rosa, widow of Phelipe Basques. She leaves a son, Pedro, she is a refugee"; "Nicolás Romero, nothing is known except that he is a Christian."[6]

Even though many died of diseases and tropical fevers contracted on arrival, many others survived the innumerable mishaps and came to leave their mark in Puerto Rican economy and society. Hence the need to examine the specific experiences of each of these groups of immigrants.

The Convicts

In Puerto Rico there has been frequent mention of slave, dependent, and salaried labor, but penal servitude has been overlooked. But this kind of work helped to erect one of the most famous landmarks of our capital: the fortifications. In a relatively short period of time, between 1763 and 1783, the convicts who came from Spain and Spanish America performed the hard labor that, over the following decades, turned San Juan into an impregnable fortress.[7]

From the sixteenth century onward, the Crown had ordered that convicts be used to row in the galleys of the Mediterranean fleet or to work in quarries and mines, especially the quicksilver mines in Almadén. With the disappearance of the galleys,[8] the possibility of using this forced labor for other activities was considered. One of the more inhuman tasks that were assigned to convicts was the operation of the water pumps in Havana's shipyard. Many convicts died carrying out such onerous tasks.

The need to update the system of fortifications in the Caribbean presented a good excuse to employ hundreds of Spanish and Spanish-American convicts in construction work at Havana and San Juan, especially former soldiers who had been sentenced for abandoning their posts or for desertion. The historian Ruth Pike has uncovered the rosters of the convicts forced to work on the fortifications San Juan between 1773 and 1783. Although the totals vary from month to month on account of the arrival of new groups, deaths, ends of sentences, and escapes, Pike's figures give a good idea of this group's importance at a time when San Juan's population barely exceeded five thousand inhabitants. Between 1773 and 1779 the monthly numbers of prisoners range from a minimum of 413 (September 1776) to a maximum of 557 (July 1773). For the period 1780–83 this fluctuates between 402 in February 1780 and 142 in June 1783.[9]

The prevailing harsh working conditions led to absenteeism on account of sickness in proportions which fluctuated monthly between 6% and 17% in 1770. The proportion of losses to death, ends of sentences, and escapes varied from year to year, as shown by Pike's statistics for the period between 1778 and 1782. The lowest proportion of deaths among the convicts was 6%, in 1779; the highest, 13.1%, in 1782. The ending of sentences shows a greater variation: 3.6% in 1778 and 28.9% in 1780. Several dozen prisoners escaped each year: from 10.4% of the total in 1778 up to 20% in 1782.[10]

O'Reilly had suggested using convicts to colonize Puerto Rico. In 1774 the Crown decided to settle on the island those inmates who had served their sentences, instead of returning them to Spain. Apparently the attempt to settle them in groups in the less-inhabited areas of the island was not successful. But a fair proportion of the foreign inmates who ended their sentences in San Juan, and probably a fair proportion of those who escaped, remained in Puerto Rico. Iñigo Abad highlights the problem of former prisoners who had no means of returning to Spain and became seminomadic squatters or smugglers. There are occasional mentions of some former convicts in the parish registers of the period.[11]

The Irish

Another group of late-eighteenth-century immigrants were the Irish, although they were not as numerous as the convicts. They begin to be mentioned occasionally in seventeenth-century sources. At that time it was probably those who had left the English Caribbean colonies where they had been taken as indentured servants for terms of six or seven years or to serve sentences for political activities. For example, in 1671, there were eight Irishmen in Puerto Rico.[12] The known cases of the second half of the eighteenth century concern Irishmen who had entered the service of the king of Spain. In Great Britain, Catholics were excluded from the army, the universities, and the public administration.

The Irish formed a close circle of *hacendados* and merchants in Loiza, Trujillo and Río Piedras. Between 1780 and 1820 the San Patricio hacienda, property of the O'Daly family, and the establishments of the Fitzpatricks, O'Neills, Powers, Kiernans, Conways, and others were responsible for the marked sugar boom of Puerto Nuevo and Monacillos, in Río Piedras, and in the area of Pueblo Viejo in Guaynabo.[13]

Although the Irish suffered ill-treatment and persecution during the British attack on San Juan in 1797, most of them were able to overcome these difficulties. They took root on the island and their descendants form an integral part of Puerto Rican society. In some cases, especially those who arrived earliest on the island, their surnames were Creolized, as Soliván (Sullivan), Morfi (Murphy), and Clas (Class).

The Africans

Out of all the groups that arrived in Puerto Rico at the end of the eighteenth and beginning of the nineteenth centuries, the most numerous and significant for the economic growth of the island and for the development of Puerto Rican national culture were the Africans. As has been seen in previous chapters, Africans were present in Puerto Rico from the early decades of colonization, and in 1531 they constituted the majority among the inhabitants who were counted. Although many of them subsequently left on the expedition to Trinidad and others took part in the colonization of Peru, many stayed and intermarried with Spaniards and Amerindians. Some foreign travelers of the seventeenth and the eighteenth centuries observed the brown and black appearance of the Puerto Rican population, the result of relationships between the population of European and African origin.

Up until the 1760s, and especially after 1784, the Afro-Caribbean characteristics of the Puerto Rican population were reinforced by the introduction of increasing numbers of black laborers. These did not generally come from the coastal areas of west Africa but from the interior. Intertribal wars, promoted by European slave traffickers in the areas between the Gambia and Congo rivers, resulted in the capture and transportation to America of millions of human beings of all ages, ranks, and linguistic groups.[14]

It is estimated that some fifteen thousand Africans arrived in Puerto Rico between 1774 and 1807.[15] Many of them were children and adolescents. For instance, Szazsdi identifies six men and six women who were transported to San Juan soon after 1800 in the brig *San Juan Nepomuceno*. He found that the average age of the males was 14 years 8 months, and of the females, 12 years and 6 months.[16]

The hunt for the captives whose work was so highly valued in Puerto Rico was carried out in regions ever more distant from the African coast. African leaders, armed with European muskets and spears, would take some enemy village by surprise at night and then burn it down, capturing its inhabitants amid the confusion. Then followed an arduous journey to the coast with youths and children in chains. There they were exchanged for cloth, tools, weapons, and liquor.

During this period Africans were transported to the Americas on ships amid inhumane conditions of overcrowding, dirt, and close confinement.[17] Slave traffickers coolly calculated their losses. It was normal for between 12 and 13% of the captives to die while crossing the Atlantic. Although the ship's outfitters wanted to minimize their losses, some calculated that they could obtain maximum profit by filling all the available space below deck with people. In any case, the cost of the dead would be deducted from the total obtained from the sale of the many survivors. Some ship captains even tossed those Africans who became infected with smallpox into the sea so as to avoid the contagion of the other captives and thus assure their sales.[18]

On many occasions the Africans rebelled against the crew even before the ship had left the African coast. In August 1764 a Massachusetts newspaper, cited by Mannix and Cowley, reported that forty-three slaves had mutinied at night on board the ship of a Captain Faggot at Gorée off the African coast. They attacked the crew, cut away the anchor, and killed the captain and two of his men. The first mate and the other sailors managed to overcome them. When it arrived in Puerto Rico the Spanish authorities occupied the brig, under the pretext of illegal trade, and confiscated the ship and the cargo.[19]

The young Africans who were disembarked in San Juan generally did not know what to expect from their new situation. The trauma of captivity and the loss of their clothing and distinctive ornaments, the horrors of a sea journey that lasted from seven to eight weeks during which they barely got to see the sun for one hour a day, and the confusion resulting from arrival in a land with a different language and customs, sometimes caused mental disorders among the slaves. Others, weakened by the voyage and exposed to new types of infections for which they had not developed immunity, died even before they were handed over to some *hacendado* or farmer.

Those who were more robust and strong in character survived, carrying their desire for freedom and their will to resist to the new tasks that were imposed on them. The next chapter discusses slavery as an economic and social institution in nineteenth-century Puerto Rico. But in addition to examining the circumstances which occasioned their arrival in Puerto Rico, one must recall the enormous influence on our society of the thousands of young Minas (from Dahomey, Ghana, and Togo), Lucumís (Yorubas), Wolofs, Angolans, Carabalís (Efut, Qua-Ejagham, Ibibio, Igbo, Ijaw), and others. This is seen in a variety of areas such as agriculture, music, food, social interaction, styles of dress and personal appearance, theater, poetry, and the sensibility and humor of Puerto Ricans. In spite of the adversity and exploitation that they experienced, they had the determination to perpetuate their spirit in a new environment.

Dominican and French Refugees

A smaller group, but one which had a huge impact on the development of the western part of the island, was that of refugees from the French and the Haitian occupations of Santo Domingo and the Haitian revolutionary war against French attempts to restore their dominion over that island.

In 1804, after the consolidation of Haitian independence, and after the Haitians occupied Santo Domingo, the ports of Mayaguez and Aguadilla were full of Dominican and French refugees. Many of them came with few belongings, although some were able to bring money, jewels, and slaves.[20]

As with the case of Santiago de Cuba,[21] the western part of Puerto Rico benefited from the expertise of French coffee growers who were fleeing the Haitian Revolution. For a long time the French colony of Saint-Domingue had been the main exporter of coffee to Europe. Now, following their expulsion from the colony where they had made huge profits with slave labor, these Frenchmen established coffee plantations in Moca, Mayaguez, and the hilly areas of the then enormous district of San Germán. Other immigrants with experience of sugar planting invested their assets and knowledge in the plains of Aguadilla, Aguada, Mayaguez, and Añasco.

Dominicans also contributed their expertise. Among the refugees was a group of professionals: notaries, doctors, teachers, and officials. There were also cattlemen and farmers, priests, soldiers, sailors, and artisans. Many of the Dominican immigrants blended easily into the ruling classes in western Puerto Rico, and from there they maintained close contact with Hispaniola. There were also some refugees from Santo Domingo in San Juan and the surrounding areas, according to the parish registers.[22]

The common language and traditions meant that this Dominican immigration in the first years of the nineteenth century passed unnoticed, in spite of its many contributions to the island. This wave of immigration was an important factor in the subsequent economic transformation of the Mayaguez area. Dominicans also made their mark on the development of schools and of the professions. Many Puerto Ricans will remember that among the Dominicans who settled in western Puerto Rico at the time were the grandfather of Eugenio María de Hostos and the father of Ramón Emeterio Betances.

European Immigrants of the Napoleonic Postwar Era

With the ending of hostilities in Europe, many hundreds of thousands of soldiers and sailors returned to civilian life. Accustomed to the life of camps, marches, and voyages, many of them found returning to farms, domestic service, or workshops tedious. Some had saved money, while others, in the course of their military service, had learned techniques or developed skills which they wanted to put into practice. But Europe was flooded with veteran soldiers and sailors and offered few opportunities for their aspirations. Thus there began a great migration to all corners of the globe by those in search of fortune.

The Spanish government promoted emigration to its American territories for some sectors of the great human tide then set in motion. However, not all potential immigrants were seen as desirable by Spain. In general, those with some capital to invest and who were willing to accept the prevailing political and religious order were sought. That is why some immigrants exaggerated the resources they had and tried to dissemble or hide their political and religious convictions so as to obtain the permit for residence and the financial privileges offered by Spain.[23]

In the years following 1815, thousands of French, English, Scottish, Irish, Danish, German, and Italian immigrants arrived. Also during that period came, although in smaller numbers, Slavs, Portuguese, Maltese, Swiss, and Dutch.

A study by Pedro Juan Hernández of Italian immigration to the area of Ponce may illustrate the process of integration of Europeans into Puerto Rican economy and society.[24] At the end of the eighteenth century there were already Italians in Ponce. In fact, the Cédula de Gracias of 1815 gives Rubaldos, Capas, Bonanos, Enrigos, and others the opportunity to legalize their residence. In the early decades of the nineteenth century the Italians in Ponce were connected with the sea. They were the owners, outfitters, or sailors of vessels that ply the coastal trade, or they had occupations related to the preparation of merchandise for export, such as coopers. Some were small tradesmen selling groceries, refreshments, knicknacks, and cloth. There were also artisans and others, such as a barber, who offered services. Some were able to acquire small and medium-sized properties and faced the usual difficulties in obtaining financing and marketing. To judge from their testimonies and the notarized transactions they constituted an active sector, but were not necessarily dominant. Some Creolized their surnames, and by the second or third generation were fully integrated into Ponce's community. They were a stable group and showed no inclination to return to their native land.

Thanks to a family chronicle kept by a Frenchman who settled in Guayama we can trace the career of an immigrant who became a *hacendado*.[25] Simon Moret was born in Orleans in February 1789, and was baptized in the Saint-Marceau parish.[26] When he was seventeen or eighteen years old he arrived, in unexplained circumstances, in Louisiana, which was already in North American hands. In New Orleans he married Adelaide Calandreau, daughter of French migrants from Saint-Domingue. Moret arrived in Puerto Rico in 1816 with his seventeen-year-old wife, his son Louis, aged three, and his brother-in-law Joseph, aged fourteen. He brought as capital 2,200 pesos acquired from the sale of his late father-in-law's properties in New Orleans.

In the first few years after his arrival Moret lived in Trujillo Bajo and the Monacillos ward of Río Piedras, apparently working as the administrator of a fellow countryman's sugar *hacienda*. In 1819 he brought his father over from France and in 1820 wanted to bring his mother and his two brothers. In his chronicle he notes: "1820 December 20. My mother and two brothers arrive in St. Thomas. All died within four days."

In 1829 Moret moved to Guayama where he worked as a surveyor. At that time great tracts of untitled land were being granted in Guayama, Patillas, Cayey, and the area of the district of Coamo that would eventually become the municipalities of Salinas and Santa Isabel. Surveyors were needed to carry out the measurement and division of the land, tasks which Moret frequently undertook.

His descendants claim that Moret was responsible for planning the central streets and town square of Guayama after it was devastated by a fire in 1832 and the center of the town had to be rebuilt. According to this tradition, which has not been backed by documentary evidence, he received as payment the land at Jobos where he eventually built a sugar mill. In 1842 Moret requested plots of land covered with mangroves in Jobos, which bordered his *hacienda*, so as to provide enough firewood for his mill.

Moret became a widower in 1838 and was remarried in 1840 to the Frenchwoman Adele Morin. All the family events are recorded in his notebook, reflecting his particular world view: the marriages of his children, the births of his slaves' children, the debts owed to him by his compatriots, the scandals of his small circle, in short, all the affairs that merited his patriarchal attention. Here is his summing up of the year 1873:

> The year 1873 has been terrible on account of the bad business of Mr. McCormick, the emancipation of slaves, and above all, a terrible drought, which has resulted in two poor harvests, and a third one, that of 1874, which will be poor also, and the low price of sugar. To complete the misfortunes, the death of my excellent daughter, Sylvie Ramu.

Although it appears that he never returned to France, he maintained links with his country, buying property there in 1853, which he later bequeathed to his French nephews. His sons and grandsons went to France to study and to visit. He also maintained close friendships with other Frenchmen in Guayama and preferred to make his personal notes in his mother tongue. When he died in 1884 it was written that he had been one of the founders of the Freemasons' lodge in Guayama.[27] His children and his grandchildren married the daughters of Spaniards or Creoles. One of his grandchildren, who had the same name, was mayor of Ponce in 1898. Moret's lands were repeatedly subdivided among his heirs and the memory of the French ancestor remained as a curiosity, a point of contact with a remote past. Even his original notebook was lost. Only a copy remained as an echo of the patriarch.

Not all the European immigrants who arrived after the Napoleonic wars had similar life stories. Most of them made modest contributions to agriculture, crafts, the professions, and trade. Many died relatively young and poor. Of those who were single when they immigrated, some did not have families and others returned to their place of origin, or left for other places in search of better opportunities. The non-Spanish European immigration was responsible for only a small portion of the demographic increase in the nineteenth century. Perhaps their impact on the economy and the culture of the country has been somewhat exaggerated. For a relatively short period of time, this wave of immigrants had a degree of preeminence in business and in sugar production in some southern municipalities, especially Ponce, Guayama, and Arroyo.[28] That overwhelming participation of several dozen of them in the sugar economy between the 1820s and the 1840s allowed them to display their economic success in different ways. This included building and furnishing costly houses, the European education of their children, and patronage of recreational activities which served to reinforce their prestige. This display is perhaps responsible for the degree of importance assigned by some historians to these immigrants, suggesting that they played a greater role in the political and social history of Puerto Rico than is warranted by their technological innovations and sugar marketing abilities. Much research still needs to be carried out into this subject, but perhaps the first step would be to demythologize them, to put into perspective the essential elements of their contribution to the economic development of the country over the two and a half decades of the sugar boom.

Subsequent chapters will deal with other groups of immigrants who arrived in substantial numbers in the years following 1823.

The Settlement of the Interior

While the island's coasts were opened up for immigration, the mountains were populated by Puerto Ricans who moved inland in search of better agricultural opportunities. The division and demarcation of the former *hatos* and the distribution of untitled land made large quantities of cheap land available. In 1819 the *Junta de Terrenos Baldíos* began granting plots and titles for uncultivated land. But much of the settlement of the interior, especially in the last decades of the eighteenth century, was spontaneous. A family chose a piece of land in the mountains, set fire to it, cleared it, planted, built a hut, and started raising chickens and pigs nearby. Sometimes this was done with the consent of a big landowner to whom a portion of the crop and the livestock would be handed in exchange for his permission. This informal squatting had the advantage of requiring no major commitment from either party.[29]

Between 1765 and 1824 all the districts in the interior show a notable increase in population. The four municipal districts furthest from the coast in 1765 show the following changes:

TABLE 9. 4

Population Increase, 1765–1824,
in Four Municipalities in the Interior

	1765	1824
Utuado	608	4,468
Pepino	614	5,939
Caguas	604	5,380
Las Piedras	834	3,058

Still more interesting is the foundation of new towns. Under the governorship of Miguel de Muesas (1769–76), Rincón, Cabo Rojo, Moca, Cayey, Aguadilla, and La Vega were founded. The latter was soon divided into Vega Baja and Vega Alta. Muesas also recognized the autonomy of Cangrejos, which up until then had been linked to Río Piedras.[30]

In the 1790s there was another spate of town foundations: Corozal, Peñuelas, Juana Díaz, Juncos, Maunabo, Luquillo, Yabucoa, Humacao, and Naguabo. In 1810 Trujillo was established, which twenty years later split into Trujillo Alto and Trujillo Bajo. In 1807 a district called Camuy was recognized which lay amid the bucolic surroundings of the area between the River Guajataca and the banks of the Camuy River. In 1823 it would be subdivided to create Hatillo and Quebradillas. In 1809 the inhabitants of Cidra obtained separation from Cayey. In 1811 Patillas was founded, in 1812 Hato Grande (San Lorenzo), in 1815 Adjuntas, in 1823 Ciales, initially named Lacy after a Liberal soldier killed in Spain.[31]

The new towns, especially those in the interior, initially had a predominantly Puerto Rican population engaged in subsistence farming and some cattle raising. But the subsequent development of external markets for coffee and the investment of capital in agriculture would eventually make the social structure of those districts significantly different from that of the era of their founders.

CHAPTER 10 | The Transition to Monoculture, 1765–1823

In the three centuries following Spanish colonization, the governors of Puerto Rico alternately defined the island's main problem as the lack of a market or the lack of a workforce. Because ships did not come to trade, production was lost. Because there was a shortage of manpower, there were not enough products to export.

These explanations, however, only served to excuse the low figures for the official trade. Smuggling flourished. The inhabitants, whose timber, cattle, leather, tobacco, and other crops were destined for that contraband trade, did not view the problem in the same way as those who governed. In fact, the problem for the residents was the expenses incurred in giving gifts and bribes to government officials so that they did not intervene in trade with foreigners.

As the eighteenth century progressed, those who ruled began to define the problem in another way. What was needed, they said, for the island to be "productive" along the lines of neighboring islands belonging to other European countries, was to remove impediments to the investment of capital. Legislation must be liberalized to allow for more frequent and cheaper importation of slaves. Property titles should to be granted to those who held land so that the land could easily be mortgaged, sold, and exchanged. Producers should be granted some reduction in export taxes. Exports should be promoted by offering the trading companies more facilities and exemptions from the laws regulating commerce between the Indies and Spain.[1]

When all this was achieved, by means of a series of measures implemented between 1765 and 1815, the official trade figures for Puerto Rico rose and those who governed began to congratulate themselves on the level of economic development reached by the island. But very few stopped to ask who benefited from all that production and volume of trade. Was it the slaves, squatters, and paid workers? Economic change did not improve living and working conditions for everyone in the same way. In fact, for many inhabitants of Puerto Rico, the situation deteriorated significantly as the burden of producing sugar and coffee for export fell more heavily on their shoulders.

Slaves for Sugar

Between 1765 and 1823 the slaves came to assume responsibility of the production of what became Puerto Rico's primary product, sugar. Several directives from the Crown made it possible to increase the numbers of slaves on the island, from 5,037 in 1765 to 21,730 in 1821. In 1765 the Aguirre-Aristegui Company was granted a franchise to introduce between five and six hundred slaves into Puerto Rico each year. In 1784 the crown abolished the *carimbo*, the mark with which slaves were branded at the time of their legal importation. When customs duties were reduced, importation became cheaper. This incentive had an immediate effect. Over the following ten years the number of slaves rose from 9,567 (10.4% of the population) to 17,822 (13.9%).[2]

With abundant and cheap slave labor, proprietors began to clear the lands near the ports, displacing cattle from the meadowlands. Río Piedras, the Toa Valley, and Loiza provided the setting for the new *haciendas*. In 1811 more than 60% of the sugar production was concentrated in that zone. The extremely fertile southern coastal plains were then plowed and planted with rows of cane. Ponce and Guayama became the main centers of sugar production.[3]

In the north, between Vega Baja and Arecibo, new *haciendas* were developed. The time of the sugar plantations also arrived on the eastern coast, which up until then had been neglected by investors. Several English investors established sugar mills in Fajardo, Humacao, and Naguabo. Further down the southeastern coast, in the districts of Yabucoa, Maunabo, Patillas, and Arroyo, the French predominated.

Later still, some interior valleys were turned into cane fields: Juncos, Caguas, Cayey. In the northwest, property began to be concentrated in fewer hands. As slaves began to replace the former untitled landholders of Aguadilla, Aguada, and Moca, the latter were forced to move into the interior. The western zone also turned to sugar; Mayaguez, Añasco, the plains surrounding the hilly hermitage of Hormigueros, Sabana Grande, and the plains of Yauco.

Everywhere cattle were retreating to the mountains or the drier zones, but never too far from the *haciendas* that needed them for traction and for meat. In this way, Salinas, Lajas, Camuy, Hatillo, and Luquillo began to acquire a role complementary to the sugar economy, which in some cases allowed them to later become independent districts. *Haciendas* competed for water rights and firewood, and at the same time began to secure their food supplies in the interior, in the mountains of Jayuya, Adjuntas, Barros, Ciales, and Corozal. One enterprising Catalan who had migrated from Venezuela established a farm on Ponce's heights to supply the sugar *haciendas* of the plain with cornmeal.[4] Thus the island began to insert itself into a system of production that soon would make obsolete the old mountain tracks and require a better network of communications.

But the operation of this system required a higher yield from the labor of slaves. The *hacendados* needed to pay off their debts, build better mills, acquire more oxen, have barrels made, transport their sugar more securely, and buy additional land on the banks of rivers and creeks. Merchants, perennially insecure on account of price fluctuations, short of capital, and apprehensive about the political turmoil in the Atlantic world, wanted fast profits and kept the interest rates high. These pressures filtered down to the cane fields, requiring longer workdays from the slaves who cut down the underbrush, cleared the land, plowed, cut, and carried the cane, and worked the mills. In short, all the additional work needed to pay the interest and reduce production costs fell onto the backs of the slaves.[5]

In subsequent years, the efforts by abolitionists to demonstrate that slave labor was not profitable, and that therefore slavery should end, for a long time obscured the profitability of this type of workforce for Puerto Rican sugar production. The research done by Andrés Ramos Mattei, José Curet, and Francisco Scarano have prompted a reconsideration and clarification of this crucial problem in Puerto Rican economic and social history.[6] Ramos Mattei has demonstrated the crucial contribution of slaves to the prosperity of Mercedita *hacienda* in Ponce, and the role played by slaves, when considered as capital, in financing improved technology in the centers of sugar production. Curet has emphasized how much more profitable slave labor was for the *hacendado* than free labor. Scarano has calculated the approximate yield of *haciendas* run by a predominantly slave workforce and has found it to be higher than that using mainly free labor.

The period of the harvest demanded exceptional efforts. Therefore it is not surprising that slaves, many of whom knew what had happened in Haiti, expressed their resentment at the conditions in which they lived and worked and began to talk about the possibility of freedom. Since the sixteenth century, when there were slave uprisings,[7] there had been no recurrence of rebellions. But from the 1790s on there began to be conspiracies to resist, flee, or take up arms and capture the towns.

Guillermo Baralt in *Esclavos rebeldes*[8] recounts the main collective attempts at rebellion by Puerto Rican slaves in the first half of the nineteenth century. There are recurrent patterns: isolated discussions, furtive meetings concealed by the *bomba* drums on the nights of festivities, communication with slaves on neighboring *haciendas*, information passed to the authorities by some Creole slave, then arrests, trials, executions, and prison sentences. Only in Toa Baja was there momentary success, followed by severe repression.[9]

If the attempted slave rebellions met with harsh repression, there were other forms of resistance which were more successful. Group or individual escapes, for instance, were frequent. In the 1820s and the 1830s the pattern was to flee to Santo Domingo, then ruled by the Haitians. How the routes of freedom have changed! In the seventeenth and eighteenth centuries slaves from the eastern Caribbean fled to Puerto Rico, where their liberty was guaranteed. Now the slaves of the new sugar era had to flee from Puerto Rico to Haiti. Nevertheless, many runaway slaves remained in Puerto Rico and tried to blend in with the free workers in other districts. In this way they successfully avoided capture for a long time. Others hid in the mountains and tried to live off whatever they could find in the forest.

There were others who showed their resistance to slavery by doing the least possible amount of work or selling items which they took from the *hacienda* in the market. Finally, there were those who were no longer able to stand the workload and the oppression and killed themselves by drowning, hanging, or drinking poison.[10]

The possibility of slaves acquiring their freedom by paying their owner the full market price of their value or having someone else pay it was apparently better in the eighteenth century than in the nineteenth. Szazsdi reckoned that at the end of the eighteenth century in San Germán one out of every eight slaves attained their freedom. For San Juan in the first decade of the nineteenth century he calculated that the proportion was smaller: one in twelve. Studying the transactions involving slaves in Naguabo between 1820 and 1873, Consuelo Vázquez found that one hundred out of 1,193 slaves sold, that is, 8.3%, had part of their price credited to them. The proportion is equivalent to one in twelve. It is likely that in areas of the island further away from the market, as is the case of Utuado, the savings generated by slaves played a larger part in their obtaining manumission. Despite this means of redeeming the market price of a slave, the intensification of sugar production meant more work and worse conditions. This hampered the slaves' efforts to save the price of their freedom.[11]

In Puerto Rico as in other regions, slavery was an odious institution which forcibly extracted labor from the many to make possible a comfortable life for the few. It matters not that there were institutional procedures supposedly designed to mitigate the abuse implicit in the institution of slavery. Nothing can excuse the central fact that some Puerto Ricans held other inhabitants of their own country in captivity and submitted them to a regime of forced labor.

The Land

In 1775, more than three-quarters of the land in Puerto Rico was still held in *hatos* (see table 10.1). The 5,581 farms were owned by 5,048 inhabitants while the 234 *hatos* belonged to 1,847 inhabitants. It was calculated that the 48 larger *hatos* comprised an average of 50 *caballerías* (some 10,000 acres) each; the 80 medium-sized *hatos* between 25 and 37.5 *caballerías;* and the 106 small ones between 12.5 and 25.[12] If we estimate that there were some 12,000 free heads of household in the island at the time, one could conclude that one out of every two had a farm or a share of an *hato*. The difference between those who had more land and those who had less must have been more marked than that between the small farmers and those who squatted on other people's land. But the fundamental difference rested on the usage of the land held.

Since the 1720s, rivalry between farmers and cattlemen had delayed the foundation of towns. Plowing the land constituted an act of defiance against the *hato* owners. In the mid-eighteenth century, efforts to reform land tenure and to begin the cultivation of the *hatos* closest to the capital had scant success. With the development of markets, both legal and illegal, there were more calls for the division and delimitation of the *hatos* and for titles to be granted to the holders of the land.

A royal charter of 1778 enacted a crucial reform by granting title to the residents of divided *hatos*.[13] The title was conditional on the productive use of the land and the payment of annual taxes at the rate of 1 peso 4 *reales* and 17 *maravedís* for every 200 acres.

TABLE 10.1

Land Distribution in Puerto Rico in 1775

Units	Total extension in *caballerías*	Rough equivalent in acres	Percentage of total surface	Rough average of unit sizes, in acres
5,039 small farms	994	198,800	11.8%	39.4
185 medium-sized farms	236	47,200	2.8%	255.1
87 large farms	248	49,600	2.9%	570.1
234 *hatos*, large, medium-sized, and small	6,913	1,382,600	82.4%	see text
(Totals)	8,391	1,678,200	99.9%	

Source: Torres Ramírez, *Isla de Puerto Rico*, 34–36.

The guarantee of property titles spurred the division of the *hatos* in the areas closest to the coast. Even then the legal proceedings were slow, litigious, and therefore costly. Some people preferred to give up their share rather than face the proceedings, expense, and obligations entailed in obtaining the titles.

An important point complicated the process of the division and titling of the land. Since the seventeenth century the *hato* owners had been obliged to supply the capital with meat at a fixed price which was often unfavorable for the cattlemen.[14]

During the course of the eighteenth century, quotas and supply rotas had been established for the different municipal districts. An estimate of the heads of cattle in each jurisdiction was used as the basis for the quotas. For example, in 1764, Arecibo had to provide 320 heads of cattle, while Utuado owed only 60.[15] However, this system did not ensure that enough animals were taken to the San Juan slaughterhouse. Cattlemen evaded their individual quotas by claiming that they were experiencing losses or reporting fewer animals than they actually owned. The San Juan *cabildo* then agreed upon another system in 1802, based on the amount of land possessed, rather than heads of cattle. Whoever did not have cattle would have

to pay the equivalent. This system prompted worse protests and some
of Ramón Power's more eloquent speeches at the Cadiz Cortes.[16] But
resentment at the system reflected not so much concern about a
jíbaro's single cow, but the burden it entailed for the new sugar and
coffee *hacendados,* among whom were Power's own mother, Josefa
Giralt. For them it seemed intolerable that the land which they used
more productively in agriculture should be used as an index for calculating the number of animals needed to supply the capital.

The compulsory supply of meat was abolished by the Cadiz Cortes
in November 1811, but it was not until 1820 that a free system for
supplying meat to the capital was established.[17] The citizens of San
Juan suffered from the resulting higher prices for meat, and beef
began to disappear from the diet of the workers. In exchange, the
land of the *hacendados* was freed from the obligation to supply the
capital. One more institutional impediment to the development of
agriculture had been removed.

By 1819 the government had begun to distribute the untitled land
which generally was located in the mountainous areas and in the
northeast of Puerto Rico. In a subsequent chapter we will consider
who benefited from this policy of land distribution and what were
the problems entailed by this.

In 1822 it was calculated that out of the total area of land, some
12.5%—approximately 175,142 acres—were *hatos,* and 96,139 acres
or 6.9% was untitled land. By contrast, some 1,130,456 acres (80.6%)
were farmland.[18] This marked a radical change from the situation that
had prevailed in 1775.

Capital and Credit

The available workforce and the supply of uncultivated land were not
sufficient to launch Puerto Rico into sugar and coffee production. An
essential component was needed to complete the classic formula that
had propelled other European colonies into the vertiginous development of monoculture. This was capital.[19] For a long time Puerto Rico,
like Santo Domingo, suffered from the flight of capital. The contri-

butions from the *situado*, never sufficient to pay off the debts previously incurred by the government, tended to leave the island. Once officials and soldiers paid off their debts to artisans, merchants, and farmers, these in turn paid what they owed to the leading merchants, who invested their income in importing more cloth and luxury items. The country still lacked liquid capital to promote agriculture.

In an article published in 1963, Adam Szaszdi reviewed the financial alternatives to liquid capital that were available at the beginning of the nineteenth century.[20] One of them, which merits more detailed research, was the allocation of sums of money as the principal for ongoing returns from chaplaincies and annuities. Those who wished to establish annual religious commemorations on the anniversary of their deaths could specify in their wills for the settling of annuities on their real estate property. This annuity constituted a lien or mortgage, five percent of which would be paid annually to a parish or convent for a mass or other religious ceremony specified by the late testator. For instance, when she made her will on July 31, 1809, Juana Manuela Hernández founded two chaplaincies in the parish of Río Piedras. She assigned 200 pesos of capital for annual sung masses in honor of the patron saints of Río Piedras, Our Lady of the Pillar and St. John Nepomucene.[21]

This arrangement had the advantage that the family of the deceased never had to pay off the sum pledged. Instead, each year they paid five per cent of the total. In the case cited above this was 10 pesos. As the chaplaincies and annuities were in effect a lien, in the event that the affected property was to be sold, the total sum of the annuity would be deducted from the price. The new owner was committed to continuing to pay the rent annually. This meant that a *hacienda* worth 11,000 pesos, but with 7,000 pesos of chaplaincies and annuities tied up in it, could change hands for only 4,000. There was a risk, of course, of falling behind with the annual payments and losing the land in order to pay off the debt. The accumulation of such debts ruined some landholders. Thence the popular saying, "you weigh more than an annuity" (*tú pesas más que un censo*).

Chaplaincies were like annuities, with the difference that the annual income was destined for a particular priest, frequently a relative of the testator. Some old curacies, like that of Coamo, were endowed with a number of chaplaincies, which meant that the priest who occupied that post could have a substantial income. This explains why some dignitaries of the Catholic Church had their own substantial resources to invest. The circumstances were different in the case of annuities. Then it was a layman, the church steward, elected by the heads of household, who administered the funds. If by chance someone paid off the principal of an annuity—"redeemed it," the expression was—the church steward was responsible for choosing someone to whom he handed the sum as a loan, thus guaranteeing the continuity of the annuities. For the person chosen this sum meant an opportunity to finance the development of his property at a relatively low rate of interest. At the end of the eighteenth century and the beginning of the nineteenth, the income from annuities and chaplaincies played an important part in financing *haciendas* in the San Juan area.

Some of the dignitaries of the cathedral chapter took an interest in making their land profitable. These included Nicolás Alonso de Andrade in Bayamón and Puerto Nuevo, José Gutierrez del Arroyo in Ponce, and José de Rivera in Arecibo.[22] The capital for agricultural investment came from another religious source: the tithes. Thus, income produced by their prebends, which were partly endowed by the tithes on agricultural production, were reinvested in agriculture. This helped to ease the country's lack of capital.

Just as some cathedral canons invested the income from their prebends in their *haciendas*, so too some soldiers assigned a good portion of the credits for their salaries to agricultural societies for the planting of sugarcane or coffee. Szaszdi has found several cases in San Juan's notarized records from the first decade of the nineteenth century in which officers from the garrison joined forces with French immigrants to establish plantations.[23] Capital and agricultural experience thus became partners for mutual benefit.

Commercial credit was harder to obtain and interest rates, which at that time were not declared because the law still prohibited loans bearing interest, must have been high. In spite of the delay and the insecurity of the payments, credit tied the debtor to the merchant in two convenient ways. As a consumer the debtor was forced to accept the prices set by the merchant, and as a producer, he was bound by the prices paid by the creditor for his crops. In this way, money hardly had to change hands since the loan was frequently equivalent to goods taken on credit, and the debt was paid off with the harvest. This system, which was so burdensome for producers, existed because there were no banks and money was scarce. By becoming the usual source of credit for farmers, commerce became the arbiter of production. Only those who had credit would be able to remain in production.

The government encouraged the importing of capital. Nonetheless, the immigrants who brought in their own resources, rapidly tied them up in the purchase and development of land, in buying sugar mills and slaves, or in the extension of commercial credit. Sometimes the latter could only be paid by selling off the land.

Technology

Another important element for the economic take-off in this period was the introduction of French, English, and Cuban techniques for sugar manufacture.[24] The huge volume of production attained by the other islands at the beginning of the nineteenth century was not only due to the large slave workforce and the injection of capital, but also to techniques that lowered the production costs. These techniques simplified the production and transportation of sugar. The artisans who came to Puerto Rico in the first decades of the nineteenth century adapted those techniques to the local mills. One of them was the Jamaican mill, which was a more efficient way of organizing the process of purifying the cane juice.

In the 1820s the investment in boilers, chimneys, and hydraulic and steam power did not yet represent a significant proportion of the expense of running a sugar *hacienda*. But when market demands required that the *hacendados* manufacture a more refined product than the traditional brown sugar, it was necessary to mortgage a higher proportion of the land to introduce technical advances.

Production for the Foreign Market

The production estimates collected by different historians for the period between the end of the eighteenth century and the first decades of the nineteenth confirm that, in the 1780s, coffee had overtaken tobacco as the most profitable export crop. But coffee was, in its turn, displaced in the 1810s by sugar.[25] Lower down on the list of exports were cattle, timber, cotton, and some minor crops. The difference was due in part to the changes in the principal market, and in part to the greater or lesser competition faced by different Puerto Rican crops in different periods.

Spain was still the only permanent destination recognized by the monopolistic commercial regime until the 1770s, although under certain circumstances there were already numerous exceptions to the commercial relations with Spanish America and the foreign colonies.[26] But the American Revolution opened up an official space for trade with the insurgent colonies, and this gave a significant boost to sugar. In the 1780s, trade with Amsterdam was promoted through the Real Factoría. This company, which was initially developed to export tobacco from Puerto Rico to the Netherlands, soon found greater profits in the resale of coffee than in the tobacco and timber trade.[27]

The wars that followed the French Revolution ended the Dutch connection and the Real Factoría disappeared. But the collapse of the Haitian competition for the coffee markets and the promotion of this crop by French refugees guaranteed new European markets for this Puerto Rican product, which became the main one in 1812. St. Thomas was the preferred port for shipments of coffee. It was through this port, neutral for the greater part of the period under consideration, that Puerto Rico conquered markets in northern Europe.[28]

While coffee linked Puerto Rico to St. Thomas and Europe, sugar, which made great advances after 1812, began to tighten the commercial relations with Philadelphia, Boston, and New York. The competition between sugar and coffee for the remainder of the nineteenth century was also linked to competition by foreign markets to supply manufactured goods to Puerto Rico.

In this interplay of interests, traders formed commercial companies that were intended to be short-term but which would later play a leading role in the economy.[29]

Puerto Rican Religious Culture in the Revolutionary Era

If Puerto Rico underwent such a dramatic transformation in the heady decades between the 1760s and the 1820s, it is not surprising that the religious culture of the country accelerated its own process of change. A study of the island's religious institutions during this period offers clues for understanding the thinking behind the delicate interplay of hierarchical initiatives and popular views of the world.

What stands out in this period in terms of religion is the disjunction between the religious conceptions of the ecclesiastical authorities and the devotional practices and human values of the masses. The reports of the bishops' pastoral visits reveal the contrasts. While for the bishop, what is fundamental to religious conduct is imparting the sacraments and catechesis; the faithful, who can only rarely visit a church on account of the distances, center their religious experience on domestic altars, rosaries, and the major festivities of the liturgical calendar. While the bishop counts the confirmations, the faithful relate the agricultural cycle to the phases of the liturgical year. Inevitably each bishop finds the people are uncultured and ignorant. The faithful, on the other hand, base the expression of their values in religious terms which are not always in accordance with the scholastic definitions of the episcopal library.

In the long run, the Christian works of mercy—of generosity, hospitality, and solidarity—were more important than the errors made by ordinary people when expressing their most intimate aspirations in terms acceptable to the prevailing orthodoxy. While Bishop Antolino ruled that one had to keep pure what little white blood there was on the island,[30] rural socializing led to interracial relationships. While in other societies, where slavery had a greater influence, contempt for interracial marriage was institutionalized, Puerto Rican popular discourse ridiculed the whitey who would not mix with his neighbors. The bishops thundered at the priests, saying that they should only socialize with "people in good standing." But the good Creole clergy attended cockfights, parties, feasts, and the town celebrations of their parishioners.[31] The innately Christian principles of the Creole faithful prevailed over the subtlety of the Spanish bishops' class-conscious distinctions. Puerto Ricans learned that racial segregation was against Jesus' gospel, not from the learned admonitions of the prelates who were appointed by the king, but from the daily practice of solidarity which they imbibed with their mothers' milk.

But if the bishops and the faithful disagreed in practice as to what constituted the essence of Christian life, their outlook on the world had in common doubts about what the age of monoculture foreboded. The merchants and *hacendados* who were striving to develop sugar plantations, sugar mills, and coffee groves had a different sense of time from the families of farmers and squatters who made up the mass of the population at the end of the eighteenth century. For those who drove the Atlantic market economy, there were periods which needed to be anticipated and exploited to make a profit. Cane had to be planted at specific intervals so that it would not all ripen at once. It had to be cut down at the right moment and immediately ground, so that it would not lose its juice. The juice had to be strained at the right time and it was necessary to watch for the moment of crystallization. The sugar had to be packed and shipped in a certain way. The promissory notes, bills of exchange, and mortgages were due on specific days. The notarized protests were drawn up, pocket watch in hand. Interest mounted inexorably with each page of the calendar of the lender, for whom each and every day was equally valuable.

Life for the bishops and the people in the countryside had a different pace. In the eighteenth century there were more than forty feast days, apart from Sundays, on which Mass had to be heard. These included all the feasts of Our Lady, the Apostles, the great saints of antiquity, St. Rose, because she was considered Puerto Rican,[32] St. Anthony, who blessed the animals, Saint Francis, St. Blaise, St.

Michael the Archangel . . . [33] Each day was different. There were days for bearing candles or receiving ashes or palm fronds or blessing throats. There were days for racing horses or lighting bonfires or singing at dawn. There were days on which no stove was lit nor nails hammered and days for throwing flowers at processions or digging yams. There were nights for singing the rosary or attending midnight mass. Some days were for work, and other days were for keeping holy.

Thus while the bishops complained that the *hacendados* set the slaves to work on holy days, the *hacendados* were lobbying to have peasants work for more days in the year. Two conceptions of time, two calendars, two ideas of how long it was fair to work, two methods of accounting. Eventually the owners of the cane fields and the coffee groves would prevail over the octaves and the *octavitas* of Epiphany, which delayed the harvests. The religious calendars of the Roman missal and of popular devotional observances began to give way. But although the investors' time prevailed, absenteeism and the *relajo*[34] would cushion the rigors of the victorious calendar.

This secular change in the notion of sacred time was accompanied by a change in attitude towards the secular celebrations and social activities shared by men and women. The reports of the episcopal visits and circulars would lead one to believe that eighteenth century society was wanton. But we know that in the dancing only fingers touched;[35] extended family gatherings perhaps began with prayers, and then the statue of the saint was covered with a veil, so that his ears were not offended by the music. In 1760, Bishop Martínez del Olmo forbade, on pain of a fine, those who were engaged to be married from visiting each other's houses before the wedding.[36]

Bishop Arizmendi, who in other ways reflected the closed provincial mentality of San Juan at the end of the eighteenth century, could still object to the mere suggestion that a theater be opened. His opposition was based on the occasions of danger and scandal represented by its functions and shows. But a generation later, Bishop Gutierrez de Cos, instead of threats, saw opportunities, and became one of the main patrons of the new Municipal Theater. There were fewer prohibitions against feasts and shows attended by both men and women. It is notable that this process coincided with another one whereby women began to acquire greater individuality. In 1787 Bishop Trespalacios complained that women were not simply named María, and he forbade names with suffixes like Montserrate, Pilar, Altagracia, or Carmen.[37] By the 1820s the Marian variations proliferate and the full potential of the names from Roman martyrology has been exploited. It is true that at times some censuses and baptismal entries omit the name of the wife or the mother, but by the 1820s those cases were isolated and indicated a certain reluctance by peasants to reveal domestic details.

In the nineteenth century the Catholic parish clergy was identified less with the island than in previous centuries. In earlier periods there had been a shortage of priests to serve the population. Twenty-five priests died in the smallpox epidemic of 1790. At the beginning of the eighteenth century, Bishop Urtiaga had to bring in and ordain eleven seminarians from Caracas to fill the vacant curacies. Although most of the clergy in the eighteenth century seem to have been born in Puerto Rico, at specific times, such as in 1772, there were vacant curacies on account of the shortage of priests. But the Creole clergy made up for their lack of numbers with their sociability and conviviality. In vain did the bishops admonish and warn local clerics about their fondness for Creole social activities. Bishop Martínez de Oneca did not want priests watching dances or parties, even from a distance. Trespalacios ordered that they only mingle with decent people. But in the 1830s, Ralph Waldo Emerson's brothers found priests attending cockfights. And in the piquant Creole poem, "Las Fiestas del Otoao," it was the priest who stopped the fight at a party and told the mayor to put the troublemakers in jail.[38]

But although the priests were keen partygoers, they were also fully involved in the concerns of their parishioners. Who, if not the priest, would confront an autocratic *teniente a guerra* or a despotic *hacendado*? Who could speak after mass about the measures to be taken to alleviate the drought, or the best way of transplanting tobacco seedlings, or the advantages of expanding the coffee plantations? Who else in Río Piedras would have the necessary courage to protest the arbitrary deeds of a Josefa Giralt, take complaining slaves to the council's attorney in Isabela, or openly contest the cost of the marriage dispensations for consanguinity with the omnipotent Vicar General Nicolás Alonso de Andrade, if not some gray-headed, stubborn and courageous priest? That is why the saying "this person has not yet encountered his town's pastor" says much about an era and its mentality.

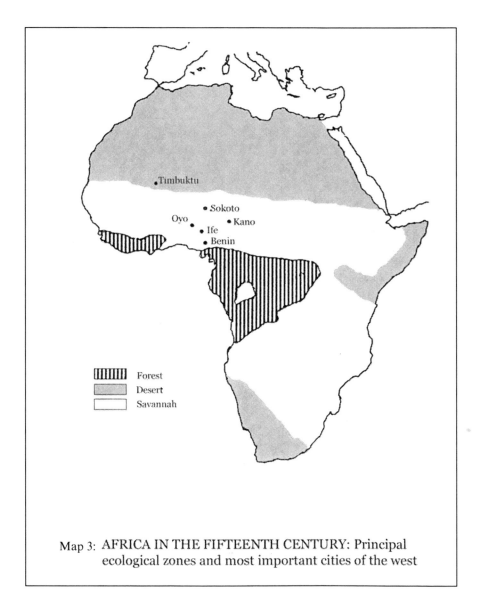

Map 3: AFRICA IN THE FIFTEENTH CENTURY: Principal
ecological zones and most important cities of the west

CHAPTER 11

A Slaveholding Society, 1824–1868

In the period between the repeal of the Constitution of Cadiz by Ferdinand VII in 1823 and the September 1868 revolution against his daughter, Queen Isabella II, Puerto Rico lived under a political regime based on the notion of exceptions. During this period the governors' full powers resided in supplementing or detracting from the norms of the Laws of Indies and the existing statutes in Spain, according to the specific case. There was little hope that the successive liberalizations which widened the social basis of the state in Spain would be extended to Puerto Rico. As some Puerto Rican historians of the nineteenth century have pointed out, although the governors boasted that they were progressives in the peninsula, once they crossed the ocean, they lost all semblance of liberality.

Or did they? Perhaps the autocracy they exercised on the island at

times represented an effort to hasten the modernization and secularization resisted by the Puerto Rican elite. In any case, the regime of
exceptions and repression was repeatedly justified by rumors of pro-
independence conspiracies and slave rebellions. Thus the idea took
hold in the minds of many Puerto Ricans that only the strong authority of the absolute governor could enable the country to maintain the
peace and order needed for security and economic prosperity. The
regime's apologists, like Pedro Tomás de Córdoba, a Spanish officer
who became the governor's secretary, sought on every occasion to
contrast the peace in Puerto Rico with the upheaval prevailing in the
Spanish-American republics.[1] On the other hand the abolition of
slavery was presented as implying the total ruin of the country.[2]
Independence and abolition came to be synonymous with political
radicalism. Neither the one nor the other was sufficiently acceptable
to be the subject of open discussion in the press, at public meetings,
or even at private gatherings.[3]

The economic development achieved during those decades generated sufficient income for the Puerto Rican treasury to pay the
island's own administrative expenses and to contribute to Spain's
overseas ventures.[4] Although the state's priorities continued to be
security and order, the availability of greater resources made it possible to undertake construction, welfare, and urban development projects. But none of these could compensate the country for its lack of
political development.

The Regime of Governor De La Torre

Between 1823 and 1837, Miguel de la Torre governed with a firm
hand and a sharp eye. He chose immigrants from Venezuela and
other former Spanish possessions and Spaniards to be *tenientes a guerra* for many districts. For instance, three of Utuado's *tenientes a guerra* under De la Torre were immigrants: Silvestre de Aibar, from Santo
Domingo, and Pedro Manuel de Quero and Manuel Muñoz, from
Venezuela. Of the previous eighteen *tenientes a guerra* and mayors in
Utuado before De la Torre, all had been Creoles, with the exception

of one Spaniard. The regional elites which controlled local government had lost their social pre-eminence under this governor.

But the new *hacendados* found De la Torre to be protective of their interests. Although Spain had signed a treaty with Great Britain promising to end the legal importation of slaves after the 30th of May 1820, more slaves than ever arrived in Puerto Rico from Africa and the neighboring islands over the following seventeen years.[5] Repeatedly, De la Torre granted special licenses to the slavers—to whom the rest of the world's markets were closed—to sell their cargos of shackled adolescents and children in Ponce, Guayama, Mayaguez, and San Juan. That steady and relatively cheap supply of a slave workforce was what the sugar *hacendados* needed to expand their canefields and put their mills to work at full capacity. At the risk of gaining a notorious reputation throughout the world by continuing the trade in human misery, which was condemned by all progressive sectors, in those years Puerto Rico occupied the second place, after Cuba, in Caribbean sugar production.

Merchants also found a staunch ally in De la Torre's government. The state's repressive mechanisms made it possible for many to take out mortgages that were increased by interest rates which were, at least in theory, illegal. In the ports opened up for official trade by the reforms of the previous decade, huge amounts of merchandise were loaded and unloaded. The ships sailed with the naval protection of the state. Under De la Torre the area of the Caribbean was purged of pirates. Cofresí, the scourge of non-Hispanic trade, was captured and shot.[6] As the main focus of Puerto Rican trade, St. Thomas enjoyed preferential treatment from De la Torre's government.

But while the new elite took advantage of the opportunities granted them by the regime, other sectors resented the greater burden placed on their shoulders by the development of the sugar monoculture economy. The African slaves in particular had reasons for attempting to shake off the yoke of their exploitation. But out of the twenty-two slave conspiracies between 1795 and 1848 identified by Guillermo Baralt, only five took place during the governorship of De la Torre (1823–37).[7]

Let us examine one of these conspiracies as an example of the general's repressive policies. On July 10, 1826, four slaves confided to their master, Dámaso Rodríguez, of Capitanejo ward in Ponce, that a slave conspiracy was afoot. The conspirators planned to set Ponce on fire, take up arms, kill their masters and, in the confusion, obtain their freedom. Rodríguez denounced the plan to the authorities, who swiftly arrested the slaves implicated in the plot, interrogated them, and put them on trial. They were judged by a military tribunal. After a speedy trial, Francisco José, Antonio, Federico, Benito, Pablo Viejo, Oguis, José Félix, Faustino, Francisco Antonio, Manuel, and Inés were sentenced to death. Felipe, Manuel, José Ubaldito, Antonio Congo, and Luis were sentenced to work in Havana's shipyards, and Pedro Congo, Felipe, Nicolás, Silvestre, Salvador, and Faustino were condemned to work in shackles on their masters' *haciendas*. Since there was no hangman in Ponce, De la Torre ordered that those who had been sentenced to death be shot on August 31, in the presence of all the slaves implicated in the denunciations. After the executions took place, the rest of the country was informed of what had happened through a notice in *La Gaceta*.[8] Naturally a moralizing report was drawn up, stressing that once again the country owed its peace to the protective attention of its rulers. The informers were given their freedom and 25 pesos.

It is interesting to note that, according to their names, several slaves born in Africa appear among the conspirators. It is also noteworthy that they had taken advantage of a *bomba* dance to plan their attack. According to the published notice, several of the conspirators were overseers. Also interesting is the fact that most of the slaves executed belonged to the Quemado, the first great Ponce sugar *hacienda*, and that those who informed on the conspirators were slaves belonging to Capitanejo ward's delegate, the owner of a medium-sized property. But what stands out more than anything is the government's definition of the problem and its solution: it was a military problem and must be tried by a military tribunal. They were punished by execution for merely attempting an uprising. Whoever believes that our past has not been violent must bear in mind all the slaves who were victims of the garrote, the gallows, or the firing squad for desiring their freedom.

Under De la Torre there was also a pro-independence conspiracy which resulted in the exile of María Mercedes Barbudo.[9] In the 1820s there was great expectation that the Venezuelans would carry their war against Spain to Puerto Rican shores. In fact, there were attacks on Fajardo in 1816 and on Aguadilla in 1825, but the action did not go beyond skirmishes.[10] Much has been written about the plans of Bolívar and his aide, the Puerto Rican Valero de Bernabé, but the enormous impact of slave interests on the island has not been sufficiently emphasized, nor has their hostility to any attempt at invasion by Bolívar.[11] In a period in which the economically dominant sectors of the country owed their solvency to the support of the Spanish state, it was unrealistic to expect that conditions favoring an uprising against Spain would develop. Among Puerto Rican slaves, squatters, and small and medium-sized farmers, only a common awareness of the benefits of removing the Spanish regime could have led to a struggle similar to that elsewhere in Spanish America. It was not because it was an island, but because it was a slave-owning society, that Puerto Rico did not become independent at that time.[12]

The Promise of Special Laws

In Spain, the death of Ferdinand VII in 1833 precipitated polarization between the liberals, who gathered around the queen regent, and conservatives, who rose in the north in favor of the succession of Carlos, brother of the late king.[13] The liberal regime that had assumed power in Madrid convoked the Cortes, and in 1836 reinstated the constitution. Puerto Rico was invited to send a deputy to the Cortes and to elect constitutional town councils. Naturally the island responded with the by now customary signs of gratitude and fervor and proceeded to hold elections.

But this time the liberalization did not take hold. In 1837 the deputies from Cuba and Puerto Rico were excluded from the Cortes, under the pretext that the laws relating to the special governance of their islands would be revised in due course.[14] In this way, with the promise of laws that would pay special attention to their overseas status, the colonial relationship that would henceforth characterize the situation of the only two remaining Spanish dominions in America was becoming apparent. The deputy returned and the constitutional town councils were abolished. Rubbing salt into the wounds, in January 1838 Governor López de Baños published a repressive police edict forbidding even the flying of kites.[15]

The disillusionment provoked by these events sparked off the conspiracy known as the "Regimiento de Granada." A group of Creole *hacendados* and soldiers, together with some Spaniards, plotted to capture the forts in San Juan and proclaim the independent republic. The attempt was scheduled for July 14, 1838. A sergeant informed on the conspirators to the regimental commander. Several of the accused were imprisoned, but the brothers Andrés and Juan Vizcarrondo managed to flee to Caracas. Buenaventura Quiñones, their brother-in-law, a *hacendado* and former constitutional mayor of Trujillo Bajo, was found hanging in his cell in el Morro. Following the military trial, five people were executed, and several others sentenced to jail. Governor López de Baños dissolved the Granada Regiment, among whose ranks had been many Creoles, and he intimidated various progressive elements in the capital.[16]

Between 1838 and 1868 the government refined its mechanisms of control over the movements and activities of the population. To enter or leave a district it became necessary to hold a passport. The *tenientes a guerra* had to make a note each day of the comings and goings of those who resided in their districts. López de Baños instituted the registration of day laborers. A day laborer was defined as any man between the age of 16 and 60 who was not a property owner or a *rentier*.[17] Day laborers had to provide evidence of their employment to the *Juntas de Vagos*, which were the municipal *juntas*. These met once a month with the local priest in attendance to deliberate on the denunciations relating to unemployment, which was considered to be vagrancy.

The government also took the initiative of developing a system of roads and tracks. In the 1830s the system of communications was rudimentary. The road to Caguas, for instance, went along the banks of the Loiza River, or, alternatively, followed old tracks through the territories of Río Piedras and Guaynabo, so that one could eventually reach the Turabo valley. It was easier to go to Ponce by schooner than on horseback. Between Utuado and Arecibo one had to wade through the Río Grande de Arecibo 23 times. Guayama had limited communications with the rest of the island. It was more difficult to travel from Arroyo to San Juan that from Arroyo to St. Thomas. The vast majority of the island's inhabitants never got to see the capital city during their lifetime. Only the great merchants and property owners who traveled there for business, or prisoners who had to serve time in la Puntilla, managed to enter the walled city. Few persons had traveled round the entire island. Only the government and the Church were able to form an idea of the totality of insular reality.

Barriers to Absolute Authority

In 1832 the Audiencia was for the first time located on the island.[18] Up until 1795 Puerto Rico came under the authority of the Audiencia of Santo Domingo. On many occasions it intervened to mitigate a governor's arbitrary actions and to bring greater perspective and clarity to bear on the legal petitions of the island's residents. When Spanish jurisdiction over Santo Domingo ceased on account of the Treaty of Basle, Puerto Rico was included within the jurisdiction of the Audiencia of Puerto Príncipe in Cuba. Insistent petitions that the island be granted a court of appeal closer to home eventually bore fruit, and in 1831 the Crown decreed the establishment of a Territorial Audiencia. This was installed on July 23, 1832, with the governor as its *ex officio* president, a regent, three judges, a prosecutor, a *relator*, and a clerk notary.

More research is needed to illustrate how the Audiencia's proximity operated to curb the excesses of the executive authority. An example of the confrontation with authorities was the critical reaction of the Audiencia to Governor López de Baños' 1838 circular on day laborers. In Madrid the Supreme Tribunal ratified the Audiencia's opinion that the circular's requirements were prejudicial to the rights of the individuals.[19] But that ratification did not forestall the *Juntas de*

Vagos continuing to force day laborers to work on *haciendas*. If they refused, they were sent to forced labor in la Puntilla.

Other institutions also made the island the object of their systematic attention. Foreign consulates, especially those of Great Britain, the United States, and France, were instrumental in curbing the governor of Puerto Rico's capricious use of authority. In 1844 a British consul was posted to San Juan, despite the objections of the local Board of Trade. Through the intervention of their consuls, the British manifested their obsession with ending the importation of slaves into Puerto Rico.[20] Not until the 1840s was the official slave traffic ended, although in the 1850s there were still indications of clandestine imports. The mission of the consuls was to further the commercial interests of their countries and to forestall the possibility of their nationals coming into conflict with the authorities. The presence of a large number of European immigrants on the island meant that British and French consuls remained alert and attentive to the main shifts in island politics. The information they provided was used to enable the other powers to occasionally exert pressure on Spain in defense of their own interests.

If the presence of the British consul was bothersome, that of the American consul could be humiliating. Several incidents in the 1820s, in particular the unprecedented outrage of Commodore David Porter's carrying out a military landing in Fajardo,[21] had shown the benefits of channeling problems and differences through a permanent consular representative. North American traders did not miss an opportunity to press for their interests. Thus, while the government suppressed any appearance of protest or disaffection among the Creoles, it was forced to pay attention to the consuls' requests. The leading *hacendados* and merchants soon became aware of the benefits that could accrue from maintaining good relations with the representatives of foreign powers. Thus, on occasion the consuls became the spokespeople for those sectors in Puerto Rico which were more closely linked to the commercial interests of the metropolis.

The Government Response to the Landless

In the 1840s the vulnerability of the Spanish dominion of Puerto Rico became evident. The sharp fall in the price of muscovado sugar on the international markets, in addition to prolonged droughts, the contraction of credit, and the scarcity of African slaves, were a blow to the stability of the economy. There were some instances of social upheaval. In 1847, crowds of men, women, and children, oppressed by a famine provoked by a long drought, thronged the roads leading to Ponce and other urban centers.[22] News of the revolution in Paris in 1848 and the subsequent slave rebellions in Martinique and Guadeloupe unsettled the elite. Governor Prim's edict of 1848, with its display of crass racial discrimination, decreed exceptional punishments for all persons of African ancestry who committed violent crimes or transgressions against property.[23]

Prim, who lost the governorship for having a murderer shot without the due process of law,[24] was succeeded by a young petulant general called Juan de la Pezuela who translated Italian and English verse as a hobby. He addressed the main problems of the island, as he perceived them, with censorious policies. He was determined to establish a closer bond between municipal authorities and the governor's office, so that any public initiative not issued by la Fortaleza was doomed. He reinforced the measures of public security and disciplined urban life. He even forbade the traditional horse races through the city during the festivities of St. John the Baptist and Ss. Peter and Paul. But the most indelible trace left by Pezuela was the promulgation of an edict on day laborers in June of 1849.[25]

The dispositions of this edict in many ways reiterated those of López de Baños, but they had the effect of making visible the dependency of the landless. They were required to carry a passbook at all times. Their employers would write in this any comments they judged pertinent to their conduct at work. Municipal authorities would make periodic reviews and would charge with vagrancy anyone whose passbook did not provide evidence of gainful employment or which had negative comments from their employers. Lastly, Pezuela decreed the end of squatting. The landless had to become tenants or waged day laborers. If they did not attain either situation, they had to move to the towns.

Perhaps it is premature to state that Pezuela was responsible for creating a market for free labor in Puerto Rico. The effect of his circular on day laborers has not been studied in detail, and certainly insufficient attention has been paid to the fact that the majority of those defined as day laborers became tenants.[26] Although many of these notarized leases with the landowners, in practice the tenants were the same as the former squatters. However, this legal fiction served the purpose of establishing accounts of what was planted and of the obligations incurred by the tenants. Thus the squatters made the transition from a situation where they personally cultivated the piece of land and shared livestock and crops with the landowner to one where they had limited access to the land. They were also obliged to work for the *hacendado* in order to pay off the debts incurred by the lease.

After Pezuela's term of office, the number of tenants and the number of charges of vagrancy in the municipalities fell.[27] The passbook regulations remained as yet another restriction on the free movement of people. What finally led the free laborers to become dependent on the landowners was not so much the state's initiatives as the very dynamics of the monoculture economy.

Fernando de Norzagaray, Pezuela's successor, increased the state's intervention in the lives of the workers in another way. As a soldier interested in engineering, he noticed the grave economic and military need for a system of roads on the island. He attempted to systematize the old system of corvées, by which residents were obliged to contribute, with money, tools, draft animals, or their personal labor, to the construction and repair of roads. Between 1852 and 1854 an ambitious program for road construction was drawn up.[28] Although it would take the rest of the century and then some more years to make it a reality, the system of communications devised during Norzagaray's governorship would provide the insular administration with a vision of all the roads needed on the island for marketing and provisioning. The road from San Juan to Ponce was defined as the main artery, with two necessary intermediate points, the Turabo and Coamo valleys. The Central Road, as it came to be known, took until 1886 to be completed,[29] but from the time of Norzagaray on, the main axis of traffic towards the interior was defined. The road did not help Guayama, which remained on the margins of the principal highway, but it supported the development of Cayey and Aibonito.

The Cholera Epidemic

In November 1855, a cholera epidemic which broke out at the port of Naguabo followed the course of the island's roads. It advanced steadily and alarmingly along the commercial routes of Puerto Rico. In November it reached Caguas and Cayey and in the following months it scourged a series of population centers.[30] Few municipalities seem to have escaped, although Adjuntas, a district in the highlands that had controlled access to isolate itself from neighboring municipalities, apparently managed to do so.

The cholera epidemic left some thirty thousand dead. It revealed the unsatisfactory nature of the urban centers. Pezuela's order forcing thousands of people to move into the towns had resulted in the proliferation of shacks in shantytowns, without any type of services.[31] There, polluting the water with their excrement and without facilities for garbage disposal or transportation, the former squatters were dying, the victims of the enlightened policy of a governor who wanted to guarantee their payment for their labor. This link between Pezuela's decrees and the ravages of cholera in the urban centers calls for a more detailed study.

The Struggle for Emancipation

The outbreak of the Civil War in the United States in 1861 opened up economic opportunities for the sugar producers. Moreover, during the four years of the conflict, it spurred the planting and export of cotton. With the ending of the Civil War in 1865, pressure mounted on the Spanish government to abolish slavery in its possessions. At that time the only remaining slavery zones in the Americas were Brazil, Cuba, and Puerto Rico. Writers like Victor Hugo had encouraged the development in Europe of strong public opinion against slavery, and this was echoed in Madrid and Barcelona. In Cuba, more than in Puerto Rico, the debate around slavery became linked to the desire for independence.[32]

Román Baldorioty de Castro, José Julián Acosta, Ramón Emeterio Betances, and other Puerto Ricans, most of whom had received their higher education in Europe, developed personal standpoints as to what were the fundamental problems of the country. When they joined forces to mitigate the rigors of slavery in Puerto Rico, they had become well known to the authorities. For this reason they were suspected of entertaining radical ideas and plans.

The need to reform the statutes in force in the Antilles and the pressure exercised by different sectors on the Spanish government led to the convocation of a *Junta Informativa* in 1866. It was made up of representatives of the principal town councils of Puerto Rico and Cuba. Progressives on the island waited impatiently for its inauguration because they hoped that this was the opportunity to bring an end to arbitrary and omnipotent rule by military men. Two of the six Puerto Rican delegates were unable to travel to Spain. Three out of the four who did go—Segundo Ruiz Belvis, José Julián Acosta, and Francisco Mariano Quiñones—after prolonged debate were able to reach agreement on a proposal for abolishing slavery in Puerto Rico.[33]

Instead of resulting in a program of reform for the islands, the *Junta Informativa* of 1866 multiplied the differences between Spain and its colonies in Cuba and Puerto Rico. The Cuban delegates, most of them committed to pro-slavery interests, did not express solidarity with the abolitionist declarations of the Puerto Ricans, but they proposed political reforms in line with their interests. The line of discussion pursued by the Spanish authorities made little impression on the Caribbean representatives. In short, the meetings were suspended without achieving anything that could satisfy the expectations that had been raised.[34]

Ramón Emeterio Betances, a doctor from Cabo Rojo who was a resident of Mayaguez, and Segundo Ruiz Belvis, a *hacendado* from

Hormigueros (which then formed part of the district of San Germán) publicly voiced their disappointment with the *Junta's* achievements. This led the Spanish authorities to decide to deport them to Spain. Warned of this, the two friends left Puerto Rico and began to seek the resources to launch a revolution. Ruiz Belvis left for Chile, but died suddenly there in 1867. Betances tried to organize an uprising from Santo Domingo, St. Thomas and New York. He found sympathy and cooperation among the Dominicans, who had just waged a war of independence against Spain.[35]

In 1867 the political malaise on the island intensified. It was a time when the effect of the ending of the U.S. Civil War was beginning to have repercussions throughout the Atlantic world. When the former Confederate states re-entered the Atlantic market from which they had been largely excluded by the blockade during the war, there was no longer external demand for cotton harvested in Puerto Rico. Sugar prices similarly fell. There was a contraction of credit, and several leading commercial houses went bankrupt. In October 1867, a hurricane on St. Narcissus' day wreaked havoc on the eastern and central parts of the island. The following month, severe earthquakes shook San Juan and resulted in the cessation of commercial and administrative activity.

All these problems had the effect of reducing the income in the government coffers and by 1868 this provoked a serious financial crisis.[36] Finding itself short of funds, the government decided to bring forward the collection of taxes, and to press for the payment of all outstanding taxes. Landowners who did not pay had part of their property seized and auctioned off to pay the debt. When these measures were added to existing grievances about the government's budgetary priorities, the dissatisfaction grew to the point that by the middle of 1868 the island was seething with rumors of a revolution.

El Grito de Lares

The rumors had a foundation. Betances and other exiles in contact with Cuban independence supporters planned a simultaneous upris-

ing in both islands.[37] In Puerto Rico, revolutionary cells were founded in Mayaguez (Capá Prieto), Lares (Centro Bravo), Camuy
(Lanzador del Norte), and Pepino (Porvenir).[38] Although only the first
two cells were endorsed by the revolutionary committee that was
coordinated by Betances, it was agreed that the revolution should
break out in Camuy on September 29, Saint Michael's Day. Traditio-
nally it was a feast day for slaves, and the conspirators were counting
on their participation. The conspirators of Camuy shared doubts
about the adequacy of the supplies of weapons and munitions at
their disposal, but the eager insistence of their colleagues from Lares
induced them to promise to go ahead with the uprising.[39]

It is possible that Camuy was chosen on account of the fact that
its mayor, Pablo de Rivera y García, implicitly or explicitly supported
the cause. The mayor's son was one of the conspirators. It is also possible that launching the uprising in a coastal district would give
Betances a place on the littoral for unloading the weapons he had
obtained. Or perhaps they were counting on taking Arecibo by surprise. Because the level of support in other towns has not been established, it is not possible to determine what support the Camuy conspirators could count on, beyond a few sympathizers identified in
Arecibo and Quebradillas.

Manuel María González, a Venezuelan who was the president of
the Lanzador del Norte cell, could not prevent knowledge of the conspiracy from reaching the Spanish authorities. Consequently, his
house was searched and compromising evidence was found. News
about the arrest of González reached Lares, and as a result it was
decided to bring forward the date of the revolution to the 23rd of
September and to inform the conspirators in Mayaguez and Pepino
of this change, so that they would join in the effort.[40]

The president of the Centro Bravo organization in Lares was
Manuel Rojas, a Venezuelan coffee *hacendado*. The capture of Lares
was planned on his property in Bartolo ward. On the night of
September 23, some 600 or more people armed with shotguns,
revolvers, and machetes entered Lares. They arrested the municipal
authorities and the Spanish merchants, proclaimed the Republic of
Puerto Rico, and set up a provisional government which was com-

posed of residents of Lares, almost all of whom were related by marriage. On the following day the revolutionaries persuaded the priest at Lares to sing a Te Deum in the church in thanksgiving for the establishment of the republic. Then they marched on Pepino, which they hoped to take with the help of Manuel Cebollero, a native of Aguada, and the leader of the Porvenir cell.[41]

In order to prevent members of the militia from joining Cebollero, one of their officers, the Pepino authorities had confined the militia to their quarters. They had also requested the help of the mayor of Aguadilla, who ordered the assembly of the militias from Aguadilla and Moca and himself went to Pepino. The revolutionaries were not able to take Pepino, and faced with the imminent arrival of troops with better weaponry, they fell back on Lares, leaving behind seven wounded who later died in the Aguadilla jail.

In Lares a force coordinated by Matías Brugman, a North American *hacendado* in Mayaguez and the head of the Capá Prieto cell, joined the revolutionaries. The leaders decided to start what was later called a guerrilla operation in the mountains, while awaiting the arms and munitions assembled by Betances and for other Puerto Ricans to join in the uprising. However, measures taken by the government prevented both of these from happening. The schooner *El Telégrafo* was confiscated with arms and munitions in Saint Thomas, and numerous arrests throughout the island forestalled other uprisings in solidarity.[42]

According to Olga Jiménez, 551 people were arrested in connection with the Grito de Lares.[43] Eighty of them died in jail during the yellow fever outbreaks in Aguadilla and Arecibo, where most rebels were held. The civil and military tribunals entered into dispute over which had jurisdiction over the accused. Governor Pavía decided that those who had been captured with weapons in their hands or who had participated in the attack on Pepino would fall under the more severe martial law. Under this arrangement, seven of the insurgents were tried in November and condemned to death. Nevertheless, following the intercession of numerous people, the penalty was commuted to prison and they were sent to Cádiz.

No other prisoner was judged or sentenced. Judge Navascués, from

Ponce, delegated by the Audiencia to draw up a brief of the cause, interrogated most of them. The huge number of the accused, and the difficulties in taking depositions in Aguadilla, Arecibo, and Lares, made the summary proceedings extremely slow. In January 1869, the new governor, José Laureano Sanz, taking advantage of the fact that a revolution in Spain had dethroned Queen Isabella II in September, declared an amnesty for all the imprisoned. The seven who had reached Cadiz returned to Puerto Rico.[44]

In order to evaluate the importance of the Grito de Lares one has to place the revolution within the context of those years. Although headed by foreign *hacendados* who were in economic straits, the Grito de Lares represented the interests of most of the population. For slaves, it meant the abolition of their bondage; for day laborers, the end of the passbook regulations; for the farmers, the end of extortion by the Spanish merchants; and for Puerto Rican professionals and *rentiers*, it meant a chance to play a part in the running of the country.

The Grito de Lares happened in 1868 because at that moment the problems of the country had reached a critical state and because there were enough people committed to the revolutionary movement to give it a wide organizational base. It failed to achieve the desired success not because it was set in motion earlier than planned and had been transferred from Camuy to Lares, but because the organizational structure and the level of political awareness of the plotters was still rudimentary. When the success of a revolution relied on a particular conversation not being overheard or on some incriminating papers not being found, anything could have sufficed to undo it.

Nevertheless, it is important to study the different aspects of the Grito de Lares because it represents the first major concerted effort by Puerto Ricans to radically alter their common situation. In the face of the government's arbitrary actions and the failure of every political solution, a revolution to reclaim the most basic human rights turned out to be the only available route. In its aftermath the Spanish authorities would be more sensitive to the climate of public opinion in the country, although no less vigilant of activities considered to be anti-Spanish. The situation had changed considerably since Miguel de la Torre's time, when watchfulness was enough.

The Population

According to the censuses, the population continued to grow between 1824 and 1867 but the rate of increase was slower than in previous periods. The number of slaves grew rapidly until the beginning of the 1840s. Then, thanks to greater vigilance on the coast of Africa and increased diplomatic pressure on Spain, the illegal trade started to decline.[45] The population of free blacks and coloreds grew more rapidly than that of whites between the 1820s and the 1840s, but suffered proportionately more than whites in the epidemics of the 1850s. Either because of changes in the way people were categorized racially, or because the black and mixed-race population suffered disproportionately from the deterioration in public health during the second half of the nineteenth century, the fact is that, after 1850, those counted as white began to grow more rapidly than the black and mixed-race population.

Immigrants were numerous during this period, but there has been a tendency to over-estimate the proportion of that sector of the population. In the 1820s refugees from other Spanish American nations, especially Venezuela, settled in the area of Ponce. It is curious that historians have insisted on seeing these Venezuelan immigrants as reactionary when, in fact, the few nineteenth-century Venezuelans in Puerto Rico whom people can name participated readily in vanguard political movements. Perhaps it has been forgotten that the circumstances that led to their emigration were varied, and that in many cases their departure was due to the post-independence political struggles. In any case, many of the immigrants came from the urban sector and the professions and had a level of formal education higher than that commonly found on the island at the time. This soon placed them in situations in which they could push for the modernization of institutions.[46] The question of who were the proponents of change in nineteenth-century Puerto Rico and who resisted it deserves more detailed analysis.

During this period the largest number of immigrants came from Spain. In the sixteenth century it had been Andalusia, Castile, and Extremadura that had sent settlers to Puerto Rico. At the beginning of

the seventeenth century, the Portuguese in the garrison had established families in Puerto Rico. Canary Islanders predominated among
the few immigrants at the end of the seventeenth and beginning of
the eighteenth centuries. However, throughout the eighteenth century, immigration became much more generalized. People came not
only from all the regions of Spain but also from Spanish America,
especially convicts sent from Mexico or Cuba to serve time and who
remained afterwards. But from the 1820s on, it was the fringes of
Spain and its coastal provinces that provided the majority of immigrants. Catalans were the largest group and then those from the
Balearic Islands, along with Valencians, Basques, Asturians, and Gali-
cians, as well as another wave of Andalusians and Canary Islanders.[47]

Many of these immigrants came to occupy positions that were
opened up by the expansion and organization of the government.
Others came as soldiers and stayed on after their period of service.
Those who set up in business as traders or farmers often brought their
brothers, nephews, and in-laws. Although not all the Spanish immigrants were literate, the level of schooling of the majority was vastly
superior to that received by Creoles in the few schools on the island.
This advantage was one of the reasons why immigrants tended to
dominate commerce and the professions in some districts.

Between 1823 and 1868, immigrants from Great Britain, France,
and other parts of Europe continued to arrive. One group which out-
numbered others was the Corsicans, who were French citizens but
had their own collective personality and traditions.[48] Although the
development of the port of Marseilles in the south of France provided a stimulus for the Corsican economy, the tension and displacement resulting from changes in land tenure and commerce led many
young people to seek opportunities in other latitudes.

Corsican immigration was linked to the development of coffee cultivation in Puerto Rico, especially in the area of Yauco.[49] Coffee had
its first boom at the end of the eighteenth century and the beginning
of the nineteenth with the arrival of the French and the Dominicans
on the western coast. Although there were many towns in the highlands that cultivated coffee and did not have a significant influx of
Corsicans, the Corsican contribution to the coffee boom in the sec-

ond half of the nineteenth century was not restricted to the *hacien-das*, but was especially evident in the important commercial houses that prepared the coffee for export. In this way the Corsicans were instrumental in introducing Puerto Rican coffee onto the French market, where its quality was long appreciated. A similar service was rendered by German immigrants from the Hamburg area who helped to make Puerto Rican coffee known and appreciated in Northern Europe.

The forced immigration of Africans continued until the 1840s. Over the long term their role in the formation of the Puerto Rican collective personality was much more important than that of the nineteenth-century European immigrants. Although at the time the latter played a more prominent role in the sugar industry or in trade, they later became diluted into the general population. The last wave of Africans to arrive on the island was generally very young and came from the interior of what is today Nigeria, Ghana, and the Congo.

No less interesting than immigration from the outside world are the internal migratory movements. Between 1863 and 1868, the mountainous areas were populated by many Creoles who had been displaced from the coasts by the spread of the sugarcane fields. The northwest, which was more densely populated than the rest of the island at the beginning of the nineteenth century, contributed settlers to Lares and Utuado. The losses suffered by small farmers on the southern coast on account of the droughts in the 1840s led them to go inland to Adjuntas, Jayuya (then a ward of Utuado), Barranquitas, Barros, and the part of Juana Díaz that eventually would become Villalba. Cayey and Hato Grande (San Lorenzo) received settlers from Guayama. People from Vega Baja and Manatí migrated to Ciales and Morovis, and Corozal emerged from Toa Alta. In this period several more towns were founded including Aguas Buenas, Salinas, Santa Isabel, and Ceiba, whose founders had been tilling the soil there for many decades. Vieques was also legally constituted, with a governor of its own who reported to the governor of Puerto Rico. Immigrants flocked to Vieques, not only from the "Big Island" (San Juan), but also from the eastern Caribbean, with whose struggles it had been linked for a long time.[50]

Untitled Lands

According to government calculations, in 1822 there were more than 96,000 acres of untitled land.[51] Most of this land and that left over from the dividing-up of the *hatos* was distributed between 1820 and 1868. The land tended to be in the highland districts, although land in Naguabo, Salinas, Cabo Rojo, San Germán, and Arecibo was also distributed in this period.

Who benefited from these land grants?[52] A calculation of all the grants made in Utuado by the *Junta de Terrenos Baldíos* between 1826 and 1843 may reveal the origins of the grantees and the size of the lots allocated. The *Junta* considered 187 applications for land in Utuado during this period, to which it gave a positive response to 165, refused 7, and postponed giving an answer in 15 cases. The total amount of land solicited was approximately 64,700 acres, but only some 29,600 acres were granted, that is, 45.7% of the extensions solicited. Although the average request was for some 350 acres, the average grantee received some 180 acres.

Eight women asked for land. It was granted to seven and the eighth case was under consideration at the end of the period under study. Of the seven cases rejected by the *Junta*, six were applications by residents of Utuado and the other was from Arecibo. Apparently the main objection was that they were the sons of landowners. The average grant was around 100 acres. Table 11.1 lists the geographic origins of the grantees.

Only in 19 of the 187 applications was some connection with military service mentioned, and out of these there were only two cases of officers from San Juan. The remaining ones are militia members. A French cleric requested 800 acres in 1836 and received 400. But prominent personalities and moneyed immigrants seem not have been interested in Utuado lands in this period.

An analysis of these concessions would give the impression that land was available for Creoles. But when, in Utuado's municipal records and in the series of Public Property in the Public Works, one finds a great many dossiers which were never considered by the *Junta*, one realizes that it was very difficult for those without means to

TABLE 11.1

Municipality of Residence	Number of grants
Utuado	79
Arecibo	14
Pepino	10
Ciales	9
Toa Baja	7
San Juan	5
Lares	2
Isabela, Vega Alta, Camuy, Moca, Quebradillas, and Toa Alta	1 each

Source: Acts of the Superior Junta de Terrenos Baldíos, Books 1 and 2.

obtain untitled land. Once the *Junta* considered the case the possibilities were good, but the greatest problem for the landless was reaching the earlier stages of the procedure.

Many of those who obtained land ended up selling it for small amounts of money to neighboring *hacendados*. These joined together to purchase grants of 200 acres to form the great coffee *latifundios* and, in the case of Salinas, Luquillo, and Lajas, extensive ranches.

Sugar and Slaves

In the 1820s the municipalities with a higher proportion of slaves— Ponce, Mayaguez, and Guayama—became the great sugar producers of Puerto Rico.[53] The former sugar-producing area between the Loiza and Toa valleys was displaced at the very time when sugar was becoming the main item for export. Moreover, sugar production began to be concentrated in larger land units, with a greater number of slaves and more complex machinery. In the case of sugar, small producers could only survive by having a dependent relationship on the larger plantations. Many families opted to sell their farms to the neighboring *hacendados* and move inland.

After 1828, sugar dominated the economy of Puerto Rico to the extent that the main problems of the island began to be defined in terms of the needs of the sugar-producing sector.[54] There were three crucial aspects: financing, the workforce, and external markets. Since no banks were as yet established in Puerto Rico, credit was in the hands of the principal merchants of the urban centers of the island. The *hacendados* took articles on credit and paid off their accounts by handing over their brown sugar to the merchants.

This made sugar production subject to fluctuations in trade. The island's merchants in their turn received their goods on credit from the great exporters, initially from St. Thomas[55] and then from the ports of the United States, England, France, and the free German cities. As a result, each time there was a credit contraction in the North Atlantic on account of financial speculation or cyclical economic fluctuations, the merchants and *hacendados* of Puerto Rico found themselves in dire straits. In spite of the lack of adequate financing, the island's sugar industry was not left behind technologically. One way or another, the more prosperous *haciendas* managed to obtain the necessary machinery.[56]

The shortage of workers in the sugar-producing areas was a perennial topic for discussion once the importing of African slaves had almost completely ceased. Added to this was the level of mortality among slaves on account of various epidemics, especially smallpox and cholera in 1855–56. Since in the short term the regulations relating to the day laborers did not succeed in incorporating the landless into the *hacienda* workforce, one alternative suggested was the massive introduction of workers from Yucatán, China, the Cape Verde islands, or the Canary Islands.[57] None of these projects came to fruition, although some three hundred Canary Islanders came to work on the island.[58] It was natural population growth and the completion of the process of dispossessing the established Creole population that would eventually guarantee the labor needed to supply the demand by the sugar sector. For the time being, the lack of an adequate workforce was one of the factors that contributed to the economic vulnerability of the *hacendados*.

Markets for Puerto Rican muscovado sugar were unstable between 1823 and 1868. Scarano has discerned three stages during this period.[59] Spain had sugarcane fields in its own territory and therefore could not absorb all the sugar production of Puerto Rico and Cuba. For this reason, around 1840, the United States became the principal market for Puerto Rican sugar. But when the cane fields in Louisiana and Mississippi began producing at full capacity there was global overproduction and the American market became relatively saturated. As a result, the price of sugar fell in the 1840s. These low prices coincided with a series of droughts in Puerto Rico, culminating in the great drought of 1847. That first severe crisis of Puerto Rican sugar was mitigated by the British market's partially compensating for a fall in North American demand.[60] Throughout the 1850s and 1860s the United States and Great Britain received most of Puerto Rico's sugar exports. With the crisis of the American Civil War (1861–65), the Union's demand for Caribbean sugar grew. Meanwhile, as the production of refined beet sugar in France and Germany rose, European demand for Puerto Rican sugar fell. The end of the Civil War in the United States meant a reduction in North American demand, which exacerbated the situation created by the stagnation of European demand for brown sugar. Thus in the 1870s there would be new problems for Puerto Rican muscovado. Its export would eventually depend on the import tariffs imposed by the United States.[61]

Upswings and Downturns for Coffee

When sugar wavered, coffee began to impose itself as an alternative. It had a period of expansion which ended in 1837 when the double disaster of a hurricane and falling demand in St. Thomas discouraged the development of coffee plantations.[62] Coffee declined in the following years, but towards 1850 it began to expand once more. This new phase would center on the highlands, which up until then had only played a secondary role in the coffee market. Several factors coincided to stimulate the expansion of coffee cultivation. These included: the enormous amount of unfarmed land which had been allocated in the preceding years by the *Junta de Terrenos Baldíos*; access to labor, in many cases that of the family itself; the availability of finance and markets; the fact that little machinery and equipment was needed for the processing of coffee; and the opening up of new roads and tracks in the highland districts.

This period of growth and expansion experienced a slowing-down in 1867–68. At that time the country was undergoing an economic crisis which led to a contraction in credit and intensified conflicts between merchants and coffee growers, but this did not affect the process of expansion in the following period.[63]

Trade

The period between 1823 and 1868 was marked by the proliferation and diversification of merchants. Up until 1840 the import trade was centered on St. Thomas.[64] Perhaps one of the unforeseen consequences of the establishment of foreign consulates in Puerto Rico was that it linked Puerto Rican merchants with the exporters of the Atlantic colonial powers. This direct contact in turn promoted the development of great commercial societies, which competed for the supply and marketing of the main items of the country's import-export trade.

The great merchant houses of Ponce, San Juan, Arecibo, Mayaguez, and Aguadilla set up systems of credit and financing which made it possible to set up small stores in the towns and in the countryside.[65] Some of the merchant houses had representatives in neighboring towns. Perhaps one day a commercial map of Puerto Rico will show the spheres of influence of the main merchant houses of the time. That would give some idea of the economic regions and economic configuration of Puerto Rico.

Financed by the wholesalers, small traders began turning the houses around the plazas into stores and also sought convenient sites along the rural highways. According to the testimony of Alejandro

Tapia,[66] by the 1870s San Juan no longer had the dreary and under-stocked stores of his childhood, but shops crammed with cloth, pots and pans, glassware, and provisions. In Ponce and Mayaguez, stores underwent a similar transformation.

In 1857 a reform of the coinage replaced the *peso macuquino* intro-duced by Alejandro Ramírez as commercial specie with a provincial coin that was divided into pesos and cents but which never fully met the needs of trade.[67] This shortage of coinage reinforced the practice of taking goods on credit to pay later when the crops were harvested, overdue wages were paid, or the promissory note was cashed.

The shop owner was always a Spaniard, according to popular belief. In fact, the lists of traders we have for that period show that in many towns the Spanish were in the minority, but they were much more conspicuous on account of the importance of their establish-ments or the modernity of their trading practices. In Utuado, for instance, 11 out of the 49 traders registered in 1848 were Spanish, and, according to the fiscal declarations, they owned only 25.5% of the total commercial capital of the district.[68] Twenty years later the principal commercial establishments in Utuado belonged to Creoles who had arrived from the coast. Although this pattern contrasts notably with that of the neighboring town of Lares, where trade was dominated by Catalans and Balearic Islanders, one would need to determine which pattern predominated on the island at the time.

History of a Small Tradesman

The career of a Catalan small tradesman whose life was cut off by pre-mature death may illustrate the nature of the business of a Spanish trader in Puerto Rico in the mid-nineteenth century. Benito Tort, born in San Feliu de Guixols in Catalonia, arrived in Puerto Rico around 1850. In 1851 he married an Utuadeña, Manuela Colón Ribera, who was the sister-in-law of the Creole merchant Felipe Casalduc. In 1860 he opened his own store in Utuado.[69]

If we follow Tort's progress in the notarized records alone, we would gain the impression that he was not very active in business.

For instance, the total worth of notarized deeds of obligations in his favor is 79 pesos 9 cents; in 1863, 116.14; and in 1864, 1,085.08. These debts were payable, variously, in coffee, rice, cotton, plantains, and money. The debtors pledged land, crops, and even a slave as guarantees. In several cases the debt was paid off with the pledged goods.[70]

When we examine the existing fragments of municipal judicial records for 1862 and 1863, we get a better picture of this small tradesman's aggressiveness. Here are some examples: On March 28, 1862, Tort sued Juan Maldonado Montalvo for 17 pesos and 6 *reales* that were owed. Maldonado acknowledged the debt and promised to pay it off at the rate of 6 *reales* a week, probably with his labor. On March 29, Tort sued Ramón Vélez for 5 pesos and 63 cents, according to the account. Vélez answered that Tort actually owed him 2 pesos and 75 cents and the case was set to go to trial in 6 days. On April 30, he sued Marcelino de Jesús for 32 pesos and 37 cents that he owed, according to the account he presented, and for having insulted him with obscenities in his store. De Jesús answered that he did not owe him anything and that he had not insulted him. The case was set to go to trial in 15 days. On February 14, 1863, he sued Manuel de los Reyes Pérez for 30 pesos and 57 cents and asked for a piece of land Pérez that was intending to sell. The debtor acknowledged the sum and asked for a month in which to pay. Tort refused and the mayor, acting as judge, ruled that Pérez had to pay within 10 days.[71]

There were other cases, dated between February and April 1863, but the reader will have got the idea by now. Tort insisted on being paid on time, and if he was not, was prepared to press for the confiscation of his debtors' belongings. The notarized records of these years show him acquiring small plots of land in Utuado. Sometimes he resold them, some times he leased them. When Tort died in 1866, farms in the wards of Roncador, Arenas, and Caguana were divided between his wife and his mother. The latter inherited most of his estate and she lived in Catalonia.[72]

But if we only look at this aspect of Tort's business, it would give the impression that he was a bully who victimized his clients. But he too was a debtor. In February 1862 he acknowledged owing Eduardo Palau, a merchant from Arecibo, 815 pesos and 19 cents and promised to pay it off in installments by 1865. That same year he mortgaged the residence he had built in Utuado. On April 25, 1864, he acknowledged his debt to Prudencio García, an Arecibo merchant of Arecibo, for 1,569 pesos which he had lent him in the form of a number of deliveries of provisions for his merchant house. He promised to pay him back in February 1865, and he mortgaged two houses and a bread oven.[73] It seems that Tort paid off both debts in the agreed installments. But the same pressure placed by the trader on his debtors he also received from his creditors on the coast.

In Tort's business dealings we may find some clues as to why the Creoles identified commerce with Spanish domination. Not only did he charge interest on late payments, he also drew up mortgage deeds with clauses pledging the handover of property if the debt was not paid. He was also a bidder at the auctions of the properties belonging to Creoles, which had been foreclosed to pay off debts to third parties or to the Exchequer. He did not hesitate to take his adversaries to the municipal court. He was married to a daughter of one of the old landowning families living on the outskirts of town and held a position on the Utuado town council. In a very short space of time he had made a modest fortune and a good marriage, and had acquired public influence. For his Creole contemporaries, the social triumph achieved so rapidly by Tort must have seemed impressive. An early death prevented this tradesman from playing a larger role in the region's economy, but this specific case illustrates both success and the discontent which that success induced.

A Slave Society

The achievements that followed the enormous efforts to develop agriculture in the mid-nineteenth century did not conceal the stamp of slavery upon society. The essential dichotomy between the free and the enslaved produced social divisions which had the effect of preventing conscientious reflection on the political nature of the country. The civil condition of the slaves was so radically different that they could not enjoy the basic rights due to every human being. The crucial question in a discussion of Puerto Rico's slave past is not whether slaves were well- or ill-treated, but the fact that they were stripped of the most basic rights in order to further the economic interests of their owners. Slaveholders perpetuated myths about Africans' intellectual and social capacities in order to justify the rapacious expropriation of the strength and the energies of their slave laborers. Racial prejudice was rooted in those visions of the other. Even if it is disguised today because it attracts criticism and contempt, racial prejudice still has a pernicious influence on our society. It distorts many attitudes, values, and perceptions among Puerto Ricans. From popular conceptions about what constitutes "good" or "bad" hair to the immoral prejudices of high society, there are echoes everywhere of a social system that allowed the fruits of the labor of the many to be appropiated to satisfy the needs and pleasures of the few.[74]

Racial divisions have a serious effect on the development of national identities.[75] This is a problem that Puerto Rico shares with the rest of Spanish America, where there have been similar examples of prejudice against the indigenous peoples. But the desperate attempt to gain the approval of the leading cultural institutions in the metropolis led many Puerto Ricans to turn their back on their Caribbean reality, to assume exaggerated Hispanophile poses. For a long time our culture defined itself as Spanish.

That is why the attempts in the 1840s to highlight the Creole elements are so interesting.[76] To begin to emphasize the cultural forms of the Puerto Rican highlands instead of continuing to imitate those of Spain, was a progressive step. In that initial, exuberant phase, the enthusiasm for everything Creole took on the appearance of a collective personality. Puerto Rico began to be conceived as a whole, different from Spain, original, natural and guileless. It was the view from the *hacendado*'s veranda. The time would come when the *hacendado* would step down from that balcony to see the sordid misery of the huts and the double-dealing in the country store. When that moment arrived, the writings of Manuel Zeno Gandía, Nemesio Canales, Salvador Brau, Matías Gonzálezn Miguel Meléndez Muñoz, and others would enable the *hacendado* to interpret the country from his perspective and he would attempt to moralize.

CHAPTER 12

The Hour of the Mountains, 1868–1898

The following events mark a watershed between two periods in Puerto Rican history: the Spanish revolution which dethroned Isabella II, the *gritos* of Lares and Yara in Puerto Rico and Cuba, the worldwide fall in the price of brown sugar, the first Spanish Republic, and the abolition of slavery.[1] Those years witnessed changes in Puerto Rico's political system and its economic base, which in turn foreshadowed the even more fundamental changes that would occur at the end of the nineteenth century. But the three decades between the Grito de Lares and the North American invasion are more than simply the final act of the drama of Spanish rule. They represent a significative shift in the center of gravity of the Puerto Rican economy. The population, credit, agrarian production, and social conflicts moved towards the highland districts. The country found that, for

199

the first time since the colonization of the sixteenth century, the most important developments were taking place in the mountains rather than on the coast. The coffee from the mountains vitalized the ports on the coast, especially Ponce and Mayaguez. The ascendancy of the mountains, albeit brief, lives on in the country's consciousness. It was responsible for making the *jíbaro*, the peasant, into the typical Puerto Rican. The country wished its identity to be rooted inland. Hence the tendency to idealize that period which produced great achievements, but paid for them in human lives.

The Population

A comparison between the censuses of 1867 and 1899 reveals the extent of the changes that had taken place in such a short space of time.[2] In 1867 the three municipalities with the largest population in Puerto Rico were San Germán, Mayaguez, and Ponce. In 1899 they were Ponce, Utuado, and Arecibo.[3] Although the island's population rose by 45% in that period, that of the principal coffee-growing districts, with the exception of Lares, rose in greater proportion: Yauco by 71%, Ciales 169%, Adjuntas 134%, and Utuado 121%. Las Marías and Maricao achieved municipal autonomy in the 1870s. The future districts of Jayuya (1911) and Villalba (1917) acquired their urban centers in this period. At the time the mountains were the open frontier of the country.

Changes in population patterns did not relieve the deterioration in living conditions which affected the second half of the nineteenth century. The mortality rate for all of Puerto Rico in 1867 was 28.8 deaths per thousand inhabitants. In 1897 it was 35.7 per thousand. In some districts the balance between life and death was slight. In 1867 Camuy registered 56 deaths for every thousand inhabitants and 43.3 births. In Morovis there were 50 deaths per thousand and 40.2 births. That same year more people died than were born in San Juan, Quebradillas, Aguadilla, and Fajardo.[4] In the 1890s the same was true for Aguadilla, Río Piedras, Cayey, Mayaguez, Ponce, Lares, Humacao, and San Juan.[5]

Nevertheless, the calamitous course of public health for the period when sugar and coffee dominated agricultural production is better illustrated by long-range changes. All the data collected on the historical demography of Utuado, Humacao, Ciales, Río Piedras, and Cayey point in the same direction.[6] Advances in the cultivation of sugarcane and coffee were linked to higher mortality rates. Malaria, schistosomiasis, and yellow fever proliferated in the irrigation channels on the coast. The humid coffee groves in the interior harbored uncinariasis and tuberculosis. When the amount of land given over to the cultivation of plantains, bananas, and vegetables was reduced in favor of cash crops, the diet of the workers worsened.[7]

The deterioration in living conditions is also reflected in the breakup of families. As the nineteenth century advanced, the proportion of children born out of wedlock rose in practically every district. Río Piedras was one of the more dramatic; by 1898 two out every three children baptized were born out of wedlock.[8] But it was not merely a question of formalizing unions before the state or the church. The census also revealed the breakup of the households of working men. By 1860, the census taken in Camuy showed the absence of husbands who had migrated.[9] In the following decades it became more common to find families abandoned by the father, children without a home, and servants aged 10 or 12 living in the houses of well-to-do families.

One consequence of the reversal in family values was the appearance of other forms of solidarity. There were many foster children on the censuses and godparents took the place of deceased parents. It may be that the extended family was not a timeless institution which has endured until the twenty-first century, but a defense mechanism developed by the nineteenth century landless and smallholders for their mutual protection. Grandmothers and grandchildren lived under the same roof, and that guaranteed support for the aging as well as the education and support of the rising generation. Further studies on these patterns of solidarity and their relationship to the economic pressures suffered by the landless at that time would be useful.

On the other hand, the growing poverty led many to leave the island. From the 1870s on, the possible destinations were Cuba and Santo Domingo, both of which needed cheap workers and were willing to recruit Puerto Ricans.[10] There were also constant comings and goings between the coast and the mountains as canecutters went to the highlands for the coffee harvest during the dead season for sugar. Migration to the city, although it was gradual and was discouraged by the authorities, began to provide Ponce, Mayaguez, and Arecibo with a reserve of labor for construction, tobacco factories, dressmaking, the docks, and domestic service.

By the 1880s the untitled lands in the interior had all been allocated. Only on the island of Culebra did there remain common land, and after 1879 there were systematic attempts to populate that island. The government distributed plots of land and the first town was founded there. Between 1881 and 1883 there was also a free port. In 1897 there were on Culebra 756 persons involved in cattle raising (with 2,215 heads of cattle) and subsistence farming and some tobacco cultivation. But the limited water supply discouraged agriculture and ranching, while fishing had a limited market in the absence of refrigeration.[11]

The limited water supply hampered the settlement of the island of Mona. Nevertheless, there was ongoing exploitation of the guano deposits. Its use as a fertilizer meant that it could be sold at a good price.[12]

Sugar plays Second Fiddle

The Puerto Rican economy in the last three decades of the nineteenth century maintained a steady rate of growth, but it was not exempt from the cyclical and sectorial crises which required serious readjustment by producers. Sugar, which had been the main player at the beginning of the period, had to play second fiddle during the 1890s. Meanwhile coffee conquered the European markets and enjoyed high prices for a dozen years. The interest in both products affected the planting of food crops. It is in this period, as Luis Muñoz Marín noted in 1925, that Puerto Rico became the producer of the items consumed at the end of a meal—sugar, coffee, and tobacco—and would forget to produce the food itself.[13]

In 1868 Puerto Rico exported *moscabado* (muscovado) sugar.[14] The international markets had come to prefer more refined white sugar, either from sugarcane or from beets. Consequently the prices for Puerto Rican sugar remained at 2.9 cents a pound for the greater part of this period. This coincided with the triumph of abolitionism and the ending of slavery in Puerto Rico. Many *hacendados* believed they would be ruined by the low prices and by abolition. In fact, the money they received as compensation for the freed slaves offered some the opportunity to modernize their mills. Since slaveholders were indemnified for their former slaves, and since the credits for that compensation were as negotiable as any other form of exchange, some former slaveholders saw this as an opportunity to improve production. However, this was limited by several factors. The Spanish government objected to the credits or coupons for indemnification being acquired by foreign companies, and this significantly reduced the opportunity of financing the reforms. Another factor was that, in order to pay the compensation, additional export taxes were placed on sugar. In the end it was the former slaveholders who ended up paying a sizable portion of the cost of freeing their slaves.

In spite of these difficulties, some set out along the risky road to modernization. Some, like Leonardo Igaravidez, rushed to acquire machinery, the cost of which was never recovered from the price they could obtain for their crops. San Vicente in Vega Baja, the first Puerto Rican sugar mill to fail, made this mistake.[15] But other investors preferred a more steady pace of change, culminating at the beginning of the 1890s in the installation of centrifugal machines for crystallizing sugar. The best known example is that of the Mercedita sugar mill, which has been studied by Andrés Ramos Mattei.[16]

The concentration of the milling phase accelerated the consolidation of sugarcane farms into fewer hands. The poor prices, droughts, and the uncertainties of the tariff wars between Spain and the United States pushed many sugar producers out of competition, either because they went bankrupt or because they moved on to other economic enterprises. In fact, after reaching its export peak in 1878, sugar's contribution to Puerto Rican trade was reduced in subsequent years. By the 1890s it had fallen off significantly in comparison with fifty years before.

Some observers then suggested that sugar could pull out of its crisis if producers joined forces to develop sugar mills. In that way, with a better product, they could obtain the higher prices paid for white sugar.[17] But others believed that the key to lifting Puerto Rican sugar out of its stagnation was renegotiating tariffs with the principal market, the United States. But Spanish manufacturing and commercial interests were not interested in such a renegotiation. Thus some observers in the sugar sector thought that the problem would only be solved if Puerto Rico had the power to negotiate tariff matters pertaining to sugar directly with the United States. For some, that solution was equivalent to autonomy. But there were already those who thought that annexation to the United States would offer the best solution. In the same way that sugar production had been linked with slavery in a previous period, now it came to be intimately related to tariff policies and the public discussion of the role of the United States in Cuba and Puerto Rico.[18]

Café, s'il vous plait

In the nineteenth century, the Europeans reveled in a marvelous social institution which had already gained some degree of importance in the last three decades of the eighteenth century. It was a place for family reunions, for conversation, for reflection, for rest, and even for study, preferably situated outdoors. On account of its principal item of consumption this place came to be known as the *café*. The "aromatic drink," as its promoters insisted on calling it, had some advantages over wine and liquor. It could be drunk at all hours and in all kinds of company, in the middle of a working day as well as at the start or end of work. It was also cheap, stimulating, and lent itself to interesting variants. While the English remained loyal to their imperial drink, tea, the rest of Europe became keen coffee drinkers. Both coffee and the favored place for its consumption acquired followers in all the great cities.

The Dutch developed their taste for coffee early on and had promoted large coffee plantations on their island of Java. Brazilian coffee was in great demand, and Cuba developed great coffee *haciendas* in the province of Oriente, spurred on by immigrants from Haiti at the beginning of the nineteenth century. These three areas were the main producers in the mid-nineteenth century. But, for different reasons, they were not able to satisfy the rising demand. What is more, two of them greatly reduced their production. Java suffered a blight that ruined its coffee groves and turned instead to cultivating rice.[19] In Cuba, the Ten Years' War which started with the Grito de Yara was fought mainly in the coffee-growing area of Oriente. Eventually Cuba ceased exporting large quantities of coffee.[20] Lastly, Brazil had to reduce production as the slaves in the coffee *haciendas* aged, coffee plantations fell into disuse, and transportation costs became prohibitive. Lacking workers and the necessary credit to launch new plantations, the existing Brazilian coffee growers experienced a reduction in their harvests in the 1880s.[21]

This favored coffee planting in other lands with the right soil and climate. Puerto Rico was in a good position to take advantage of the opportunity, because it had been producing coffee for a long time, although in moderate quantities for export. By the 1870s a series of circumstances that promoted the production and export of coffee coincided: the incentive of favorable prices, the accessibility of credit, the improvement in the road system, the opening up of new land, and above all, the availability of cheap labor.[22] The highland farms began to concentrate on the production of coffee. Small neighboring coffee growers became subordinate to the large producers as they handed in their harvests to pay off debts incurred in the *hacendado's* country store. Experiences varied from one district to the next. While in Yauco *haciendas* dominated production, in Utuado it was the small and medium-sized coffee farms that supplied more than sixty percent of the crop. But merchants, who were the ultimate providers of credit, were best placed to profit from the economic juncture. The need to extend the areas of cultivation and improve their processing equipment induced *hacendados* to continually incur debt with the merchants. For that reason, the crisis at the end of the century found them in a situation of extreme vulnerability.

Agriculture and Politics

In the 1880s and the 1890s Puerto Rico staged an intense debate on the direction, if any, of the country's agrarian development. The sugar crisis and the boom in coffee exports were not the only subjects under discussion. José Ramón Abad and Fernando López Tuero argued in favor of government encouragement of the planting and export of alternate crops, such as cacao, pineapple, oranges, lemons, and corn.[23] Furthermore, they alerted public opinion to the notable decline in production of foodstuffs for the local market. To depend on the favorable prices for cash crops on the world markets was to court disaster in terms of feeding the population. Diversification became their slogan. The scarcity during the North American blockade in 1898 and the famine that followed the hurricane on the feast of St. Cyriacus in 1899 showed how right they were.

Investment in the long-term development of agriculture for the benefit of the country came to be a high priority in the discussion of the country's public affairs. But the clarity of thought of these late-nineteenth-century writers did not fundamentally alter investors' priorities and governmental apathy. The history of agronomic thinking in Puerto Rico in the hundred years following the publication of José Ramón Abad's work on the fair of Ponce of 1882 remains to be explored. It is possible that, in many cases, this reflection on the nature of the country's problems had more value than the eloquent statements of politicians on the stump whose rhetoric has not always been matched by the originality of their ideas.

Commerce, Markets, Money, and Tariffs

But the course of agriculture in the 1880s was not so straightforward that it could be changed by the mere decision of producers to experiment with new crops. The financing of agricultural development was closely linked to marketing. Merchants extended credit for commodities, and in this way they induced producers to hand over their harvests in payment.[24] On account of the credit mechanisms, merchants, for their part, were beholden to their European and North American suppliers.

The lack of banks and coinage was at the root of all these relations of dependency.[25] On account of the close connection between financing and marketing, production was tied to the immediate exigencies of international demand. Meanwhile, long-term investment as well as the promotion and development of new markets and the introduction of technology remained subordinate to the need to liquidate accounts on the short term. The lack of a stable and abundant coinage subjected merchants to fluctuations in silver and the unfavorable prices for their exports in the face of the abundant merchandise from the North Atlantic. Circulation problems accentuated the structures of personal dependency and discouraged any fundamental change to production.

All of this turned trade into a hazardous occupation and ultimately intensified the flight of capital. The merchant who retired preferred to invest his savings in real estate or in enterprises in Spain, than risk incurring losses in businesses that were no longer under his control. In that way, each generation denied the next one access to the capital which had accumulated on the island. This reduced commercial wealth, and as a result, led to complications and the scarcity of credit facilities.[26]

Another factor was added to the uncertainty surrounding commerce. The fact that Cuba and Puerto Rico depended mainly on the North American market for the sale of their sugar led both islands to increase their acquisition of manufactured and agricultural products from the United States. But the development of Cuban and Puerto Rican trade with North America deprived Spanish manufacturers of the full enjoyment of markets that they considered to belong to them. Thus pressure grew on the Spanish government to raise tariffs for North American imports to the Antilles. In United States there was a vehement reaction to these measures. North American diplomats threatened in turn to raise the tariffs on Antillean sugar. Naturally, the sugar interests of Mississippi, Louisiana, and Minnesota favored those raises, as this would better protect their cane and beet sugar. North American investors in Cuba lobbied to defend their interests.[27]

Although Spain had at various times yielded to tariff pressures from the United States, in 1895 a serious confrontation occurred. Both nations raised their tariffs. The rise in the price of commodities from the United States and the difficulty of selling their sugarcane harvest provoked a crisis in Puerto Rico. Never before had the island's powerlessness to solve its basic problems been so obvious.[28]

Eventually the crisis found a diplomatic solution, but the memory of commercial bankruptcies and labor protests in 1895 left a deep impression in public opinion. If political structures were not modified, the crisis could repeat itself. In this dramatic way the question of the relationship between Spain and Puerto Rico, and between Puerto Rico and the United States, came under consideration.

Conflicts and Solidarities

If the urban strikes and closing of commercial houses in 1895 brought the island's political tensions to the surface, there were even deeper social conflicts which repeatedly manifested themselves in the public consciousness. The antagonism between rival sectors of society assumed different forms: from open violence to the different shades of social differentiation. All of this delayed the formation of a collective sense of identity. As long as slavery lasted, a sector of the population had remained beyond the consideration of those Puerto Ricans who attempted to define a common purpose for the people. When the legal traffic in slaves ended, the majority of the last generation of slaves had been born on the island. That perhaps explains the changes in the forms of resistance to slavery in its last years. Rather than slave conspiracies, it was individual acts of resistance against abuse, along with escapes, which were common during that final phase of slavery. But abolition did not guarantee the totality of civil liberties to those who were emancipated. Thus began the long and painful process of claiming the rights which were now denied them by the invocation of outdated privileges.

The integration of the freed slaves into the ranks of the free laborers was not without its frictions.[29] Many of the former sugar mill operators possessed skills that were now valued more highly by the labor market than the free day laborers. The freed slave, who stood out among other workers on account of his degree of specialization, also experienced problems with his employer, often his former master, who wanted to bind him to a salary scale that did not recognize the demand for his working skills.

But the most critical conflict in the post-emancipation period revolved around labor that was contracted on the basis of indebtedness, of which day laborers were the victims.[30] The chain of debt binding the merchant houses on the coast to local traders, and farmers to the latter, had its final and weakest link in the worker. As he did not own property, he could offer only his labor as a pledge for what he bought on credit in the farmers' stores. But the network of tariffs, interest, money exchange, freight, and the cost of foreign goods raised the price of consumption so high that the worker was always in debt for his purchases. This meant a reduction in the compensation for his work.

Indebtedness was in fact the basic premise of the relationship between employer and worker. As long as he worked he ensured the prolongation of his credit. It could be the labor of the head of the household or that of his wife and children. It could be work during the harvest or domestic chores in the *hacendado*'s house. That relationship, which included and bound the whole family, sometimes took on the appearance of paternalism that purported to lessen the innate injustice of the situation. But the cohesion of a society based on such weak foundations could not last. At times social relations became strained. It was then that *hacendados* carried their shotguns and large guard dogs deterred people from passing through their property.[31]

Rural workers were not as passive as some folklorists, nostalgic for the lost agrarian society, would have us believe. One can detect movements of resistance in the legal files and private correspondence of the period.[32] The sugar sector, shaken by the crisis of the 1890s, witnessed some strikes for higher wages in that decade.[33] In the mountains, where working conditions limited the possibility of strikes, other forms of resistance appeared which revealed fundamental social conflicts. When the exploitation became too blatant, workers and smallholders threatened to use fire and machetes on the stores and the houses of the *hacendados*. In the novel *La Charca*, Manuel Zeno Gandía portrays a society with tensions that could not be assuaged by the law or the interplay of bonds of solidarity.

The existence of intermediary sectors between the great *hacendados* and the workers meant that social conflict in the rural areas did not have a markedly class-conscious aspect. Farmers, hucksters, artisans, muleteers, professionals, teachers, rural guards, and priests played changing roles in the rural struggles. In particular, the large number of small- and medium-sized property owners prevented a marked polarization in social relations.

For this reason, the social conflicts at the end of the 1880s and in the 1890s, whether overt or covert, may have been categorized too readily as antagonism between Creoles and Spaniards. Such a definition of the problem prevents the adequate examination of the nature of the conflict. When one examines the legal files for specific cases of conflict, one sees that *hacendados* and merchants, Creoles as well as Spaniards, are involved in these struggles. Only the bands of the *tiznados* of 1898–99 resorted to attacking "the Spaniards." Of course there were also Creole *hacendados* among those attacked by the bands.[34]

In the towns the social conflicts did not yet involve the large numbers which create mass movements out of the protests, marches, and strikes that were beginning to be organized.[35] Typesetters, a group which generally had some education and some political consciousness, were at the forefront of the salaried workers who protested. Artisans, who had a long experience of urban life and who also had experience of joint action through association, began to map out the course of the incipient labor movement.[36]

At the time, in addition to the urban labor struggles, were other clashes which merit further study. This includes those between landlords and tenants, consumers and storekeepers, the military and civilians in San Juan, immigrants from the rural areas and long-established urban residents, and the professionals who studied outside the island and the members of the elite who hired their services.

A Creole Bourgeosie?

Not all conflicts in Puerto Rican society were along class or sectorial lines. Among the economically dominant groups, there were less visible but no less acute conflicts. Besides the frictions between merchants and *hacendados* there were ongoing quarrels among members of each group.[37]

The most obvious clash was between Spanish merchants and Creoles. The stereotypical view that all merchants were Spanish loses credibility when one examines the municipal rosters of the principal commercial taxpayers. Puerto Ricans appear alongside Catalans, Corsicans, and Asturians. Occasionally distrust and competitiveness surfaced, and in moments of crisis, such as in 1886–87, the additional support of steady clients was sought.[38]

More detailed studies of these rivalries are needed, because it has been assumed too readily that they are merely clashes of nationalities. Not all foreign merchants became the object of boycott and of ridicule. Not all Creoles were involved in the disputes. Why? Was it a question of a clash between wholesale merchants attempting to corner the market in some key commodities? Or were the conflicts generated by municipal tradesmen competing among themselves for clients who hesitated in times of crisis over which of their creditors should receive their coffee crop in payment? What importance should be attributed the denial of credit to storekeepers when unexpected crises force them to go to their creditors, the wholesale dealers, to request extensions for payment?

The hypothesis of a creole bourgeoisie rests on the premise that there was a degree of homogeneity among the dominant sectors which facilitated the definition of a national identity based on their common interests. But racial, regional, and occupational factors produced diverse, rather than unified, ways of feeling Puerto Rican. Above all, the fact that Puerto Rican nineteenth-century elites did not prevail over the rest of society weakens the hypothesis of the crystallization of a Creole bourgeoisie.

Marriages and the institution of godparents may offer clues to the social interplay of merchants and *hacendados*, whether Spanish or

Creole, wholesalers or storekeepers, coffee growers or sugar producers, autonomists or assimilationists, white or black, Catholic or
freemason. Thus one might find Creole merchants with Spanish
sons-in-law and vice versa, and Creoles and Spaniards being godparents or witnesses at the weddings of each other's children. They
belonged to the same recreational associations, they attended the
same celebrations and feasts, their children had the same tutors. In
the cloistered environment of town life, where recreational facilities
and social activities were few, it was not unusual for the families of
the merchants to socialize together. National differences that might
perhaps have kept their parents apart did not last into the second
generation. Today, in many towns, the families that are considered
"old" were in their first generation in the 1880s. Their claim usually
derives from the intermarriage of second generations with families
who were formerly socially prominent.

The Political Cauldron

In the last three decades of Spanish rule, the political changes in the
peninsula had more rapid repercussions on the public life of Puerto
Rico than in previous eras. It was now easier to travel between Spain
and Puerto Rico by steamship. The Spanish press and continual correspondence meant that political life on the island began to be dominated by the great political debates in Spain. Those debates aroused
great interest, since the economic and fiscal problems of the island
were linked to shifts in peninsular politics.

The dethronement of Isabella II following the revolt of 1868 ushered in a particularly fertile period for political debate.[39] The
Constituent Assembly, which was convened to deliberate on the
future of Spain, included representatives from Cuba and Puerto Rico.
In successive regimes—the monarchy of Amadeo of Savoy, the
Republic, and the Restored Bourbon Monarchy—delegates from Cuba
and Puerto Rico participated as members of the Cortes.

The political life of both islands between 1868 and 1873 was centered on two very different, but not unrelated, debates. For Cuba the

main question was the war of independence that had begun with the Grito de Yara in October 1868, and which would continue until the Pact of Zanjón in 1878.[40] But for Puerto Rico the main order of business was the abolition of slavery. Sugar played an important role in both situations. In Cuba, the war would be ended in the name of sugar interests. In Puerto Rico, in consideration of those same interests, abolition would be decreed with indemnification to the slave owners. But the consequences were different. In Cuba the solution to the problems of the Ten Years' War would be postponed, while in Puerto Rico the abolition of slavery ended one debate to open up political discussion at another level.

Between 1870 and 1873 Puerto Rico experienced the greatest political liberalization of the whole of the nineteenth century,[41] although these liberties did not appear simultaneously. The Spanish constitution of 1869 and subsequent legislation were applied gradually on the island. An example of this process is the belated implementation of the legislation concerning the election of mayors and members of the town councils.

One reason behind these delays was the opposition of the conservatives, who had initiated a debate with the liberals about the applicability to the island of the political reforms in Spain. The discussion had the effect of polarizing public opinion into two opposing camps. The existence of relative freedom of the press in those years allowed the differences between liberals and conservatives to be publicized, defined, and reinforced. The debate also enabled the public to know whom the spokesmen for each side was. From that moment on, the open political debate was developed in the island which has continued uninterrupted to the present day.

Although different channels, such as the elections, the press, the debates in the provincial Deputation, and formal and informal meetings, were available for reaching a decision on controversial issues, the trickery and manipulation of former times lingered. One representative incident was known as the Estrellada de Camuy.[42] Cayetano Estrella, a Dominican and longtime resident of Camuy and a landowner in the Zanja de Agua ward, received an anonymous warning that his house would be attacked by some bandits at night.

Another anonymous note advised the Civil Guard that an armed conspiracy was brewing in Estrella's house. The patrol which went that night to investigate Estrella's house was met by gunshots. The patrol fired back. The incident resulted in the loss of several lives. Estrella and his relatives were arrested and put in prison in Arecibo until the matter was cleared up. Apparently, the purpose of the anonymous notes was to create uneasiness and suspicion, so that people would believe that revolution was being planned in a district that had once been involved in the Grito de Lares. The intention may have been to provide obstacles for the bill abolishing slavery which was under consideration in the Spanish Cortes.

Abolition

In the 1860s continued resistance by slaves to the work regime imposed on them and to the deprivation of their basic human rights took different forms. These included isolated acts of violence against foremen and overseers, escapes, robbery, and slacking.[43] A few slave-holders had seen the necessity of providing incentives to slaves in the form of some kind of remuneration. The government itself instituted an annual lottery awarding freedom to a deserving slave chosen from a list of names submitted by the slaveholders. A number of slaves saved enough to buy the freedom of their children at the baptismal font. According to a disposition introduced by Pezuela, they had to pay 25 pesos for the emancipation of the newly born.[44]

Evidence of the victims' repudiation of slavery shows that abolition was not only the result of the will of the rulers, but responded to urgent demands by the slaves themselves. Public punishments, rumors of flight and of fights with overseers, sensitized public opinion about the outdated nature of a system which treated people as if they were things. In the *Gaceta*, the government's official journal, one can find examples of popular sympathy for the slaves. In 1854, for instance, twenty-two people in a ward of Manatí were fined for harboring a fugitive slave. The interesting thing about the list is that it comprises a great variety of men and women, from landholders to freedmen, to Modesto the slave, for whom his master had to pay the fine. Obviously a whole neighborhood was complicit in helping the unnamed fugitive. Other fines appearing in the *Gaceta* are no less revealing. In January of 1844 a *hacendado* from Naguabo had to pay a fine because his foreman had given seven slaves permission to go to Ceiba, play *bomba*, on Epiphany eve and ask for Christmas tips. In Yabucoa, Don Ramón Cintrón held a card game in his house, and among the participants appeared not only several "dons," but also several slaves. These and many other examples show that people continually undermined the laws relating to the slaves. The government sought to keep the slaves apart from the rest of the population, but daily interaction ignored the governors' circulars. The state did not achieve consistent vigilance over and management of the slave population.[45]

The seed of abolitionism had a chance to sprout among the Puerto Ricans who had lived outside the island. Residence in foreign countries, especially for study, gave young Puerto Ricans a wider perspective from which to reject slavery as an institution. The return of these young students to the island and the impact of seeing the slaves working at harvest time led some of them to take sides in support of abolition. By then freemasons had begun to found a series of lodges throughout the island. The period from 1870–73 was a particularly propitious one for the lodges recruiting militant members from among the liberal and abolitionist youth.

The proclamation of a republic in Spain following the abdication of Amadeus I at the beginning of 1873 provided a favorable juncture for abolition. The United States and Great Britain were applying diplomatic pressure on Spain.[46] The Puerto Rican delegation at the Cortes advocated approving the measure, even if the Cuban deputies failed to back the universal emancipation of the slaves. The Spanish liberal leadership, still euphoric from the proclamation of the republic, helped to pass the bill. On March 22, 1873, the Cortes decreed the emancipation of all slaves in Puerto Rico. Nevertheless, the condition of working under contract to an employer for three years was imposed. The former masters would be indemnified for the value of their slaves in installments to be paid annually over ten years.[47]

In Puerto Rico the news of abolition was received with much rejoicing. There were celebrations and public festivities everywhere. But the freed slaves soon discovered that becoming waged did not solve many of their problems. In theory they had the option of free contracts, but in reality the vast majority had to choose to be contracted to their former masters. One must remember that by the time of abolition, more than 90% of the slaves had been born on the island. Their ties of solidarity were in the districts where they had been born and worked, and it was in those places where they were well-known that, with the few resources at their disposal, they had the best chance of obtaining reasonable accommodation and working conditions.[48]

The First Spanish Republic

It was not too long ago that old people in Puerto Rico would rebuke children with the question: "Do you think this is a republic?" The allusion was to the First Spanish Republic (1873–74) and the spate of freedoms that it made possible in Puerto Rico. For the liberals it was an occasion to participate in the exercise of power, especially through the Diputación Provincial and the town councils. Freedom of the press, of assembly, of worship, and of association allowed for experimentation with new forms of expression, which up until then had been offered only by the printed word. But the tensions between conservatives and liberals and the political agitation that erupted in 1873 were sufficient for subsequent periods to associate the notion of republic with disorder.

If the changes under the Republic were sudden, even more so was its 1874 collapse as a result of the military revolt that eventually brought Alfonso XII, son of Isabella II, to the throne of Spain. The governor charged with implementing the restoration of the monarchy in Puerto Rico was José Laureano Sanz, who had already been governor in 1869. The arbitrary manner in which Sanz behaved during his second period of governorship prompted Labor Gómez Acevedo to dub him "Promoter of Separatism in Puerto Rico."[49]

Sanz was consistent in his objective of concentrating Puerto Rican legislative and executive initiatives in the hands of the governor once again. Teachers were one of the sectors most affected by his measures. A number of Creole teachers were deprived of their posts and replaced by Spanish teachers, who were, in theory, better educated. Sanz's offensive against Creole teachers turned the schools into instruments of control where lessons in Spanish patriotism were taught along with catechism and grammar.[50]

The Province

Under the new statutes drawn up by the restorers of the monarchy, Puerto Rico in theory had the status of a Spanish province. However, legislation approved in Spain did not automatically apply to the island. This reluctance to make the island's situation equivalent to that of other provinces in Spain reinforced the fact that its relationship with Spain was a colonial one.

The effective limitation of suffrage to the wealthier male taxpayers made the fictitious nature of the island's provincial status even more obvious. Although several laws regulated electoral participation in Puerto Rico, in every case the right was limited to a minority, which at times was tiny. For instance, in the 1885 election for deputy to the Cortes for the district of Río Piedras, Loíza, and Río Grande, out of ten thousand inhabitants in Río Piedras, barely thirty had the right to vote, and only sixteen actually exercised it. In this way it was possible to send a triumphant candidate as Puerto Rican deputy to the Cortes with a total of forty votes. The candidate was a Spaniard who did not live on the island. In the face of that evidence, it is absurd to speak of democratic elections in Puerto Rico in the 1880s.[51]

Between 1874 and 1886 a factional quarrel developed as a result of this inequality. The Liberal Reformist Party, born in the heat of the struggles from 1870 to 1873 to extend the freedoms enacted in Spain to Puerto Rico, lost ground. Confronted by a situation in which the vote was restricted to major taxpayers and in which the governors arranged the election of non-resident deputies who were aligned with the ruling party in Madrid, it became difficult to achieve representation in the Cortes for broad sectors of Puerto Rican society. Even the liberal deputy to Cortes from the Sabana Grande district, Rafael María Labra, was never a resident of the island. Labra was a Cuban who lived in Madrid for many years where he steadfastly defended Puerto Rican interests, and he was elected by the only district in Puerto Rico which the conservatives were not able to win.[52]

Who were these conservatives who managed to control the elections to the Spanish Cortes and to the Provincial Deputation for such a long time? Some studies of their leaders present an interesting paradox.[53] In nineteenth-century Europe, those who were interested in modernizing trade, manufacture, and agriculture generally identified themselves with political parties of liberal tendencies. They considered excessive regulation and supervision of the enterprising sector to be anachronistic and a hindrance, so they advocated less governmental control of the economy. But in Puerto Rico the conservative groups chose notable merchants and *hacendados* as their leaders. These were the ones who resisted liberalization and wanted strong government. Why this apparent contradiction between their economic interests and their political ideology?

It is generally assumed that the conservative leadership placed their identification with Spain ahead of economic interests. Pablo Ubarri and José M. Fernández, the Marquis of la Esperanza, were examples of defenders of national interests at all costs. If the only criterion was personal allegiance to Spain, the argument might seem convincing. But if one considers the wider context of the island's socioeconomic reality, the perspective changes. Then the opposition by the economically dominant sectors to a substantial modification of the colonial regime appears more rational. The increasing interference of the United States in the Puerto Rican economy meant that those who advocated economic change on the island were sidelined. Moreover, the liberalization of the political structures facilitated that greater degree of interference. In other words, maintaining Spanish control over exports and credit, making foreign investment more difficult while easing the import of cheaper goods, and reinforcing the dependence of farmers and shopkeepers on the chief merchants would help to avoid serious economic disruption. The conservatives saw the development of the Spanish market as fundamental. They guaranteed the ties of dependency by aiming to appoint those who were identified with the colonial relationship as government officials. They also blocked the development in Puerto Rico of a nationalist sentiment which would overturn the colonial system of checks and balances.

During the period of their ascendancy, conservatives believed that the principal threat to the system would emerge not from the Puerto Rican political scene, but from a change in the ruling party in Spain. For that reason, one of the pillars of their politics was to support any governor arriving in Puerto Rico, regardless of his political affiliation in Spain. Naturally, the governors found it convenient to count on the backing of the majority party on the island, which they could use to prop up their own party in the Cortes. This pragmatic reconciliation between the powers, however, began to diminish on account of the political evolution of the Spanish parties, whose ideologies were less and less in tune with that of the conservatives in Puerto Rico. It was also affected by the growth of greater political consciousness in Puerto Rico, as new generations educated outside the island returned to join in the political debate.

It was mainly in the press that the major issues of Puerto Rican politics were discussed after 1880.[54] At that time the liberal press was weak, a victim of arbitrary censorship, threats of closure, and low literacy rates in the country. But almost all municipalities had their own newspaper. These were publications of four pages, with editions of some 300, and they tended to survive for only five or six issues. Even so, they succeeded in raising awareness and generating discussion. Even those who did not read could hear about the latest major debate from conversations in the town square or the *botica*.

The Reforms

In the 1880s a series of reforms was implemented in Puerto Rico which promoted economic growth and helped mitigate the obstructive effects of some of the colonial institutions. The reform of the Civil Code,[55] which extended to Puerto Rico the procedures of the Spanish tribunals, established basic terms for contracts, and assured the supremacy of property rights. Other aspects of the Code, such as the removal of the sale with a clause of resale if a debt was not paid, an abusive device which had been used to dispossess smallholders, represented a significant advance over former legal practices. But the implementation of the Spanish Civil Code in Puerto Rico before the U.S. invasion above all ensured the continued enforcement of Spanish law and the Roman legal tradition in Puerto Rican jurisprudence.

In May 1880, the Property Registry began operations. Besides signifying an enormous advance in terms of property titles, the Registry also provided a mechanism for the verification of successive mortgages, rights of way and other obligations, divisions, and sales. Although the process of registering a large part of the real estate in Puerto Rico was exceedingly slow, the new measures simplified the procedures for obtaining financing and for transferring property rights.

In 1880 the governor, Eugenio Despujols, also launched a reform of education.[56] Although this reform did not immediately achieve its aims, in the long run it produced a significant increase in the number of schools and in the literacy rate. The sectors which up until then had been neglected by the public education system—girls, the rural areas, and the secondary level (equivalent to what would later be known as the intermediate school)— benefited greatly from these reforms. The population census of 1910 also demonstrates their effectiveness. In the towns more than half of those born after 1880 were literate.

The setting up of the Population Registry in 1885 was another welcome reform. Up until then Catholic priests had been in charge of registering births, marriages, and deaths. Many people took a long time to become aware of their obligation to register newborns. When one compares baptismal records from the 1890s with births registered at the Population Registry, the totals for baptisms are noticeably higher than those for births.[57] But by the first decade of the twentieth century a greater proportion of the children born are registered. The need to obtain a certificate for burial forced familes to register the deceased.

In Puerto Rico there were several attempts to reform municipal law. By the 1880s the municipal law in force in Spain was implemented, but with provisos making the governor the arbiter of municipal debates. Even so, the municipalities' functions were defined and procedures were regulated.[58]

All these reforms implied the regimentation of life in accordance with the requirements of a state that attempted to guarantee its own interests. But in the latter part of the 1880s, the Spanish state in Puerto Rico had entered a critical phase which ended with its dismantling after the U.S. invasion of 1898.

The Autonomist Movement

A general financial crisis shook the countries that produced tropical crops in 1886–87.[59] The resulting economic recession revealed the Spanish government's inability to protect the economies of Cuba and Puerto Rico and the powerlessness of the islands' elites to protect their own interests. At the same time the effects of the crisis heightened social conflicts.

An influential segment of public opinion in Puerto Rico believed that in order to avoid such alarming developments in the future it was necessary to modernize agriculture and the related industrial activities. But in order to carry out such changes it was necessary for Puerto Rico to have control over decisions relating to tariffs, customs duties, taxes, the export and import of commodities, and agricultural and industrial development. The autonomist ideology was based on an appreciation that the fundamental issues of the country are economic in nature and that their solution was linked to the political capacity to guarantee the entry of Puerto Rican products onto foreign markets.

The weakness of the Liberal Reformist Party in the mid-1880s prevented it from being the appropriate instrument to further the objectives of the modernizing sectors.[60] The liberals' struggles had revolved around the need to implement in Puerto Rico the reforms passed in Spain. As a basic premise, it was desirable that the political structures of the island and those of Spain were homogeneous. But what now entered into the discussion was the specificity of Puerto Rico's problems. Although they approached it from different perspectives, it was the same argument that the conservatives had made for maintaining the colonial structures.

Preliminary discussions among liberals interested in these proposals led to the convocation of an assembly held in Ponce at the beginning of 1887.[61] Out of that assembly emerged the new Autonomist Party, whose leading light was Román Baldorioty de Castro. People from different ideological positions joined the Autonomist Party and from the beginning the fundamental issues of the country were defined in different ways. In the end, the diversity of interests and of strategy occasioned intense internal debates which eventually led to divisions.

The Autonomist Party immediately became organized at the municipal level, and its initial force alarmed extremist elements within the conservative movement. Many voters had stopped exercising the electoral rights they held by virtue of their taxed income. Now they gave signs of wishing to join the autonomists, which could produce a new political balance among the deputies elected to the Spanish Cortes and to the Diputación Provincial.

Extremist conservative sectors considered the appearance of what seemed to be the beginning of open hostility directed at the commercial houses owned by Spaniards as an even more terrible development. In some districts there was a boycott of the Spaniards' stores and this was attributed to the orders of secret societies, such as the Torre del Viejo, which were encouraged by the autonomists.

These extremist elements succeeded in making an impression on General Romualdo Palacios, the new governor. They convinced him that the rise of autonomism represented a serious threat to Spain's interests. They argued that separatist interests were behind the efforts of the new party. They informed him about the threat of the secret societies whose influence was growing in the rural areas.

The Compontes

Governor Palacios had a summer residence in Aibonito. In the summer of 1887, convinced by the denunciations of the activities of the secret societies, he unleashed a wave of repression on the entire island. The districts of Juana Díaz and Ponce were particularly affected.[62] During the following weeks, arbitrary arrests, the torture and abuse of those arrested, and threats against the press and against free expression proliferated. The state's efforts to spread panic throughout the countryside led some conservatives to carry out their own investigations and acts of aggression. Everywhere the institutional order fell into abeyance. Local leaders exerted their influence, either to persecute enemies or to protect friends, and the state's inability to guarantee and maintain public order became evident.[63]

Besides testifying to the arrogance of a colonial power, the *compontes*, a term that was coined to refer to torture during that period, showed that the colonial state was incapable of governing its own territory according to its own laws and procedures. The government that had introduced the Penal Code was providing an example of its violation. The Terrible Year of '87 may have been a much more decisive factor in Spain's loss of Puerto Rico than the U.S. invasion of 1898.

The main autonomist leaders were jailed in Ponce and then sent by ship to San Juan to be incarcerated in El Morro. Some observers feared that Palacios' arbitrariness would lead him to put the autonomists before a firing squad, following a court martial without adequate guarantee of due process. However, the fact that those accused were prominent members of society served to protect them. But many peasants on the southern coast, anonymously accused of backing the boycott against Spanish commerce, suffered beatings which in some cases resulted in death.

A cable dispatched from St. Thomas informed Deputy Labra and the Spanish authorities of the abuses perpetrated in Puerto Rico on the governor's initiative. The extremist conservative sectors waited too long to present a defense of the governor who had so efficiently reacted to their insinuations. The government relieved Palacios of his command on November 9.[64]

The Political Parties, 1888–1898

Palacios' replacement did not bring an end to the difficulties faced by the new Autonomist Party, but these took a different turn. Following a weak showing in the initial electoral contests, the Autonomist Party became involved in a long series of internal wrangles. Although the disputes ostensibly revolved around the appropriate method of obtaining autonomy, the real and important issue was the kind of autonomy that was desired. For the proponents of autonomism, their ideal was the different models of home rule which some dependencies of the British Empire had achieved or were pushing to achieve. Since 1867, Canada had enjoyed the status of a dominion, which guaranteed self-rule within the British Commonwealth. In the 1880s Ireland debated the desirability of a status which guaranteed self-government while allowing free access to English markets.

Some autonomists considered that the model to follow was that of Canada, which enjoyed the full extent of self-government within the legal framework of common institutions with Great Britain. For others, what was desired was simply the flexibility to reach tariff agreements with the United States. Within those extremes was a plurality of models for autonomy.

Baldorioty, ailing, prematurely aged, and impoverished, resigned the leadership of the autonomist movement and died shortly afterwards.[65] None of the leaders who succeeded him would enjoy as much unchallenged authority over the party. Around 1892, a young newspaperman from Barranquitas called Luis Muñoz Rivera began to promote the idea that autonomy could be attained by means of an alliance with one of the main Spanish parties. In exchange for offering their support to candidates for the Cortes, the autonomists would obtain the assurance that Puerto Rico would be granted self-government.

Muñoz Rivera initially met with much opposition to his project, but at the start of 1897, along with other autonomists, he obtained a specific commitment from the Liberal Monarchists, led by Práxedes Sagasta. This promise was valuable because Sagasta had a real chance of becoming the prime minister of Spain.

A group of autonomists did not accept this arrangement, which was endorsed by the party's assembly. They argued that, by entering into an alliance with the monarchists, they were compromising their republican principles. Nor did they want obtaining autonomy to depend on Sagasta's fulfilling his promises.[66]

This division came to a head in 1895 and led to the establishment of a "pure" and "orthodox" autonomist movement, centered on San Juan and its surrounding districts. Among its leading exponents was José Celso Barbosa, a doctor from Bayamón who was a graduate of the University of Michigan at Ann Arbor and a fervent believer in republican institutions of government.[67]

In the summer of 1897 the Spanish Prime Minister Antonio Cánovas del Castillo was murdered by an anarchist. The Queen Regent invited Sagasta to take up the post of prime minister. On November 25, 1897, by the decree of the regent, Puerto Rico was granted autonomous status. This did not fully meet the expectations of more radical autonomists, but it guaranteed the island its own parliament, cabinet, and municipal councils elected by the people.[68]

The autonomous cabinet was installed on February 9, 1898. It was composed of a president and a number of secretaries for the departments of Justice and Government; Treasury; Public Education; Public Works and Communications; and Agriculture, Industry, and Commerce. These officials took up their posts on February 11. On March 27, elections were held and the autonomists, led by Muñoz Rivera, won a majority in the new parliament. The start of the Spanish-American War meant that this parliament did not meet until July 13. The municipal elections under the autonomous charter were never held.[69]

The Origins of the Spanish-American War

The economic crisis of 1895 led to strikes and unprecedented popular demonstrations in Puerto Rico. In Cuba it sharpened political discussion and led to the resumption of the War of Independence. Coordinated and well-armed, the Cuban revolutionaries seized the initiative in their old power bases on the eastern side of the island and managed to extend the war to the western region.[70]

According to the ideas of José Martí and other pro-independence leaders of the Cuban revolution, the war had as its aim the independence of both Cuba and Puerto Rico.[71] More than a hundred Puerto Ricans participated in the actions of the Cuban war between 1895 and 1898.[72] Several Puerto Ricans advocated that the military operations be extended to Puerto Rico. From Paris, Betances maintained a steady correspondence with the revolutionary committee in New York and with Cuban revolutionary agents in other parts.[73]

In May 1897 there was an attempt to start a rising in Yauco, but the vigilance of the Spanish authorities succeeded in suppressing it. The failure of the "intentona de Yauco" did not discourage Puerto Rican revolutionaries who were active in Cuba, some of whom, like the poet from Arecibo, Pachín Marín, lost their lives fighting for Cuban independence. The Spanish government redoubled its vigilance, especially in the area between Mayaguez and Yauco, which was considered to be less loyal to the Spanish government.[74]

The government of the United States had tolerated the activities of Cuban revolutionaries in New York and Florida, but from 1895 on it was urged to intervene in Cuba. The great sugar interests had their investments concentrated on the western part of the island, a prime sugar-growing area. As the revolution spread towards the west, these interests began to suffer losses. The Spanish policy of concentrating the population of the eastern provinces in camps guarded by troops offended the humanitarian sensibilities of world public opinion. The sensationalist North American press condemned the Spanish administration of Cuba and began advocating direct intervention by the United States. William McKinley, elected president in 1896, increased the North American pressure on Spain.

Everyone was uneasy with the idea of a North American intervention in the Cuban war, but no one knew how to avoid it. In February 1898, an explosion in the boilers of the battleship Maine, anchored in Havana, accelerated events. The United States accused Spain of being responsible for the loss of the ship. The Spanish government, using all the diplomatic means to hand, insisted on resolving the confrontation with the United States. Nevertheless, diplomacy failed and the war began on April 21.[75]

Puerto Rico's Nineteenth-Century Cultures

In his frequently discussed essay, *El país de cuatro pisos*,[76] José Luis González has advanced the thesis that four cultures have been super-imposed in Puerto Rico since the sixteenth century. According to this scheme, each stage would reflect the economic changes that led to the crystallization of successive dominant cultures.

Towards the end of the nineteenth century, the cultural worlds of the black, the *jíbaro*, and the Europeanized Creole existed side by side with a precision that social fissures would reveal. The fourth story, that of Americanized Puerto Ricans, had not yet begun.

In spite of the social divisions, Puerto Rican cultures in the nineteenth century proved to be mutually permeable, as evidenced by patterns of solidarity, the codification of social norms, popular religiosity, the spoken language, music, poetry, and religious iconography. It is true that Europeanized creoles succeeded in imposing their culture as the dominant one and that most of them valued only those forms that imitated the creative trends then fashionable in France and Spain. But the creativity of the peasants and the workers from the mountains and from the coast triumphed over the disdain of the elite. This change in attitudes has been gradual and has not yet resulted in the effective synthesis of the competing values.

It is not surprising, therefore, that much of the influence exercised by popular cultures on the dominant one has remained implicit, and that only now is it being uncovered and valued.[77] In the case of the *danza*, the formal nineteenth-century Puerto Rican ballroom dance, Federico Cordero and others have attempted to demonstrate how European and Afro-Caribbean elements came together to develop this musical form. The *bomba* and the *plena*, whose rhythms are patently African, today barely retain remnants of the African languages which originally resounded in their verbal expressions. They have been hispanicized in the same way as the descendants of Africans have become creolized, and they incorporate social concepts and turns of phrase from the Puerto Rican scene. Thus music became a vehicle of criticism and of social celebration and its playing spread beyond the specific communities which created it.

Painting found patrons among the owners of houses built in towns as a result of the sugar and coffee booms. We move from the religious themes that displayed the genius of Campeche and filled the solemn living rooms and sacristies of San Juan in the eighteenth century[78] to the portraits of the new Ponceño dynasties. The aristocratic portraits that adorned the halls and offices substituted for lineage and provided evidence of their owners' social success. The portrait painter had a specific task, but if he was a rebel educated in Paris, like Francisco Oller,[79] he would spend his moments of forced leisure persistently observing the landscape and the light which Creole lattices attempted to keep out. A talent for capturing social realities did not prevent his accepting commissions to paint *haciendas* and cane fields. Oller gave an illusory quality to those tracks and paths over which sugar wealth was carried. On the walls his impressions of landscapes hung, like moral warnings.

El velorio (The Wake) dominates the totality of Oller's work and Puerto Pican painting with the same naturalness as those who wield inherited power.[80] The heart-rending topic of the dead *jíbaro* child— an incident which seemed commonplace at the time as it was a daily occurrence —is portrayed by Oller with the irate cynicism of one who still wants to believe. The technical aspects of the painting have been extensively studied in sketches of its component parts, but what is more important is that this technique is at the service of a vision of society that goes beyond the subject of the eternal juxtaposition of life and death. All the characters are there on account of the child's death, but this does not bring them together. Each one follows his own path and his own interests. All gazes avoid the body. Life has been briefly interrupted by the ritual of the wake and each symbolic detail underscores the general indifference. The painting sums up the dilemma of Puerto Rican formal art at the end of the nineteenth century. The artist can only be faithful to his creative vocation by pointing towards what goes on outside the houses of the powerful, but in doing so, he is met with indifference by those who could offer him patronage.

The *Ateneo*

The need for a meeting place to promote and discuss the country's cultural activities led to the foundation of the *Ateneo Puertorriqueño* in 1876. Manuel Elzaburu and the cofounders of "the learned house" had in mind the type of cultural association found in Spain. In the last two decades of the nineteenth century there was still no university in Puerto Rico, nor were there many opportunities for openly discussing the important topics of the day. The *Ateneo* met those perceived needs in San Juan and came to play a wider role than that of similar institutions in Spain.[81]

The *Ateneo* has for a long time been identified with the literary culture of the country. Although its statutes and internal structure dictated that scientific matters form part of the ordinary agenda of the institution, after 1898 literary and philosophical matters dominated those related to technology and the natural sciences. In the end, this unfortunate cultural division was a reflection of the limited exposure of engineers and doctors to the humanities. This was typical of the North American education they received. Only those who had philosophical and literary interests beyond those of their profession found the *Ateneo* a place to experience enlightened debate. But in general, professionals represented a new breed of people who had little in common with the *Ateneo* men of letters. A study of the universities chosen by the leading families for their sons before 1898 shows the split which developed between two dominant cultures: Latin and North American. Neither the *Ateneo* nor any similar institutions were able to prevent the subsequent dispersal of the intellectual talent of the country.

The institution of the *Ateneo* offered at least one of the leading sectors an alternative to the cultural politics of successive governments. But the diverse manifestations of popular culture did not have similar institutions to promote and preserve their creative works.

Religious Manifestations

The Catholic Church, which for over three centuries had held the monopoly on permitted public worship, was rejected by some sectors of the Puerto Rican community in the last three decades of the nineteenth century.

With the immigration of Europeans from Protestant countries, their respective denominational churches also entered the country. The currents of liberalism which characterized the period from 1870–73 promoted the tolerance of groups that had been practicing their religions in private. The establishment of the first Episcopal church in Ponce in that period opened up a new period in the country's religious history.[82]

The old Christian churches of Europe found favorable ground for expansion in Ponce, Mayaguez, Aguada, Vieques, and other districts. Meanwhile, some members of the country's elite dabbled in belief systems and ethical principles which had an affinity to Christianity but were derived from the esoteric discussions then common in France, Great Britain, and other industrialized countries. Theosophy, Rosicrucianism, spiritualism, and other movements began to gain a following among many of the island's elite. A more detailed study of such groups and of their publications during that period would be worthwhile.

One would also need to study in greater detail the expressions of popular religious syncretism, both in regions which had significant African influences, such as Guayama and Arroyo, as well as isolated regions in the mountains where pre-Christian European traditions blended with Christian elements from different Hispanic and European traditions.

Puerto Rico Becomes a Vast Sugar Plantation

The United States invaded and occupied Puerto Rico in 1898. The Treaty of Paris, which marked the end of the war between the United States and Spain, forced the latter to cede its rights over Puerto Rico and the Philippines to its adversary.

The United States and the Hispanic Caribbean

The United States' interest in acquiring control over one of the Greater Antilles predated the Spanish-American War. Thomas Jefferson, third president of the U.S. (1801–1809), believed that the Greater Antilles were destined to spin in the orbit of the new nation. James Monroe, the fifth president (1871–1825), expressed concern that another power might replace Spanish rule over Cuba and Puerto Rico. In 1852, the United States was interested in acquiring Samaná Bay in the Dominican Republic. At the end of the 1860s it entered into negotiations concerning annexation with some sectors in the Dominican Republic. At the end of the nineteenth century, Henry Adams wrote that he knew the Antilles sufficiently well to be sure that "whatever the American people might think or say about it, they would sooner or later come to police those islands, not against Europe, but for Europe, and America too."[1]

Over the course of the nineteenth century, the United States had moved from being a supplier of of flour, tobacco, cotton, wood and its products, furs, and other raw materials to being an exporter of manufactured goods. The avalanche of immigrants to its vast territory, the wealth of its mines and oil fields, its innovative technology and entrepeneurial skill, and the fierce tariff barriers which protected national industry all provided strong incentives for the large-scale production of a multitude of artifacts, appliances, and instruments which were marketed to a world keen for domestic convenience and efficiency in the office and the workshop.

But the United States was not the only country that had industrialized so radically. Great Britain, Germany, and France, and, to a lesser degree, other European nations also had undergone similar industrial revolutions. These powers competed with the United States for markets for their products and for raw materials for their factories. This competition, which had accelerated since the 1870s, brought with it a division of the globe. In those areas where weakness and internal division permitted, the European powers established protectorates and colonies. Thus they effectively provided their national enterprises with markets, raw materials, and ports for storage and distribution. In other areas, where the states were able to successfully resist foreign control, the industrialized powers ensured that their investments and their property were respected and given the advantage. In that way British capital came to hold sway over the production and circulation of goods in the Argentine Republic. The Germans had a strong interest in Guatemalan and Haitian coffee production, and the French undertook the construction of the Panama

Canal in what was then a province of Colombia.

Successive Spanish rulers were fearful of the North American interest in Cuba and Puerto Rico. Nevertheless, the structure of the sugar trade reinforced the relationship that existed between the Spanish Caribbean colonies and the northeastern United States. It came to be said in the 1880s that Spain administered its two colonies in the Caribbean for the economic benefit of the United States.

The North Americans had invested heavily in Cuba and thus friction between Spanish and North American interests was common. The Cuban aspiration for independence and the repressive measures adopted by the Spanish government to quell the Cuban independence movement exacerbated existing differences regarding economic matters. For influential sectors in the United States, Cuba's independence came to mean the opening up of the Cuban market, free of the tariffs with which Spain protected its own manufactures.

The war between Spain and the United States was the result of North American allegations about the explosion of the battleship Maine, which was anchored in Havana. The eagerness for war displayed by North American newspapers like the *New York World* and the *Herald* had a great effect on public opinion. This has prompted some historians to refer to this armed confrontation as "the Correspondents' War" or as "Hearst's War," after the owner of one of the more warmongering newspapers.[2]

For this reason, opinions about the causes of the war among the majority of North Americans and the positions they assumed were based more on the heated opinions of war correspondents like Richard Harding Davis than on the political debate waged in Washington.[3] These same correspondents were responsible for bringing Puerto Rico to the attention of the man on the street in the United States for the first time. Their reporting introduced absurd notions about Puerto Rico which neither time nor the long history of association have been successful in dispelling among some sectors in the United States.

The Bombardment of San Juan

The North American blockade of Puerto Rico exposed the island's incapacity to feed itself. Ships from Spain were kept out and those from the United States did not arrive. Although there were some ships from Canada and other nations, flour became scarce; salted meat, ham, rice, potatoes, and many types of canned food were not available. There was no bread in the bakeries. Even the sale of plantains was rationed. In short, the agronomists' predictions about the consequences of an excessive reliance on export crops were fulfilled.

The war came even closer to home when Admiral Sampson's squadron bombarded the fortifications of San Juan on May 12, 1898.[4] This exploratory bombardment tested the city's defenses and resulted in a number of dead and wounded civilians, and caused general panic among the population.

Meanwhile in Washington the possibility of invading Puerto Rico was considered. The Puerto Rican section of the Cuban Committee in New York believed that an invasion was the most effective way to achieve the independence of Puerto Rico. But a division was already evident among the revolutionaries in New York between those who favored North American intervention on the island to ensure its independence and those who feared the annexation of the island to the United States.

It was not a new debate. It had been pending since the 1850s, when Narciso López attempted to free Cuba from Spanish domination by having it annexed to the United States. Revolutionaries like Betances were aware of the consequences for Puerto Rico of North American intervention in the Caribbean. But at that time, spurred on by the idea of shaking off Spanish rule in Puerto Rico, there was insufficient consideration of the island's destiny after the departure of the Spanish authorities.[5]

Since the beginning of the war the military had considered the advantages that a rapid annexation of Puerto Rico might represent for the United States, which for a long time had been looking for a naval base to protect its interests in the Caribbean. As the construction of a canal through Central America was being considered, there was a need to provide for the strategic defense of that future link between the Atlantic and the Pacific.[6] Thus the Puerto Ricans who were interested in intervention found it easy to convince President McKinley to arrange it.

Once Santiago de Cuba had been captured, the invasion of Puerto Rico was the next logical move in order to force Spain to give in to North American demands. The key question was where the troops were going to land.

The Invasion

The invasion fleet that left from Cuban waters had planned to steam into Fajardo, from where the North Americans would advance to take San Juan and, with a single stroke, bring an end to Spanish rule. The plan to disembark the troops at Fajardo was widely known.[7] They were expected there both by the Spaniards and by the Puerto Ricans who intended to cooperate with the North Americans.

General Nelson Miles, the commander of the expedition, decided to land in Guánica on the southern coast. This beachhead would allow for the swift capture of Ponce, where they expected to meet widespread sympathy in the city. It would also facilitate the capture of Yauco, where there had been a separatist attempt in 1897.

The decision to land at Guánica instead of Fajardo gave a different aspect to North American military operations in Puerto Rico. The effect might have been different if the North Americans had directly tackled their principal military objective on the island. Without confronting much military resistance, and with the help of Creoles, the North American army was able to occupy the principal towns in the south and the west of the country. There was no likelihood that a sentiment different from that encouraged by Miles' proclamation on landing would surface.

From Guánica Miles published a manifesto emphasizing the invaders' benevolent intentions towards the country's inhabitants. The ambiguous terminology of the proclamation could satisfy a broad range of Creole expectations, but it did not explicitly commit itself to recognizing the political sovereignty of Puerto Ricans.[8]

On the way to Yauco little Spanish resistance was encountered. Through the intervention of the foreign consuls, Ponce surrendered on July 28 and was spared the bombardment of its civilian population. The people greeted the North American troops with cheering as that triumphal arrival portended the beginning of a regime of freedom.[9]

1898, The Year of Illusions

In the days following the occupation of Ponce, the North American troops, wearing heavy blue woolen uniforms, advanced in all directions. One column turned towards the west and captured Mayaguez. Another marched along the excellent central highway and occupied Juana Díaz and Coamo. In both towns the war correspondents, Stephen Crane in Juana Díaz and Richard Harding Davis in Coamo, entered ahead of the troops and later boasted of having accepted the respective surrenders But the Spaniards were entrenched on Asomante mountain and blocked the way to Aibonito. Although General Wilson exchanged fire with Spanish troops in Asomante, the plan was for General Brooke to march down from Guayama, which had been occupied by the Americans after they disembarked in Arroyo on August 2, to Cayey, which lay behind the Aibonito line of defense, and from there to San Juan.[10]

A small column led by General Roy Stone and escorted by several dozen Creole sympathizers left Ponce and climbed the mountains. Before taking Adjuntas, the troops stopped at the place later called the Alto de la Bandera, the Flag's Halting Place. The objective of this column was to seize Utuado; it was achieved on August 3. The escort of Creole sympathizers, some of them affiliated with the pro-independence cause, preceded the North American troops into the city.[11]

In general, when a town was occupied, the mayor was replaced and military authority was proclaimed, reiterating Miles' affirmation that the war was not against the Puerto Ricans, and supplies and services for the troops were bought and hired. It was understood that normal government services would continue to operate. For instance, the Population Registry in Utuado closed at 10 a.m. on the day of occupation, but at 7 o'clock the next morning it had re-opened with the same clerks as on the previous day.[12]

Nevertheless, the appearance of normality did not last for long. The spirit of revenge came over many Creoles. The memory of the *compontes* or tortures of 1887 and of the climate of vigilance and suspicion which had accompanied the start of the war was too recent. Soon bands of *tiznados* or individuals who smeared themselves with charcoal began to haunt the mountain coffee *haciendas*.[13] Personal reprisals combined with the collective settling of scores, leaving conflagration, murder, violations, and threats in their wake.[14]

The North American troops found themselves in the paradoxical situation of having to mobilize in defense of the Spanish *hacendados* and merchants against the Creoles whom they presumably had come to rescue from the Spanish yoke.

The Armistice

French mediation led to an armistice between the countries at war. This came into effect on August 12. While the negotiations were taking place in Paris, a cessation of hostilities was expected. But the power vacuum which occurred in some towns after the departure of the Spaniards, and as the North American troops approached, led to confrontation of another kind. In Ciales, for instance, a large group of people occupied the town. The pro-Spanish auxiliary volunteers who had left Ciales returned with reinforcements and there was a bloody encounter between these and the occupiers, with the result that thirteen people died. Although the volunteers prevailed because they were better armed and militarily trained, the event underscored the uncertainty which hovered over Puerto Rico.[15]

It was evident that in Washington the government intended to obtain the cession of the island from Spain. North American businessmen came in droves to Ponce, with the intention of sharing in the market which was now fully opened up for northern investors.[16]

Some Puerto Rican businessmen and *hacendados* believed that the annexation of Puerto Rico to the United States was imminent and that this would bring an immediate boom for the sugar industry.

Among the separatists who had been active in New York, the preference for annexation was already evident. Some had moved to Puerto Rico to serve as interpreters for the troops, or reckoned on their chances of serving in the territorial government. Meanwhile, Betances died in Paris in September without seeing his dream realized, while the educator Eugenio María de Hostos, in New York at the time, nurtured hopes of returning to promote a pro-independence plebiscite.

In 1898 the ranks of the traditional nineteenth-century pro-independence movement underwent a drastic division. While some became stalwart defenders of annexation to the United States, others saw that they had to begin anew the task of planning a strategy for liberation. The latter were joined by those who were disappointed with the new state of affairs.[17]

The Treaty of Paris

According to the terms agreed upon by the two countries, Spain handed over all the districts by October 18, 1898.[18] The last Spanish troops departed soon afterwards. General John Brooke was installed as military governor in San Juan.

On December 10 the treaty which officially ended the war between Spain and the United States was signed in Paris. In April 1899, it was ratified by the United States Senate. Under its second article Spain ceded to the United States the island of Puerto Rico with its neighboring islands. The treaty safeguarded the rights of Spaniards who resided there, as well as guaranteeing religious freedom for all the inhabitants. For a period of ten years there would be free trade between Spain and its former possessions, and the entry, free from customs duties, of books, works of art, and other cultural materials, so long as they were not for subversive purposes. Spain could establish consulates in Puerto Rico and in the Philippines.[19]

But while the Treaty spelled out the rights which Spain ceded and retained in Puerto Rico, it said little about the political condition of Puerto Rico.

The Military Government

While awaiting the definition of its future regime, Puerto Rico remained under the rule of military governors until June of 1900.[20] This period was particularly harsh. The sugar industry was on tenterhooks on account of the uncertainty about the decisions Congress might take regarding Puerto Rico. On August 8, 1899, a hurricane later named after St. Cyriacus' day traversed the island and laid waste to the coffee groves. The terrible famine it caused was only partially relieved by North American supplies.

In the countryide there were still bands of *tiznados* who attacked Spanish property. The military government repressed these with a heavy hand, but in some parts of the island it took time to reestablish the institutional order.

Municipalities were confronted by the residents' reluctance to pay their taxes. Between August and October 1898, resignations from government posts multiplied, some as a result of pressure from their rivals and others because their salaries were not being paid.[21]

The military government devised solutions. The complex public administration had at last fallen on the shoulders of the former Creole functionaries, but these had neither the power nor the resources to make fundamental decisions about public policy.

Two of the military government's measures were to be especially important for the life of the country. The first, taken by Governor Guy Henry, gave debtors a period of one year in which to pay their debts. This measure favored the farmers but was disadvantageous for the merchants. As they were not able to settle their accounts, they became short of capital at the precise moment when they were facing the North American competition which was appearing on the island. The second decision, also disadvantageous for Creole capital, established the official exchange rate for provincial money at 60 U.S. cents for each provincial peso.[22]

It was not the first time that an obligatory exchange rate had been set. In 1857 the *macuquino* coinage had been withdrawn from circulation with 12.5% depreciation. Successive introductions of coinage were made with losses of 5% of the value of the previous money. In 1895 the Mexican peso, which was put into circulation on the island with an inflated value, 40% above the real value of silver on the international markets, had been exchanged for the new provincial money at the cost of 787,000 pesetas.[23]

The provincial peso had never been equivalent to one hundred U.S. cents. Like all national coinage, its value had fluctuated against the dollar. Luis Muñoz Rivera had already predicted in September 1898 that the exchange would be made at the rate of 1 peso for 70 U.S. cents.[24] But in the months preceding the official exchange the value of the peso had hovered at around 80 cents. The rate imposed by the military government represented a devaluation. The U.S. dollar had been in circulation throughout the island even before the invasion and came to be the official currency of Puerto Rico. Merchants protested at the exchange rate, for they realized that their future credits would be worth fewer dollars than when they were extended.

The Foraker Law

Meanwhile the U.S. Congress in Washington was the scene of a lively debate between the supporters and the opponents of the imperialist policies of William McKinley and the dominant faction of the Republican Party.[25] Puerto Rican politicians, not yet attuned to the dynamics of North American politics, had little to contribute to this debate. Among the followers of Muñoz Rivera as well as those of his old rival Barbosa, the hope prevailed that the new instrument of government that emerged from the Washington debate would serve the country's best interests. At no previous juncture of Puerto Rico's political history since 1868 had the country been so powerless in the face of legislation issued outside the island as in those initial months of 1900.

Political leaders could have mobilized public opinion in the country but they seemed unsure as to whether that would prove to be of lasting value. There was the risk of reprisals, and they were also unsure to what extent the new metropole would exercise its power. Under the military government, several newspapers in Ponce and Mayaguez were closed or threatened with closure.[26] If the autonomists waited expectantly, the pro-independence sector had scattered. Eugenio María de Hostos tried unsuccessfully to rouse public opinion. He was not well known in Puerto Rico on account of his long years in exile and he was not able to establish effective communications with the professional and business classes in such a short space of time. Disillusioned, De Hostos returned to Santo Domingo, where he died in 1903.[27]

The law eventually passed by Congress to establish a civil government in Puerto Rico was the result of several agreements between congressional factions, but scarcely reflected the aspirations of the country's elites.[28]

In its principal clauses the Foraker Law granted Puerto Ricans an elected House of Delegates, to be chosen every two years. The House of Delegates was linked to an Executive Council composed of 11 members nominated by the President of the United States to enact legislation. In theory, the legislature would have ample powers, but these were subject to the governor's veto and Congressional review.

The separation of the executive and the legislature was limited on account of the creation of the Executive Council. The contradiction between its legislative character and the fact that the majority of its members were also members of the cabinet created many problems. The country's judicial system would become subject to revision by a committee appointed by the governor. This committee would submit recommendations for a projected revision within a convenient time frame.

The governor would not be elected by Puerto Ricans, but would be nominated by the President and approved by the United States Senate. The members of the governor's cabinet, who would also occupy *ex officio* places on the Executive Council, would also be nominated by the President and ratified by the Senate.

To appease the anti-imperialists and also in accordance with U.S. sugar interests, a 500-acre limit was imposed on the amount of property could be owned by a corporation in Puerto Rico. However, the clause did not set any penalties for noncompliance.

As for trade, the Foraker Law established free trade between the United States and Puerto Rico, only imposing a 15% excise duty on the shipping of rum and sugar. The income from that duty would revert to the Puerto Rican treasury.

The Elections of 1900

McKinley named Charles Allen as the first civilian governor. Allen kept on most of the military government's officials until after the legislative elections specified by the Foraker Law. The Executive Council came into existence in June. Among the procedures adopted was the ruling that Secretary of State Hunt, its president, could nominate all the members of committees charged with drawing up plans. José de Diego and Manuel Camuñas protested against this in vain; the majority of the Council voted against them.[29]

Hunt then proceeded to nominate a special committee to draw up the electoral districts for the House of Delegates. The designated committee presented majority and minority reports. The majority report recommended the creation of seven districts, with five representatives to be elected from each district. But the electoral boundaries for the third district aroused furious objections from De Diego and Camuñas. This district stretched from Isabela and Aguadilla in the north down to Yauco and Lajas in the south, which left Mayaguez and its surrounding districts to form a fourth district. In the United States such demarcation was known as gerrymandering.

The Executive Council approved the electoral districts drawn up by the majority of its special committee.[30] De Diego and Camuñas resigned from the Council, and the Federal Party, presided over by Luis Muñoz Rivera, chose not to participate in the elections in November of that year because it did not trust the government to be impartial. That abstention resulted in the Republican Party winning all the seats for the House of Delegates in the 1900 elections and electing Federico Degetau as its delegate without vote to the House of Representatives in Washington.

With the elections of 1900 and 1902 the political life of the country acquired some aspects of intolerance between the parties which still characterize elections in Puerto Rico.

Demographic Changes

The devastation wrought by the hurricane on St. Cyriacus' day made 1899 the year which witnessed the greatest loss of life in the nineteenth century. The destruction of the coffee groves had no short-term remedy because the new plantings would take five years to produce their first harvest. This acutely affected the mountain region. The crisis was exacerbated by the lack of capital to finance reconstruction. After some initial hesitations about the profits to be made from coffee, North American capital clearly opted for sugar and tobacco.[31] In the long term this option led to coffee-growing being considered the typical Puerto Rican agricultural investment, as opposed to sugar, which was dominated by North Americans.

In those difficult times emigration was promoted as an alternative to hardship. The first great exodus was to Hawaii, then recently annexed by the United States. There was a demand for cheap labor to work in the sugarcane fields and the citrus groves. Carmelo Rosario Natal has retold the dramatic story of the several thousand migrants who departed for Hawaii to face living and working conditions that were quite different from those they had been promised.[32]

But the largest population shift was from the mountains to the coast, as can be seen from a comparison of the censuses of 1899 and 1910. In subsequent decades the differences between the two zones became more marked. San Juan, Ponce, and Mayaguez acquired great urban sprawls, which in turn attracted the development of manufacturing and services. By the 1910s the shortage of housing for workers in those cities had become chronic.[33]

A notable improvement in health between 1900 and 1930 was

reflected in a sustained drop in mortality rates. There was also a slow but steady fall in the birth rate.[34] The discovery by Dr. Bailey K. Ashford and his research team of an effective treatment for anemia (*uncinariasis*) mitigated the effects of an illness that had killed so many people in the highlands over the previous decades. Similar advances in the treatment of malaria made some coastal zones less unhealthy. These included Guánica and its sugar-producing ward, Ensenada, where the abundance of mosquitoes had hindered efforts to develop sugarcane. These advances and the government policies that promoted them were the subject of lively discussions in the period.[35]

In the 1930s the fall in the mortality rate slackened off but the birth rate continued to fall steadily. It is interesting to note that in the century preceding the introduction of artificial methods of birth control, the birth rate fell faster than in the period in which these became available.[36]

Sugar and Capital

From 1900 onward, the sugar industry experienced a period of dizzy expansion. The abundance of external capital, especially from investors in the Boston and New York areas, resulted in the establishment of new sugar *centrales*. Aguirre and Guánica were prominent in this new phase. The number of sugar *centrales* increased until 1910, but after that the concentration of the manufacturing phase resulted in their decrease. Competition developed between the five major sugar corporations with majority North American capital and the Creole owners of *centrales*, whose number declined.[37]

This competitiveness related to the problem of the entry of Puerto Rican sugar onto the North American market. The fall in sugar beet production in France and Germany during the First World War had kept demand and sugar prices high, but in 1920 there had been a drastic fall in the prices. Many landowners, who had incurred debts to extend their plantations and improve their machinery, suffered heavy losses.

The 1920s saw the maximum expansion of sugar production on the island. But the capacity of the sugar sector to generate employment had already reached its peak. Moreover, when sugarcane cultivation was extended to marginal land it affected the ecological balance. The system of quotas which limited the amount of unrefined sugar that could enter the North American market acted as a brake on the optimal development of the plantations. As a result, by the end of the 1920s, the need to find alternatives to the sugar industry was under public consideration.[38]

Tobacco

One alternative that had been explored in the previous decades was tobacco. In the interior of the island there was a great deal of land suitable for its cultivation. After the 1899 hurricane, tobacco became a frequent replacement for the coffee plantations. Moreover, in the inland municipalities tobacco provided jobs in the factories where cigars and cigarettes were made, and loose tobacco was prepared for export.

The expansion of the tobacco industry was achieved at the cost of the domestic manufacturers. Regulations were imposed that penalized traditional cigar makers, who used to work at home. These unwitting lawbreakers were persecuted by internal revenue agents. Thus the law forced the concentration of tobacco manufacturing in urban factories, many of which were owned by external capital.

The tobacco factories were the first great manufacturing centers on the island and they contributed to urban development. For the first time women entered the wage labor market on a large scale. The *despalilladoras* who stripped the stems from the leaves were the vanguard of the new female working class.[39]

Labor Movements

The concentration of workers in cane fields and tobacco factories accelerated the organization and mobilization of the waged workers and gave them great strength. Gervasio García has shown that the origins of the workers' movement in Puerto Rico can be traced back to the urban artisans' workshops. At the beginning of the 1870s artisans founded clubs and other social and credit organizations in the principal towns. Their contact with European labor literature brought them in touch with the struggles in other parts of the world to obtain and consolidate workers' rights.[40]

The crises of the 1890s prompted the awakening of the labor movement. In 1891, for example, some sugar mill workers at Jerónimo Landrau's mill in Monacillos ward in Río Piedras stopped work. This is the message sent by Landrau to the mayor of Río Piedras:

> I wish to advise you that yesterday, Monday 18th of the month, very few workers came to work, protesting that it was a feast day and they would not work, and today Tuesday those who came stated that if they were not paid 5 *reales* a day, that is 61.5 cents, they would not work, and they would withdraw, leaving the cane cut and piled up beside the mill. Sugar has been selling at 2.75 and 2.85 and it is likely to go lower, it is not possible to pay such high wages, when by paying just 50 cents we are already losing and are not able to meet the high expenses that arise.[41]

The higher cost of living and the crisis of sugar in world markets trapped workers. Under those circumstances joint action became more likely.

There are references to different strikes in 1895 and 1896 which coincided with the problems following the exchange of the coinage in 1895 and the tariff wars between Spain and the United States. In April 1898, between two and three hundred workers went on strike at the Canóvanas *central*, demanding wages of one peso a day.[42] We know about some of these difficult struggles of the early labor movement from the memoirs of Rafael Alonso Torres and other early labor leaders. Strikes were outlawed at the time, as well as any alliance among workers "to make the workforce more expensive."[43]

After 1898 workers began to claim their right to assemble, express themselves, and act jointly, which were guaranteed by the Bill of Rights amendments to the U.S. Constitution. With the protection of those constitutional rights they began to hold assemblies and marches and to organize unions. After the labor movement was consolidated, they created an extremely useful link with the American Federation of Labor (AFL), one of the great labor confederations then existing in the United States.

The person who contributed most to that link with the AFL was a Galician immigrant called Santiago Iglesias Pantín, an anarchist by inclination and a carpenter by profession.[44] Imprisoned by the Spanish authorities in 1898 for his activities in organizing labor, Iglesias succeeded in overcoming the suspicions of the North American military authorities in the period following the invasion. Soon he perceived the enormous advantage to be gained by the Puerto Rican labor movement if direct contact was established with North American labor leaders. He traveled diligently to congresses and meetings of the AFL. In this way he eventually obtained the support of that body for strikes and legislative lobbying. It should be pointed out that, out of the great labor federations in the United States at the time, the AFL was the most conservative.

Iglesias was one of the founders of the Federation of Laborers. Early in the history of the federation it was necessary to decide whether to choose labor organization or party political activism. In the first fifteen years of its existence, the Federation vacillated between both courses of action. In the 1904 elections several labor leaders were candidates for the Union Party. Several local labor parties participated in elections between 1906 and 1914. In Arecibo, the workers' party won the municipality in the elections of 1914.

By 1915 enthusiasm for the political activism that prevailed in different sectors of the Federation resulted in the decision, taken at a meeting held in Cayey, to found a working men's party: the Socialist Party.[45]

The period between 1915 and 1919 was favorable for the growth of the labor movement. The First World War brought an intense demand for sugarcane and tobacco products and this translated itself into higher prices. It also lent greater force to labor demands for better salaries and working conditions. But although strikes happened at a favorable period for the workers, they had to face determined opposition by management. The sugarcane strike of 1917, for instance, resulted in two deaths.

In those early days the labor movement had huge celebrations for the First of May—International Labor Day. It readily quoted the European labor literature, including the works of Marx and Engels. The 1917 triumph of the Bolshevik Revolution in Russia and the ensuing reaction among the Western industrialized powers brought about changes. The Federation decided to rein in its ideological position and followed the guidelines set by the AFL in the United States.

By the middle of the 1920s, the Free Federation of Laborers was a significant force on the island. But the course of the workers' movement would be firmly tied to the electoral tactics of the Socialist Party.

From Foraker to the Jones Law

The Republicans won again in the 1902 elections. This time the Federals had agreed to participate and won two of the seven representative districts in the House. These elections were the most violent of the entire twentieth century.[46]

In 1904 Rosendo Matienzo Cintrón, Manuel Zeno Gandía, and other political leaders promoted the foundation of the Union of Puerto Rico, a civic association.[47] In a short space of time this association, which had as its aim the defense of Puerto Rican interests, transformed itself into a political party. The new political entity drew its membership from the Federal and Republican parties and from new participants in political affairs, including labor leaders like Ramón Romero Rosa.[48]

The Union Party won the 1904 elections and all subsequent elections in which it participated up until 1928. Prominent among its leaders was Luis Muñoz Rivera, but Tulio Larrinaga, José de Diego, Rosendo Matienzo Cintrón, Luis Llorens Torres, Nemesio Canales, Eduardo Georgetti, Antonio R. Barceló, Jorge Córdova Dávila, and many other well-known figures, both in business and in the professions, also played important roles.

The party was not committed to any specific political solution to the question of Puerto Rico's status. Instead it sought to achieve, in the short term, the replacement of the Foraker Law by a more comprehensive statute which would offer Puerto Ricans effective participation in the government of the island. It was with that understanding that they strove to have an elected Senate replace the Executive Council, which exercised both executive and legislative powers.

In its early years all the efforts of the Union Party to obtain amendments to the Foraker Law failed. At the beginning of 1909 the party leadership's frustration with the intransigence of the Executive Council, and the governor's indifference to the claims of the elected House delegates, reached a point where, during a caucus of Union legislators, Luis Lloréns Torres proposed a legislative strike. This meant that the House should abstain from passing any bills until the executive branch agreed to listen to its key proposals. Although the caucus did not approve Llorens Torres' motion, it came to adopt the proposal by Luis Muñoz Rivera that gave the legislative leadership greater flexibility in its negotiations with the governor and the Executive Council. The House then went on to consider and approve bills on public health, irrigation, public education, juvenile delinquency, the problems of Vieques and Culebra, and public works. When Governor Regis Post asked the House to be tough in its approval of the budget submitted by the Executive Council, the House proceeded to reduce the salaries of all high-ranking government officials, including the heads of the departments. The Executive Council refused to endorse these amendments made by the House to the budget.[49]

Thus a deadlock arose between the two legislative bodies. In an extraordinary session, the House refused to approve the budget unless two specific proposals were taken into account. One was to improve the credit situation of farmers, and the other that certain positions filled by the governor's appointment become elected ones. As a result of this deadlock, both sides appealed to the United States Congress. The Republican majority in Congress backed the governor and the Executive Council, while the Democratic minority supported the arguments of the House of Delegates. Although President Taft proposed amendments to the Foraker Law, which would deprive the

House of any decision-making powers over the budget, the President finally supported the so-called Olmstead Amendment. This established that Puerto Rico's budget for the preceding year would remain in force whenever the Legislature of Puerto Rico did not approve a budget for the incoming year.

Although defeated in Congress, the Union Party's leaders believed that their battle had not been in vain, because it had highlighted the limitations and the contradictions in the political clauses of the Foraker Law. In this way, the battle over the 1909 budget helped intensify the Union Party campaign to replace the Foraker Law with more comprehensive and fairer legislation.

One of the thorniest issues was that of citizenship. By 1910 Puerto Ricans were citizens of Puerto Rico, but that citizenship did not have any internationally recognized legal meaning. In order to travel abroad Puerto Ricans needed the endorsement of the American authorities. The legal limbo of citizenship forced Puerto Ricans to ask themselves who they really were. In 1898, the relatively few foreigners residing in Puerto Rico at the time, especially Spaniards, retained the citizenship of their countries of origin. This can be established from the census returns for 1910. After 1898, some Puerto Ricans who had spent some time in the United States time as students took advantage of their stay to apply for and obtain American citizenship on an individual basis. This was the case of Martín Travieso, for instance. In March of 1914 the House of Delegates passed a resolution rejecting any attempt to impose American citizenship on Puerto Ricans collectively. American citizenship was finally accepted by the Union Party when it became clear that it was a condition of having Congress authorize a fully elective legislature in Puerto Rico.[50]

In face of the prevailing legal ambiguity, the Puerto Rican Republican Party, which was then the minority party, included in its political platform the objective of obtaining United States citizenship for Puerto Ricans by means of an amendment to the Foraker Law. Republicans sought equality before the law, and also that Puerto Ricans could have the same legal capacity to exercise their constitutional rights as the North Americans who lived in Puerto Rico.[51]

The Jones Law

The year 1916 was full of expectation. The elections slated for November were postponed, in face of an imminent new law which would restructure the government of the island. Luis Muñoz Rivera, Resident Commissioner in Congress, lobbied different representatives and senators for a law which would fulfill the political aspirations of the Union Party. Nevertheless, the political realities did not give Muñoz Rivera much bargaining power. His health worsened considerably over the course of the negotiations in Washington and those with his own party's leadership held on the island. He died on November 15, 1916, without having achieved his goal. An impressive funeral procession testified to Muñoz Rivera's popularity with the Union masses.[52]

It was not until March of 1917 that the new law, approved by Congress and signed by President Woodrow Wilson, came into force. Known as the Jones Law after its proponent in the House of Representatives, William Jones, the new law granted American citizenship to everyone born in Puerto Rico who did not specifically refuse it within a period of six months. It established an elective Senate in lieu of the Executive Council, with two senators elected from each of the seven districts into which the Island would be divided and five senators elected by the entire electorate. Several other adjustments made to the political structure did not obscure the fact that the governor continued to be appointed by the President of the United States. Also, the confirmation of the cabinet members would be done, not by the Legislature of Puerto Rico, but by the United States Senate.[53]

Several clauses of the Jones Law reinforced the island's economic dependence. Puerto Rico could only refine a portion of the sugar it produced. Trade between the United States and Puerto Rico had to be carried in ships registered in the United States. This had the effect of increasing the cost of living, because hire charges for the North American ships was higher than for ships belonging to other nations.[54]

All in all, the Jones Law represented progress in relation to the Foraker Law. With few amendments, it regulated the life of the country up until 1952, and some substantial clauses are still in force.

The First World War

Shortly after the approval of the Jones Law, the United States entered the First World War on the side of Great Britain, France, and their allies against Germany, Austria-Hungary, and their allies. The war, which had broken out in August 1914, had become one of attrition in the trenches on the Western front. Meanwhile, the demoralized armies of the Tsar of Russia could barely hold off German troops in Eastern Europe.[55]

The United States' entry into the war meant the implementation of compulsory military service in Puerto Rico. Although many Puerto Ricans were recruited into the Army, only a few of them actually saw armed service in Europe, as the war ended in November 1918 with a victory for Great Britain and its allies. But this first participation of Puerto Ricans in an armed conflict fought by the United States in foreign lands established a norm which was followed in subsequent wars in the twentieth and the twenty-first centuries. American citizenship, although it granted limited political rights to Puerto Ricans, imposed military service. Several hundred Puerto Ricans refused to join the Army and were arrested either for evasion or for disobeying enlistment orders.[56]

On the other hand, the development of war industries created a need for labor on the east coast of the United States. Several thousand Puerto Ricans migrated to New York, looking for the jobs offered by that opportunity.[57] The affluence of the workers strengthened and gave a stronger identity to the Puerto Rican community on Manhattan's east side in New York, which dated back to the final decades of the nineteenth century.

Prohibition

In the elections of July 16, 1917, there was also a referendum on the planned prohibition of the sale of alcoholic beverages in Puerto Rico. This measure was the result of lobbying by a number of religious leaders, in United States and in Puerto Rico, who believed that the solution to the social problems of the country was to eradicate alcoholism. For them, a sure method of achieving it was to forbid the manufacture and sale of intoxicating beverages.

Several religious groups and the Socialist Party supported the measure in the electoral campaign, while the Union and the Republican parties did not take a stance on the issue. Prohibition won the referendum with 102,423 votes in favor and 64,227 against.[58]

Although it was adopted with great enthusiasm, before the United States approved a similar constitutional amendment, prohibition, as it was popularly known, became a major headache for the authorities and a symbol of the country's cultural alienation. The state's intervention in the personal decisions and conduct of individuals became a parody of the government's responsibility to watch over the security and the welfare of citizens. Numerous arrests for the operation of liquor stills and for the possession of alcoholic beverages only underscored the impossibility of legislating for a morality that was alien to the country's customs. Liquor fermented in clandestine stills was not always distilled and placed in containers according to minimal norms of hygiene, and this in turn exacerbated the public health problems. A subculture of smuggling and clandestine activities reduced the state's capacity to intervene in more important matters, and the police who were charged with searching and confiscating stills lost prestige.

Prohibition finally ended in 1933, when the constitutional amendment that had made it possible was revoked in the United States. Meanwhile, it had contributed to the criminalization of some sectors of the country. The experience with this statute showed the futility and arbitrariness of attempting to impose an alien moral code on the entire population.

The Crisis of the Depression

Throughout the 1920s the problems of agriculture in Puerto Rico monopolized the attention of the ruling classes. In response to the stimulus of the First World War, the sugar sector had overextended itself and now faced serious marketing problems. There was an attempt to address the problem by establishing candy factories and finding other uses for sugarcane derivatives, but this was not enough to solve it. The tobacco sector faced a fall in prices for its harvests. As for coffee growers, the First World War had reduced spending power in the countries which were the main consumers of Puerto Rican coffee. Cuba, one of the most important markets, had begun to produce the majority of the coffee that it consumed. Coffee growers faced falling prices and difficulties in obtaining financing.[59]

All these problems were compounded by the hurricane of St. Philip's Day in September 1928, Puerto Rico's greatest natural disaster of the twentieth century. It was probably what today would be a Category 5 hurricane. Several hundred people died. The winds and floods destroyed farms and thousands of houses in the cities and countryside. The country was brought to its knees.

If the economy had been on an upward path, the pace of recovery after the hurricane could perhaps have been faster. But 1929 was the last year of postwar economic expansion for the United States. By the end of the year, the enormous tensions within U.S. financial structures had given way and Wall Street crashed.

North American farmers had been hastily mechanizing their operations in the postwar years. As long as prices kept up with their expectations they were able to keep up the payments for the machinery they had bought on credit. But as the 1920s advanced, the agrarian sector in the United States, though still important for the economic balance of the nation, could not meet the increased costs of financing because their income from crop and livestock sales had fallen. This weakness of the agricultural sector showed that the domestic market was not capable of absorbing the country's increasing manufacturing production. On the other hand, the relative strength of the dollar and the competition generated by other manufacturing countries with cheaper labor costs limited access to foreign markets. To avoid the stagnation that threatened the North American economy it was necessary to guide a dramatic new technological breakthrough which would open up new demand on the internal market. What happened on Wall Street was the investors' admission that the shares negotiated on credit were inflated in relation to their real value in terms of production and trade.[60]

The Depression that began in 1929 in the United States represented a death knell for the battered agrarian economy of Puerto Rico. Sugar and tobacco prices on the North American market fell. There was also a reduction in financial facilities, public income, commercial activity, employment, private and public construction, and investment in the manufacturing sector. The general despondency which had started with the hurricane was sapping people's vitality, cutting jobs, restricting consumption, and limiting the possibilities for personal development.

All the economic indicators during the Depression were worse in Puerto Rico than in the United States, with the additional factor that the crisis in the United States halted the emigration of Puerto Ricans to the mainland as a way to escape the crisis. The suicide rate rose and the homicide rate climbed to 18 per hundred thousand in 1936.[61] There was a huge wave of crimes against property and various signs of severe social malaise. A sense of hopelessness gripped the country. The song "Lamento Borincano" (Puerto Rican Lament) by the composer Rafael Hernández dates from that sad period. The song sums up the bitterness of a people prostrated by economic forces beyond their control.

The Nationalists

The Union Party brought together all those political elements for which independence was the only acceptable alternative. But after the 1915 assembly, when Antonio Barceló replaced José de Diego as party president, the independence sympathizers had begun to gravitate outside the orbit of the Unionists. While the objective was to achieve a greater degree of self-government for Puerto Rico through a new constitutional law which would replace the Foraker Law, it was not difficult for autonomists and pro-independence supporters to join ranks within the same party. But after Muñoz Rivera's death in 1916, the legislation of American citizenship in 1917, the death of De

Diego in 1918, and the elimination from the platform of the Union Party in 1922 of independence as one of the future options, the old pro-independence sympathizers distanced themselves from the party. In any case, the younger generation was not very attracted to a party which, after winning elections over such a long period, had only achieved the reforms of the Jones Law.

In 1922 a group of dissidents from the Union Party and young independence sympathizers founded the Nationalist Party.[62] Its first president was José Alegría. In the 1920s, the nationalists took an active part in the debate on the obligatory use of English as the language of instruction in public schools. They placed much emphasis on the symbols of national identity and advocated the study and contemplation of Puerto Rico's historical reality. Aside from putting up some candidates in municipal campaigns, they did not participate in general electoral campaigns.

In 1929, a young Ponce lawyer, a former militant of the Union Party, Pedro Albizu Campos,[63] became president of the Nationalist Party. The change of leadership led to greater mobilization of the municipal leadership of the party. The Nationalist Party registered for the 1932 elections and had candidates for municipal and legislative office in the municipalities of San Juan, Arecibo, Ponce, Guayama, and Humacao. Pedro Albizu Campos was a candidate for senator-at-large and obtained more than 3% of the vote. In Caguas, Utuado, and some other municipalities Albizu received more votes than did members from other parties, a reflection of the acceptance of his candidacy in those towns.[64]

The defeat in 1932 created a split among the nationalists. Albizu and a sector of the party became convinced that they would never achieve their goal by the electoral route. Consequently they decided to escalate their militancy. But other nationalists were disgusted with this trend and abandoned active politics or joined the Liberal Party.

In 1934, Albizu tried to approach the sugar workers who were on strike in the eastern region.[65] Although many workers came to listen to his speeches, this did not translate itself into a lasting following. In fact, Albizu had a greater impact in the towns, where his followers were teachers, students, shopkeepers, artisans, and white-collar workers, rather than among the cane workers.

Relations between the nationalists and the police deteriorated rapidly between 1933 and 1936. In Río Piedras, for example, a confrontation following an arrest developed into an exchange of gunfire in which five persons were killed. Albizu blamed those deaths on the Island Police Chief Francis Riggs. On February 23, 1936 in two consecutive incidents, the nationalists Elías Beauchamp and Hiram Rosado attacked and fatally wounded the police chief. Afterwards both young men were shot to death at police headquarters on San Francisco Street in San Juan.[66]

The three deaths divided the country. Riggs' death had a profound effect on the United States. Senator Tydings from Maryland, a personal friend of Riggs, presented a resolution in Congress to grant immediate independence to Puerto Rio, without any safeguards for the immediate economic future of the country. On the other hand, the funeral of the two nationalists was accompanied by an enormous show of emotion. The governor initiated proceedings against the nationalist leadership in Federal court, where Albizu and others were found guilty of instigating Riggs' murder and were sentenced to prison. In 1937 Albizu was transferred to Atlanta, Georgia, and for the next ten years was absent from the everyday politics of the country. His followers remained politically active to the extent that the circumstances allowed.

On Palm Sunday, 1937, which coincided with the anniversary of the abolition of slavery in Puerto Rico, the Nationalist Party had programmed a march in Ponce. At the last minute the mayor of Ponce revoked the permit he had granted for the event. The nationalists decided to go ahead with the march, and twenty-one people were killed in confrontations with the police who blocked the route. This incident is known in Puerto Rican history as the Ponce Massacre.[67]

The event aroused widespread indignation, especially because the investigations carried out by order of Governor Winship produced unconvincing results. The American Civil Liberties Union, together with members of the Colegio de Abogados de Puerto Rico, carried out an investigation in which the governor was named as being responsible for the massacre.

Although in its heyday in the 1930s, the Nationalist Party did not succeed in consolidating its grip on the masses as the labor movement had done in the 1920s. Its militant character led the country to turn its attention to North American cultural domination and the deficiencies of the political programs of the parties that shared power. The crisis of the 1930s made clear the failure of the North American model, if one existed, for Puerto Rican economic and social development. In the face of this failure the Nationalists recalled the situation of Puerto Ricans before 1898, but in doing so, somewhat idealized it. On the other hand, they placed a great deal of importance on those cultural elements they considered to be inherent in Puerto Rico's Hispanic roots. Among those values were the Catholic faith, the traditional Hispanic concept of the role of women in society, and the dignity of the work of smallholders and artisans.

In the 1970s some thinkers began to ask whether that invoking of the Hispanic Puerto Rico explained the limited response of the workers to the Nationalist program.[68] Collective memories of the slave system, the tortures (*compontes*) of 1887, the inhuman conditions of life in the old *haciendas*, and the domination of the *hacendados* were at odds with Albizu's expressed nostalgia for the past. Women, who in the 1930s were entering the waged job market in force and were shaping their own images as producers, might not trust rhetoric which mainly recognized their role as housewives and child-minders. Then again, Puerto Ricans who joined the Protestant churches in growing numbers could disagree with the idea that nationality was identified with Catholicism. And the new world of professionals and technicians who were trained in North American institutions, and were accustomed to North American ways of thinking, would have little enthusiasm for calls to return to the pre-industrial past.

Plans for Reconstruction and Social Welfare

Between 1924 and 1932 there was a realignment of political forces. The growing influence of the Socialist Party, evident in the elections of 1917 and 1920, prompted conservatives among the ruling Union

Party to seek an alliance with their old rivals, the Republicans. In the elections of 1924 and 1928 the resulting alliance won the elections. But factionalism and disagreements over public policy divided the Union Republican Party. Antonio R. Barceló lost out in those internal struggles. He organized his followers into a party, but was not allowed to use the symbols or the name of the Union Party, so it became the Liberal Party.[69]

The Union Republican Party, on the other hand, entered into discussions with the Socialist Party, which seemed most likely to gain from the granting of the vote to women.[70] They agreed to form a coalition, which won the elections of 1932 and 1936. In Puerto Rico's political history that period is frequently called "the time of the Coalition."

In this way the socialists finally got into power. Santiago Iglesias was elected resident commissioner in Washington, and that responsibility kept him away from immediate supervision of his party's political interests. Although the socialists obtained some legislation that benefited their interests, some party members felt that their political allies, the Republicans, were getting more advantages from wielding legislative power.

The socialist leadership's capacity to overcome these tensions was seriously challenged in 1933–34. The terrible conditions of the Depression led workers to demonstrate the urgency of their demands with a wave of strikes in the tobacco and needlework industries, bakeries, public transportation, and haulage. Foreseeing a strike during the coming sugarcane harvest, the leading sugar producers proposed an agreement with negotiators of the Free Federation of Workers to fix salaries for the 1934 harvest. But when the agreement was published many workers expressed their intention to reject it. As a result, a strike broke out in the first weeks of 1934, which was not supported by the union leadership, but which affected the sugar plantations in the east and southeast of the island.[71]

Although the strike eventually petered out and the workers returned to cutting cane, the strike left profound divisions among the socialist masses. The dissident socialist leadership grouped together in Socialist Affirmation, and assumed positions that were increasingly distant from those of the Party's leadership. In 1936 some dissident leaders joined other new elements in politics and in labor organizing to found the Communist Party. The new party, although it partici- pated in the 1936 election in the municipalities of Utuado and Jayuya, focused its attention more on the labor unions than on elec- toral politics. By 1938 it had a great deal of influence among the dockworkers, who held an important strike in that year.[72]

While the workers' sector tried out new approaches and discussed the future of the labor movement, the ruling coalition and the Liberal legislative minority were concerned with other problems. President Franklin Delano Roosevelt's administration, inaugurated in 1933, confronted the effects of the Depression in the United States by attempting to promote a plan of national economic renewal. Part of the strategy consisted in revitalizing economic life through public works projects which created jobs. Thus, the government of the United States assigned funds to Puerto Rico for an emergency aid project, which was known by its initials, PRERA, Puerto Rico Emergency Relief Act. Roads and bridges were built with these funds and a reforestation project was begun. These initiatives gave thou- sands of young people their first experience of paid employment.[73]

The lack of employment on the island was so acute, however, that the available funds barely scratched the surface of the problem. Competition for the few jobs that were being created gave a boost to political patronage. It was inevitable that heated debates should develop around the control of hiring. The Coalition accused the administrator of the program, James Bourne, of favoring Liberals. In some towns there were violent confrontations among those who aspired to jobs from the PRERA.

Meanwhile, various Puerto Rican figures, who perceived that wel- fare programs were incapable of solving the structural problems of the Puerto Rican economy in the long run, worked on drafting a comprehensive plan of national reconstruction. This eventually became known as the Chardón Plan, as its coordinator was the University of Puerto Rico professor Carlos E. Chardón.[74]

The Chardón Plan had four main objectives. Firstly, it proposed the literal application of the 500-acre limit clause of the Foraker Act.

Secondly, it held that the government should acquire land exceeding the 500-acre limit through a public corporation created by law. This corporation would then distribute the land among landless laborers. These in turn would be organized into cooperatives to cultivate their land and market their crops. The Plan also considered the gradual industrialization of the island, the coordination of the public education system, and the development needs of Puerto Rico. It also looked at the expansion of public health services, the creation of a system of public housing, and various programs for community education.

Although it enjoyed the backing of influential members of Roosevelt's administration, the Chardón Plan faced enormous political and institutional hurdles. The Coalition majority in the Legislature saw it as a creation of the Liberal minority and mistrusted the endorsement of the Plan by Roosevelt's administration. Governor Winship did not show much enthusiasm for the main concepts of the Plan. Finally, the tribunals obstructed the Plan by refusing to recognize the sanctions placed by some recently enacted legislation on holdings in excess of 500 acres.[75]

Nevertheless, the Chardón Plan gave results over the long term. Its ideas fed into the political program of the Popular Party in the 1940 electoral campaign. The discussion of the plan helped to educate Puerto Rican public opinion on the merits of economic planning and the need for an integrated view of the country's problems.

Public Education

The University of Puerto Rico was established by the Legislature in 1903, with the transfer to Río Piedras of a teachers' training college founded in Fajardo through local initiative in 1900. It grew slowly and in its first decades it focused on the education of teachers, though a law faculty had been founded by 1913. In the 1920s the University entered a new phase of expansion.[76] In the mid-1920s a department of Hispanic studies gained distinction and by the 1930s it was recruiting talented young Puerto Rican professors who had been educated in Europe and the United States. By the 1930s, programs in the natural sciences and the social sciences began to be developed, but it was not until the 1940s that the University was divided into the faculties (*facultades*) that it has today. As the university grew, its campus developed into an architectural complex which served its needs and fostered an academic ambience.[77] Meanwhile, in Mayaguez a branch of the University specializing in agronomy and engineering developed its own full-fledged curriculum. In San Germán a private university, initially called the Instituto Politécnico, and now known as the Inter-American University, was founded in 1911 to offer a college education to several hundred students.

In the twentieth century, Puerto Rico achieved something that many thinkers throughout the world have desired for their countries: that the most substantial item in the budget be dedicated to education. In the first half of the century the amounts were relatively modest, as was the island's budget. When those allocations were made, various priorities were considered. Was it preferable to achieve a minimal level of education for all school-age children, or to develop a system for intermediate and higher education? Should new schools be built or should the existing ones receive more resources? Should teachers be better paid or should funds be assigned instead to creating a greater number of teaching posts?

No discussion on educational priorities aroused greater passion than that related to the language of instruction in public schools.[78] Since the creation of the Department of Public Education, the commissioners had steadfastly pursued the stated aim of achieving the Americanization of Puerto Ricans through the schools. In particular, they insisted that English be used to teach all the school subjects except Spanish. This priority required a great many North American teachers to be brought to the island, since few Puerto Rican teachers at the beginning of the century had sufficient mastery of English to teach in that language.[79]

In the 1920s and the 1930s the controversy surrounding the official language of instruction intensified. In many schoolrooms the requirement only managed to satisfy appearances. Textbooks were in English, and that made learning more difficult for many students. In the Central High School in Santurce, for instance, Latin was taught with textbooks in English, even though Latin is much closer to Spanish than to English.

A poor grasp of English made it more difficult to gain access to higher levels of instruction. Students who came from homes with little contact with North American culture found it very difficult to gain a degree which required a competent level of English. The battle around the language of instruction acquired connotations of class consciousness and had a bearing on other areas of school life. For instance, there were debates about the routines associated with the pledge of allegiance to the American flag, commencement ceremonies, school yearbooks, and extracurricular activities. Several strikes by high school students over these issues accelerated the politicization of many students.

In spite of its limited budget and its serious internal wrangles, the school system expanded considerably between 1900 and 1940 and this benefited many children of workers, artisans, retailers, and public employees in the urban areas.

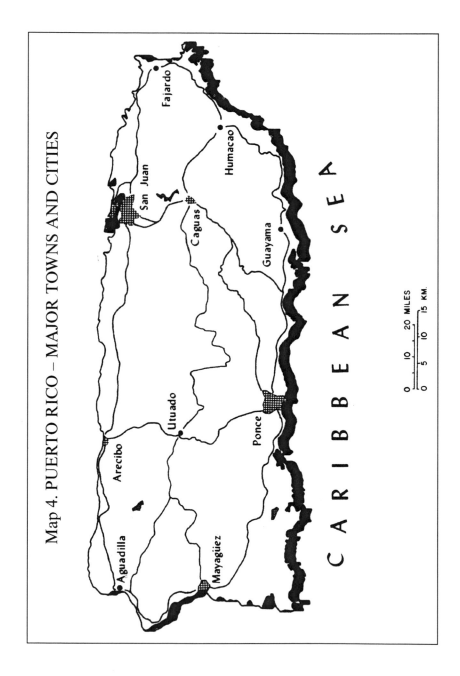

Map 4. PUERTO RICO – MAJOR TOWNS AND CITIES

Aguadilla

Arecibo

Utuado

Mayagüez

Ponce

San Juan

Caguas

Guayama

Fajardo

Humacao

CARIBBEAN SEA

0   10   20 MILES
0   5   10   15 KM.

<table>
<tr>
<td>CHAPTER
14</td>
<td>

The New Industrial and Urban Order, 1940–1980

</td>
</tr>
</table>

Different societies confronted the Depression in different ways. Some countries installed dictatorships which designed and imposed economic policies which were aimed at protecting the interests of their ruling classes. Other countries sought consensual solutions, but that consensus did not always favor the interests of the dispossessed. For others, war was the way out. At the cost of a significant increase in the public debt and the accelerated acquisition of military equipment, they generated jobs and transformed their economies.

All of this was prompting a new concept of the state, different from the nineteenth-century liberal model. The state was no longer merely the arbiter of free economic forces, but was itself becoming the principal and defining economic force. According to the new doctrines, the state could no longer be neutral in economic interplay, as some nineteenth-century thinkers had suggested, because that neutrality already implied taking a position. On the other hand, the public debt could turn into an instrument of the state to be used for improving the economy without necessarily becoming a burden. According to these theories, the way to emerge from a cycle of economic recession was not to curb government spending so as to keep it within the budget guaranteed by fiscal income. Instead the government should launch new public works, welfare, and housing projects, among others, to fuel economic activity by putting the workers back into productive roles. In the long run the deficit would be covered by the new income generated by a regenerated economy.[1]

Under the presidency of Franklin Delano Roosevelt, the United States tested some of the formulas derived from the economic thinking of John Maynard Keynes, a British economist who had challenged the premises of the classical liberal economy. In spite of the reluctance of the more conservative judges, the state implemented economic initiatives which jurists had previously only associated with private enterprise. It was along the lines of Keynes' thinking that some models of economic reconstruction were attempted in Puerto Rico.

The Crisis of the Political Parties

The operation of the PRERA and PRRA plans was partly responsible for the perception that there was a parallel government operating in Puerto Rico. These plans reported, not to the Legislature of Puerto Rico, but directly to the presidency of the United States. As these programs had at their disposal an amount of funds which the legislature did not have, they attained a level of prestige and a thrust that called into question the merits of the elected government and its capacity to understand the population's demands.

This shake-up of the traditional mechanisms of political patronage happened at a time when a generational change in political leadership was in the air. Antonio R. Barceló, president of the Liberal Party, died in 1938 after vainly trying to maintain his party's unity.

Santiago Iglesias, wounded during a Nationalist attack in 1936, died in 1939 of an illness contracted while on a trip. Rafael Martínez Nadal, leader of the Republicans, faced divisions within his party, and these divisions became more acute after his death in 1941.

In the runup to the elections of 1940, all three parties suffered from internal divisions which resulted in the foundation of new parties. Out of the Liberals' crisis in 1938 a new party had emerged. It united workers and smallholders from the mountains, professionals, intellectuals, owners and tenants of small sugarcane plantations, retailers, and drivers of public transport.[2] Although the San Juan press paid little attention to it, the Popular Democratic Party, registered in 1938, had been growing steadily in the interior districts of the island. Even on the eve of the elections, a newspaper column in *El Mundo* reported that Rafael Martínez Nadal predicted that the new party only had the possibility of winning in Barranquitas.

The Divided Victory of 1940

The candidate of the Socialist and Republican coalition, the journalist Bolívar Pagán, son-in-law of the late Santiago Iglesias, won the post of Resident Commissioner in Washington in the 1940 elections. The Popular Democratic Party won ten of the seventeen Senate seats, ensuring the election of Luis Muñoz Marín as its president. But the *Populares* only obtained eighteen of the thirty-nine seats in the House of Representatives. The coalition of Republicans and Socialists won eighteen seats, and the Tripartite Unification Party, which was also a new party, won three seats. In order to gain the approval of their proposed legislation in the House, the *Populares* had to win the support of opposition legislators.

The cohesion among the *Populares* and the rapport between their leaders, especially Muñoz Marín, and President Roosevelt's aides and officials meant that a great many of the measures that they legislated from their political platform were approved. In 1942 the economist Rexford G. Tugwell, former professor of the University of Columbia and a presidential adviser, was named Governor of Puerto Rico.[3] This appointment served to reinforce the *Populares'* activities in the legislature.[4]

In 1941 a Land Law was approved which implemented the dispositions of the Chardón Plan that the lands exceeding the 500-acre limit which the sugar corporations had to sell to the government be turned into cooperatives. These lands were given over to the cultivation of pineapples, oranges, and grapefruit, vegetables, and other food items that were in short supply owing to the navigational hazards brought about by World War II. On Tugwell's initiative a Planning Board was created to regulate economic development and to draw up plans for the orderly development of the urban areas. An Economic Development Administration, *Fomento*, was established to promote industrial development. Two public corporations were created, one for the provision of electricity throughout the island and another to provide drinking water for Puerto Rican homes. Urban public transportation in the San Juan area was reorganized under government aegis with the establishment of the Metropolitan Bus Authority.

The government intensified efforts to massively extend public schooling. A Community Education Division was eventually created within the Department of Education. Health programs were set in motion and their radius of action was extended to the rural areas. Other government services were mobilized to make them more accessible to the general population, which at the time was mainly rural. Much of this determination to dramatically improve living conditions was carried out with reduced budgets, but the new party made ample use of young professionals who were willing to work for the people. This populist orientation of government employees gave a particular zest to the campaigns for the eradication of the more obvious signs of poverty.

The Second World War

During the first four years of their legislature the *Populares* confronted the grave shortages in Puerto Rico resulting from the entry of the

United States into the Second World War.[5] Up until December 1941, the United States had been an interested observer in the war that had broken out in 1939 between Germany and the Allied countries (Great Britain, France, Poland, and others). Almost all the European nations, willingly or otherwise, had become involved in the war. The Soviet Union was invaded in June 1941 by its former ally, Germany. Japan and Italy were the main allies of the German government, which was headed by Adolf Hitler, the leader of the National Socialist Party.

On December 7, 1941, a Japanese air squadron bombed Pearl Harbor, the principal North American naval base in Hawaii. This led the United States to immediately declare war on Japan and its allies. Tens of thousands of Puerto Ricans were drafted into the United States military and served in the Pacific, North Africa, and Europe. For many of these soldiers, this was the first time they had left the island. The military training received and the experience gained during the years of military service had a profound effect on most of them. Some left the service with a robust attachment to North American institutions. For others the experience was a turning point in their lives which sharpened their anti-militarist sentiments, their notions of Puerto Rican identity, and their aspirations for collective justice.

The World War II generation of veterans had a modernizing influence on the country. The access these veterans had to higher education, finance for purchasing a house, federal employment, and other services and rights gave them a collective image of activism and leadership. From their ranks emerged candidates for political office in the various parties, civil and labor leaders, professionals, and tradesmen. The experience of war distinguished this generation from the preceding ones and gave it a sense of security and well-being which has not been as evident among veterans of subsequent wars.

The Second World War ended with total victory for the Allies. The moral prestige of having vanquished the National Socialist German state, whose atrocities became patent at the end of the war, was shared between the United States and the Soviet Union, the two emerging powers whose leadership was consolidated.

Puerto Rico suffered from shortages of many imported articles during the war. The reforms instituted under Tugwell's administration had not yet operated in peacetime. The Allied victory of 1945 was met with great exuberance and great expectations on the island. In the November 1944 election, several months earlier, the dominance of the Popular Party had been ratified by unprecedented margins.

The Puerto Rican Independence Party

In Puerto Rico a number of questions hung in the air in 1945, but the main one was the possibility of self-government for the country, an aspiration shared by many Puerto Ricans. The leaders of the Popular Democratic Party, which included many known supporters of independence, had postponed any consideration of the future relationship between the United States and Puerto Rico and of the statutory instrument which would regulate this until the war was over. In 1945, after an overwhelming victory by the Populares in the 1944 elections, some felt that the push for independence should no longer be postponed.

Luis Muñoz Marín, the main leader of the Popular Democratic Party, had come to believe that real economic growth in the country was more urgent that the issue of political status. His position became clearer throughout 1945. He accepted the industrialization of the island as necessary to solve the chronic problems of poverty. The efforts to achieve political independence would prolong economic dependence on monoculture and would make it hard to obtain capital for new areas of economic activity. Muñoz considered that it was imperative to take advantage of the favorable postwar juncture to lift the country out of its economic morass.

Some legislators and leaders of the Popular Party were of the opinion that independence should be the first priority. Positions became inflexible. Finally in 1946 Gilberto Concepción de Gracia and many former sympathizers of the Popular Party founded a new political body: the Puerto Rican Independence Party. Its main objective was the attainment of independence by electoral means.[6]

The Economic Development Administration
and Economic Take-Off

In 1946 a Puerto Rican was named governor of Puerto Rico, Jesús T. Piñero, a collaborator of Muñoz Marin and Resident Commissioner in Washington. In 1947 Congress approved an amendment to the Jones Law which made the position of governor of Puerto Rico an elective one. When the Popular Party won the elections in November 1948, Luis Muñoz Marín became the first elected governor. In that election the Popular Party won all the districts except San Lorenzo. The Puerto Rican Independence Party came in second. After 1948 the Populares gave a new twist to their efforts to industrialize the country. Initially the state had contributed industrial capital, with which to set up glass, cement, and paper factories. Now the Populares proposed to encourage external investment by offering tax exemptions, for a period of to seventeen years, to manufacturing firms which established themselves in Puerto Rico. Teodoro Moscoso, a pharmacist from Ponce, was in charge of the Economic Development Administration.

The incentives program of Fomento (as the administration was generally known) delivered results in the short term. In the two decades following the tax exemption, hundreds of factories were set up on the island, generating over 130,000 jobs. The factories that were opened in those initial years required little technology but an abundant workforce. Towards the mid-1960s, when those original factories were being phased out, Fomento promoted the development of heavy industry by establishing petrochemical plants in the south and southeast of the island. From the mid-1970s on, the most important industrial plants were pharmaceutical and electronics factories.

Although the debates about the merits of the Fomento program have been intense and thorough, there is little doubt that it was responsible for radically transforming the country's socioeconomic structure. Tens of thousands of women entered the paid job market and secured their own role in the economy. Agriculture stopped being the main source of employment in the island. Industrial salaries, much higher than those in agriculture, allowed workers to become homeowners. The houses were generally built from cement,

TABLE 14.1

Salaried employment in Agriculture and Manufacture in Puerto Rico, 1940–1984, by thousands of workers.*

Year	Agriculture (includes fishing)	Manufacture (excludes domestic needlework)
1940	230	56
1950	216	55
1960	125	81
1970	68	132
1975	48	130
1980	40	143
1984	39	142

*Note: Employment in other sectors, including commerce and government, rose from 226,000 in 1940 to 561,000 in 1984.
Source: Puerto Rico Planning Board, *Estadísticas Socioeconómicas, 1984*, pp. 3–4.

following the guidelines of the insurance industry, and were equipped with furniture and electrical appliances typical of modern societies. Industrial activity fueled other sectors of the economy, such as construction, professional services, banking, and tourism. Commercial activity expanded significantly.

Migration to the United States

After the Second World War, employment opportunities in the expanding economy and the low cost of air travel acted as incentives for hundreds of thousands of Puerto Ricans to migrate to the United States in search of work.[7]

With the protection of migrant workers for the fruit and vegetable harvests in mind, the Office of Employment and Migration was created under the Puerto Rican Department of Labor. The Office's role was to ensure that the laborers did not fall victim to misleading or fraudulent contracts and that the agreements were honored. But many workers who went to the United States at harvest time, after working for one or two years on contracts protected by the Department of Labor, accepted other job opportunities independently. Sometimes they became victims of abuse.

A high proportion of the workers opted to migrate to cities, where they could find jobs in light industry or in services. The old Puerto Rican neighborhoods in Manhattan grew rapidly with the affluent new migrants.[8] They established important neighborhoods in the Bronx and Brooklyn and in nearby towns in New Jersey. In Chicago and Philadelphia, Puerto Rican communities expanded rapidly in the 1950s and 1960s.[9] Communities also developed in Cleveland, Buffalo, Connecticut, and Indiana.[10]

Many of the Puerto Ricans who moved to the United States encountered serious problems. The cities of the northeastern states, following rapid growth in the second half of the nineteenth and the early decades of the twentieth centuries, had experienced a rapid process of suburbanization, which was facilitated by the mass production of automobiles and the construction of expressways. The old brick and mortar houses in the cities, abandoned in the flight to the suburbs, were subdivided by (often unscrupulous) speculators who leased them to Puerto Rican migrants. They faced problems with plumbing maintenance, antiquated heating systems, leaky roofs, and humid basements. They also suffered from the proliferation of vermin, the decaying urban systems of waste disposal, and the lack of security. These migrants from rural areas had little previous experience of urban living with which to confront the labyrinth they were entering.[11]

On top of all of this was the prejudice and contempt faced by many in the workplace and on the street. Their accent, the color of their skin, their Hispanic origins, and even their religious beliefs and their traditional code of honor were reasons for belittling and discriminating against Puerto Ricans. Children and adolescents who grew up in Puerto Rican communities, and witnessed their parents' perplexity in the face of unforeseen circumstances, soon developed their own lifestyles, in which they combined elements from the Puerto Rican and North American worlds. Some joined gangs who lorded it over particular streets and parks. They became the object of the press sensationalism[12] and were portrayed as exotic by the world of show business. Thus there arose a stereotype of Puerto Rican youth in New York City which has endured not only in the United States and in Puerto Rico, but also in other countries.

TABLE 14.2
Puerto Ricans Residing in the United States

Year	Total of Puerto Ricans in the U.S.	Percentage in New York City
1910	1,513	36.6
1920	11,811	62.3
1930	52,774	not indicated
1940	69,967	87.8
1950	301,375	81.6
1960	887,662	69.0
1970	1,429,396	56.8

Source: Kal Wagenheim, *A Survey of Puerto Ricans on the U.S. Mainland in the 1970s* (New York: 1975), 71.

Less visible, but in the long run more important, were the numerous civic and religious associations which participated in the collective struggles of Puerto Rican communities for their rights. These gave their members a sense of achievement, stability, and dignity. The civic projects and celebrations, the networks of solidarity, information, and necessary support provided by these organizations which had been created and supported by the migrants acted as a counterbalance to the burdens of economic necessity and social injustice. Many of those who went on to became political and civic leaders started out in these clubs, associations, and churches. The same can be said of many women who would later demonstrate a capacity for leadership and civil action in the United States.

Eventually the second and third generations of Puerto Ricans born in the United States to migrant parents followed a different path from their predecessors. The old Puerto Rican neighborhoods in some cities disappeared, giving way to Dominican communities or those from other Latin American and European countries. Puerto Ricans born in the United States began to make their mark in the professions, politics, the artistic and literary world, and in the media. Thus began a new stage in the history of the Puerto Rican communities. Although they still passionately identify with Puerto Rico, as is evident in the annual New York City Puerto Rican Day Parade, the development of new Puerto Rican communities with their own characteristics in the United States begins a new chapter in the historical experience of Puerto Ricans.

The Nationalists: 1950 and 1954

While Puerto Rico entered a period of urban and industrial transformation, Albizu Campos and his followers pushed the unfinished agenda of the 1930s, obtaining sovereignty and independence for Puerto Rico.

Albizu had been released from prison in Atlanta and had remained in New York. During his long years in prison he had given a definitive form to the essential elements of his 1930s thesis. But his absence from Puerto Rico, during the Second World War and the period when the new urban and industrial order was developing, had distanced Albizu from the perceptions and expectations of the younger generation.

In 1948, university students at Río Piedras, wishing to hear the legendary and compelling figure speak, insisted that Albizu should come to the University of Puerto Rico. They lowered the American flag at the University and replaced it with the Puerto Rican flag. The resulting clash with the university authorities unleashed a long and heated strike by students. The situation became even more tense when the issue of the exclusion from campus, suspension, and expulsion of student leaders was added to the original motivation for the strike.[13] In fact, the original motive was quickly forgotten. In any case, the nationalistic rhetoric of the 1930s, with its urgent insistence and its evocation of the glorious nineteenth century, held little attraction for the postwar university generation.

But if Albizu made little headway with the new generation in the capital city, his message had a profound impact on some groups in the towns of the interior where the traditional pace of life seemed threatened by cultural changes and where many of the expectations created by the reforms of the 1940s had yet to be met.

At the start of November 1950, Nationalist groups joined forces in the attack on police headquarters and other government establishments, including la Fortaleza.[14] The gunfire in San Juan and in the urban centers of more than fifteen municipalities alarmed the population, who listened to the radio for news of the events.

Twenty-eight people died as the result of these exchanges of gunfire. In Utuado, five nationalists who had surrendered died in circumstances which were never satisfactorily explained. In Jayuya, a group of nationalists from Coabey ward captured the police headquarters and proclaimed the republic. A fire which broke out during the gun battle burned down numerous houses and businesses in the town.

Two nationalists attacked Blair House in Washington, where President Truman was residing while the White House was being refurbished. One of the nationalists and one policeman died in the exchange of gunfire. Nationalist Oscar Collazo was tried and condemned to death for killing the policeman but the sentence was commuted to life imprisonment by President Truman. Collazo was released from prison in the 1970s.

Albizu Campos and a large number of nationalists were tried and jailed following these occurrences. Also, in the hours following the nationalist attacks there were arrests and searches in the homes of hundreds of independence sympathizers who were not affiliated with the Nationalist Party. The memory of these arrests and searches, and of the prejudice and persecution suffered by many independence sympathizers in the years that followed, poisoned relations between Independentistas and Populares for long afterwards.

Albizu Campos was found guilty of conspiring to overthrow the government and was put in jail. In 1953 Governor Muñoz granted him conditional liberty.

In Washington, in March 1954, three young Nationalists fired bullets in the chamber during a meeting of the U.S. House of Representatives. Six congressmen were wounded. North American public opinion was outraged by this attack on Congress. The nationalists were arrested in the Capitol along with another accomplice seized in Washington. They were tried and sentenced to long prison terms. President Carter eventually secured their release.

Albizu Campos was arrested and jailed once more. He remained in prison until the deterioration of his health required his transfer to the Presbyterian Hospital in Santurce. In November 1964 he was pardoned by the governor, and he died in April 1965.

In 1954, figures from across the political spectrum condemned the attack on Congress in statements made to the press. They reaffirmed their support for electoral and democratic institutions. It was not until the Pro-Independence Movement (MPI) claimed Albizu's figure as an emblem of the struggle for independence in the late 1960s that his name appeared again as one of the most revered figures of the new Puerto Rican Left.

The events of 1950 and 1954 placed new obstacles in the path of the Puerto Rican independence movement, which was attempting to convince people of the desirability and viability of independence. Although Albizu's image was later rehabilitated and he was regarded with affection and understanding, it was for a long time associated with acts of violence. A critical examination of the key texts produced by the pro-independence sectors since 1954 shows how difficult it is to reconcile the repeated commitment of its leadership to democratic processes on the one hand, and on the other, the idealization of armed struggle which was occasionally advocated by nationalist sectors.[15]

A similar tension is evident among other political sectors, who profess the same commitment to democracy but have periodically manifested civic and institutional intolerance toward the free exercise of political rights by the Independentistas.[16] Of special concern were the revelations in the late 1980s that tens of thousands of police files were kept on suspected independence supporters. Although in Puerto Rico most people believe that the island's destiny can only be determined freely and openly by Puerto Ricans themselves, there are still traces of intolerance and authoritarianism which hinder the open discussion of the constitutional process.

The Commonwealth Constitution of 1952

Ever since the period of military government that followed the U.S. invasion, the possibility had been raised of Puerto Rico having autonomous status within the United States, similar to that which it had under Spain in 1897–98. But that model of autonomy had long been considered as a transitional period to foster the growth and consolidation of political and economic institutions. Once this was achieved, Puerto Ricans would be in a position to opt for independence or statehood. After the approval of the Jones Act in 1918, the main obstacle to this type of self-government was seen to be the reluctance of the United States Congress to concede greater power to the Puerto Rican people.

Muñoz Marín was an independence supporter in the 1920s and the 1930s.[17] For many of his followers, postponing the issue of status during the 1940 and 1944 electoral campaigns did not mean that Muñoz had lost interest in independence. Instead it showed that he saw commitment to solving the island's socioeconomic problems as being of greater urgency.

After 1943 it was clear that Muñoz had regained his interest in the model of autonomy, not as a short-term constitutional transitional measure, but as a lasting political instrument. In 1946 this led him, along with Resident Commissioner Fernós Isern and other leaders of his party, to outline possible models of autonomy which had a chance of being approved by Congress and which would meet the immediate political needs. The approval in 1947 of the procedure which made the office of governor an elected one raised expectations that it would not be long before a constitution could be enacted. This should be a more ambitious statute than an organic act such as those of Foraker or Jones.

In 1950 Congress authorized the convocation of a constituent assembly in Puerto Rico. This assembly was elected in 1951. Most of its members were affiliated with the Popular Party and a minority represented the Republican Statehood and Socialist parties. The Independence Party did not wish to participate.

The Constituent Convention met from September 1951 to February 1952 and was headed by Antonio Fernós Isern. In a referendum held on March 3, 1952, the people of Puerto Rico approved the proposed constitution by a margin of 374,649 votes to 82,923.

The constitution met with opposition from various sectors in Congress. Vito Marcantonio, the most liberal of the New York City congressmen, opposed it because he favored independence for Puerto Rico.[18] Some southern congressmen opposed it because they believed that there were dangerous inclinations towards socialism in Puerto Rico. Others based their opposition on fears that the law enabling the Constitution implied that Congress was relinquishing its jurisdiction over Puerto Rico. Even those who supported the idea of statehood for Puerto Rico thought that the constitution would discourage statist sentiments on the island.[19]

The opposition gained two amendments, one weakening the Bill of Rights included in the constitution by excluding Section 20 on economic rights and another explicitly stating that any amendment to the constitution had to be consistent with the Constitution of the United States, the Federal Relations Act, and Law 600 of the 81st Congress.[20]

Estado Libre Asociado (Free Associated State) was the name given to the system of government in Puerto Rico after July 25, 1952. This formula for status ratified the concepts of self-government and permanent union with the United States. The constitution did not exclude the possibility of either independence or statehood, or the possible development of an autonomous status that consolidated self-government within a permanent union with the United States.

The "Peaceful" Decade, 1955–1965

Puerto Ricans were involved in the military campaigns in Korea from 1950 onward. On account of a technicality, this was never described as a war between the United States and its allies against the People's Republic of Korea and the People's Republic of China. The 65th Infantry Regiment from Puerto Rico distinguished itself during the retreat from the Yalu River under the heavy Chinese bombardment, while covering the retreat of other sectors of the United States Army. According to the armistice in 1954, the Korean War ended in stalemate. A line was drawn between North and South Korea, not too far from the 38th parallel, the original boundary of both jurisdictions.

The 65th Infantry Regiment returned to Puerto Rico after serving in Korea to be greeted with an impressive reception in San Juan harbor. The ending of the Korean War began a decade which subsequently became a period of nostalgia for many Puerto Ricans.[21] The economy was then in full expansion and there were positive signs of social mobility. The crime rate reached its lowest level since 1931.[22] Emigration to the United States had peaked in 1954 and had begun to fall. There was a degree of social order as a result of the new employment opportunities and the relatively high salaries in manufacturing as compared with agriculture. There were also opportunities for obtaining a university degree and moving up the social ladder and for achieving material goals. In general there was a feeling of success.

This apparent calm and contentment was also due to other factors. As the nature of production had changed, so the labor movement found itself in a transitional phase. The so-called "international" unions, based in the United States, dominated the new factories and enterprises. This meant that there were relatively few strikes.[23] An intensive program to relocate those on a low income to public housing gave the impression that the chronic shortages of housing in San Juan were being addressed.

In the rural areas, the *Program de Esfuerzo Propio y Ayuda Mutua* (Program of Self-Help and Mutual Aid) supported the construction of cement housing, the development of building skills, and the formation of rural communities. The most remote rural areas now had schools.[24] An intensive program of rural electrification eventually reached almost the entire population. The Aqueducts Authority sought to do the same with the water supply. A massive program to eradicate tuberculosis was beginning to produce satisfactory results.

In 1955 the Institute of Puerto Rican Culture was founded to promote cultural activities. The Board of Directors of this new institution chose the young archeologist Ricardo Alegría as its first executive director. In the following years the Institute supported the restoration of public and private buildings in the historic zone of San Juan and also the knowledge and preservation of artisans' skills, music, the plastic arts, literature, drama in all its forms, historical research, dance, and the study of folklore.

At the University of Puerto Rico, the chancellor, Jaime Benítez, and a dynamic group of administrators and advisors employed the talents of renowned visiting academics from Spain and Latin America to strengthen the humanities and science curricula. The poet Juan Ramón Jiménez, who taught at the University and lived in Puerto Rico, received the Nobel Prize for Literature in 1956. The University established its School of Medicine and extension programs in other Puerto Rican cities. Legislation passed in 1966 instituted a reform of the university, which had among its aims the management of the rapid growth of the institution. Under the guidance of the Council of Higher Education and the supervision of the university president, Benítez, there grew a system of university campuses, with a board of trustees and academic senates. From their inception the academic senates provided for representation for professors, and eventually for students.

During those years there was talk of a "peaceful revolution" in Puerto Rico, which had permitted a dramatic rise in income levels and had improved public health and education. The United States sponsored a program to allow foreign visitors to observe Puerto Rican social and economic programs. The Casals Festival, promoted by the government and directed by the Catalán cellist Pablo Casals, became world-renowned and drew classical music lovers to the island each year.

These visitors were soon followed by tens of thousands of tourists who came to the beaches of the San Juan area in search of sun and tranquility during the traditional U.S. winter holiday season. Spurred on by the success of the Caribe Hilton hotel, which was built in 1950, some hotel chains began to put up luxurious buildings in El Condado in Santurce and Isla Verde in Carolina. The tourism industry, which had been promoted for some time, now began to appear as one of the main providers of employment.

TABLE 14.3
Guests registered at hotels, 1950–1984

Year	Number of Registered Guests
1950	57,721
1960	207,638
1970	734,981
1975	778,366
1980	817,061
1984	637,944

Source: Planning Board of Puerto Rico, *Estadísticas socioeconómicas 1984*, pp. 7–8.

The Popular Party maintained its electoral lead throughout this period. From 1956 onward, the Puerto Rican Statehood Party replaced the Independence Party as the second party in general elections. The internal crises of the Independence Party and the regrouping of various independence sympathizers resulted in the foundation in 1958 of the Movement for Independence. This became known some thirteen years later as the Puerto Rican Socialist Party.

In 1960 there were ideological differences on the issue of religious education, which some groups wanted to introduce into the public school curriculum, and on government promotion of artificial contraception. The Catholic bishops of San Juan and Ponce denounced some of the points in the Popular Party's program. The upshot of this politico-religious debate was the foundation of the Christian Action Party.[25] This party gained the support of some religious sectors, especially the Catholics. It came in third in the 1960 elections, but was no longer a significant force by the elections of 1964.

Urban Issues

Industrialization and urban growth went hand in hand. In a relatively short space of time hundreds of thousands of Puerto Ricans came to own cars.

TABLE 14.4
Number of Motor Vehicles Registered on 30 June

Year	Vehicles
1940	26,847
1950	60,727
1960	179,657
1970	614,202
1975	773,742
1980	1,129,312
1984	1,227,000
	(approximate number)

Source: Planning Board of Puerto Rico, *Estadísticas Socioeconómicas, 1984*, pp. 9–10.

The unconscious goal of large sectors of the population was to own their own houses and cars. The housing developments that proliferated in the postwar era attracted many residents from the rural areas and also reduced population density in the old urban centers. A new lifestyle accompanied the suburban house and the car. The mall replaced the old shopping streets as the focus of economic activity. The workplace, rather than the place of residence, became, for many, the focus of friendship and social interaction.

From 1960 onward, the push towards urban life with its related values was also boosted by the extension of credit facilities and the huge diversity of consumer goods. The consumerist mentality that seized the country transformed old patterns of life.

The new society promoted greater educational and economic independence for the Puerto Rican woman.[26] Her lifestyle changed radically. She drove her own car, had her own bank account, formed associations or planned her own activities, and had access to a range of professional and academic careers.[27] The participation of women in politics was no longer symbolic or patronizing. Felisa Rincón, María Libertad Gómez, and María Arroyo had their own political power base. In the civic organizations, Clara Luz Vizcarrondo and other leaders headed the drive to serve the marginalized sectors of society. Nilita Vientós Gastón presided over the Ateneo Puertorriqueño and directed the literary journal *Asomante* (later called *Sin Nombre*). Margot Arce and Concha Meléndez were at the forefront of a literary renaissance at the university. Although Julía de Burgos obtained little recognition during her lifetime, she became known as one of Puerto Rico's foremost poets after her death in 1954 in New York. Celia Bunker established the Instituto de la Familia (Institute for the Family). Sister Isolina Ferré headed a successful community project in Playa de Ponce, which was later replicated elsewhere. Many other women ran their own businesses or farms, assumed leadership roles in labor unions, distinguished themselves as judges, in research, in public administration, and in the field of communications and the world of show business. In the year 2000, Sila María Calderón became the first woman governor of Puerto Rico.

The Impact of the Cuban Revolution in Puerto Rico

The debate around the Cuban revolution of 1959 has influenced political behavior in Puerto Rico in a number of ways. The initial reaction to the victory of Fidel Castro and his bearded revolutionaries from the July 26th Movement was one of jubilation and solidarity. In an editorial on January 2, 1959, *El Mundo*, the conservative daily newspaper, expressed joy at the ending of civil conflict in Cuba and the collapse of Fulgencio Batista's corrupt regime.

Some time later the media began to express negative reactions. The arrival on the island of exiled Cubans not affiliated with the former Cuban regime,[28] the growing distance between the churches and the revolutionaries, the ending of relations between the United States and Cuba, and the formalization of the Marxist-Leninist nature of the new government all had an impact on public opinion in Puerto Rico.

But while many in government, business, the churches, and the field of education in Puerto Rico were largely opposed to the political changes in Cuba, the new pro-independence generation that was entering the political fray began to find affinities with the theoretical approaches and the public positions adopted by the Cuban government. A pro-independence Left, which sympathized with liberation struggles in the Third World and which was identified with the labor movement and the new student movements protesting against military service and institutional paternalism, coalesced around figures such as Juan Mari Brás, Juan Antonio Corretjer, and Rubén Berríos.

After the death of its founding president Gilberto Concepción de Gracia, there was a difficult generational transition within the Puerto Rican Independence Party. For some time several tendencies co-existed within the party, but after various shifts Rubén Berríos consolidated his hold on the party. Until the 1972 elections this new phase of the Independence Party was marked by socialism that adopted Marxist rhetoric. Following a period of painful internal struggles, after 1973 the PIP moved towards the center of the political spectrum and emphasized its ideological distance from the Cuban regime.[29]

But if the PIP avoided identification with Cuba, the Movement for Independence (PSP, or Puerto Rican Socialist Party after 1971) used its widely-read weekly, *Claridad*, and its public activities in its attempt to identify with the successes of the Cuban Revolution. While the Revolution was in its ascendant phase, and the moral prestige of Ernesto "Che" Guevara captivated the youth of the Americas, the PSP exploited this in its affiliated youth organizations, FUPI and FEPI, and in labor militancy. Thus it became the most vocal mouthpiece of the new protest movements.

The Vietnam War

President Lyndon Johnson won easily over his Republican opponent, Senator Barry Goldwater of Arizona, in the 1964 elections. A key factor in this victory was the electoral promise he made not to escalate U.S. intervention in the war waged by the Vietcong against the government of South Vietnam in southeastern Asia. But in the summer of 1965 it was evident that, in order to avoid the collapse of its ally in Saigon, the United States government was ready to intervene on a large scale in a war which was never declared and which was not supported by Congress.

The mobilization of North American troops in southeast Asia had the immediate effect of reactivating compulsory military service in Puerto Rico. Between 1965 and 1975, tens of thousands of Puerto Ricans undertook military tours of duty in Vietnam. The frustration of a war that did not enjoy widespread support in the United States, and in which Vietnamese civilians were at times an ally and at times the target of military operations, disillusioned many Puerto Rican soldiers. When they returned to civilian life, these former combatants, in different ways, showed a reluctance to be identified with Vietnam. On the other hand, there were soldiers who accepted U.S. military policy in its various stages of intervention, vietnamization, and disengagement, but this did not make them derive any satisfaction from their experience in Vietnam.

Although in the United States, opposition to the military escalation in southeast Asia united people and organizations of different political tendencies and from different backgrounds, public opinion in Puerto Rico was much more restrained. It was among sectors on the left that there was large-scale overt opposition to the war. Among other sectors, only some figures, like the Representative Benny Frankie Cerezo from the New Progressive Party, spoke out against the war, and then at some considerable political risk.

The 1967 Plebiscite

The leaders of the Popular Democratic Party were dissatisfied with the limited autonomy offered by the Commonwealth Constitution of 1952. They sought legislation which would develop autonomous status to its fullest extent. Approaches to Washington were channeled through Resident Commissioner Fernós Isern, who in 1959 pressed for the approval of the Fernós-Murray bill, which was not passed by Congress. An agreement between Governor Muñoz Marín and President John F. Kennedy resulted in dialogue aimed at achieving the constitutional adjustments that were considered necessary. A joint commission of North Americans and Puerto Ricans was selected, the Status Commission, which held public hearings in Puerto Rico.[30]

Muñoz had left the governorship after the 1964 elections, but he recommended a plebiscite in which the three alternative forms of status were presented. The Popular leadership nurtured hopes that the mandate obtained in the referendum would allow them to seek the hoped-for achievement of autonomy in Congress.

The Puerto Rican Independence Party announced its decision not to take part in the plebiscite in support of the independence model. The Republican Statehood Party was split. Its president, Miguel Angel García Méndez, and an important group of its officials refused to take part in the referendum to uphold the model of statehood. Nevertheless, Luis Ferré, gubernatorial candidate for that party in the elections of 1956, 1960, and 1964, agreed to participate. To that end, along with numerous civic leaders, he founded an organization called United Statehooders (Estadistas Unidos).[31]

In the plebiscite held in July 1967, the commonwealth model obtained the backing of 60% of voters, while statehood received 39% of the vote and fewer than 1% signaled their preference for independence.[32] The figures were interpreted in different ways. The Populares claimed that they had the necessary mandate. Those who supported statehood were jubilant because their model had triumphed in Ponce, Cataño, San Lorenzo, Corozal and several precincts in San Juan. They saw the results as a foretaste of their first victory against the Populares. And for the *independentistas*, the massive abstention of their supporters indicated the strength of their party's discipline.

After the plebiscite, both the Republican Statehood Party and the Populares suffered internal divisions. The militants among the United Statehooders decided to found a different statehood party, which they named the New Progressive Party (NPP). Between August 1967 and the general election of 1968, this new party was able to attract the vast majority of the former members of the Statehood Party, as well as unaffiliated voters and people who had previously voted for the Populares.

There was competition among the Populares for the gubernatorial nomination as a result of a disagreement between Roberto Sánchez Vilella, Muñoz's successor, and members of the legislature. A sizable number of Populares opted to channel their political aspirations and their desire for internal democracy within their party into a new political party. Governor Sánchez Vilella and his followers joined the People's Party, which had been previously been registered with a different political orientation.

These political divisions diverted attention away from the results of the plebiscite and centered all expectations on the 1968 elections in which the New Progressive Party won the governorship, the House of Representatives, and twenty-four municipalities, mainly those with the largest populations.

The Bipartisan Era

The governorship of Luis Ferré (1969–73) initiated a period during which two powerful political parties, the New Progressives and the Populares, competed for the exercise of authority at both the national and the municipal levels.[33] The Populares found it hard to learn how to share the responsibility which they had held unchallenged for such a long time. But this institutionalized exercise of authority generated a greater awareness that the functions of the legislative and executive branches of the government are different, and there was a greater capacity to reconcile positions through intense negotiation.

This capacity was most severely tested after the 1980 and the 2004 elections in which the governor and the legislative majorities were chosen from different parties.

Perhaps even more important than the parties' alternation in power was the strengthening of the media. The need to go beyond press releases and press conferences inspired investigative and critical reporting. Reporters from the radio, television, and the press have continually monitored political and civil life.

In the short run, the competition between the leading parties resulted in an inescapable sense of the politicization of every aspect of social life. But once the initial stages of excessive favoritism and partisanship had passed, the increasingly energetic discussion of all public matters made successive governments more responsive to public opinion and more inclined to provide as much information as possible about their operations.

Continual demands by the media and the opposition parties for accountability from the government encouraged civic groups to make their problems and aspirations public, in the expectation that this would immediately attract public attention. For example, citizens' groups concerned about health hazards in public schools, environmental groups lobbying for the regulation of emissions or protesting about deforestation, and university students pressing their specific demands all learned to contact the media and explain the issues to the whole country.

The fact that the various communities and civic groups continually express their needs and issues in the media may mean that the political debate on the island has tended to revolve more around the nature and scope of public services than around alternative models of political status. This shift in focus from the status debate reflects the main political parties' competition for the vital support of the increasingly non-partisan middle class, which supports some candidates in one election and others in the next. In 1968, the differences in the composition of the militant sectors of the parties were more evident than in 2005. In 1968 the NPP had the most support among the young and in the urban areas, while the Populares' support base was stronger among older people and in the rural areas.[34] Four decades later, the situation is much more complex, with the northern part of the island supporting the statehooders and the southern part the commonwealthers, but the latter predominate in the governor's election results in four out of the five largest cities. More significantly, the background of the political leaders has tended to become more uniform in terms of profession, place of abode, and political style.

On the other hand, the ending of the era of rapid economic growth after the 1973–74 oil crisis was reflected in the stagnant job market and increased dependency on Federal fund transfers.[35] In 1976 the federal Food Stamp program was instituted on the island and more than half of Puerto Rican families were provided with a regular basic diet. The federal plans for housing subsidies and Medicare for the elderly fulfilled many needs and expectations. These developments served to center the political debate on the quality of government services. The status debate fell into the background once more.

By the beginning of the twenty-first century there was less consensus in Puerto Rico about the kind of political status preferred for the island. However, the two main political parties had a more common view as to which basic public services the government should provide and what part the government should play in fostering economic growth. By skirting the issue of status, a matter that profoundly divides Puerto Ricans, the political leaders have made socioeconomic problems their priority on the political agenda.

The Maravilla Case

The so-called "Maravilla" case dominated the campaigns of the elections of 1980 and 1984.[36] On July 15, 1978, two young pro-independence militants, Arnaldo Darío Rosado and Carlos Soto Arriví, died on Maravilla mountain at the hands of the Puerto Rican police. These young men, along with an undercover police agent, had forced Julio Ortíz Molina, the driver of a collective taxi, to take them to the mountain. According to the testimony of the undercover agent they were planning to sabotage the communications installations there.

In the 1980 campaign, it was alleged that the young men had surrendered when they found themselves surrounded by police and that they had later been killed. That version circulated widely but was not corroborated. When the Populares gained control of the Senate in the 1980 elections, Miguel Hernández Agosto, Senate president, and Francisco Aponte Pérez, president of the Senate's Juridical Commission, succeeded in having the Senate initiate a thorough investigation into the incident. A young lawyer, Héctor Rivera Cruz, charged by Aponte with leading the investigation, was able to gather numerous testimonies and carry out cross-examinations during the public hearings which were televised in 1983. Rivera Cruz was able to show that Rosado and Soto Arriví had been executed by the agents involved who had committed perjury in their initial statements.

The Maravilla case held the public's attention for several months and the dramatic outcome of the hearings profoundly touched the collective sentiment. Subsequent attempts to prove that the agents were acting on instructions from above failed.

Puerto Rico and the 936 Clause

After the rapid rise in the cost of energy in 1973–74, the economic model based on the development of manufacturing faced serious problems in Puerto Rico.[37] In 1976 it was believed that a solution had been found with the implementation of the so-called clause 936 of the U.S. Internal Revenue Code. According to that clause, profits made by North American companies based in overseas territories of the United States could be repatriated free of tax.

While this disposition was in force, significant amounts of capital flowed into the banks established in Puerto Rico. According to the economist Eliezer Curet, there were more than 5 billion dollars in 936 funds in 1982, and by 1996 they had reached 10.6 billion dollars.[38] The banking sector experienced unprecedented growth in the following years. But the expectation that the 936 funds would generate many more jobs through long term investment in Puerto Rican industry did not materialize. Instead, the available funds went into consumption and very few factories were built or developed using the capital generated by the "936" firms.

The deficit in the Federal budget led the United States Congress to re-examine the operation of clause 936. As there was little evidence that this mechanism had fostered the growth of employment, some Congressmen insisted that the clause be amended to make those companies' funds liable to taxation. Some amendments were introduced in the mid-1980s to avoid the more obvious abuses. Although under Governor Rafael Hernández Colón, Puerto Rico lobbied to retain clause 936, Congress abrogated it in 1996, but gave a ten-year transition period before the full implementation of the changes.

CHAPTER 15

Changes in Perceptions and Values from the 1960s to 2005

In Latin America as well as in the United States, the decade of the 1960s was characterized by an extreme clash between generations and mentalities. The proportion of young people in the total population had risen in almost all Western societies. Millions of those born after the Second World War reached university age just as the old institutions and ways of thinking were beginning to give way.

The Second World War had accelerated the displacement of the former European elites. In Great Britain the postwar Labor government had significantly increased taxation on inheritance and real estate and had nationalized large-scale enterprises and the health service. In other countries a greater rationalization of financial and economic systems had resulted in a questioning of the old structures of privilege. The generation that grew up under the shadow of debates on the outmoded nature of the old orders and styles developed its own criteria about the social norms that they considered should remain.

The music of the British group the Beatles was in various ways symbolic of the generation gap. Not only did the rhythms and lyrics defy convention, but the place of music in daily life was also important. The proliferation of radios and portable cassette players meant that the young were able to go about their daily routines while listening to their favorite music. In earlier times people had stopped their activities in order to listen to instrumental music; now it was the normal background to their usual pursuits.[1] Along with lively and rebellious music, the youth also favored hairstyles and clothes that were strikingly different from those of previous generations.

The defiant sound of the new rock music was not the only way in which the youth challenged the established order. The production line method of manufacturing motor vehicles had put cars within reach of all incomes. Many young people in the 1960s aspired to buy their own automobile, even if it had been owned several times before. Continual mobility, like the nonstop music, offered a freedom of action that was not always guaranteed by the actual possibilities of economic production and social struggles. The car was turned into a quasi-cultic object, painted, fixed up, and even upholstered to reflect the fantasies and aspirations of its driver. It came to be a loud signifier of youth counterculture.[2]

The popularity of artificial methods of birth control, especially the contraceptive pill, launched a revolution in sexual relations. Efforts to maintain the old codes of conduct in Latin America, whereby a single woman was always chaperoned, clashed with the constant images from the movies, television, and advertising which showed the unchaperoned young woman perfectly at ease in the presence of a young man. The new mobility of the youth, combined with the media's indifference to the former sexual mores and the secularization of individual morality, encouraged experimentation. Homosexuals, who had long been excluded from mainstream consideration, rebelled against the prevailing prejudices. They experienced a degree of tolerance, initially in a few societies, and then in most

Western ones. Time and again the adherence to a different sexual morality resulted in confrontations between parents and children, authorities and students, and between lay people and the representatives of the churches and religious communities.

On the other hand, from the 1960s onward, young people confronted their governments with generational demands. These included the abolition of compulsory military service in the United States. In France it was the democratization of public education, in Czechoslovakia it was the liberalization of social life, in Mexico it was the ending of corrupt administration, and in Japan, respect for the environment. Young Argentinians were pushing for political liberalization, and in China, the youth sought the eradication of inherited class consciousness. These confrontations met with repressive measures in Argentina, Czechoslovakia, and Mexico. As a reaction to repression or harrassment, clandestine armed struggles emerged in West Germany, Italy, and the Basque Country. The battle between the generations, in its political form, sometimes led to the modification of regulations and constitutions. Thus the voting age was lowered to 18 years in many countries and the age for occupying elected office was also lowered. Other countries recognized 18 as the age of majority. Some countries also facilitated the financing of university studies, modified the system of compulsory military service by offering the option of community service, and agreed to include student or youth representatives on the governing boards of universities, city councils, and legislatures.

As consumers, the young defined themselves as a new and vigorous market which tested the imaginative resources of advertisers. The adjective "young" became a must for any item aimed at a wide market. Public relations agencies assumed the new styles of the youth counterculture. Soon trends which had developed spontaneously became jumbled together with those designed to target the market. The same rhythms and color schemes that denounced militarism were used to sell soap, deodorants, or presidential candidates.[3]

The aspirations of young people to a new lifestyle were also threatened by the association of addictive drugs with the counterculture of the 1960s.[4] In their eagerness to experiment with whatever was forbidden and to defy convention, many young people became trapped into chemical or psychological dependency on illegal substances. Rapidly coming into conflict with the authorities, the young addict was forced to steal or mug people in order to maintain a habit that was expensive because it was illegal. Powerful drug traffickers set up businesses in the greater urban and industrial world centers. By means of their vulnerable intermediaries, recruited among the youth, they sponsored multimillion-dollar smuggling operations which undermined the official economy in several countries.

In Puerto Rico all of this had an effect on the 60s generation and it also modified the prevailing attitudes and outlook. There were the predictable struggles over rock music, long hair and short skirts, and the rejection of the established social norms. But the importance of the youth phenomenon was underscored by the energy of the student struggles to alter university structures, the rejection of compulsory military service and the Vietnam War, and the desire to solve the problem of status in the short term. The student movement, however, was out of step with similar movements in Latin America, Europe, and the United States. In the case of Puerto Rico its most important manifestations, such as student strikes, marches, protests, publications, and associations, reached their peak between 1969 and 1982, somewhat later than the countries named above.

The Struggle for Housing

Even more important than the confrontations with the establishment over the demands of their generation was the participation of the youth in social campaigns. One of the most pressing problems in Puerto Rico at the end of the 1960s was that of housing for low-income families.[5] The proliferation of cars and suburban development had resulted in urban sprawl. The time came when workers and the unemployed found that there were not enough low-cost housing units near urban workplaces. The price of land in the suburbs had risen so much that it was now beyond the reach of workers.

Urban renewal programs had been clearing the old neighborhoods where so many people who had recently arrived from the countryside had their first experience of urban living. The existing shantytowns in Santurce, Hato Rey, Ponce, and Cataño were an all-too-visible sign of the country's serious economic and social ills. Therefore, successive governments yielded, perhaps too easily, to the temptation to eradicate them and transfer the residents to public housing. By doing this, they broke up the old residential communities. Families with higher incomes did not live permanently in public housing. However, these were the families that had, on many occasions, provided stability and continuity in the old communities. Old people were relocated to places where their experience and contacts were no longer of any use. Moving meant that people were separated from the churches and the schools where they knew community leaders and were known to them. The final result of dispersing these so-called slums was that it became difficult for families to develop new social ties and solidarity in public housing. For example, the strength of religious and civic groups and the importance of other ties of solidarity are more evident in the older public housing than in the new.

TABLE 15.1

Number and value of new units of housing, according to construction permits, 1950–1984

Year	Private Sector		Public Sector*	
	No. of Permits	Average unit value	No. of Permits	Average Unit Value
1950	5,777	$8,887.65	276	$128,358.49
1960	8,951	10,728.63	472	75,995.76
1970	12,549	16,468.43	276	419,108.70
1975	5,422	43,276.46	397	398,090.68
1980	6,259	44,052.24	169	797,514.79
1984	4,419	55,927.13	291	499,323.02

*Note: In general, the public sector's housing consists of multi-family units.
Source: Junta de Planificación de Puerto Rico,
Estadísticas socioeconómicas 1984, pp. 5–6.

As the old neighborhoods disappeared, many families who needed housing at the end of the 1960s occupied vacant land near Carolina, Caguas, Rio Grande, Vega Baja, Ponce and Loiza. Shantytowns were traditional on the island. There was already in the seventeenth century one near el Morro which eventually became known as La Perla.[6] But the founders of the new settlements discovered that the government did not approve of the occupation of land and the construction of housing on lots already designated by planners for other uses or which were vulnerable to flooding. For a time it seemed as if the government found it easier to reiterate its prohibitions and escalate its penalties against the "liberators of land" than to find solutions for the housing problem. In some cases the government had to accept new neighborhoods such as Villa Justicia in Carolina, or Punta Diamante in Ponce. In other cases it sought alternatives such as the restoration of the old urban centers. By the 1990s the problem had eased, but the high cost of construction made it more difficult for young couples to obtain their own homes.

Food Stamps

The old agrarian order vanished rapidly in the 1960s and 1970s. Several consecutive years of drought in the 1960s compounded the problems of farmers and cattlemen. The gradual consolidation of the sugar *centrales* led to the foundation of the Sugar Corporation and state incorporation of most of the remaining *centrales*. A long span of years with low coffee prices accelerated the disappearance of many coffee farms. The coffee that was still produced by 1980 (256,000 hundredweights) came from small and middle-sized farms in a few coffee- growing districts. Tobacco production fell rapidly. By 1980, production (21,000 hundredweight) was limited to some isolated wards in the center and northwest of the island.[7] Sugarcane fields were increasingly only found in some parts of the south.

The disappearance of commercial agriculture left hundreds of thousands of people who had depended on their harvests without a fixed income. Former tobacco processing centers like Comerío were

TABLE 15.2

Sugarcane harvested in Puerto Rico, by thousands of tons, 1940–1984

Year	Thousands of Tons
1940	1,019
1950	1,286
1960	1,006
1970	453
1975	299
1980	175
1984	96

Source: Junta de Planificación de Puerto Rico,
Estadísticas socioeconómicas 1984, pp. 7–8

not able to develop industrial plants, nor create the number of jobs needed to compensate for those lost in the workshops and on the farms that had disappeared. The marked difference in salaries between the manufacturing and agricultural sectors discouraged people from working in the coffee harvests.

By the beginning of the 1970s it was clear that living conditions in districts like Maunabo, Arroyo, and Jayuya, where industrialization had made little progress, were close to collapse.[8] The death from starvation of a girl in San Lorenzo caused a scandal. The former welfare programs of the island government did not meet the needs of the marginal sectors, for whom the achievements of the industrialization program had not meant a significant improvement in their lives. On the other hand, textile factories and other low-tech enterprises were beginning to withdraw from the island as their financial incentives lapsed. In 1973, the former governor Luis Muñoz Marín began to talk about the need for a new social revolution:

Its economic progress has placed Puerto Rico among the leading countries of the world. In terms of what we have done with this progress we are stuck at the level of the unjust and confused world that surrounds us. . . . We increased the creation of wealth twenty-fold . . . but the improvement has not been as noticeable as it should be on account of the unjust way in which that production is distributed among Puerto Ricans. We can say that there has been a change from poverty exacerbated by the unjust way that whatever was scarce was shared out, to a prosperity which challenges us by the unjust way that wealth is distributed.[9]

The debate in the media did not provide a short-term solution to the hunger that was reappearing among the marginalized sectors of the island. On behalf of those sectors, Resident Commissioners Jorge Luis Córdova Díaz and Jaime Benítez succeeded in having Puerto Rico included in the Nutritional Assistance Plan. This federal program provided low-income families who qualified with a monthly sum of money to purchase food. In the first years in which the Plan was in force, the amount was assigned in food stamps which could be redeemed in grocery stores and supermarkets. Later it was changed to checks.

Food stamps were a short-term solution. Few people believed at the time that they would become a permanent and necessary component of the family budget of most Puerto Ricans. Unfortunately, the ills they were intended to address became more acute. The dismantling of light industry was followed by the collapse of the petrochemical industry. Commercial agriculture was disappearing. Thus a large sector of the population became even more dependent on food stamps.

The former reliance on credit at the old neighborhood grocery store declined with the food stamps. Supermarkets were given a boost by the new spending power of the masses, and their influence modified the traditional Creole diet. At the same time, the food stamp program did not stimulate Puerto Rican commercial agriculture, as had been hoped.

Some critics have pointed out that the inability of the food stamp program to fuel productivity was a bad omen and that the program can lead to perpetual dependency.[10] Instead of stimulating the consumption of what the land produces, food stamp income has

TABLE 15.3

**Participants in the Nutritional Assistance Plan,
1977–78 to 1983–84**

Fiscal Year	Families Participating	Cost of the Program
1977–78	397,133	$869,144,997
1978–79	439,058	821,703,784
1979–80	493,179	810,562,153
1980–81	492,932	851,281,661
1981–82	506,248	893,614,414
1982–83	433,987	780,184,214
1983–84	412,645	776,143,510

Source: Junta de Planificación de Puerto Rico,
Compendio de Estadísticas Sociales 1984, p. 103.

increased the preference for imported food, especially fast foods. On the other hand, the social cost of reducing the number of beneficiaries has been evident. Even then, there are those who advocate phasing out food checks, but their arguments are not convincing. It would be unjust to cancel them in order to provide cheap labor for landholders. How to rescue Puerto Rican agriculture from its inertia without once again subjecting the masses to a degrading work regime is one of the main problems in Puerto Rico today.

The New World of the Universities

The rise in the number of jobs in the service sector prompted the hope that a university education would enable people to obtain work. The extension to Puerto Rico of the Federal Pell grants (Basic Educational Opportunity Grants, or BEOG) saw a dramatic increase in the number of university students and an unprecedented expansion in enrollment at private universities.

TABLE 15.4

**Numbers of University Students Enrolled in Puerto Rico,
1940–1984**

Year	University of Puerto Rico	Private Universities	Total Number
1940	4,987	384	5,371
1950	11,348	1,286	12,634
1960	18,223	6,306	24,529
1970	37,839	19,499	57,338
1975	52,055	44,259	96,314
1980	50,837	79,268	130,105
1984	53,816	106,156	159,972

Source: Junta de Planificación de Puerto Rico,
Estadísticas Socioeconómicas, 1984, pp. 9–10.

Attending university delays entry into the job market and in general it doubles the chances of obtaining work. In 1986 it was reckoned that 22% of the population was unemployed but only 11% of university graduates were actively seeking work. University studies also provide a space for critical reflection and socializing outside the home. It is within that context that a particular lifestyle developed in the university residential areas.

This new university world was accompanied by the *nueva canción*. The cafe-theater flourished. In the 1970s and 1980s, the different styles and messages of Roy Brown, Wilkins, Haciendo Punto en Otro Son, Moliendo Vidrio, Lucecita Benítez, Danny Rivera, Antonio Cabán Vale "El Topo," Glenn Monroig, and Tony Croato all offered access to a world which was not known at first hand. They had the attraction of poetry that is almost never read aloud in a classroom, and which causes a stir outside university concert halls or the crowds of young people in outdoor concerts. The same was true of the new style of satire of Los Rayos Gamma and Benigno Orante and the new popular theater.[11] The new and irreverent narrative works of Luis Rafael Sánchez, Ana Lydia Vega, Carmen Lugo Filippi, Magali García

Ramis, Edgardo Rodríguez Juliá, Rosario Ferré, Mayra Santos and others who keep those who think in declarative sentences awake, also found a niche there. A suitable environment for all this creativity is provided by the universities where people have come to knock on the doors of the former cultural establishment.

It is there, perhaps, that the country is also best able to re-encounter and celebrate itself.

CHAPTER 16

From Alternation in Power to Shared Government, 1980–2005

Economic Alternatives

In the 1990s it became clear that the strategy of boosting the economy by promoting North American and foreign investment in the manufacturing sector had become obsolete. The inclusion of Mexico in the North American Free Trade Agreement with the United States and Canada gave an advantage to Mexico. North American factories were based in Mexico as the free entry of their products into the American market and lower wages made it more attractive to investors. In any case, the globalization of the economy meant that many American enterprises extended their manufacturing centers in Asia. Only the pharmaceutical companies maintained their substantive long-range commitment to the Puerto Rican economy.

In the face of these changes in manufacturing opportunities, there was an imperative need for alternative routes to the development of the Puerto Rican economy. The need for a new model of economic development was discussed at the same time as neoliberal sectors in the United States and Latin America were advocating government divestment of public corporations. The idea was broached that Puerto Rico would become more competitive in marketing its tourist amenities and services if the infrastructure was radically improved. In order to finance these improvements and to fund the long-range overhaul of education, the government had to sell the state-owned Puerto Rico Telephone Company.

Although this had first been attempted under Governor Rafael Hernández Colón in 1990, the sale of La Telefónica was not actually carried out until the mid-1990s under Governor Pedro Rosselló. Because the sale was fiercely opposed by labor militants and by a wide range of sectors, only half of the stocks were initially sold, and a tiny portion was reserved for the employees. Eventually, the government completed the sale under Governor Sila Calderón. Other government assets were also disposed of, most notably the shipping company Navieras de Puerto Rico, and the pineapple juice company, Lotus, which dated from the 1940s. The militant union of the publicly-owned energy company, Autoridad de Energía Eléctrica, has remained vigilant against any attempt to privatize this government asset.

Much of the infrastructure built in the 1990s was intended to make the metropolitan area of San Juan more modern and convenient. The reservoir of the Río Grande de Arecibo was tapped and an impressive system for water conveyance was built to supply the new suburban housing on the north coast. The initial phase of an urban railway connecting San Juan and Bayamón was opened in 2005. It will eventually link Carolina and other towns. A stadium capable of holding 35,000 spectators opened in late 2004. It was named after the late José Miguel Agrelot, a popular actor and comedian. A new expressway linking San Juan to Fajardo was temporarily halted by environmental concerns, but was eventually approved and completed. A new convention center was built near the old Isla Grande airport in Santurce.

Social Concerns

Surveys taken over the last three decades of public opinion about Puerto Ricans' primary concerns always place crime at the top, closely followed by drugs. Both problems are generally seen as closely related. The homicide rates rose steadily throughout the 1970s and 1980s and did not fall significantly in the first years of the twenty-first century, as has happened in the main cities of the United States. The general consensus is that drug consumption has not decreased. Puerto Rico has become a stopover on the cocaine trafficking route between Colombia and the United States, but it is heroin addiction that has become prevalent among drug users.

As public insecurity about these issues grew, so did calls to close off access to the middle- and upper-class suburban areas. In the 1990s the Legislature authorized neighborhood associations to take charge of their own security. These associations built walls around the housing developments, hired private guards, and controlled the traffic on their streets. By acknowledging that it could not protect the citizens, the state had recognized that it did not govern its own streets.

Instead, the state used diversion tactics to conceal its own weakness. In the 1990s, under Governor Pedro Rosselló, the government staged well-publicized raids on public housing units, especially in the metropolitan area of San Juan. These places were identified as drug distribution centers and were put under permanent surveillance by the police and units of the National Guard. The result, however, was that the drug distribution centers, popularly called *puntos*, spread throughout the island. What had been largely a problem of the major urban centers now became widespread.

Some tentative attempts have been made to deal with the central issue of drug addiction, mainly through treating addicts with substitute legal drugs. But the enormous profits from the illegal drug trade fuel the gangs' open warfare and drive the recruitment of new addicts.

While the government was publicizing its efforts to control the sale of illegal drugs and reduce crime, a wave of government corruption cases hit the media. The corruption was partly linked to political fundraising efforts. The skyrocketing costs of campaigning and the three referenda held in the 1990s had required an enormous outlay of funds by the political parties. In an attempt to address this situation, legislation was enacted to provide public funds for the political parties and to control private donations. Some observers were not convinced that this would be effective.

Another concern that repeatedly surfaced in the media was domestic violence. Increased awareness of the need to protect the victims of abuse led to the enactment of Law 54, which provided mechanisms for the reporting, regulation, and prosecution of such cases. But the problem has not diminished, either because people are now less reluctant to mention specific cases in public, or because changes in the workplace, where women have become more evident, have not yet been accompanied by new ways of running the household and settling conjugal differences. Some critics, notably Trina Rivera de Ríos, have argued that family courts should be given greater powers and flexibility to deal with these cases.

New Cultural Movements

With the proliferation of the use of personal computers and access to the internet, instant and constant contact with cultural movements abroad have become common. On the popular level this has resulted in the ready adoption or abandonment of music and lifestyles as soon as they appear on or disappear from global markets. The globalization of cinema and show business icons has created an instant following on the island. On the other hand, there is greater awareness of issues and problems beyond the immediate concerns of the island population. Young people are more interested than previous generations in travel and in seeing the world glimpsed on their screens. The ultimate consequences of this insertion into the new global culture and its market remain to be seen.

Among academics there has also been a readier integration into the debates and projects of their peers elsewhere. Of particular interest is the impact of European trends in literary and philosophical crit-

icism. A lively debate on the constructions of Puerto Rican identity[1] has sparked an interest in re-reading and discussing the writings of authors like Antonio S. Pedreira, José Luis González, and Tomás Blanco, who attempted to define the main features of the Puerto Rican character. The challenge to the entrenched canon of the 1930s generation and its heirs has also provoked a heated defense of the hallowed values of Puerto Rican nationality.[2]

Peace for Vieques

One issue that created surprising consensus in the 1990s was the continued use of the island of Vieques by the U.S. Navy for target practice and joint exercises with naval and military units from other countries. The accidental death of a naval employee during one of those exercises sparked furious protests. The grounds of the naval base were occupied by militants and the Navy was forced to suspend exercises for a time. Governor Pedro Rosselló negotiated a staged withdrawal of the Navy from Vieques with President Clinton's administration. A huge march along the expressway in Hato Rey, the largest public demonstration in Puerto Rican history, demonstrated general rejection of the island's continued use for military exercises. Of crucial importance was the support given by Puerto Rican communities in the United States to the "Peace for Vieques" movement. Many militants, including prominent figures from all three political parties, such as the PIP president Rubén Berríos, Carolina mayor José Aponte, and NPP senator Norma Burgos, were arrested and spent time in Federal detention centers for acts of civil disobedience challenging the resumption of the bombing. However, in the end, President George W. Bush honored President Clinton's commitment and the Navy withdrew from Vieques. The Federal government also closed down Roosevelt Roads, the naval base in Ceiba. This led to severe economic hardship in the eastern part of the island. One issue that is still outstanding is the promised Federal removal of the military debris on the islands of Vieques and Culebra.

From Twentieth- to Twenty-First-Century Politics

The growth and expansion of the federal government in the second half of the twentieth century resulted in the erosion of commonwealth self-government. Whereas in the United States this development was generally welcomed by liberals, in Puerto Rico it has challenged the premises and assumptions of all political groups.

Independence supporters are pessimistic because they believe that unless Puerto Rico acts now to reclaim its sovereignty, it will soon be encompassed in the growing morass of federal legislation, regulations, and monitoring. Commonwealth supporters are critical because they see the encroachment of federal jurisdiction as the negation of the autonomous state that they envisage, similar to those found in Catalonia, Wales, and elsewhere in Europe. Most proponents of statehood are not happy either, because the premise they have taken for granted all along, that full incorporation into the American union would not destroy that which is peculiar and proper to the Puerto Ricans, loses credibility in face of the all-powerful federal government.

While status politics still formally mark the boundaries of electoral allegiance, recent elections have demonstrated a significant willingness by voters to cross over and choose candidates over parties. Although the Independence Party barely gathers 3% of the votes cast for governor, its at-large candidates for the Senate and the legislature regularly top the list with upwards of 150,000 votes each. But the traffic also runs in the other direction. In the 2004 elections, the support of pro-independence voters was crucial for the narrow victory of Aníbal Acevedo Vilá as governor. Also important was the reluctance of some twelve thousand statehooders to vote for their party's gubernatorial candidate, although they readily endorsed the nominee for Resident Commissioner, Luis Fortuño. In Carolina, the Popular candidate for mayor, José Aponte, has won the elections regularly since 1984, although statehooders constitute the majority of the electorate. In Bayamón it is the NPP candidate, Ramón Luis Rivera, Jr., who benefits from the crossover vote from the Populares. Similar electoral preferences have been observed in other municipalities. Voters

seemed to be less concerned about the options for status than about good management and administration. General election figures are not necessarily a reliable indication of status allegiances.

Pluralism in Puerto Rico

It is hard to find a subject that does not provoke divisions among Puerto Ricans today. Even the Puerto Rican flag, which should be a symbol of harmony and unity, is sometimes flown in a display of exclusiveness, rejection, and ethnocentric self-affirmation. A nation's symbols should signify unity rather than division. However, as so often happens, as part of the struggle to establish a people's unity, those elements that are considered representative of the common identity are affirmed so repeatedly that, in the end, it becomes difficult to admit that there is room for diversity in unity. If you have made the religious practice of the majority a key to the identity of a people, it then becomes difficult to concede that religious minorities are also part of the nation. That is the challenge for some modern nations such as Egypt, Sri Lanka, and Russia. If you have defined as part of the national identity the use of only one language, as Spain did in the recent past, you undermine efforts to unite under the same flag those who speak different languages. Unity does not mean uniformity but rather community of purpose. In order to achieve this one must guarantee that every sector of society has the respect and equality needed for the pursuit of happiness. One of the most neglected aspects of the historical formation of a Puerto Rican collective identity has been precisely this failure to pay due attention to the plurality of our experience as a people. In the rush to produce a narrative of our past which affirms some common values and achievements, we have forgotten to also give space to those particular expressions and alternative experiences which have impelled our development as a people.

It is the diversity of our ancestors that helps to account for the wealth and complexity of our culture. If we take pride in Roberto Clemente-Walker or Bernie Williams, we must acknowledge that the

Eastern Caribbean, place of origin of some of their forefathers, has a share in the formation of our nation. If we celebrate Hollywood actors José Ferrer or Raúl Juliá we must remember that Catalonia also nurtured us. Governor Jesús Piñero reminds us that we must remember the immigrants from the Canary Islands. Just as Betances and Hostos recall the Dominicans, so does the historian Salvador Brau recall the Venezuelans, the naturalist Agustín Stahl, the Swiss, and the painter José Campeche, the novelist Enrique Laguerre, and the composer Rafael Hernández, our African forebears. They grafted onto our society cuttings from very different cultural traditions, which made it possible for our arts, letters, and sciences to flourish. That is why ethnocentric discourses which undervalue and exclude recent arrivals to our island reveal crass ignorance about how our nation was formed. In Puerto Rico, at a given moment, we were all immigrants, from the early indigenous people in their canoes to the Dominican who arrived just the other day via Rincón and today works on a building site.

The Pluralities of Today

By affirming the complexity and diversity of the formation of the Puerto Rican nation we celebrate the richness and breadth of our traditions, from the festival of the Holy Innocents in Hatillo to the carnival masks of Ponce, from St John's Eve celebrations in the capital to sung rosaries on the eve of Epiphany in Lares. And that diversity and wonderfully expressive creativity does not have an end-by date, a year after which no innovation or alteration is permitted. One example from the local calendar of this capacity for renewal and reinvention are the Fiestas of Calle San Sebastian, which began in the nineteenth century, were revived in mid-twentieth century, and have been ingeniously added to the post-Christmas calendar in the last few decades. Other examples include the marathon of Saint Blas in Coamo, Mother's Day celebrations throughout Puerto Rico, the feasts of Santiago (St. James) in Loiza, Thanksgiving Day, and the nine days of caroling masses before Christmas. In each case Puerto Ricans have appropriated a traditional or foreign celebration, and have adapted or hybridized it at will. We have given it our own form and meaning and made it our own, something characteristic and memorable, adapted to fit our needs and our requirements. If we carefully examine the development and nature of our celebrations we will see that this very appropriation and adaptation has occurred in all of them. There never has been a defining moment, because what was celebrated with *cañas* (horse races) and bullfights in the eighteenth century, by the nineteenth century is celebrated with fanfares at daybreak and cavalcades, and in the twentieth century with parades and carnival floats. The process has always been an open one, because the people have always combined tradition with a touch of innovation. It is true that we have given up celebrating Candlemas with bonfires on the eve of February 2. Nor do we associate eating *funche* (cornmeal) with the feast of St. Peter and St. Paul (June 29). We no longer sow tobacco on the feastday of St. Rose of Lima on August 30, nor do we sing *bomba* at Michaelmas on September 29. Halloween has replaced the solemnities of the Feast of All Souls on November 2. But along the way we have incorporated St. Valentine (February 14), graduation days, and those memorable festivities held when one of our own achieves fame and glory in the outside world.

We have become so accustomed to bemoaning our misfortunes, and complaining about the politicians who live by talking about them, that we forget what we do have, in spite of our misfortunes and politicians. Our history has been one of struggles and challenges, but also of successes and satisfactions. We tend to always compare ourselves with richer countries, and by doing so we underline our deficiencies. However, only rarely do we try to see how we measure up to happier societies. There is an exaggerated tendency to claim that we have the highest indices of whatever is deemed antisocial or inhumane. We are not told how those indices were obtained, nor even whether every society keeps such statistics. Without being naive, I think we should also take note of our achievements. The prophets of doom are forever trying to restrict our youth to a certain degree of conformity and routine. But our very culture counters the asphyxia of sterile fundamentalism and slavish imitation.

One must educate people for life in a pluralistic world, teach them how to handle diversity, how to face doubt as the spark of creativity, rather than a stumbling block. The capacity to adjust to very different situations, the eagerness to seek solutions for the perennial problems, the will to consider all the possible solutions and not only those that flatter tribal vanities, this is what a sound education offers. Other societies dedicate the greater part of their national budget to sustain armies that are paraded before the public, but the people of Puerto Rico are proud of the fact that the greatest recurring item of public expenditure is education. Let others play with their boats and airplanes; we form consciences, launch keen minds onto the path of learning, and are building a society free of racial prejudice and religious intolerance, firm in its commitment to equality and social justice.

To strengthen that commitment to education by incorporating the most fundamental values of our national character is the challenge for all Puerto Ricans, from whatever political party, rich or poor, young or old, Protestant or Catholic. It is healthy for us to be perennially dissatisfied with the results of our endeavors, because it means that we will never give up. As long as there is some form of exploitation, abuse, or misfortune to be addressed, we will never be satisfied. That unity of purpose sustains all our endeavors and binds us together.

Unity of purpose, but plurality of means by which that purpose is achieved. We are all united in the desire for general happiness, and we differ in identifying the means to that end. We celebrate this plurality and we learn from it. This means that we have to value those who think and act differently.

Our flag was not adopted to shelter only those who are considered virtuous or worthy. It is a symbol of all Puerto Ricans; it covers the rights of all. It is the flag of the maximum-security prisoner who seeks access to rehabilitation programs. It is also the flag of the disabled, who struggle to retain their independence in their wheelchairs, and of fishermen who are constantly harassed by the authorities, and of the homosexual who demands his human rights, and of expatriates working to assure the future of their children. It is not only the flag of triumphant boxers and beauty queens, it is also a spur in defeat, it is hope amid the silence, and a proof of perseverance. Our flag celebrates our community of purpose and our diversity as a people.

Notes

Chapter 1

1. See Eric Williams, *From Columbus to Castro* (London, 1970); Gordon Lewis, *The Growth of the Modern West Indies* (New York and London, 1968); *The Unesco General History of the Caribbean*.
2. See Charles Schuchert, *Historical Geology of the Antillean-Caribbean Region or The Lands Bordering the Gulf of Mexico and the Caribbean Sea* (New York, 1935); Instituto Cubano de Recursos Minerales, *Geología de Cuba* (La Habana, 1964); Watson Monroe, "Las divisiones geomórficas de Puerto Rico," in María Teresa B. de Galiñanes, ed., *Geovisión de Puerto Rico: Apotaciones recientes al estudio de la geografía* (Rio Piedras, 1977), 3–43.
3. It is interesting to note that the comparison between the Mediterranean and the Caribbean has been attempted by writers of different perspectives and backgrounds. We still lack a historian who might do for the Caribbean what Fernand Braudel did for the Mediterranean in his classic, *The Mediterranean and the Mediterranean World in the Age of Philip II*, trans. Siân Reynolds (New York: Harper & Row, 1972–73).
4. See Monroe, op. cit.; Howard A. Meyerhoff, *Geology of Puerto Rico* (Río Piedras, 1933); Raoul C. Mitchell, *A Survey of the Geology of Puerto Rico* (Río Piedras, 1954); Clifford Kaye, *Coastal Geology of Puerto Rico, Geological Survey, Professional Paper 317* (Washington, D.C., 1959).
5. See Angela Kay Kepler, *Helechos comunes del Bosque de Luquillo. Puerto Rico* (San Juan, 1975).
6. See Rafael Picó et al., *Nueva geografía de Puerto Rico* (Río Piedras, 1969), 189ff.; Virgilio Biaggi, *Las aves de Puerto Rico* (Río Piedras, 1974); *Puerto Rico y el Mar: Un programa de acción sobre asuntos marinos: Informa el Gobernador, San Juan 1972* (Río Piedras, 1974); Elbert L. Little, Jr., Frank H. Wadsworth, and José Marrero, *Arboles comunes de Puerto Rico y las islas Vírgenes* (Río Piedras, 1977).
7. See *Los sistemas de mangles de Puerto Rico. Programa de la zona costanera* (San Juan: Departamento de Recursos Naturales, 1978). In 1940 there were 16,000 acres of mangroves in Puerto Rico. Of these, 11,800 belonged to the government and the rest to private owners. On the mangrove swamp vegetation and the uses of its wood in the 1930s see I.R. Holdridge, "Some Notes on the Mangrove Swamps of Puerto Rico," *The Caribbean Forester* 1, no. 4 (1940), 19–29.
8. See Monroe, op. cit., 19–20.
9. Mark D. Spalding, *A Guide to the Coral Reefs of the Caribbean* (Berkeley, 2004).
10. Vicente Murga, ed., *Puerto Rico en los manuscritos de don Juan Bautista Muñoz* (Río Piedras, 1960), 36 and 136. See Ovidio Dávila, *Arqueología de la Isla de la Mona* (San Juan, 2003).

Chapter 2

1. See Labor Gómez and Manuel Ballesteros, *Culturas indígenas de Puerto Rico* (Río Piedras, 1978); Ricardo Alegría, "La población aborigen antillana y su relación con otras áreas de América," in Aida Caro, *Antología de lecturas de Historia de Puerto Rico (siglos XV–XVIII)* (3rd printing; Río Piedras, 1977), 47–63; Jalil Sued Badillo, *Los caríbes: realidad o fábula: Ensayo de rectificación histórica* (Rio Piedras, 1978).

2. Gómez and Ballesteros, op. cit., 33–36; Alegría, loc. cit., 48–54.
3. Gómez and Ballesteros, 37–38.
4. Luis A. Chanlatte, *La Hueca y Sorcé* (Vieques, Puerto Rico); *Primeras migraciones agroalfareras antillanas* (Santo Domingo, 1981); Luis A. Chanlatte Baik and Ivonne M. Narganes Storde, *Vieques, Puerto Rico: Asiento de una nueva cultura aborígen antillana* (Río Piedras, 1983); Diana López Sotomayor, "Vieques: un momento en la historia" (thesis, UNAM, Mexico City, 1975); Luis A. Chanlatte Baik, *Cultura ostionoide: un desarrollo agroalfarero antillano* (offprint from *Homines* 10, no. 1 [1986]); *La cultura saladoide en Puerto Rico: su rostro multicolor* (Río Piedras, 2002).
5. See Fray Ramón Pané, *Relación acerca de las antiguedades de los indios*, translated by José Juan Arrom (5th ed.; Mexico City, 1984); Gonzalo Fernández de Oviedo, *Sumario de la natural historia de las Indias*, edited by José Miranda (2nd printing; Mexico City, 1979); Bartolomé de las Casas, *Apologética historia de las Indias* (Madrid, 1958); Irving Rouse, *The Tainos: Rise & Decline of the People Who Greeted Columbus* (New Haven: Yale University Press, 1992).
6. See Robert Cassá, *Los taínos de la Española* (Santo Domingo, 1974), 34.
7. Frank Moya Pons, *Historia colonial de Santo Domingo* (2nd ed.; Santiago, 1976), p. 16 (my translation).
8. See Sherburne F. Cook and Woodrow Borah, "La población aborigen de la Española," in *Ensayos sobre Historia de la Población: México y el Caribe*, translated by Clementina Zamora (Mexico City, 1977), 359–87.
9. See Francisco Moscoso, "Parentesco y clase en los cacicazgos taínos: el caso de los naborías," paper presented at the Ninth International Congress for the Study of Pre-Columbian Cultures of the Antilles (Santo Domingo, 1981).
10. Luis Chanlatte, "Los arcaicos y el formativo antillano (6000 B.C.–1492 A.D.)," paper presented at the 16th International Congress of Caribbean Archeology (Guadeloupe, 1995).
11. See Moscoso, op. cit.
12. Jalil Sued Badillo, "Las cacicas indo-antillanas," *Revista del Instituto de Cultura Puertorriqueña*, no. 87 (1985): 17–26.
13. See Ricardo Alegría, "Las relaciones entre los taínos de Puerto Rico y los de la Española," *Revista del Instituto de Cultura Puertorriqueña*, no. 63 (1974): 31–33.
14. Gómez and Ballesteros, 128; Las Casas, in Pané, op. cit., 117; Eugenio Fernández Méndez, *Art and Mythology of the Taíno Indians of the Greater West Indies* (San Juan, 1972), 32, 35–37.
15. Pané, 33–40; on the cojoba tree, see Little and others, op. cit., 190–92.
16. See Cassá, op. cit., 174–75; Mercedes López Baralt, *El mito taíno: raíz y proyecciones en la Amazonía continental* (Río Piedras, 1976), 23.
17. Gonzalo Fernández de Oviedo y Valdés, *Historia general y natural de las Indias, Islas y Tierra-Firme del Mar Océano* (Madrid, 1851), 1:465.

Chapter 3

1. See J.A. García de Cortázar, *La época medieval*, vol. II of *La Historia de España Alfaguara* (2nd ed., Madrid, 1974), 49ff.
2. Ibid., 111ff., Reyna Pastor de Togneri, *Del Islam al Cristianismo: En las fronteras de dos formaciones económico-sociales: Toledo, siglos XI–XIII* (Barcelona, 1975), Charles-E. Dufourcq and J. Gautier Dalché, *Histoire économique et sociale de l'Espagne chrétienne au Moyen Age* (Paris, 1976), chapters 2 and 3.
3. García de Cortazar, chapters 3 and 4; Dufourcq and Gautier Falché, op. cit., chapters 3 and 4.
4. Pastor de Togneri, op. cit. and *Conflictos sociales y estancamiento económico en la España medieval* (Barcelona, 1973), 131–71 and 175–95; Dufourcq and Gautier Dalché, chapter 5; García de Cortázar, chapters 4 and 5.
5. See Antonio Domínguez Ortíz, *El Antiguo Régimen: Los Reyes Católicos y los Austrias*,

    vol. 3 of *La Historia de España Alfaguara* (8th ed., Madrid, 1981), chapters 1 and 2.
4. Oliver Davies, *West Africa Before the Europeans: Archeology and Prehistory* (London, 1967), 149–50.
5. Ibid., 238.
6. Ibid., 239.
7. Ibid., 258; Robert and Marianne Cornevin, *Histoire de l'Afrique: des origines a la deuxième guerre mondiale* (4th ed.; Paris, 1974), 136, 163–65; Joseph Ki-Zerbo, *Historia del Africa negra*, vol. 1: *De los orígenes al siglo xix*, translated by Carlo Caranci (Madrid, 1980), 150–60, 184–215; Roland Oliver and J.D. Fage, *Breve historia de Africa*, translated by Cristina Rodríguez-Salmones (Madrid, 1972), chapter 7.
8. Davies, 265; Cornevin, 165–66; Ki-Zerbo, 193.
9. Cornevin, 163.
10. Ibid., 169; Davies, 306–7.
11. Cornevin, 169; Ki-Zerbo, 230–36.
12. Cornevin, 167–70; Davies, 272; Robert Cornevin, *Histoire du Dahomey* (Paris, 1962).
13. Cornevin, *Histoire de l'Afrique*, 167, 170.
14. Ibid., 161.
15. See Cheik Anta Diop, *L'Afrique noire pre-coloniale* (Paris, 1960). This author sometimes idealizes premodern work relations.
16. Ibid., 161.
17. See Cheik Anta Diop, *L'Afrique noire pre-coloniale* (Paris, 1960). This author sometimes idealizes premodern work relations.

Chapter 4

1. See Jacques Heers, *Occidente durante los siglos XIV y XV: Aspectos económicos y sociales*, translated by E. Bagué (Barcelona, 1968); David Herlihy, *Medieval and Renaissance Pistoia: The Social History of an Italian Town, 1200–1430* (New Haven, 1967); Reyna Pastor de Togneri, *Conflictos sociales y estancamiento económico en la España medieval* (Barcelona, 1973); Rodney Hilton, *Bond Men Made Free: Medieval Peasant Movements and the English Rising of 1381* (New York, 1973); Guy Bois, *Crise du féodalisme: Economie rurale et démographie en Normandie orientale du début du 14e siècle au milieu du 16me siècle* (Paris, 1976).
2. See Alberto Tenenti, "The Sense of Space and Time in the Venetian World of the Fifteenth and Sixteenth Centuries," in J.R. Hale, ed., *Renaissance Venice* (London, 1973), 17–37; Frederic C. Lane, *Venice: A Maritime Republic* (Baltimore, 1973), 67–82, 234–37.
3. See Christian Bec, *Les marchands écrivains: affaires et humanisme a Florence, 1375–1434* (Paris, 1967); Nicolai Rubinstein, "Italian Reactions to Terraferma Expansion in the Fifteenth Century," in Hale, ed., *Renaissance Venice*, 197–209; S.J. Woolf, "Venice and the Terraferma Problems of the Change from Commercial to Landed Activities," in Brian Pullan, ed., *Crisis and Change in the Venetian Economy in the Sixteenth and Seventeenth Centuries* (London, 1968), 175–203. Woolf considers that the principal investments in land by the Venetians were made after 1510; Gene Brucker, *Renaissance Florence* (New York, 1969), 51–88; L.F. Marks, "The Financial Oligarchy in Florence under Lorenzo," in E.F. Jacob, ed., *Italian Renaissance Studies* (New York, 1960), 123–47.
4. Jacques Heers, *Génes au XVe siècle: Civilisation mediterranéenne, grand capitalisme et capitalisme populaire* (Paris, 1971), 96–152.
5. See Peter Russell, *Prince Henry the Navigator: A Life* (New Haven, 2000).
6. Chaunu, *La expansión europea*, 105ff.; Samuel Eliot Morison, *Admiral of the Ocean Era: A Life of Christopher Columbus* (Boston, 1942), 64–68.
7. See "Capitulaciones de Santa Fé 17 de abril de 1492," in Aida R. Caro Costas, *Antología de lecturas de Historia de Puerto Rico (siglos XV–XVIII)* (3rd impression; Río Piedras, 1977), 13–15; Morison, op. cit., 104–7; Chaunu, 115, 118.
8. Morison, 109ff.

9. See Felipe Fernández-Armesto, *The Canary Islands After the Conquest: The Making of a Colonial Society in the Early Sixteenth Century* (Oxford, 1982).

10. See Morison, chapters 11 to 20. Adam Szasdy has suggested that Pinzón, who had been exploring the northern coast of Hispaniola, at that time discovered what would eventually become known as Puerto Rico.

11. See Demetrio Ramos, "El problema de la fundación del Real Consejo de las Indias y la fecha de su creación," in Demetrio Ramos et al., *El Consejo de Indias en el siglo XVI* (Valladolid, 1970), 11–39.

12. Morison, chapter 28; Moya Pons, 53; Chaunu, 118, 132.

13. Morrison, 420.

14. Salvador Brau, *La colonización de Puerto Rico* (4th ed., annotated by Isabel Gutierrez del Arroyo; San Juan, 1969), 37ff. In 1514, Gonzalo de Sevilla, a witness in a notarized testimony, said he was on Columbus' second journey and that Columbus personally landed in Marigalante, Guadeloupe, and San Juan, and not the other islands (note by Isabel Gutierrez del Arroyo, ibid., p. 38). See also Aurelio Tió, *Doctor Diego Alvarez Chanca (Estudio biográfico)* (San Juan, 1966).

15. See Ricardo Alegría, "Las relaciones," loc. cit.; Cayetano Coll y Toste, ed., "Asiento y capitulación que se tomó con Vicente Yañez Pinzón, para poblar la isla de San Juan, como capitán y corregidor," *Boletín Histórico de Puerto Rico* 1 (1914): 214–17; "Título de Capitán y Corregidor de la Isla de San Juan, en la persona de Vicente Yañez Pinzón," ibid., 217–19; "Real cédula haciendo merced de la tenencia en la isla de San Juan, a favor de Vicente Yañez Pinzón," 220–21.

16. See Vicente Murga Sanz, *Juan Ponce de León* (2nd rev. ed., Río Piedras, 1971), 35ff; Ovidio Dávila, "Apuntes para una interpretación histórico-arqueológica del primer intento de asentamiento de Juan Ponce de León en Puerto Rico, 1508," *Revista del Instituto de Cultura Puertorriqueña*, no. 87 (1985): 1–7.

17. Murga, *Ponce de León*, 37–40; see a communication of the king to Pasamonte on June 6, 1511, in Murga, *Puerto Rico en los manuscritos de don Juan Bautista Muñoz* (Río Piedras, 1960), 38 and 47. See also Alvaro Jara, "Ocupación de la tierra, poblamiento y frontera (Elementos de interpretación)," in Enrique Florescano et al., *Tierras nuevas: Expansión territorial y ocupación del suelo en América (siglos XVI–XIX)* (Mexico City, 1973), 1–10.

18. Murga, *Ponce de León*, 51; Manuel Ballesteros Gaibrois, *La idea colonial de Ponce de León* (San Juan, 1960), 158ff.

19. Murga, *Puerto Rico en Manuscritos Muñoz*, 30, 32, 47, 57, 58, 60.

20. See Jalil Sued Badillo, *El Dorado borincano: La economía de la conquista, 1510–1550* (San Juan, 2001).

21. Murga, *Ponce de León*, 63–65; Brau, *Colonización*, 147–50.

22. Murga, *Puerto Rico en Manuscritos Muñoz*, 71; Brau, *Colonización*, 230–39.

23. Letter of the officials of San Juan to the King on August 8, 1515, in Murga, *Puerto Rico en Manuscritos Muñoz*, 150; "Memoria y descripción de la isla de Puerto Rico mandada a hacer por S.A. el Rey Don Felipe II en el año 1582 y sometida por el ilustre señor capitán Jhoan Melgarejo, Gobernador y Justicia Mayor en esta ciudad e isla," in Eugenio Fernández Méndez, *Crónicas de Puerto Rico*, 114 (cited hereafter as Melgarejo): "their numbers were reduced by illnesses such as measles, colds and smallpox and other harsh treatments, they passed to other islands with the Caribs." On the extinction of the Amerindians in the Greater Antilles, Pierre Chaunu suggests that women's labor in mining affected lactation. The Amerindians lacked cow's milk, and children were breastfed until the age of four. This resulted in a low fertility rate for women. In a population whose average age must have been around 20, the interruption of the reproductive cycle by work in the gold mines would lead to a marked fall in the population of 70 or 80 percent over a period of 15 years. Pierre Chaunu, *Seville et l'Amérique aux XVIe et XVIIe siècles* (Paris, 1977), 83–85.

24. Brau, *Colonización*, 127–32, 189.

25. Instituto Hispano-Cubano de Historia de América, *Documentos Americanos del*

Archivo de Protocolos de Sevilla Siglo XVI, Publicación extraordinaria del Comité Organizador del XXVI Congreso Internacional de Americanistas (Madrid, 1935), nos. 39, 104, 143, 181, 186, 327, 358–60, 429, 466, 486, 506, 739–43, 753.

26. See Ricardo E. Alegría, ed., *El pleito por indios de encomienda entre el ex-contador Antonio Sedeño y el contador Miguel de Castellanos. Puerto Rico, 1527* (San Juan, 1993).
27. See Salvador Brau, *Historia de Puerto Rico* (2nd facsimile edition; San Juan, 1966), 69; Jalil Sued Badillo, *El Dorado borincano.*
28. Jean Gaudemet et al., *Les élections dans l'eglise latines des origines au XVIe siècle* (Paris, 1979).
29. See Demetrio Mansilla Reoyo, *Iglesia castellano-leonesa y curia romana en los tiempos del rey San Fernando* (Madrid, 1945), and Peter Linehan, *The Spanish Church and the Papacy in the Thirteenth Century* (Cambridge, 1971), 111, 323.
30. Cristina Campo Lacasa, *Historia de la iglesia en Puerto Rico (1511–1802)* (San Juan, 1977); Vicente Murga y Alvaro Huerga, *Episcopologio de Puerto Rico I* (Ponce, 1987).
31. Ibid.; Murga, *Puerto Rico en Manuscritos Muñoz*, 150, 152; Campo Lacasa, op. cit., 34.
32. Hortensia Pichardo Viñals, *Las ordenanzas antiguas para los indios: Las leyes de Burgos, 1512* (La Habana, 1984), 25–26.
33. Ibid., 28–40; Luis M. Díaz Soler, *Historia de la esclavitud negra en Puerto Rico (1493–1890)* (Río Piedras, 1967), 20.
34. Pichardo, 60.
35. See Lewis Hanke, *The Spanish Struggle for Justice in the Conquest of America* (3rd impression; Boston, 1965); Enrique Dussel, *El episcopado latinoamericano y la liberación de los pobres, 1504–1620* (Mexico City, 1979).
36. See "Carta del lysenciado Figueroa a Su Maxestad describiendo la ysleta y la cibdad de Puerto Rico," in Coll y Toste, *Boletín histórico de Puerto Rico* 3 (1916): 114–18.
37. "Carta del obispo de Puerto-Rico Don Fray Damián López de Haro, a Juan Diez de la Calle con una relación muy curiosa de su viaje y otras cosas. Año 1644," in Fernández Méndez, *Crónicas*, 165–66 (henceforth cited as López de Haro).
38. Brau, *Colonización*, 188, note; Murga, *Puerto Rico en Manuscritos Muñoz*, 69–70.
39. Brau, *Colonización*, Appendix 14, 559.
40. Ibid., 382–83, 561–63; Paul E. Hoffman, *The Spanish Crown and the Defense of the Caribbean, 1535–1585: Precedent, Patrimonialism and Royal Parsimony* (Baton Rouge, 1980), 52.
41. Huguette and Pierre Chaunu, *Seville et l'Atlantique (1504–1650)* (Paris, 1955), vol. 6, part 2, tables 544ff., pp. 690ff.
42. See Francisco Lluch Mora, *Orígenes y fundación de Guayanilla (siglos XVI–XIX)* (Boston, 1977), 27–29.
43. On Lando see Francisco Moscoso, "Encomendero y esclavista. Francisco Manuel de Lando," *Anuario de Estudios Americanos* 49 (1993): 119–42.
44. Aida R. Caro Costas, "Esclavos y esclavistas en Puerto Rico en el primer tercio del siglo XVI (1531)," *Revista del Museo de Antropología, Historia y Arte de la Universidad de Puerto Rico*, no. 1 (1979): 17; Julio Damiani Cósimi, *Estratificación social, esclavos y naborías en el Puerto Rico minero del siglo XVI. La información de Francisco Manuel de Lando. Ensayo de cuantificación y transcripción paleográfica. Cuadernos de Investigación Histórica*, no. 1 (1994) (Río Piedras, 1995).
45. Murga, *Puerto Rico en Manuscritos Muñoz*, 364.
46. See "Real Provisión del Emperador Carlos V a los Concejos, regidores, caballeros y hombres buenos de la ciudad de San Juan, comunicándoles han cesado los derechos de los sucesores de Colón en la isla, y hasta nueva orden, los alcaldes electos cada año, ejercen la jurisdicción del gobernador" (January 19, 1537), in Caro, *Antología*, 123–25.
47. Murga, *Puerto Rico en Manuscritos Muñoz*, 310.
48. Angel López Cantos, "Historia de una poesía," *Revista del Instituto de Cultura Puertorriqueña*, no. 63 (1974): 1–6.
49. See Francisco Moscoso, *Juicio al gobernador: Episodios coloniales de Puerto Rico, 1550* (Hato Rey: Publicaciones Puertorriqueñas, 1998).

50. See Javier Malagón Barceló, *El distrito de la Audiencia de Santo Domingo en los siglos XV a XIX* (2nd ed.; Santiago, 1977).
51. Murga, *Puerto Rico en Manuscritos Muñoz*, 359, 374, 383; see Eugenio Fernández Méndez, *Las encomiendas y la esclavitud de los indios de Puerto Rico, 1508–1550* (5th ed.; Río Piedras, 1976), 79.
52. Archivo General de Puerto Rico, Colección Francisco Scarano, "Estado general que comprehende el número de vecinos y Habitantes que existen en la Ysla de Puerto Rico con inclusión de los Párvulos de ambos sexos y distinción de clases, estados, y castas hasta fin del año de 1802."

Chapter 5

1. Moya Pons, 71.
2. Frederic C. Lane, *Venice: A Maritime Republic*, 297–98; Fernández Armesto, 79–83.
3. Moya Pons, 73, 78.
4. Ibid., 79.
5. Brau, *Colonización*, 459; Ruth Pike, "Tomás de Castellón, empresario genovés en San Germán a principios del siglo XVI," *Revista del Instituto de Cultura Puertorriqueña* no. 79 (1976): 6–9; Jorge Lizardi Pollock, "Tratos y contratos cotidianos en Puerto Rico, 1509–1530: Vida material del mercader Tomás de Castellón," *Cuadernos de Investigación Histórica* no. 2 (Río Piedras, 1996).
6. Murga, *Puerto Rico en Manuscritos Muñoz*, 326, 364, 370, 373. In 1529 Charles V decreed that sugar mills could not be judicially impounded for debts (Moya Pons, 76). This privilege remained in force until the nineteenth century, when its derogation was solicited because it inhibited the financing of sugar haciendas.
7. One *arroba* was equivalent to 25 pounds; four *arrobas* made a hundredweight. Eufemio Lorenzo Sanz, *Comercio de España con América en la Época de Felipe II* (Valladolid, 1979), 1:617 n. 73.
8. Elsa Gelpí Baiz, *Siglo en Blanco: Estudio de la Economía Azucarera en Puerto Rico, siglo XVI* (San Juan, 2000).
9. Antonio Rivera, ed., "Relación que da un marino llamado Juan Bocquel natural de la Campiña en Brabante venido de Inglaterra habrá un mes habiéndose hallado en el último viaje de Indias hecho por el conde de Comerlant y a su entrada y salida de San Juan de Puerto Rico," *Historia* 1, no. 1 (1951): 81. Cited henceforth as Bocquel, "Relación."
10. Huguette and Pierre Chaunu, *Seville et l'Atlantique (1504–1650)* (Paris, 1955–59), 7:142–43.
11. Melgarejo, 123–24.
12. Jalil Sued Badillo, *Guayama: Notas para su historia* (San Juan, 1983) 35, 38, 39; Melgarejo, 122. Sued observes that the only known sugar mill in the south at the time was the one named Nuestra Señora de Vallehermoso, in Yabucoa, established in 1545 by Gonzalo de Santolalla (op. cit., 37).
13. Melgarejo, 130.
14. "Descripción de la Isla y Ciudad de Puerto Rico, y de su Vecindad y Poblaciones, Presidio, Gobernadores y Obispos; Frutos y Minerales, Enviada por el Licenciado Don Diego de Torres Vargas, Canónigo de la Santa Iglesia de esta Isla en el Aviso que Llegó a España en 23 de Abril de 1647," in Eugenio Fernández Méndez, *Crónicas de Puerto Rico desde la conquista hasta nuestros días (1493–1955)* (2nd ed.; Río Piedras, 1976), 177. Cited henceforth as Torres Vargas.
15. Lugardo García Fuentes, *El comercio español con América, 1650–1700* (Seville, 1980), 347.
16. Murga, *Puerto Rico en Manuscritos Muñoz*, 351–52.
17. See Linda A. Newson, *Aboriginal and Colonial Trinidad: A Study in Cultural Contact* (London, 1976).
18. Moya Pons, 107–8.
19. "Relación del viaje a Puerto Rico de la expedición de Sir George Clifford, tercer

conde de Cumberland, escrito por el reverendo doctor John Layfield, capellán de la expedición (1598)," in Eugenio Fernández Méndez, ed., *Crónicas de Puerto Rico*, 148. Cited henceforth as Layfield.

20. Moya Pons, 126ff., Plank Peña Pérez, Antonio Osorio: Monopolio, Contrabando y *Despoblación* (Santiago, 1980).
21. Francisco Lluch Mora, *Fundación de la villa de San Germán en las Lomas de Santa Marta* (Mayaguez-Yauco, 1971); Ramón Rivera Bermúdez, *Historia de Coamo: La Villa Añeja siglos XVI al XX* (3rd ed. rev.; Coamo, 1980), 34–39.
22. Torres Vargas, 178.
23. Pierre and Huguette Chaunu, *Seville et l'Amérique aux XVIe et XVIIe siècles* (Paris, 1977), 74. This work is an abridged and revised version of the classic *Seville et l'Atlantique* cited above.
24. Cayetano Coll y Toste, "La propiedad territorial en Puerto Rico: su desenvolvimiento histórico," *Boletín de Historia de Puerto Rico* 1 (1913): 253–54; Fréderic Mauro, *Le Portugal et l'Atlantique au XVIIe siècle (1570–1670): Étude économique* (Paris, 1960), 368.
25. Melgarejo, 130.
26. Bocquel, "Relación," 81.
27. Layfield, 148.
28. López de Haro, 166.
29. García Fuentes, 356, table 70.
30. Chaunu, *Seville et l'Atlantique* vol. 6, 2, 1026, table 731; Lorenzo Sanz, *Comercio*, 1:609–11; see Esteban Nuñez Meléndez, *Plantas medicinales de Puerto Rico: Folklore y fundamentos científicos* (Río Piedras, 1982), 164–65.
31. Melgarejo, 123–24.
32. García Fuentes, *Comercio* 1:369, 531–33; Torres Vargas, 178; Enriqueta Vilá Vilar, "Condicionamientos y limitaciones en Puerto Rico durante el siglo XVII," *Anuario de Estudios Americanos* 28 (1971): 229; Carl and Roberta Bridenbaugh, *No Peace Beyond the Line: The English in the Caribbean, 1624–1690* (New York, 1972), 53–54, 65, 154.
33. Torres Vargas, loc. cit.; García Fuentes, 524–26 and 352; John Esquemeling, *The Buccaneers of America: A True Account of the Most Remarkable Assaults Committed of Late Years Upon the Coast of the West Indies by the Bucaneers of Jamaica and Tortuga, Both English and French*, edited by W.S. Stallybrass (London-New York, n.d.), 88.
34. López de Haro, 164, 166; Layfield, 153; Melgarejo, 126.
35. Gilberto Aponte, *San Mateo de Cangrejos (Comunidad cimarrona en Puerto Rico): Notas para su historia* (San Juan, 1985), 11.
36. François Chevalier, *La formación de los latifundios en México: Tierra y sociedad en los siglos XVI y XVII*, translated from the French by A. Alatorre (2nd ed. revised; Mexico City, 1976).
37. See Orlando Patterson, *The Sociology of Slavery: An Analysis of the Origins, Development, and Structure of Negro Slave Society in Jamaica* (London, 1973).
38. In 1579 the bishop wrote to Philip II: "I have visited on my own all of this island. Although it is thinly populated, the inhabitants are spread out and it is necessary to travel all of it and this is difficult on account of the broken terrain, and this is one of the major inconveniences here that I know of for its good spiritual and temporal rule . . ." (in Lluch Mora, *Fundación de la Villa de San Germán*, 57).
39. Torres Vargas, 209–10.

Chapter 6

1. See Eileen Power, "The Wool Trade in the Fifteenth Century," in Power, ed., *Studies in English Trade in the Fifteenth Century* (New York, 1960), 39–44 and 72–79; S.T. Bindoff, *Tudor England* (8th impression; Harmondsworth, 1972), 17; Mauro, *Europa en el siglo XVI*, 137–43.
2. Ismael Sánchez-Bella, *La organización financiera de las Indias, siglo XVI* (Seville,

1968), 13–14; J.M. Ots Capdequí, *El estado español en las Indias* (4th impression; Mexico City, 1975), 63–64; Moya Pons, 91–92; Charles Gibson, *Spain in America* (New York, 1966), 100–101.

3. See the works already cited by Huguette and Pierre Chaunu, *Seville et l'Atlantique* and *Seville et l'Amérique*.
4. Ruth Pike, *Aristocrats and Traders: Sevillian Society in the Sixteenth Century* (Ithaca: Cornell University Press, 1972); Antonio Domínguez Ortíz, "Delitos y suplicios en la Sevilla imperial," in *Crisis y decadencia de la España de los Austrias* (Barcelona, 1969), 13–71.
5. In addition to the works cited above, see Eufemio Lorenzo Sanz, *Comercio de España con América en la época de Felipe II* (Valladolid, 1980), 2 vols.; Moya Pons, 159–60.
6. See the contributions to the subject of sixteenth-century inflation by Vilar, Chaunu, and Mauro: Pierre Vilar, "El problema de la formación del capitalismo," in *Crecimiento y desarrollo* (2nd ed.; Barcelona, 1974), 106–34; Pierre Chaunu, *La España de Carlos V*, translated into Spanish by E. Riambau Sauri (Barcelona, 1976), 36–40; Fréderic Mauro, *Europa en el siglo XVI*, chapter 3, "El juego de la oferta y la demanda," 103–44.
7. See Chaunu, *La España de Carlos V*, 1:33ff.; 2:13–15, 36–40; J.H. Elliott, *Imperial Spain 1469–1716* (New York, 1966), 178–96.
8. Murga, *Puerto Rico en Manuscritos Muñoz*, p. 111; Geoffrey J. Walker, *Spanish Politics and Imperial Trade, 1700–1789* (Bloomington, 1979), 1–2.
9. Paul E. Hoffman, *The Spanish Crown and the Defense of the Caribbean, 1535–1585* (Baton Rouge, 1980), 7.
10. For the narration of a crossing, see López de Haro, 160–61.
11. Hoffman, op. cit., 5–6.
12. Ibid., 6.
13. Chaunu, *Seville et l'Amérique*, 79.
14. Hoffman, loc. cit.
15. Bibiano Torres Ramírez, *La armada de Barlovento* (Sevilla, 1981), 2–3, 8, 30–31, 36–37, 147.
16. See Manuel Alvarado Morales, *La ciudad de México ante la fundación de la Armada de Barlovento* (Mexico City, 1983).
17. See Philippe Braunstein and R. Delort, *Venise: portrait historique d'une cité* (Paris, 1971), 57–58.
18. Hoffman, 25; Moya Pons, 98. Between 1551 and 1635, of the sixty-two ships sailing between Seville and the West Indies captured by corsairs, only six were captured around Puerto Rico; all six captures occurred between 1551 and 1596, and five of them were in the Mona Passage (Chaunu, *Seville et l'Atlantique* vol. 6, part 2, 878, 954, and 966). These statistics would make one think that the problem of the corsairs has been exaggerated, but one has to remember that the Chaunus have counted only the capture of ships in the route Seville-America. Vilá Vilar has verified that in the period 1621–32 only ten percent of the ships that arrived in San Juan came from Seville; the others were from Margarita, Caracas, Cumaná, or the Canary Islands, or had as their original arrival point New Spain. Perhaps in this inter-Caribbean traffic corsairs affected Puerto Rico more than the traffic with Seville. Enriqueta Vilá Vilar, "Condicionamientos y limitaciones en Puerto Rico durante el siglo XVII," *Anuario de Estudios Americanos* 28 (1971): 230.
19. Lutgardo García Fuentes, *El comercio español con América, 1650–1700* (Seville, 1980), 159–60; Chaunu, *Seville et l'Amérique*, 76–77; Moya Pons, 99.
20. García Fuentes, 160; Gibson, op. cit., 102.
21. See Cornelio C. Goslinga, *Los holandeses en el Caribe*, translated into Spanish by E. Pacios (La Habana, 1983), 164–69.
22. Moya Pons, 99.
23. Lorenzo Sanz, *Comercio de España con América* 2:282 note 38.
24. See Eduardo Aznar Vallejo, *La integración de las Islas Canarias en la corona de Castilla (1478–1526)* (Seville, 1983), 315; Chaunu, *Seville et l'Amérique*, 58; Francisco

Morales Padrón, *El comercio canario-américano (siglos XVI, XVII, y XVIII)* (Seville, 1955), 300, 322–23, 327–28, 340–46; García Fuentes, 99–102.

25. Ibid.; Angel López Cantos, *Historia de Puerto Rico, 1650–1700* (Seville, 1975), 33–34; see Manuel Alvarez Nazario, *La herencia lingüística de Canarias en Puerto Rico* (San Juan, 1972).

26. Murga, *Puerto Rico en Manuscritos Muñoz*, 329–30. According to Enriqueta Vilá Vilar, some 10% of the ships that arrived in Puerto Rico between 1621 and 1632 "were ships that sailed for New Spain and came in forced arrivals" ("Condicionamientos," loc. cit.). Forced-arrival ships supplied Puerto Rico with slaves; see Juana Gil Bermejo, *La Española, anotaciones históricas (1600–1650)* (Seville, 1983), 245.

27. López Cantos, *Historia*, 277.

28. See Domínguez Ortíz, *El Antiguo Regimen*, 240–60 and 292–316.

29. See Goslinga, 115–16. The Spanish crown even hired the services of a pirate, Simon Danzer, to attack Dutch trade. See John Lothrop Motley, *The Life and Death of John of Barneveldt* (New York, 1900) 1:236–38.

30. Hoffman, 7.

31. Murga, *Puerto Rico en Manuscritos Muñoz*, 247, 320, 326; Brau, *Colonización*, 382–83, 561–63.

32. Murga, *Puerto Rico en Manuscritos Muñoz*, 411.

33. Ibid., 320, 354; Hoffman, 38.

34. Murga, *Puerto Rico en Manuscritos Muñoz*, 370.

35. See Francisco Lluch Mora, *Fundación de la villa de San Germán en las Lomas de Santa Marta* (Mayaguez, 1971).

36. See Sued, *Guayama*, 41. Of the port of Guadianilla on the southern coast, a sailing guide of the sixteenth century said that there "our ships go on few occasions. It is more frequented by the French and other nations who sail to these parts although it is forbidden" (Murga, *Puerto Rico en Manuscritos Muñoz*, 408). Would it have been the authorities' misgivings about smuggling rather than their powerlessness before the corsairs that led the settlement to be moved to the Santa Marta hills?

37. López Cantos, *Historia*, 3.

38. Hoffman, 37–38.

39. Ibid., 53.

40. Ibid., 22, 57, 61, 141, 154, 196, 212; José Cruz de Arrigoitia, "El situado mexicano: origen y desarrollo en Puerto Rico durante los años de 1582 a 1599" (master's thesis, Universidad de Puerto Rico, Río Piedras, 1984).

41. Hoffman, 37–38.

42. See Aida R. Caro, *Villa de San Germán: Sus derechos y privilegios durante los siglos XVI, XVII y XVIII* (San Juan, 1963).

43. Cruz de Arrigoitia, op. cit., 38ff.

44. Ibid.; Moya Pons, 205, 212; Enriqueta Vilá Vilar, *Historia de Puerto Rico, 1600–1650* (Seville, 1974), 193–99; López Cantos, *Historia*, 93–105.

45. Garret Mattingly, *The Armada* (2nd impression; Boston, 1959), 82–119; A.L. Rowse, *The Expansion of Elizabethan England* (2nd impression; New York, 1965), passim.

46. Coll y Toste, *Boletín historico de Puerto Rico* 2:148ff.; 11:191.

47. Bocquel, 77–78; "La toma de la Capital por Cumberland: Extracto del Informe del Conde de Cumberland," *Boletín histórico de Puerto Rico* 5 (1918): 40.

48. Bocquel, 78–79.

49. Layfield, 145; Bocquel, 80–81.

50. Alonso de Contreras, *Vida, nacimiento, padres y crianza del capitán Alonso de Contreras*, edited by F. Reigosa (Madrid, 1967), 197.

51. Goslinga, 87ff.

52. Ibid., 52.

53. After the disappearance of King Sebastian of Portugal in a campaign in North Africa, Philip II invaded Portugal in 1580. Both kingdoms were united until the 1640s.

54. Ibid., 110ff.

55. "Fragmentos de Joannes de Laet, Historia o Anales de los Hechos de la Compañía Privilegiada de las Indias Occidentales," in Fernando Géigel Sabat, *Balduino Enrico: Asedio de la ciudad de San Juan de Puerto Rico por la flota holandesa* (Barcelona, 1934), 58–77 (cited henceforth as Laet).
56. "Relación de la entrada y cerca del enemigo Boudoyno Henrico, General de la Armada del Príncipe de Orange en la ciudad de Puerto Rico de las Indias; por el Lcdo. Diego de Larrasa, Teniente Auditor General que fue de ella," in Géigel Sabat, 158 (henceforth cited as Larrasa).
57. Laet, loc. cit.; Larrasa, 159ff.
58. Ibid., 175–77.
59. Laet, 89–100.
60. Vilá Vilar, *Historia*, 169ff.
61. Goslinga, 172.
62. Vilá Vilar, *Historia*, 180.
63. See Alvarado, op. cit.
64. Ibid.
65. Chaunu, *Seville et l'Atlantique*, vol. 6, 2, p. 490, table 233 and p. 493, table 236; J. Marino Inchaustegui, ed., *Reales cédulas y correspondencia de gobernadores de Santo Domingo* (Madrid, 1958), 4:1245, no. 367.
66. *Seville et l'Atlantique*, vol. 8, part 1, 553–54; see Vilá, "Condicionamientos," 220.
67. Torres Ramírez, *Armada*, 147. López Cantos draws a negative conclusion about the role the Armada in Puerto Rico: "It was of limited use; its mission was more negative than fruitful, it did little to improve defense, to say the least" (*Historia*, 247).
68. Carl and Roberta Bridenbaugh, *No Peace Beyond the Line*, 13.
69. See Chaunu, *Seville et l'Amerique*, 79; Sued, *Los caribes*.
70. Chaunu, loc. cit.; Vilá Vilar, *Historia*, 159–61.
71. Bridenbaugh, 13, 19.
72. Ibid., 53–54.
73. Ibid., 65, 154.
74. Ibid., 75.
75. Ibid., 93–94.
76. Ibid., 33 and 270.
77. Carlos de Siguenza y Góngora, *Infortunios de Alonso Ramírez*, annotated by Alba Vallés Formosa (San Juan, 1967).
78. López Cantos, *Historia*, chapter 6. In 1691 the Puerto Rican cleric Francisco Sanabria wrote to the King: "I have seen, Lord, evident and notorious risks of losing this island, knowing in the subjects a variety of very deliberate dispositions to favor and deliver their wills to Calvinist and Lutheran foreigners, without regard to the religion they profess, but only to human interests, on account of the good fortune which they have recognized in their smuggling of slaves, clothing and other things." (Ibid., p. 6, note 8).
79. Ibid., 275.
80. Ibid., 282–83.
81. Ibid., 274.
82. Ibid., 280.
83. See Arturo Morales Carrión, *Puerto Rico and the Non-Hispanic Caribbean: A Study in the Decline of Spanish Exclusivism* (Río Piedras, 1971).
84. See Salvador Brau, "Fundación de Pueblos en Puerto Rico. Apuntes de un Cronista," *Boletín Histórico de Puerto Rico* 7 (1920): 87.

Chapter 7

1. López Cantos, *Historia*, 15, 43; Bibiano Torres Ramírez, *La Armada de Barlovento* (Seville, 1981), 87.
2. Richard Konetzke, *Colección de Documentos para la Formación Social de Hispanoamérica 1493–1810*, vol. 2, part 1 (Madrid, 1958), 558–59.

3. Waldermar Westergaard, *The Danish West Indies under Company Rule (1671–1754)* (New York, 1917), 161.
4. Salvador Perea, *Historia de Puerto Rico 1537–1700* (San Juan, 1972), 226; López Cantos, *Historia*, 33–34.
5. Ibid., 34, note 47.
6. This total is obtained from the figure of 1,076 militiamen discovered and published by Salvador Brau and republished by Coll y Toste (Salvador Brau, "Fundación de pueblos," loc. cit., 88). Assuming that there was a population of males between the ages of 16 and 60 similar to that which can be calculated from O'Reilly's 1765 census (in which the ratio of free men between the ages of 15 and 60 to the total population is 1 for every 5.4 persons), one gets a total of 5,810. The number is rounded up to 6,000 to make allowances for the probability that in 1700, the proportion of women to men was greater than in 1765. I am grateful to Salvador Padilla for suggesting the number of militiamen as a base from which to calculate the total population.
7. Francisco Lluch Mora, *La rebelión de San Germán (1701–1712)* (Mayaguez, 1981).
8. See Aida R. Caro, *Villa de San Germán: Sus derechos y privilegios durante los siglos XVI, XVII y XVIII* (San Juan, 1963).
9. Lluch Mora, *La rebelión*, 16–17. In 1589 governor Menéndez de Valdés wanted to supplement the garrison of San Juan with Sangermeños. The cabildo of San Germán appealed to the Audiencia of Santo Domingo, which twice found in favor of the cabildo, and each time the governor rejected the Audiencia's order. King Philip II backed the Governor over the Audiencia, giving higher priority to military needs than to the legal claims of the town. See José Cruz Arrigoitia, "El situado mexicano" (M.A. thesis in history), 75–76.
10. See "Real Cédula del Rey Felipe V Premiando a los Defensores de Arecibo contra los Ingleses en 1702," in Cayetano Coll y Toste, ed., *Boletín de Historia de Puerto Rico* 8:195–97, and "Patente de Capitán de Infantería Española para D. Antonio de los Reyes Correa," ibid., 198–99.
11. See Arturo Morales Carrión, *Puerto Rico and the Non-Hispanic Caribbean: A Study in the Decline of Spanish Exclusivism* (Río Piedras, 1971), 59–63; Fernando Portuondo, *Historia de Cuba (1492–1898)* (6th ed.; Havana, 1974), 174–75; Westergaard, 181 and 192n.; C.H. Haring, *The Buccaneers in the West Indies in the XVII Century* (Hamden, 1966), 271–72.
12. See Richard Pares, *War and Trade in the West Indies 1739–1763* (Oxford, 1936), 15, 18, 23–24.
13. Ibid., 15.
14. See Salvador Brau, *Historia de Puerto Rico* (2nd facsimile ed.; San Juan, 1966), 164–68; Morales Carrión, *Puerto Rico and the Non-Hispanic Caribbean*, 69ff.; Torres Ramírez, *Armada*, 194; "Documentos sobre el corsario Miguel Enríquez," *La Revista del Centro de Estudios Avanzados de Puerto Rico y el Caribe*, no. 1 (July–December 1985): 151–67.
15. Arturo Morales Carrión, "Orígenes de las relaciones entre los Estados Unidos y Puerto Rico, 1700–1815," *Historia* 2 (1952): 9–14. See "Real Orden dando patentes de corso contra los ingleses (18 de agosto de 1739)" in *Boletín Histórico de Puerto Rico* 4:134.
16. "The Journal of a Captive, 1745–1748," in Isabel M. Calder, ed., *Colonial Captivities, Marches and Journeys* (New York, 1935), 124–25.
17. Acts of April 20 and June 8, 1740, in *Actas del Cabildo de San Juan Bautista de Puerto Rico 1730–1750* (San Juan, 1949), 130 and 167–68. In 1749 Pedro Vicente de la Torre was a council member (ibid., 266–78).
18. Parish of San Felipe de Arecibo, copy of the First Book of Marriages. On the problem of consanguinity in the seventeenth century marriages see López Cantos, *Historia*, 32–33 and 36.
19. Bridenbaugh, op. cit., 127–28 and note 47.
20. López Cantos, *Historia*, 21–25.

21. See Berta Cabanillas, "La alimentación durante el siglo XVIII," chapter 11 of *El puertorriqueño y su alimentación a través de su historia (siglos XVI al XIX)* (San Juan, 1973).
22. Between 1708 and 1750, twenty-two free women in Arecibo married slaves but only four free men married slave women (Copy of the First Book of Marriages of San Felipe de Arecibo).
23. Archivo General de Indias, Audiencia de Santo Domingo, legajo 546.
24. Ibid., 18r.
25. Ibid., 24v and 25v, 41r, 43r–44r, 48v–49r, 50r, 50v–64v; Generoso Morales Muñoz, "Real Cédula de Fundación de Añasco," October 18, 1733, in "Fundación del Pueblo de San Miguel de Cabo Rojo, 1771–72," *Boletín de Historia Puertorriqueña* 1, no. 8 (1949): 232–34.
26. The late Dr. Pedro Hernández Paraliticci generously provided a photocopy of a transcription of "Documentos relativos a la fundación de Utuado. Copiado de un libro manuscrito que se conserva en el Archivo de la Parroquia de Utuado, por el P. Fray Cayetano de Carrocera, religioso franciscano capuchino. Utuado agosto de 1924." The transcription is now in Archivo General de Puerto Rico, Colecciones Particulares.
27. See F. Picó, "Lazos de solidaridad entre los fundadores de Utuado," *Revista del Instituto de Cultura Puertorriqueña*, no. 85.
28. See María Judith Colón, *Historia de Isabela y su desarrollo urbano 1750–1850* (Carolina, 1987); Juana Gil Bermejo, *Panorama histórico de la agricultura en Puerto Rico* (Seville, 1970), 253; Oscar Bunker, *Historia de Caguas*, vol. 1 (Caguas, 1975), chapters 6 and 7; Carlos Rodríguez and Gregorio Villegas, *Guaynabo: Notas para su historia* (San Juan, 1984); Marcial Ocasio, *Río Piedras: Notas para su historia* (San Juan, 1985); Gilberto Aponte, op. cit.
29. See Generoso Morales Muñoz, "Fundación del pueblo de San Miguel de Cabo Rojo," loc. cit. (for the conditions imposed, which reflect previous opposition, see 235–37); Gil Bermejo, op. cit., 256–59; Antonio Ramos and Ursula Acosta, *Cabo Rojo: Notas para su historia* (San Juan, 1985), 15–17, includes information on the families in the area at the time of the foundation.
30. See San Germán's 1735 ordinances, favoring the cattlemen, in Caro, *Legislación municipal*, 62; Gil Bermejo, 248ff.; Aida Caro, *El cabildo o régimen municipal puertorriqueño en el siglo XVIII*, vol. 2 (San Juan, 1974), 74ff.
31. Appendix no. 7 of the "Memoria de D. Alexandro O'Reylly sobre la isla de Puerto Rico," in Aida Caro, *Antología*, p. 404.
32. Ibid.
33. Parés, op. cit., 18.
34. Francisco Morales Padrón, *El comercio canario-americano (siglos XVI, XVII, y XVIII)* (Seville, 1955), 80–81.
35. Morales Carrión, *Puerto Rico and the Non-Hispanic Caribbean*, 83; Altagracia Ortíz, *Eighteenth Century Reforms in the Caribbean: Miguel de Muesas, Governor of Puerto Rico 1769–76* (Rutherford, 1983), 75–76.
36. See Appendix no. 5 in O'Reilly's Report, "Relación en que se manifiesta el precio a que los extranjeros pagan todos los frutos, ganado y madera que extraen de la Isla de Puerto Rico; y el a que venden los efectos que introducen, según las noticias más exactas que pude adquirir," in Caro, *Anthology*, p. 401.
37. For a glimpse of the capital city's life in its solemn moments, see "Relación Verídica en la Que se Da Noticia de lo Acaecido en la Ysla de Puerto Rico a fines del Año de 45 y principios del 47 con el motivo de llorar la Muerte de N. Reyu y Señor Don Phelipe Quinto y Celebrar la Exaltación a la Corona de N.S. D. Fernando Sexto. Dedícase al Señor Coronel de los Reales Exércitos Don Juan Joseph Colomo Gobernador y Capitán General de Dicha Isla. Por un Afecto Servidor Suio en 19 de Febrero de 1747," *Boletín Histórico de Puerto Rico* 5 (1918): 148–93.
38. For instance, María Verdugo Segarra, wife of Sebastián González de Mirabal, took charge of the family's cases in court in the long years of the proceedings against

the Sangermeños who refused to obey the governor's orders (Lluch, *La rebelión*, 34, 37, 46, 59); another woman, Pascuala de Figueroa, opted to go to jail rather than declare against those charged (ibid., 34).

39. See Aida R. Caro, *Legislación municipal puertorriqueña del siglo XVIII* (San Juan, 1971). For instance, San Germán's *cabildo* ordered in 1735: "That in future no houses be allowed on the square belonging to persons of lesser quality, because that place is reserved for the first families, and the same on the town's main street; and those who have them are not allowed to sell them to such persons of low quality, the penalty being 10 ducats" (ibid., p. 47).

40. For instance, on July 15, 1736, the priest at Arecibo married a couple whom Juan de la Escalera Montañez, one of the *alcaldes* of the capital city and "general visitor of this Island," had brought to the jail. The *alcalde* had a license from the bishop to "identify in each settlement he visited unmarried persons who were living in sin, put them in that town's jail and inform the pastor," so that he "without the least delay marry and bless them" (Copy of Arecibo's First Book of Marriages, 74r).

41. See Generoso Morales Muñoz, ed., "Visita del obispo al Partido y Pueblo de San Felipe en la Ribera del Arecibo," *Boletín de Historia Puertorriqueña* 1 (1948–49): 139; "Primera visita pastoral del obispo Pizarro al Pueblo e Iglesia de la Ribera del Arecibo," ibid., 214–15; "Primera visita pastoral del obispo Antolino al Pueblo de la Ribera del Arecibo, 1750," ibid., 246.

42. See Generoso Morales Muñoz, "Visita pastoral única del obispo Antolino a la Ribera de Santa Cruz del Bayamón, 1750," *Boletín de Historia Puertorriqueña* 2 (1950): 113.

43. See Morales Carrión, *Puerto Rico and the Non-Hispanic Caribbean*, 62; A.P. Thornton, *West India Policy Under the Restoration* (Oxford, 1956), 223, note 4; Cecil Headlam, ed., *Calendar of State Papers, Colonial Series, America and West Indies, 1706–1708 June* (London, 1916), nos. 473–74, 591, 717, 723; Pares, 78, 182; Westergaard, 316.

44. Pares, 605 and 608.

Chapter 8

1. See Jacques Godechot, *Las revoluciones (1770–1799)*, translated into Spanish by Pedro Jofre (2nd ed.; Barcelona, 1974), 7–8.

2. See Witold Kula, *Teoría económica del sistema feudal*, translated into Spanish by E.J. Zembrzwski (Mexico City, 1974).

3. See Carlos A. D'Ascoli, *Del mito del Dorado a la economía del café (Esquema histórico-económico de Venezuela)* (2nd ed.; Caracas, 1980), 167ff.; Tulio Halperin Donghi, *Revolución y guerra: Formación de una élite dirigente en la Argentina criolla* (2nd ed.; Mexico City, 1979), 41ff.

4. See Daniel P. Mannix and M. Cowley, *Historia de la trata negrera*, translated into Spanish by E. Bolívar Rodríguez (2nd ed.; Madrid, 1970), 76–107.

5. See Lawrence Henry Gipson, "The American Revolution as an Aftermath of the Great War for the Empire, 1754–1763," and Thad W. Tate, "The Coming of the Revolution in Virginia: Britain's Challenge to Virginia's Ruling Class, 1763–1776," in David L. Jacobson, ed., *Essays on the American Revolution* (New York, 1970), 69–81, 113–28.

6. On the reverberations in Puerto Rico of the Spanish intervention in the war between Great Britain and its thirteen rebel colonies, see Arturo Morales Carrión, "Orígenes de las relaciones entre los Estados Unidos y Puerto Rico 1700–1815," in *Albores históricos del capitalismo en Puerto Rico*, 100–102.

7. And the island of Bermuda, if one accepts the argument that it belongs to North America. Many of the supporters of the English cause in the thirteen colonies went to Canada and to Bermuda.

8. See Albert Soboul, *La Revolution française* (Paris, 1962), 1, 108.

9. See Jean Egret, *La pre-revolution française 1787–88* (Paris, 1962); Ernest Labrousse, "La crisis de la economía francesa al final del Antiguo Régimen y al principio de la Revolución," in *Fluctuaciones económicas e historia social* (2nd impression; Madrid,

1973), 339–72.

10. See Michel Vovelle, *La caída de la Monarquía 1787–1792*, translated into Spanish by Clara Campos (Barcelona, 1979), 127–28.

11. See E.P. Thompson, *The Making of the English Working Class* (New York, 1966), 102–85; Gonzalo Anés, "La Revolución francesa y España," in *Economía e Ilustración en la España del Siglo XVIII* (Barcelona, 1969), 141–98.

12. R.R. Palmer, *The Age of the Democratic Revolution*, vol. 2, *The Struggle* (Princeton, 1964), chapters 3, 5, 9, 10, 12, and 14.

13. On the Haitian revolution, see the classic work by C.L.R. James, *The Black Jacobins* (New York, 1938).

14. See "Memoria de D. Alexandro O'Reylly sobre la Isla de Puerto Rico," in Caro, *Antología*, 385–416; Altagracia Ortiz, op. cit.; Iñigo Abad y Lasierra, *Historia geográfica, civil y natural de la Isla de San Juan Bautista de Puerto Rico* (San Juan, 1970); Edgar Pérez Toledo, "Real Factoría Mercantil: Contribución a la Historia de las Instituciones Económicas de Puerto Rico (1784–1795)" (master's thesis in history, Universidad de Puerto Rico, Río Piedras, 1983), 31–32.

15. SBibiano Torres Ramírez, *La isla de Puerto Rico (1765–1800)* (San Juan, 1968), 261–62.

16. S"Bando de Policía de don Juan Dabán y Noguera. 1783," in Caro, *Antología*, 455–58.

17. See Parroquia de Nuestra Señora del Pilar de Río Piedras, Book I of Circulars (1774–1798), a copy of the circular of December 22, 1774: "Some persons have given me news that there are many who have been subjected to the major excommunication instituted by me on those who send cattle from the Island to foreign parts. And taking pity on the evil state of so many souls who, with so little fear of God, have offended him, I give faculties to all confessors so that they may absolve from it those who have been excommunicated, and I declare that this excommunication is rescinded, as I do rescind it from this moment." In a circular of November 13, 1776, Bishop Pérez Jiménez reiterates that the smugglers "sin gravely against God and against the King" "and those who practice smuggling are obliged to make restitution to the royal treasury," 3v and 20r–21r.

18. Iñigo Abad, op. cit., 123.

19. "Directorio General que ha mandado formar el Señor Don Miguel de Muesas Coronel de los Reales Ejércitos Gobernador y Capitán General de esta Isla de San Juan de Puerto Rico," in Caro, Antología, 420; Archivo General de Puerto Rico, Fondo de Gobernadores Españoles de Puerto Rico, box 283, responses of several *tenientes a guerra* to the Governor to the circular of June 5 in relation to the episcopal circular of April 12, 1798.

20. See Aida R. Caro, *El cabildo o régimen municipal en Puerto Rico*, vol. 2 (San Juan, 1974).

21. On these subjects see Adam Szaszdi, "Documentos del Archivo de Protocolos de San Juan de Puerto Rico referentes a Venezuela (1801–1811)," *Historia*, new series, 5 (196): 75–97; "Apuntes sobre la esclavitud en San Juan de Puerto Rico, 1800–1811," *Anuario de Estudios Americanos* 24 (1967): 1433–77; "Credit Without Banking in Early Nineteenth Century Puerto Rico," *The Americas* 19 (1962–63): 149–71; "La municipalidad de San Germán en Puerto Rico (1798–1808)," *Journal of Inter-American Studies* 1, no. 4 (1959): 489–513.

22. See A. Aspinall, ed., *The Later Correspondence of George III*, vol. 2, *February 1793 to December 1797* (Cambridge, 1963), 515; Julian Corbert, ed., *Private Papers of George, Second Earl of Spencer, First Lord of the Admiralty, 1794–1801*, Navy Record Society, vols. 48 (1914), 71 and 58 (1924), 220; William Belsham, *Memoirs of the Reign of George III from His Accession to the Peace of Amiens* (6th ed.; London, 1813), 3:220.

23. See Juan Manuel Zapatero, *La guerra del Caribe en el siglo XVIII* (San Juan, 1964); Torres Ramírez, *Isla de Puerto Rico*, 173ff.; Ruth Pike, *Penal Servitude in Early Modern Spain* (Madison, 1983), 136–38.

24. James Ralfe, *The Naval Biography of Great Britain* (2nd facsimile edition; Boston,

1972), II, 108–9; Zapatero, op. cit., 436–56; *The Times*, June 7, 1797, p. 2, copy of Sir Ralph Abercromby's dispatch.
25. Zapatero, 473, 491, 509.
26. Ibid., 505–26.
27. Ibid., 473–76; Corbett, ed., *Spencer Papers*, loc. cit., vol. 58 (1924), 220–21; Abercromby's Report, *The Times*, June 7, 1797, p. 2.
28. See Aida Caro, *Antología*, 465–66; Torres Ramírez, *Isla de Puerto Rico*, 256–58; Aponte, *Cangrejos*, 37.
29. Caro, *Antología*, 471–74; Torres Ramírez, *Isla de Puerto Rico*, 256–58; see the tribute to Castro in "El ataque británico a Puerto Rico de 1797 en la 'Gaceta' de Guatemala," in Luis González Vales, *Alejandro Ramírez y su tiempo* (Río Piedras, 1978), 7–8.
30. See Richard Cobb, *Les armées revolutionnaires* (Paris, 1961–63), 2 vols.
31. See Georges Lefebvre, *The French Revolution*, vol. 2, *From 1793 to 1799*, translated by J.-H. Stewart and J. Figuglieti (3rd impression; London and New York, 1965), 292–94; Denis Woronoff, *La republique bourgeoise: de Thermidor a Brumaire 1794–1799* (Paris, 1972), 78–82; Albert Soboul, *Le directoire et le consulat (1795–1804)* (Paris, 1967), 33–35.
32. See Geoffrey Bruun, *Europe and the French Imperium 1789–1814* (3rd impression; New York, 1965), 1–14; Louis Bergeron, *L'episode napoleonien: Aspects interieurs 1799–1815* (Paris, 1972).
33. Lidio Cruz Monclova, *Historia de Puerto Rico (siglo XIX)*, vol. 1 *(1808–1868)* (6th ed.; Río Piedras, 1969), 3–5; Raymond Carr, *Spain, 1808–1939* (Oxford: Clarendon Press, 1966), 79ff.
34. Ibid., 4; *Actas del Cabildo de San Juan Bautista de Puerto Rico 1803–1809*, edited by Aida Caro (San Juan, 1970), 403–5.
35. See Indalecio Liévano Aguirre, *Bolívar* (3rd ed.; Cali, 1981), 59–70; Halperin Donghi, op. cit., 160–67; Luis Villorro, "La revolución de la independencia," in El Colegio de México, *Historia general de México*, vol. 2 (Mexico City, 1976), 325–26.
36. Cruz Monclova, 19–20; Aida R. Caro, ed., *Ramón Power y Giralt* (San Juan, 1969), 35–36.
37. Ibid., 71–128.
38. Ibid., 45–69.
39. Ibid., 123–24.
40. Ibid., 95.
41. Cruz Monclova, 34–41.
42. Ibid., 37–38.
43. Ibid., 34; Luis González Vales, "Alejandro Ramírez y la crisis del papel moneda: Apuntes para la historia económica de Puerto Rico en el siglo XIX," in *Alejandro Ramírez y su tiempo*, 46.
44. Cruz Monclova, Appendix 2, 522.
45. Jose Fontana underscores the limitations of this constitution, which reflects the limited transformation at that point of Spanish society since the beginning of its war against Napoleon. *La crisis del Antiguo Régimen 1808–1833* (Barcelona, 1979), 16–18 and 82–95.
46. Cruz Monclova, 49.
47. Ibid., 53–54.
48. See Luis González Vales, "La primera Diputación Provincial, 1813–1814: Un capítulo de historia institucional," in *Alejandro Ramírez y su tiempo*, 145–251.
49. Luis González Vales, "Alejandro Ramírez y la crisis del papel moneda," loc. cit., 44.
50. Ibid.
51. Ibid., 73; Cruz Monclova, 54.
52. See Héctor Humberto Samayos Guevara, *El régimen de intendencias en el reino de Guatemala* (Guatemala, 1978), 7–30; Luis González Vales, "Alejandro Ramírez y el establecimiento de la Intendencia," loc. cit., 15–16.
53. "Alejandro Ramírez y la crisis del papel moneda," ibid., 43–44.
54. "Breves apuntes para una historia de la Lotería en Puerto Rico," ibid., 43–44.

55. González Vales, "Alejandro Ramírez y el establecimiento de la Intendencia," loc. cit., 19–20. In 1815 it was permitted to pay the fiscal quotas for the first third of the year in coinage, paper money, products, or cattle, according to an equivalency table in which coffee was valued at 8 pesos the hundredweight, rice at 4, corn at 4, and tobacco at 6. Camuy's quota was 60 hundredweight in corn, and that of Utuado in rice (125 hundredweights) and in corn (50). Only Tuna was allowed to pay in tobacco (200 hundredweight). See "Correspondencia del Intendente de Puerto Rico con el Secretario de Estado y del Despacho Universal de Indias, Año, 1814," a printed circular of January 2, 1815, in Archivo General de Indias, Audiencia de Santo Domingo, dossier 2416.
56. Cruz Monclova, 75–76. Alejandro Ramírez deplored the abolition of the town councils: "the countryside and the towns have come to be ruled again by the *tenientes a guerra*, a sort of military corporal, whom the Captain General names and dismisses at will. There is a tendency to return to the old custom of renting out and auctioning off. Those who had an interest in these practices have come again to have influence and authority. No good system of the Royal Treasury can be established on this island, if before all else are arranged the interior regulation, the administration of Justice and the items and affairs that considered politically, require such special and different rules as the island is different from all others of the King's possessions," in "Correspondencia," loc. cit.
57. Cruz Monclova, 77–78.
58. Ibid., 78–83.
59. Ibid., 84; Francisco Scarano, *Sugar and Slavery in Puerto Rico: The Plantation Economy of Ponce, 1800–1850* (Madison, 1984), 18–19.
60. Scarano, op. cit., passim.
61. See E.P. Thompson, op. cit., 603–710; L. Bergeron, F. Furet, and R. Koselleck, *La época de las revoluciones europeas, 1780–1848*, translated into Spanish by F. Pérez Gutierrez (3rd ed.; Mexico City, 1979), 175–76.
62. Carr, op. cit., 128–45; Fontana, op. cit., 31–36 and 134–38.
63. Cruz Monclova, 105–9; Delma Arrigoitia, "La segunda Diputación Provincial de Puerto Rico (1820–1823)," *Caribe* 4–5 (1983–84): 91–103.
64. See Guillermo Baralt, *Esclavos rebeldes: Conspiraciones y sublevaciones de esclavos en Puerto Rico (1795–1973)* (Río Piedras, 1982); Luis M. Díaz Soler, op. cit., 213–14.
65. Ursula Acosta, "Ducoudray Holsten: Hombre al margen de la historia," *Revista de Historia* 1, no. 2 (1985): 63–89.
66. Cruz Monclova, 141–42; Harold J. Lidnin, *History of the Puerto Rican Independence Movement*, vol. 1 (*19th century*) (San Juan, 1981), 35–37.

Chapter 9

1. For this period see Juan González Mendoza, "Demografía y sociedad en San Germán: siglo XVIII," *Anales de Investigación Histórica* 9 (1982): 1–64.
2. A. Szaszdi, "Los registros del siglo XVIII en la parroquia de San Germán," *Historia*, n.s. 1, no. 1 (1962): 56, 59–60; Gregorio Villegas, "Fluctuaciones de la población de Guaynabo en el periodo 1780–1830," *Anales de Investigación Histórica* 8 (1981): 125.
3. Parish of Our Lady of the Candelaria of Mayaguez, Book 4 of Burials.
4. Ibid., 120r, entry 232.
5. On the immigrants to Puerto Rico for this period see Estela Cifre de Loubriel, *La inmigración a Puerto Rico durante el siglo XIX* (San Juan, 1964); Rosa Marazzi, *El impacto de la inmigración a Puerto Rico 1800–1830: Análisis estadístico* (Río Piedras, n.d.); Pedro Juan Hernández, "Los inmigrantes italianos de Puerto Rico durante el siglo XIX," *Anales de Investigación Histórica* 2, no. 2 (1976): 1–63; Raquel Rosario Rivera, *Los emigrantes llegados a Puerto Rico procedentes de Venezuela entre 1810–1848 (Incluye Registro de Emigrados)* (San Juan, 1992).
6. Parroquia de la Candelaria de Mayaguez, Book 4 of Burials, entries 252, 265, 321, 332, 335.

7. Pike, *Penal Servitude*, 138ff.
8. Even to this day in Puerto Rican correctional institutions there is mention of "galleys" to allude to the divisions where convicts are housed. As Pike shows, that use of the word is a survival of the penal language of the eighteenth century.
9. Ibid., 138.
10. Ibid., 139–47.
11. Ibid., 141, 182; *Iñigo Abad, Viage a la América*, facsimile edition by Carlos Arcaya (Caracas, 1974), 74r; Parish of Río Piedras, Book 3 of Burials, 170v–171r.
12. López Cantos, *Historia*, 28.
13. Szazsdi, "Credit Without Banking," loc. cit., 61–62; Edgar Pérez Toledo, op. cit.
14. See Daniel P. Mannix and M. Cowley, *Historia de la trata de negros* (2nd ed.; Madrid, 1970), James A. Rawley, *The Transatlantic Slave Trade: A History* (New York, 1981).
15. Ibid., 74.
16. Adam Szazsdi, "Apuntes para la esclavitud en San Juan de Puerto Rico, 1800–1811," *Anuario de Estudios Americanos* 24 (1967): 1442.
17. See Mannix and Cowley, chapter 5.
18. Ibid., 127–28.
19. Ibid., 157.
20. See Szazsdi, "Credit Without Banking" and "Apuntes sobre la esclavitud," loc. cit.
21. See Fernando Portuondo, *Historia de Cuba (1492–1898)* (6th ed.; Havana, 1974), 258; Rafael Duharte Jiménez, *Seis ensayos de interpretación histórica* (Santiago, 1983).
22. Río Piedras parish, First Book of Marriages of White Persons, 29r–v, marriage of Manuel Aponte, native of Santiago de los Caballeros in the island of Santo Domingo, with María Lorenza de Castro, from Cupey. In the Third Book of Burials there are several mentions of slaves born in Santo Domingo (e.g., 135r, 149r).
23. See for instance the efforts of the Lee family to continue to belong to the Episcopal Church in the Puerto Rico of the 1850s. Albert E. Lee, *An Island Grows: Memoirs of Albert E. Lee, Puerto Rico 1873–1942* (San Juan, 1963), 5.
24. Pedro Juan Hernández, op. cit.
25. "Crónica de don Simón Moret," translated from a typescript done by Carlos R. Gadea; AGPR, FGEPR, box 106, "Expediene instruido por Don Simón Moret natural de Orleans en Francia, solicitando carta de domicilio"; ibid., box 66, untitled dossier of request made by Simon Moret to introduce between 12 and 14 slaves from Curaçao, St. Thomas, St. Croix, or Guadeloupe (March 5, 1847; refused); Obras Públicas, Propiedad Pública, Guayama, dossiers 12 bis and 34.
26. Photocopy of baptismal record sent by Ramón Gadea.
27. *El Buscapié*, July 13, 1884, p. 3.
28. Scarano, *Sugar and Slavery*, 81–90.
29. See Iñigo Abad, *Viage a la América*, 51v–52v, "Informe dado por el Alcalde don Pedro Yrisarri al Ayuntamiento de la Capital. 1809," in Caro, *Ramón Power*, 49–50.
30. Altagracia Ortíz, op. cit., 190–93. See Pío López, *Historia de Cayey* (San Juan, 1973); Antonio Ramos and Ursula Acosta, *Cabo Rojo: Notas para su historia* (San Juan, 1985); Luis de la Rosa Martínez, *Vega Baja: Notas para su historia* (San Juan, 1983); Gilberto Aponte, op. cit.
31. In Humacao there had been previous attempts to found towns; see Salvador Abreu Vega, *Apuntes para la historia de Humacao* (Humacao, 1984), 50–61. See Carmelo Rosario Natal, *Historia de Naguabo* (Río Piedras, 1979); Antonio Rodríguez Fraiz, *Historia de Corozal* (Santiago, 1966); L.A. Balsquide, *Compendio intrahistórico de Peñuelas* (San Juan, 1972); José Francisco Díaz Viera, *Historia Documental de Trujillo Alto* (Barcelona, 1962); José A. Sierra Martinez, *Camuy: Notas para su historia* (San Juan, 1984); Herminio R. Rodríguez Morales, *San Lorenzo (San Miguel de Hato Grande): Notas para su historia* (San Juan, 1985); Wilhelm Hernández, *Adjuntas: Notas para su historia* (San Juan, 1985); Carlos Domínguez Cristóbal, *La esclavitud, la instrucción pública, y la iglesia en Ciales durante el siglo XIX* (Río Piedras, 1985); Frances Ortíz Ortíz, *Cidra: Notas para su historia* (San Juan, 1986). Other towns founded in the period were Morovis, Sabana Grande, Aibonito, Barranquitas, and

Gurabo. See Joaquín Santiago and Walter Cardona Bonet, *Aibonito: Notas para su historia* (San Juan, 1985).

Chapter 10

1. See Altagracia Ortíz, op. cit.; Edgar Pérez Toledo, *Real Factoría Mercantil*; Iñigo Abad, *Historia*.
2. Díaz Soler, 117.
3. Scarano, *Sugar and Slavery*, 42–43.
4. See Guillermo Baralt, *La Buena Vista* (San Juan, 1988). In a later period it became a coffee *hacienda*.
5. Ibid., 25ff.; Pedro San Miguel, "Los trabajadores en las haciendas de Vega Baja, 1800–1873," *Caribe* 3, no. 4 (1982): 68–80.
6. See Andrés Ramos Mattei, ed., *Azúcar y esclavitud* (Río Piedras, 1982); Francisco Scarano, "Slavery and Free Labor in Puerto Rican Sugar Economy, 1815–1873," in V. Rubin and A. Tuden, eds., *Comparative Perspectives on Slavery in New World Plantation Societies*, vol. 292 (1977) of *Annals of the New York Academy of Sciences*, 553–63; José Curet, "From Slave to Liberto: A Study on Slavery and its Abolition in Puerto Rico, 1840–1880," Ph.D. thesis (Columbia University, 1979). See Fernando de Norzagaray (Governor of Puerto Rico, 1853), "Demostración de la economía que resulta en el cultivo de una hacienda de caña cuando trabajan en ella esclavos y no jornaleros," *Historia y Sociedad* 1 (1988): 179–82.
7. See Francisco Moscoso, "Formas de resistencia de los esclavos en Puerto Rico, siglos XVI–XVIII," *América Negra*, no. 10 (December, 1995): 31–48.
8. Guillermo Baralt, *Esclavos rebeldes* (Río Piedras, 1982).
9. Ibid., 111–26; Arturo Morales Carrión, "Bembé y sus compañeros Nongobás," *Boletín de la Academia Puertorriqueña de la Historia* 6 (1980): 43–51.
10. See Benjamín Nistal Moret, *Esclavos prófugos y cimarrones, Puerto Rico, 1770–1870* (Río Piedras, 1984); Iñigo Abad, *Historia*, 183. On cases of passive resistance see Antonio Rivera, "Viva Puerto Rico Li... Li... Li...," *Historia* 4, no. 1 (1954): 62.
11. Szaszdi, "Esclavitud," loc. cit., 1463–64 and 1475–76 and note 72; Consuelo Vázquez, "Las compraventas de esclavos y cartas de libertad en Naguabo durante el siglo XIX," *Anales de Investigación Histórica* 3, no. 1 (1976): 58.
12. Torres Ramírez, *Isla de Puerto Rico*, 36. See Francisco Moscoso, *Agricultura y sociedad en Puerto Rico, siglos 16 al 18: Un acercamiento desde la historia* (San Juan, 1999).
13. See "Bases para el reparto de tierra en Puerto Rico, forma de hacerlo a fin de que haya el mayor número posible de propietarios, cultivos que han de tener y organización administrativa de varios pueblos," in Caro, *Antología*, 443–47.
14. See José Eizaguirre, "Los sistemas en el régimen de abasto de carne de San Juan durante la primera mitad del siglo XIX" (master's thesis, University of Puerto Rico, Río Piedras, 1974).
15. *Actas del Cabildo de San Juan Bautista de Puerto Rico 1761–1767* (San Juan, 1954), p. 63.
16. See Caro, *Ramón Power y Giralt*, 173–74.
17. Eizaguirre, op. cit., 96ff.
18. AGPR, Fondo de Gobernadores Españoles, box 54, "Estado que demuestra los terrenos de labor, hatos y realengos que se hallan empadronados en la Isla, con expresión de los derechos que satisfacen los labradores, por las dos primeras clases, según los padrones formados en 1822."
19. See Scarano, *Sugar and Slavery*, 20–21; Manuel Moreno Fraginals, *El ingenio: complejo económico social cubano del azúcar* (Havana, 1978), 1:62–71.
20. "Credit Without Banking in 19th Century Puerto Rico," loc. cit.
21. Parish of Río Piedras, Third Book of Burials, 166v.
22. Ivette Pérez Vega, in her book, *El cielo y la tierra en sus manos* (Río Piedras, 1985), dedicates a chapter to José Gutierrez del Arroyo. Nicolás Alonso de Andrade in

1802 contracted with Jean Girardet the lease of his hacienda in Bayamón for 9 years. At the time there were 12,000 coffee trees planted. Girardet had to plant 50,000 more and set up the machinery and whatever was necessary for washing, pulping, and drying the coffee. He had to build a storehouse and devote a fifth of the land to vegetables. When the lease was up, half of the coffee trees planted would belong to Girardet and he would have the right to use the pulping machine (Szaszdi, "Credit Without Banking," 165). In the burial records of Río Piedras there are numerous entries concerning Andrade's slaves, many of them baptized just before their deaths.

23. Szaszdi, "Credit Without Banking," 163–64.
24. See Andrés Ramos Mattei, *La hacienda azucarera: Su crecimiento y crisis en Puerto Rico (Siglo XIX)* (San Juan, 1981), 66ff.; Scarano, *Sugar and Slavery*, 100–112; Moreno Fraginals, op. cit., 1, 169–75, 203–55.
25. Scarano, *Sugar and Slavery*, 5–7.
26. See Angel López Cantos, "El comercio legal de Puerto Rico con las colonias extranjeras de América, 1700–1783," *Revista de Ciencias Sociales* 24 (1985): 201–27.
27. Pérez Toledo, 115–16.
28. See Birgit Sonneson, "Puerto Rico y San Tomás en Conflicto Comercial 1839–1843" (master's thesis, University of Puerto Rico, Río Piedras, 1973), chapters 1 and 2.
29. See Carmen Campos Esteve, "La política del comercio: Los comerciantes de San Juan, 1837–1884" (M.A. thesis in history, University of Puerto Rico, Río Piedras, 1987).
30. Generoso Morales Muñoz, ed., "Primera visita pastoral del obispo Antolino al Pueblo de la Ribera del Arecibo. 1750," *Boletín de Historia Puertorriqueña* 1 (1948–49): 251.
31. Campo Lacasa, *Historia de la Iglesia*, 133.
32. As his marriage entry in Lima shows, Rose's father, Gaspar de Flores, had been born in San Germán.
33. Generoso Morales Muñoz, ed., "Edicto del Obispo sobre trabajo permisible en Puerto Rico durante los días festivos," *Boletín de Historia Puertorriqueña* 2 (1949–50): 277–78.
34. How to translate this quintessentially Puerto Rican word? *Relajo* means loosening up, with humor, mimicry, and disrespect, the dominant sense of order. It is good-natured kidding but also means resistance. One Spanish dictionary (Cuyas) even made it equivalent to depravity.
35. Iñigo Abad, *Historia*, 188–89.
36. Campo Lacasa, *Historia de la Iglesia*, 134.
37. Parish of Río Piedras, Book I of Circulars, "Mandatos del Yllmo. Sor. Dr. Dn. Felipe Josef de Trespalacios por la Gracia de Dios, y de la Sta. Sede Apostólica del Consejo de su Md.," 10r.
38. See Frank Otto Gatell, ed., "Puerto Rico Through New England Eyes, 1831–1834," *Journal of Inter-American Studies* 1, no. 3 (1959): 291; Manuel Alonso, "Las fiestas del Otoao," *Album Puertorriqueño* (2nd impression; San Juan, 1968), 105.

Chapter 11

1. See Pedro Tomás de Córdoba, *Memorias geográficas, históricas, económicas y estadísticas de la Isla de Puerto Rico* (2nd facsimile edition, San Juan, 1968), 6 vols.
2. This attitude persisted among some up to the day of abolition. See José Marcial Quiñones, *Un poco de historia colonial (incluye de 1850–1890)* (San Juan, 1978), 134.
3. See Ada Suárez, "El doctor Ramón Emeterio Betances y la abolición de la esclavitud," Revista del Colegio de Abogados de Puerto Rico (February, 1978), 13–17; Cayetano Coll y Toste, "El doctor Goico," *Boletín Histórico de Puerto Rico* 5:194–95.
4. Olga Jiménez de Wagenheim, *El grito de Lares: sus causas y sus hombres*, translated by Carmen Rivera Izcoa (Río Piedras, 1984), 50–51.
5. Arturo Morales Carrión, *Auge y decadencia de la trata negrera en Puerto Rico* (San Juan,

1978), 25, 29–55.

6. See Ursula Acosta y David Cuesta Camacho, *¿Quién era Cofresí?* (Hormigueros, 1984). As in other instances of outlaws becoming popular heroes, Cofresí has loomed large in Puerto Rican folklore. See Roberto Fernández Valledor, *El mito de Cofresí en la narrativa antillana* (Río Piedras, 1978).
7. Baralt, *Esclavos rebeldes*, 156–57.
8. Republished by Coll y Toste in *Boletín Histórico de Puerto Rico* 3 (1916): 347–49.
9. Cruz Monclova, *Historia*, 180; Germán Delgado Passapera, *Puerto Rico: Sus luchas emancipadoras (1850–1898)* (Río Piedras, 1984), 28–29; Raquel Rosario Rivera, *María de las Mercedes Barbudo: Primera Mujer Independentista de Puerto Rico 1773–1849* (San Juan, 1997).
10. Cruz Monclova, *Historia*, 85–86, 181–82.
11. See Francisco Pérez Guzmán, *Bolívar y la independencia de Cuba* (Havana, 1988); Loida Figueroa, "Puerto Rico y el sueño bolivariano respecto a la América Latina," *Revista de la Biblioteca Nacional José Martí*, 3rd series 26 (1984): 9–20; Héctor Feliciano Ramos, ed., *Antonio Valero de Bernabé: Soldado de la Libertad 1790–1863* (San Germán, 1992).
12. For the analogous situation of Cuba, see Raúl Cepero Bonilla, *Azúcar y abolición* (3rd ed.; Barcelona, 1976), 44.
13. See the timely clarification on this subject by Fontana, op. cit., 48–49 and 93–203.
14. Cruz Monclova, *Historia*, 225–29; Vázquez, *López de Baños*, 9.
15. Ibid., 51–52.
16. See Vicente Géigel Polanco, "Don Andrés Salvador Vizcarrondo y Ortíz de Zárate," *Revista del Instituto de Cultura Puertorriqueña* no. 63 (1974): 22–30; Vázquez, *López de Baños*, 38.
17. There is an abridged version of López de Baños's circular on day laborers in Labor Gómez Acevedo, *Organización y reglamentación del trabajo en el Puerto Rico del siglo XIX (propietarios y jornaleros)* (San Juan, 1970), 485; see Vázquez, *López de Baños*, 135.
18. See José Trías Monge, *El sistema judicial de Puerto Rico* (Río Piedras, 1978), 24–25.
19. Vázquez, *López de Baños*, 126–28.
20. AGPR, Fondo de Gobernadores Españoles, box 322, untitled dossier on the Board of Trade's opposition. See Morales Carrión, *Auge y decadencia*, 123ff.; David S. Murray, *Odious Commerce: Britain, Spain and the Abolition of the Cuban Slave Trade* (Cambridge, 1980).
21. Antonio Rivera, "La toma de Fajardo por el Almirante Porter," *Historia*, 2nd series 2, no. 3 (1963): 71–91. See David Porter, *An exposition of the Facts and Circumstances which Justified the Expedition to Foxardo...* (Washington, 1825); Robert Beale, *A Report on the Trial of Commodore Porter* (Washington, 1825).
22. See *Gaceta del Gobierno de Puerto Rico*, October 26, 1847, p. 4; November 11, 1847, p. 4; December 2, 1847, p. 3; and December 11, 1847, p. 3.
23. See Cayetano Coll y Toste, ed., "Bando del general Prim contra la raza africana," *Boletín histórico de Puerto Rico* 2 (1915): 122–26; Arturo Morales Carrión, "El año 1848 en Puerto Rico, aspectos del mando de Prim," *Revista de Occidente*, no. 147 (1975): 211–42.
24. Salvador Brau, in his *Historia de Puerto Rico*, asserted that Prim shot Ignacio Avila, "El Aguila," for having stolen the governor's horse. Subsequent historians repeated the story. Recent research has shown that Avila, born in the Canary Islands, was an escaped convict who murdered an hacendado in the Lajas area at a time when governor Prim was touring the west.
25. On Pezuela see Tapia, *Memorias*, 120–26; the edict is in Labor Gómez, op. cit., 449–53.
26. In January, 1850, Pezuela supplemented his circular on day laborers with one on the lease of land (Circular no. 67). In 1856, in a "Proyecto sobre Reglamento de Jornaleros," prepared by the Royal Junta for Trade and Fomentation, the effects of Pezuela's 1850 norms for renters were criticized. "The evil has been created by the

mayors who did not understand their spirit, and even more so those who seeking only their own profit, deviated the paternal instincts of the Superior Government with the notarized leases of land" (AGPR, FGEPR, box 322, "Proyecto sobre Reglamento de jornaleros," 4v–5r).

27. For instance, in Utuado, according to the Acts of the "Junta de Vagos y Amancebados," no one was denounced for vagrancy in 1868; two were in 1869, and none in 1870. Of the two denounced in 1869, one was a day laborer denounced by his wife and the other a former hacendado who had participated in the Grito de Lares and had just come out of jail in Ponce.

28. See "Diario del Gobernador Norzagaray," *Anales de Investigación Histórica* 6, no. 1 (1979): 70–132.

29. See María de los Angeles Castro Arroyo, "La construcción de la Carretera Central en Puerto Rico (Siglo XIX)" (master's thesis, University of Puerto Rico, Río Piedras, 1969).

30. See Coll y Toste, "Como fue la invasión de cólera morbo en esta isla en el siglo XIX," *Boletín Histórico de Puerto Rico* 6 (1919): 215–17.

31. In 1856 the Real Junta de Comercio y Fomento, in its projected regulations for day laborers, stated that "one would not lament today so many horrors from the cholera epidemic if day laborers had the most basic resources, at least a house to withstand the weather's inclemencies" (loc. cit., 5v–6r).

32. Cepero Bonilla, op. cit., chapters 7 to 11. See also Rebecca Scott, *Slave Emancipation in Cuba: The Transition to Free Labor, 1860–1899* (Princeton, 1985).

33. See Segundo Ruiz Belvis, José Julián Acosta, and Francisco Mariano Quiñones, *Proyecto para la abolición de la esclavitud en Puerto Rico presentado a la Junta de Información reunida en Madrid el 10 de abril de 1867*, edited by Luis M. Díaz Soler (San Juan, 1969); Ada Suárez, "El doctor Ramón Emeterio Betances y la abolición de la esclavitud," loc. cit., and "Segundo Ruiz Belvis (Hormigueros, Puerto Rico, 1829–Valparaiso, Chile, 1867)," *Caribe* 3, no. 4 (1982): 3–65; Alberto Cibes Viadé, *El abolicionismo puertorriqueño* (Río Piedras, 1975).

34. Cruz Monclova, *Historia*, 428; Cepero Bonilla, 72–74.

35. See "Oficio del Gobernador Marchessi al Ministro de Ultramar dando cuenta de los antecedentes políticos de las personas que fueron obligadas a abandonar la Isla en 1867 (14 de julio de 1867)," *Historia* 2 (1952): 98–113; Andrés A. Ramos Mattei, "Betances, Lares y el ciclo revolucionario antillano," *Revista Sin Nombre* 13, no. 3 (1983): 7ff.

36. See "Don Julián Pavía da cuenta del estado en que se encuentra el país y propone medios para fomentar su riqueza (24 de diciembre 1867)," *Historia* 2 (1952): 94–98; Paris, Ministère des Affaires Etrangères, Archives Diplomatiques, Correspondance Comerciale, Porto Rico, tome 7, 1867–69, Letter of the French consul in San Juan on November 5, 1867 (microfilm in Centro de Investigaciones Históricas, Universidad de Puerto Rico, Río Piedras).

37. Ramos Mattei, "Betances, Lares y el ciclo revolucionario antillano," loc. cit., 22–27.

38. Although the exact number of cells and of participants cannot be firmly established, Francisco Moscoso points out that there was a cell called Lanzador del Sur in Ponce. Francisco Moscoso, *La Revolución Puertorriqueña de 1868: El Grito de Lares* (San Juan, 2003), 52.

39. Olga Jiménez de Wagenheim, op. cit., 144–45.

40. Ibid., 163–66.

41. Ibid., 166–85; Harold J. Lidin, *History of the Puerto Rican Independence Movement*, vol. 1 (*19th Century*) (San Juan, 1981), 91–101; Moscoso, *La Revolución Puertorriqueña*, 62–63.

42. Moscoso, *La Revolución*, 66–67.

43. Jiménez, 217, 221.

44. Ibid., 215–20.

45. Morales Carrión, *Auge y decadencia*, 39–43, 59–61, 175.

46. Rosa Marazzi, op. cit., 53–54.

47. See Estela Cifre, *La formación del pueblo puertorriqueño: La contribución de los catalanes, balearicos y valencianos* (San Juan, 1975)

48. See María Dolores Luque de Sánchez, *La presencia corsa en Puerto Rico durante el siglo XIX* (San Juan, 1982).

49. See Guillermo A. Baralt, *Yauco o las minas de oro cafetaleras (1756–1898)* (San Juan, 1984).

50. See "Creación del pueblo de la Ceiba," *Boletín Histórico de Puerto Rico* 3 (1916): 260–62; Héctor E. Colón Ramírez, *Orocovis: Su desarrollo histórico, social económico 1825–1940* (Orocovis, 1980); Otto Sievens Irizarry, *Guayanilla: Notas para su historia* (San Juan, 1983); Generoso Morales Muñoz, *Fundación del pueblo de Lares* (San Juan, 1946) and *Fundación del Pueblo de Guadiana (Naranjito)* (San Juan, 1948).

51. AGPR, FGEPR, box 54, "Estado que demuestra los terrenos de labor, hatos y realengos... según los padrones formados en 1822."

52. On this subject see Nydia Martínez de Lajara, "Repartimiento de terrenos baldíos en el pueblo de Salinas durante el siglo XIX," *Anales de Investigación Histórica* 2, no. 2 (1975): 48–81.

53. In 1828, Mayaguez, Ponce, and Guayama produced 54% of Puerto Rican sugar (Scarano, *Sugar and Slavery*, 14).

54. See Darío de Ormaechea, "Memoria acerca de la agricultura, el comercio y las rentas internas de la isla de Puerto Rico," *Boletín Histórico de Puerto Rico* 2 (1915): 229.

55. See Birgit Sonneson, "Puerto Rico y San Tomás en conflicto comercial" (master's thesis), chapter 3, "El comercio entre Puerto Rico y San Tomás 1815–1835."

56. Ramos Mattei, *La hacienda azucarera*, 65ff.

57. See AGPR, Audiencia, Real Acuerdo, box 20 B, dossier 21, "Expediente de acuerdo sobre que se conceda permiso para introducir en esta Ysla seiscientos jornaleros o colonos libres de la de Cabo Verde" (1857), 1r–v and 5v; Obras Públicas, Asuntos Varios, Acts of the Junta for Trade and Fomentation, 1860, 38r, a project of Manuel J. Cuevas, of Mayaguez, to introduce 3,000 Indian day laborers from Yucatán and Nueva Granada; Fondo de Gobernadores Españoles de Puerto Rico, box 322, petition by Cabasa and Company, from Cabo Rojo, to introduce 500 day laborers from Curazao (1856).

58. See copy of the printed contract of the Canary Islander immigrant Salvador Plata, from Gomera Island, with Bartolomé Cifra and Ramón Mandillo, from Tenerife, in 1843, for transportation to Puerto Rico to work for two years in public works and the fortifications. The immigrant was to receive 4 reales a day as salary, and he would pay 2 pesos a month for his journey, and 4 reales a month into a mutual aid fund. After two years he would be free to settle wherever he wished. The contract hinted at, but did not promise, the concession of untitled land (AGPR, Fondo de Gobernadores Españoles de Perto Rico, box 204).

59. Scarano, *Sugar and Slavery*, chapter 1.

60. Ibid., 13. See Emma Dávila Cox, *Este inmenso comercio: Las relaciones mercantiles entre Puerto Rico y Gran Bretaña, 1844–1898* (San Juan, 1996).

61. Ramos Mattei, *La hacienda azucarera*, 83–84.

62. See Sonneson, op. cit., "Años de transición; 1835–1839."

63. See Laird W. Bergad, *Coffee and the Growth of Agrarian Capitalism in Nineteenth-Century Puerto Rico* (Princeton, 1983), 100–102.

64. Sonneson, chapter 5, "Años de conflicto, 1839–1843."

65. See Astrid Cubano, "Economía y sociedad en Arecibo en el siglo XIX: Los grandes productores y la inmigración de comerciantes," in Francisco Scarano, ed., *Inmigración y clases sociales en el Puerto Rico del siglo XIX* (Río Piedras, 1981), 175.

66. Tapia, *Mis memorias*, 12.

67. See "Real Decreto ordenando la recogida de la moneda macuquina," in *Bóletín Histórico de Puerto Rico* 2 (1915): 115–21.

68. AGPR, Fondo Municipal de Utuado, "Pueblo de Utuado. Año de 1848. Reparto de lo correspondiente al comercio de este Pueblo para el subsidio ordinario del presente año." Two other tradesmen are emigrés from Costa Firme.

69. Tort appears 13 times as a witness of notarized deeds in Utuado between September 19 and December 19, 1850. See AGPR, Protocolos Notariales, Utuado, Otros Funcionarios, 1850; Obras Públicas, Asuntos Varios, Inventario del Archivo de la Capitanía General, dossier 103, box 79A, "Yndice de los expedientes relativos al ramo de Comercio que existen en el Archivo de la Secretaría del Gobierno General," no. 1108; Parish of San Miguel de Utuado, Book 3 of Marriages, White, no. 392.

70. AGPR, Protocolos Notariales, Utuado, Osvaldo Alfonzo 1862, 38v–39v; year 1863, 79v–80v; year 1864, 50v–51r, 83r–v, 135–136r, 163v–164r, 167v–168v; year 1865, 105r–106r, 169v–170r.

71. AGPR, Tribunal Superior de Arecibo, Civil, Utuado, box 241A, dossier without cover of Verbal Judgements for 1862, 31v, 32r, 40v; dossier without cover for 1863, 20r–22r, 34r–v, 35v, 37v, 38r, 43v.

72. AGPR, Protocolos Notariales, Utuado, Osvaldo Alfonzo, 1867, 101r–102v.

73. Ibid., Alfonzo 1862, 43–45r; year 1864, 83v–84r.

74. See Arcadio Díaz Quiñones, "Tomás Blanco: Racismo, Historia y Esclavitud," preliminary study of the third edition of Tomás Blanco, *El prejuicio racial en Puerto Rico* (Río Piedras, 1985).

75. See Angel G. Quintero Rivera, José Luis González, Ricardo Campos, and Juan Flores, *Puerto Rico: Identidad Nacional y Clases Sociales (Coloquio de Princeton)* (Río Piedras, 1979).

76. See José Luis González, *Literatura y sociedad en Puerto Rico* (Mexico City, 1976), 102ff.

Chapter 12

1. On this period see Cruz Monclova, *Historia*, vols. 2 and 3; Reece Bothwell, *Puerto Rico: Cien Años de Lucha Política* (Río Piedras, 1979), vol. 1, part 1 and vol. 2; Angel G. Quintero Rivera, *Conflictos de clase y política en Puerto Rico* (Río Piedras, 1976), 9–99; Astrid Cubano Iguina, "Comercio y hegemonía social: Los comerciantes de Arecibo 1857–1887" (master's thesis in history, University of Puerto Rico, Río Piedras, 1979); Andrés Ramos Mattei, *La hacienda azucarera*; Gervasio L. García, *Historia crítica, historia sin coartadas: Algunos problemas de la historia de Puerto Rico* (Río Piedras, 1985).

2. "Isla de Puerto Rico, Censo general de su población, hasta fines de Diciembre, 1867, clasificado según los diferentes conceptos que expresa el siguiente cuadro," published in *Gaceta del Gobierno de Puerto Rico*, in consecutive numbers in July, August, and September, 1868; U.S. Department of War, *Census of Porto Rico* (Washington, D.C., 1899).

3. Ibid.

4. "Cuadro de las defunciones ocurridas durante todo el año de 1867," *La Gaceta*, September 10, 1868; "Cuadro de los nacimientos habidos durante todo el año de 1867," ibid., September 12.

5. Department of War, *Census of Porto Rico*.

6. See Angel Cuadrado Quiñones, "Estudio parcial de los registros del siglo XIX de la parroquia Dulce Nombre de Jesús del partido de Humacao," *Anales de Investigación Histórica* 1, no. 1 (1974): 1–45; Héctor Rodríguez Nieves, "Las fluctuaciones en la población de Cayey, 1815–1861" (master's thesis in history, University of Puerto Rico, Río Piedras, 1980; Hilda A. Rosario, "Estudio demográfico de Ciales en sus primeras décadas como pueblo, años 1820–1884," unpublished monograph for the history seminar at the University of Puerto Rico; Angel Rodríguez Cristóbal, "Relación de Bautismos, Matrimonios y Defunciones en Ciales durante los años 1860–1899," in *La esclavitud, la instrucción pública y la iglesia en Ciales durante el siglo XIX* (Río Piedras, 1985), 98.

7. José Marcial Quiñones described the day laborers at the end of the nineteenth century in these terms: "Today 20% of them are rachitic, flaccid, degenerate, anemic, and the causes are found in the scant food, in the lack of shelter and in the immod-

erate use of alcohol. . . . It could also be affirmed that many of them do not light a fire more than once a week, to cook themselves a stew. And on other days what do they live on? . . . They don't eat more than a few crumbs, which ever in our country a compassionate hand bestows, or some tuber, or a fruit not yet ripe . . ." (op. cit., 88–89). See Esteban López Giménez, *Crónica del '98: El testimonio de un médico puertorriqueño*, edited by Luce and Mercedes López-Baralt (Río Piedras, 1998).

8. See Parish of Río Piedras, Book 21 of Baptisms.
9. AGPR, Municipal Archive of Camuy, boxes 119, 120, and 121, "Censo de la noche del 25 al 26 de diciembre de 1860."
10. See Center for Puerto Rican Studies in New York, History Task Force, *Sources for the Study of Puerto Rican Migration 1879–1930* (New York, 1982), 10–13.
11. Cayetano Coll y Toste, *Reseña del estado social, economico e industrial de la Isla de Puerto Rico al tomar posesión de ella los Estados Unidos* (San Juan, 1899), 364–65.
12. See *Boletín Histórico de Puerto Rico* 12, 173–75; Juan Brusi y Font, *Viaje a la Isla de la Mona (1884)* (San Juan, 1997).
13. Quoted by Truman Clark, *Puerto Rico and the United States 1917–1933* (Pittsburgh, 1975), 109.
14. Ramos Mattei, *La hacienda azucarera*, 22–23.
15. Ibid., 28–30.
16. Ibid., 65–82.
17. See Jaime Sifre Tarafa, "Memoria sobre el estado de la industria azucarera hacia finales del siglo XIX," *Anales de Investigación Histórica* 6, no. 2 (1979): 115–26.
18. See Angel Quintero, *Conflictos de clase*, 18–29.
19. See Clifford Geertz, *Agricultural Involution: The Process of Ecological Change in Indonesia* (Berkeley, 1966).
20. See Portuondo, op. cit., 338, 390, 504.
21. See Stanley J. Stein, *Vassouras: A Brazilian Coffee County, 1850–1900* (New York, 1976).
22. See Laird W. Bergad, *Coffee and the Growth of Agrarian Capitalism in Nineteenth-Century Puerto Rico* (Princeton, 1983), chapter 3, "The Expansion of Coffee Production, 1850–1885."
23. See Fernando López Tuero, *La reforma agrícola* (San Juan, 1891); José Ramón Abad, *Puerto Rico en la feria exposición de Ponce en 1882* (2nd facsimile edition; Río Piedras, 1967).
24. See Carlos Buitrago Ortíz, *Haciendas cafetaleras y clases terratenientes en el Puerto Rico decimonónico* (Río Piedras, 1982), chapters 3, 6, and 7; María Isabel Bonnin Orozco, "Las fortunas vulnerables: comerciantes y agricultores en los contratos de refacción en Ponce, 1865–1875" (master's thesis in history, University of Puerto Rico, Río Piedras, 1984); Luis E. Díaz, *Castañer: Una hacienda cafetalera en Puerto Rico (1868–1930)* (2nd ed.; Río Piedras, 1983), 40.
25. See Annie Santiago de Curet, *Crédito, moneda y bancos en Puerto Rico durante el siglo XIX* (Río Piedras, 1989).
26. See Cubano, *Comercio y hegemonía social*, 225–27; Bergad, *Coffee*, 169; Díaz, *Castañer*, 125; Esperanza Mayol, *Islas* (San Juan, 1974).
27. See María Asunción García Ochoa, *La política española en Puerto Rico durante el siglo XIX* (Río Piedras, 1982), 361–67.
28. See Loida Figueroa, *Breve historia de Puerto Rico*, part 2: *Desde el crepúsculo del dominio español hasta la antesala de la Ley Foraker (1892–1900)* (Río Piedras, 1977), 74–75.
29. See Andrés Ramos Mattei, "Technical Innovations and Social Change in the Sugar Industry of Puerto Rico 1870–1880," in Manuel Moreno Fraginals, Frank Moya Pons, and Stanley Z. Engerman, *Between Slavery and Free Labor: The Spanish-Speaking Caribbean in the Nineteenth Century* (Baltimore, 1985), 170–72.
30. There are numerous dossiers of municipal judgments in Utuado for this period in which a landowner sues a worker to pay his debt of 10, 15, or 20 pesos and the worker promises to pay in labor: see AGPR, Fondo del Tribunal Superior de Arecibo,

Civil Series, Utuado, boxes 241A and following. For instance, in October, 1876, the landowner Manuel Jiménez claimed 24 pesos and 16 cents from Juan Monserrate Maldonado, from Roncador ward, plus legal costs. Maldonado acknowledged the debt "and he offers to pay it with two or three days of work a week in the claimant's place. The plaintiff accepted the offer" (ibid., box 246, "Mes de Octubre de 1876. Demanda de D. Manuel Giménez contra Juan Monserrate Maldonado. Núm. 103").

31. See Luis Díaz, *Castañer*, 56–57; Buitrago, *Haciendas cafetaleras*, 140–45.
32. See Fernando Picó, *Los irrespetuosos* (San Juan, 2000).
33. See Andrés Ramos Mattei, "Documentos para la historia de Puerto Rico en el siglo XIX," *Anales de Investigación Histórica* 9 (1982): 72–73.
34. Díaz, *Castañer*, 58–60; AGPR, Fondo de Fortaleza, letter of the mayor of Utuado on September 21, 1899; Thomas E. Sherman, S.J., "A Month in Porto Rico," *The Messenger of the Sacred Heart* 33, no. 12 (1898): 1078–79.
35. See Silvia Alvarez Curbelo, "El Motín de los Faroles y otras luminosas protestas: disturbios populares en Puerto Rico, 1894," *Historia y Sociedad*, no. 2 (1989): 120–46.
36. See Gervasio L. García and Angel G. Quintero Rivera, *Desafío y solidaridad: Breve historia del movimiento obrero puertorriqueño* (Río Piedras, 1982), chapter 1.
37. See Dulce María Tirado, "Las raíces sociales del liberalismo criollo: El Partido Liberal Reformista (1870–1875)" (master's thesis in history, University of Puerto Rico, Río Piedras, 1981).
38. See Félix Mejías, *De la crisis económica del 86 al año terrible del 87 (Apuntes para la Historia Económica de Puerto Rico)* (Río Piedras, 1972).
39. See José A. Gautier Dapena, *Trayectoria del pensamiento liberal puertorriqueño en el siglo XIX* (San Juan, 1963), 41–44.
40. See Portuondo, op. cit., 393–468.
41. See Cruz Monclova, *Historia*, vol. 2, part 1 (1868–1874).
42. See Antonio Rivera, "Viva Puerto Rico Li... Li... Li...," *Historia* 4, no. 1 (1954): 65–68; Fernando Picó, "Don Cayetano Estrella y el Camuy de la Estrellada," *Contra la Corriente* (Río Piedras, 1995), 53–72.
43. See José Curet, "About Slavery and the Order of Things, Puerto Rico, 1845–1873," in Moreno, Moya, and Engerman, *Between Slavery and Free Labor*, 117ff.
44. See Alberto Cibes Viadé, *Don Juan de la Pezuela inicia el abolicionismo puertorriqueño* (offprint from *Revista Extramuros*) (Río Piedras, 1975).
45. Fernando Picó, "Los Ocultadores de Manatí," *El Nuevo Día*, Sunday magazine, March, 2001.
46. Centro de Investigaciones Históricas, Universidad de Puerto Rico, *El proceso abolicionista en Puerto Rico: Documentos para su estudio*, vol. 2 (San Juan, 1978), 83–100.
47. Cruz Monclova, *Historia*, vol. 2, part 1, 269.
48. See Benjamín Nistal Moret, "Problems in the Social Structure of Slavery in Puerto Rico During the Process of Abolition, 1872," in Moreno, Moya, and Engerman, *Between Slavery and Free Labor*, 117–40; Ramos Mattei, "Technical Innovations," ibid.; Pedro San Miguel, "Expediente sobre la abolición de la esclavitud (Juncos, Puerto Rico, 1873)," *Historia y Sociedad* 1 (1988): 183–88.
49. Labor Gómez Acevedo, *Sanz: Promotor de la Conciencia Separatista en Puerto Rico* (San Juan, 1956).
50. Ibid., 208–14.
51. AGPR, Municipal Archives of Río Piedras, provisional box 332, bound docket titled "Archivo Municipal de Río Piedras Años 1888–89 Varios Asuntos," dossier "Lista de electores para Diputado a Cortes, ratificada con arreglo al artículo 54 de la Ley electoral para regir en la expresada sección durante el presente año de 1885," 312r–313v and 354r.
52. Cayetano Coll y Toste, "Don Rafael M. de Labra," *Boletín Histórico de Puerto Rico* 5 (1918): 376–78.
53. See Leandro Fanul González, "Don Pablo Ubarri y Puerto Rico" (master's thesis in history, University of Puerto Rico, Río Piedras, 1980).
54. See Mariano Negrón Portillo, *El autonomismo puertorriqueño: su transformación ide-*

ológica (1895–1914) (Río Piedras, 1981), 15–16. On the newspapers of that period see Antonio Pedreira, *El periodismo en Puerto Rico* (Río Piedras, 1969), vol. 5 of the *Obras Completas*; Fernando Feliú Matilla, ed., *200 años de literatura y periodismo 1803–2003* (San Juan, 2004).

55. See Trías Monge, *El sistema judicial*, 37.
56. García Ochoa, *La política española*, 386–401; Luis de la Rosa Martínez, *Historia de la instrucción pública en Vega Baja 1874–1910* (Vega Baja, 1980), 17–19.
57. Antonio Borrés Otero, in an unpublished seminar paper entitled "El cambio de soberanía y el sentimiento religioso popular en el municipio de Río Piedras 1890–1909," found that in Río Piedras in the years between 1890 and 1893 more children appear as baptized than are on the civil register.
58. See María Barceló Miller, *Política ultramarina y gobierno municipal: Isabela 1873–1887* (Río Piedras, 1984).
59. See Mejías, op. cit.
60. See Gautier, 51–52, 57–60; Cruz Monclova, *Historia*, vol. 2, part 2, 671–76; vol. 3, part 1, 27–36.
61. Lidio Cruz Monclova, *Historia del año de 1887* (3rd ed.; Río Piedras, 1970), 163–65.
62. Ibid., 203ff; 253–328; Coll y Toste, ed., "Proclama del Gobernador Don Romualdo Palacios al País, dando a conocer la carta del Jefe de la Guardia Civil sobre la Sociedad Secreta Los Secos" and "Documentos para la Historia de la Sociedad Secreta 'Los Secos y los Mojados', llamada también 'La Torre del Viejo', que diólugar a los Sucesos Políticos de 1887," *Boletín Histórico de Puerto Rico* 5 (1918): 17–20 and 263–72.
63. Cruz Monclova, *Historia del 1887*, loc. cit. An example of a conservative leader who protected his friends was Eusebio Pérez, a Jayuya hacendado; see Carlos Orama Padilla, "Don Eusebio Pérez: un caudillo del cafetal," in *Album de Jayuya 1962–63* (San Juan, 1964), 171.
64. Cruz Monclova, *Historia del 1887*, 338–39; Coll y Toste, ed., "Cablegrama puesto desde St. Thomas a Madrid, a Don Rafael M. de Labra, diputado a Cortes, por los autonomistas," *Boletín Histórico de Puerto Rico* 5 (1918): 375–76.
65. Lidio Cruz Monclova, *Baldorioty de Castro* (San Juan, 1966), 344, 377.
66. See Pilar Barbosa de Rosario, *La comisión autonomista de 1896: Historia del autonomismo puertorriqueño, 16 de septiembre de 1896 al 12 de febrero de 1897* (San Juan, 1957).
67. See Pilar Barbosa de Rosario, *El ensayo de la autonomía en Puerto Rico 1897–1898* (San Juan, 1975), 45–49.
68. See José Trías Monge, *Historia constitucional de Puerto Rico* (Río Piedras, 1980), 1:107–34.
69. Coll y Toste, *Reseña*, 3–4.
70. Portuondo, 513, 515ff.
71. See Ramón de Armas, "Acerca de la estrategia continental de José Martí: El papel de Cuba y Puerto Rico," *Anuario del Centro de Estudios Martianos* 7 (1984): 88–112.
72. Joaquín Freire, *Presencia de Puerto Rico en la Historia de Cuba (Una aportación al estudio de la historia antillana)* (San Juan, 1975).
73. See Luis Bonafoux, *Betances* (2nd ed.; San Juan, 1970); Ramón Emeterio Betances, *Las Antillas para los Antillanos*, edited by Carlos M. Rama (San Juan, 1975); Ramón Emeterio Betances, *Epistolario (1895)*, edited by Ada M. Suárez Díaz (Río Piedras, 1978); Manuel Maldonado Denis, *Betances revolucionario antillano y otros ensayos* (Río Piedras, 1978).
74. See Cruz Monclova, *Historia*, vol. 3, part 3, 42–51; Carmelo Rosario Natal, *Puerto Rico y la crisis de la Guerra Hispanoamericana* (Río Piedras, 1975), Appendix 12, pp. 319–21.
75. See Philip S. Foner, *The Spanish-Cuban-American War and the Birth of American Imperialism* (New York, 1972), 1:236–39, 254–76.
76. José Luis González, *El país de cuatro pisos y otros ensayos* (Río Piedras, 1980), 9–44; English translation by Gerald Guinness, *Puerto Rico: The Four-Storeyed Country*

(Princeton: Markus Wiener, 1993).
77. See Angel Quintero Rivera, *Salsa, sabor y control: Sociología de la música tropical* (2nd ed.; Mexico City, 1999).
78. See Edgardo Rodríguez Juliá, *Campeche o los diablejos de la melancolía* (San Juan, 1986).
79. See Osiris Delgado Mercado, *Francisco Oller y Cestero (1833–1917), Pintor de Puerto Rico* (San Juan, 1983), 90–102.
80. For a modern rendition, see Rafael Trelles, *Visitas al Velorio (Instalción en homenaje a Francisco Oller)* (Río Piedras, 1991).
81. See Josephine Rullán, "El Ateneo Puertorriqueño: Secuela y Gestor del Pensamiento Liberal, 1876–1903" (master's thesis in history, University of Puerto Rico, Río Piedras, 1982).
82. See P. Juan Jorge Rivera Torres, ed., *Documentos históricos de la Iglesia Episcopal Puertorriqueña*, vol. 1 (San Juan, 1983), 10–16; José Aracelio Cardona, *Breve historia de la Iglesia Presbiteriana en Puerto Rico* (Río Piedras, 1976), 8–12.

Chapter 13

1. See Yamila Azize, "¿Interesaban los Estados Unidos a Puerto Rico antes de 1898?" *Homines* 8, no. 1 (1984): 77–81; Norzagaray, "Diario metódico," loc. cit.; Sumner Welles, *Naboth's Vineyard: The Dominican Republic 1844–1924* (New York, 1928); Henry Adams, *The Education of Henry Adams* (New York, 1964), 145.
2. See Charles H. Brown, *The Correspondents' War: Journalists in the Spanish-American War* (New York, 1967).
3. See for instance, Richard Harding Davis, "The Rough Riders at Guasimas," in *Notes of a War Correspondent* (New York, 1911), 45–76.
4. Angel Rivero, *Crónica de la Guerra Hispanoamericana en Puerto Rico* (San Juan, 1972), 65–143.
5. See Carmelo Rosario Natal, *Puerto Rico y la crisis de la Guerra Hispanoamericana (1895–1898)* (Hato Rey, 1975), 97–98. In 1868 there was a division among revolutionaries in Mayaguez with regard to the Grito de Lares because some favored annexation to the United States (Ramos Mattei, "Betances, Lares y el ciclo revolucionario antillano," loc. cit., 21).
6. See Alfred T. Mahan, *Lessons of the War with Spain and Other Articles* (2nd impression, Freeport, 1979), 28–29.
7. Rivero, op. cit., 182–83.
8. See text in ibid., 232.
9. Ibid., 224–30; Rosario Natal, *Puerto Rico. . .*, 231.
10. Rivero, 271–73; see R.H. Davis, "The Taking of Coamo," op. cit., 101–12.
11. Julio Tomás Martínez Mirabal, *Colección Martínez: Crónicas íntimas* (Arecibo, 1946), 49–57; Rivero, 562. Several days later the brigade commanded by General Guy Henry camped in Utuado. The poet Carl Sandburg, in an autobiographical text, would remember the march of that brigade under heavy rain. *Always the Young Strangers* (New York, 1953), 425–16.
12. Department of Health, Registro Demográfico de Utuado, Defunciones, entries 614 and 615.
13. See Fernando Picó, *Puerto Rico 1898: The War After the War* (Princeton: Markus Wiener Publishers, 2004).
14. See Rivero, 421–26; Sherman, loc. cit.; Rosario Natal, *Puerto Rico*, 260–63; Mayol, 129–34.
15. Juan Manuel Delgado, *El levantamiento de Ciales* (San Juan, 1981); Picó, *Puerto Rico 1898*, 48–50.
16. Several guides for potential North American investors were published at that time. See, for instance, Robert T. Hill, *Cuba and Porto Rico with the Other Islands of the West Indies: Their Topography, Climate, Flora, Products, Industries, Cities, People, Political Conditions, Etc.* (2nd ed.; New York, 1899). Ramón Morel Campos, author of *El por-*

venir de Utuado (Ponce, 1897), was promoting his work in English on November 2, 1898 (*El Cañón*, no. 1, p. 4).

17. See Mariano Negrón Portillo, "El liderato anexionista antes y después del cambio de soberanía," *Revista del Colegio de Abogados* 33 (1972): 369–91.

18. In point of fact Toa Alta was not occupied by the Americans until October 27, and Culebra even later (Rivero, 689).

19. See *Message from the President of the United States Transmitting a Treaty of Peace Between the United States and Spain Signed at the City of Paris on December 10, 1898* (Washington, D.C., 1899).

20. See Edward Berbusse, S.J., *The United States in Puerto Rico, 1898–1900* (Chapel Hill, 1966).

21. See AGPR, Fondo Municipal de Utuado, "Acta de la reunión celebrada por los mayores contribuyentes sobre allegar recursos para el Municipio," September, 1898.

22. Berbusse, op. cit., 93.

23. Coll y Toste, *Reseña*, 13–15.

24. Bothwell, op. cit. 2:111.

25. See Carmen I. Raffucci, *El gobierno civil y la Ley Foraker (Antecedentes históricos)* (Río Piedras, 1981), 43–107; Claude Bowers, *Beveridge and the Progressive Era* (Cambridge, Mass., 1932); Robert Beisner, *Twelve Against Empire: The Anti-Imperialists 1898–1900* (New York, 1968).

26. Picó, *Puerto Rico 1898*, 114–16.

27. See Juan Bosch, *Hostos el sembrador* (3rd ed.; Santo Domingo, 1979), 176–87.

28. See María Dolores Luque de Sánchez, *La ocupación norteamericana y la Ley Foraker (La opinión pública puertorriqueña) 1898–1904* (Río Piedras, 1980), 135–87; Raffucci, op. cit., 109–35. See text in José Trías Monge, *Historia constitucional de Puerto Rico*, vol. 4 (Río Piedras, 1983), 327–38.

29. *Journal of the Executive Council of Porto Rico: Executive and Legislative Sessions*, vol. 1: *June 28, 1900 to January 31, 1901* (San Juan, n.d.), 5.

30. Ibid., 18–24; see 27 and 81; Bothwell 2:157–63.

31. See Muriel McAvoy-Weissman, "Early United States Investors in Puerto Rican Sugar," in Blanca Silvestrini, ed., *Politics, Society and Culture in the Caribbean: Selected Papers of the XIV Conference of Caribbean Historians* (San Juan, 1983), 113–30.

32. See Carmelo Rosario Natal, *Exodo puertorriqueño (Las emigraciones al Caribe y al Hawaii: 1900–1915)* (San Juan, 1983); Norma Carr, "Imágenes: El Puertorriqueño en Hawaii," in Asela Rodríguez de Laguna, ed., *Imágenes e Identidades: el puertorriqueño en la literatura* (Río Piedras, 1985), 105–16; Blase Camacho Souza and Alfred P. Souza, *De Borinquen a Hawaii: Nuestra Historia. From Puerto Rico to Hawaii* (Honolulu: Puerto Rican Heritage Society of Hawaii, 1985).

33. See Negociado del Trabajo, *Informe sobre las condiciones de vivienda de los trabajadores de Puerto Rico* (San Juan, 1914).

34. See José L. Vázquez Calzada, *La población de Puerto Rico y su trayectoria histórica* (San Juan, 1978), 214, 134, 136.

35. See Bailey K. Ashford, *A Soldier in Science* (New York, 1934), 56–104; Blanca G. Silvestrini, "El impacto de la política de salud pública de los Estados Unidos en Puerto Rico 1898–1913," in Silvestrini, ed., *Politics, Society and Culture*, 69–83; Luis Pabón Batlle, *El retorno de Polifemo: La medicina de Estado en Puerto Rico al umbral del siglo XX* (Bayamón, 2003); Marlene Duprey Colón, "La ilusión del cuerpo sano: Discursos sobre higiene, cartografías del peligro y dispositivos de vigilancia en Puerto Rico (1883–1933)" (Ph.D. dissertation in history, University of Puerto Rico, Río Piedras, 2003).

36. Vázquez Calzada, op. cit., 136; Annette B. Ramírez de Arellano and Conrad Seipp, *Colonialism, Catholicism and Contraception: A History of Birth Control in Puerto Rico* (Chapel Hill, 1983), 175. Fertility rates, however, went down from 191.9 in the first decade of the twentieth century to 173.4 in 1930; in the 1970s the rate was 95.8 (Vázquez Calzada, 139).

37. See the works already cited by Angel G. Quintero, and José A. Herrero, *La mitología del azúcar: Un ensayo en historia económica de Puerto Rico, 1900–1970*, Centro de

Estudios de la Realidad Puertorriqueña (CEREP), *Cuadernos*, 5.
38. See Victor S. Clark and others, *Porto Rico and Its Problems* (Washington, D.C., 1930), 479–514.
39. See Yamila Azize, *Luchas de la mujer en Puerto Rico 1898–1919* (San Juan, 1979); Blanca Silvestrini, "La mujer puertorriqueña y el movimiento obrero en la década de 1930," *Cuadernos de la Facultad de Humanidades* 3 (1979): 85–104; Fernando Picó, "Las trabajadoras del tabaco en Utuado según el censo de 1910," *Al Filo del Poder* (Río Piedras, 1993), 173–94.
40. See Gervasio L. García y Angel G. Quintero Rivera, *Desafío y solidaridad: Breve historia del movimiento obrero puertorriqueño* (Río Piedras, 1982), 15–27.
41. Ramos Mattei, "Documentos," loc. cit., 72–73.
42. *El Liberal*, April 15, 1898, p. 2.
43. Rafael Alonso Torres, *Cuarenta años de lucha proletaria*, edited by Nicolás Nogueras Rivera (San Juan, 1939), 60, 63, 94, 224.
44. See Ginzalo Córdova, *Santiago Iglesias: Creador del movimiento obrero de Puerto Rico* (Río Piedras, 1980); Santiago Iglesias, *Luchas emancipadoras* (2nd ed.; Río Piedras, 1956).
45. See Arturo Bird Carmona, *A lima y machete: La huelga cañera de 1915 y la fundación del Partido Socialsita* (Río Piedras, 2001).
46. See Mariano Negrón Portillo, *Las turbas republicanas, 1900–1904* (Río Piedras, 1990).
47. See José A. Gautier Dapena, "Génesis, fundación y triunfo de la Unión de Puerto Rico," *Historia* 6 (1956): 3–34; Luis M. Díaz Soler, *Rosendo Matienzo Cintrón, Orientador y Guardián de una cultura* (Río Piedras, 1960), 2:255–87; Bothwell, 2:191–97.
48. See Cayetano Coll Cuchí, *Historia del gran partido político puertorruqueño Unión de Puerto Rico* (San Juan, 1930); Amilcar Tirado Avilés, "Ramón Romero Rosa: Su participación en las luchas obreras (1896–1906)," *Caribe* 2 (1980–81): 3–25; Angel G. Quintero Rivera, "El análisis social de Ramón Romero Rosa, obrero tipógrafo puertorriqueño de principios de siglo," ibid., 27–31.
49. *Journal of the Executive Council of Porto Rico, 1909*, 129–30, 149, 154–55, 175, 177; Ramón Meléndez, "El conflicto legislativo de 1909 en Puerto Rico," *Historia*, new series 1, no. 1 (1962): 65–82.
50. See Frank Otto Gatell, "The Art of the Possible, Luis Muñoz Rivera and the Puerto Rican Jones Bill," unpublished work, pp. 10 and 17 (copy in the Puerto Rican Collection of the Lázaro General Library of the University of Puerto Rico); Bolívar Pagán, *Historia de los partidos políticos puertorriqueños (1898–1956)* (2nd ed.; San Juan, 1972), 1:174; José Cabranes, *Citizenship and the American Empire* (New Haven, 1979).
51. M. Drew, ed., *Register of Porto Rico for 1910* (San Juan, 1911), p. 231.
52. Gatell, op. cit., 20–23, Bolívar Pagán, 1:176.
53. See text in José Trías Monge, *Historia constitucional*, 4:341–65.
54. See Samuel Ewer Eastman and Daniel Marx, Jr., *Ships and Sugar: An Evaluation of Puerto Rican Offshore Shipping* (Río Piedras, 1953), chapter 10, "The Institutional Environment in Which Puerto Rican Shipping Operates," and chapter 8, "Ocean Freights and the Cost of Living: The Impact of Rates."
55. See Marc Ferro, *La Gran Guerra (1914–1918)*, translated by Soledad Ortega (Madrid, 1970).
56. See AGPR, Fondo de la Policía, Querellas, box 3, lists of persons sought by the police for evading military duty. According to police reports, one way of evading service was to migrate to work in New York.
57. Centro de Estudios Puertorriqueños de Nueva York, History Task Force, Sources, 104–28; Bernardo Vega, *Memorias de Bernardo Vega: Contribución a la historia de la comunidad puertorriqueña en Nueva York*, edited by César Andreu Iglesias (2nd ed.; Río Piedras, 1980), 139.
58. See Truman R. Clark, *Puerto Rico and the United States, 1917–1933* (Pittsburgh, 1975), 31–35.
59. See Victor Clark and others, op. cit., 479–83, 654–74, 687–97.

60. See Broadus Mitchell, *Depression Decade: From New Era Through New Deal 1929–1941*, vol. 9 of *The Economic History of the United States* (New York, 1961).
61. See Blanca Silvestrini, *Violencia y criminalidad en Puerto Rico, 1898–1973* (Río Piedras, 1980); Pedro A. Vales, Astrid A. Ortíz, and Noel A. Mattei, *Patrones de criminalidad en Puerto Rico: Apreciación socio-histórica, 1898–1980* (Río Piedras, 1982).
62. See Bothwell 1:397–400; 2:322–24.
63. See Luis Angel Ferrao, *Pedro Albizu Campos y el Nacionalismo Puertorriqueño* (San Juan, 1990).
64. Junta Insular de Elecciones, *Estadísticas de las elecciones celebradas en Puerto Rico el 8 de noviembre de 1932*.
65. On this subject, see Taller de Formación Política, *¡Huelga en la Caña! 1933–34* (Río Piedras, 1982); Georg Fromm, "La historia ficción de Benjamín Torres: Albizu y la huelga cañera de 1934," seven essays published in the literary supplement *En Rojo*, in *Claridad*, between the end of May and the beginning of July, 1977.
66. See Sonia Carbonell Ojeda, "Blanton Winship y el Partido Nacionalista (1934–1939)" (master's thesis in history, University of Puerto Rico, Río Piedras, 1984), chapters 2 and 3.
67. See Carbonell, op. cit., chapters 2 and 3; Manuel Moraza Ortíz, *La masacre de Ponce* (Hato Rey, 2001).
68. See García y Quintero, op. cit., 110; Georg Fromm, loc. cit. and *César Andreu Iglesias* (Río Piedras, 1976), 54–59; Arcadio Díaz Quiñones, *Conversación con José Luis González* (Río Piedras, 1976), 106–18.
69. See Thomas Mathews, *La política puertorriqueña del Nuevo Trato*, translated into Spanish by Antonio J. Colorado (Río Piedras, 1970), 25–26, 35–37; Bolívar Pagán, 1:314–19; II, 1–47.
70. On the recognition of women's right to vote, see Clark, op. cit., 40–45; María Barceló Miller, *La lucha por el sufragio femenino en Puerto Rico 1896–1935* (Río Piedras, 1997).
71. See Blanca Silvestrini, *Los trabajadores puertorriqueños y el Partido Socialista (1932–1940)* (Río Piedras, 1979), 46–75.
72. See García and Quintero, 112; Juan Angel Silén, *Apuntes para la historia del movimiento obrero puertorriqueño* (Río Piedras, 1978), 100; Taller de Formación Política, *No estamos pidiendo el cielo: Huelga portuaria de 1938* (Río Piedras, 1988).
73. Mathews, op. cit., 130–42.
74. Ibid., 153–82; Bothwell, 2:446–48.
75. Mathews, 196–200, 210–15, 218ff., 318–19.
76. Thomas E. Benner, *Five Years of Foundation Building: The University of Puerto Rico, 1924–1929* (Río Piedras, 1965). See also Carlos Rodríguez Fraticelli, *Education and Imperialism: The Puerto Rican Experience in Higher Education 1898–1986*, Centro de Estudios Puertorriqueños, Working Paper Series (New York, 1986).
77. María Luisa Moreno, *La arquitectura de la Universidad de Puerto Rico* (Río Piedras, 2002).
78. See Aida Negrón Montilla, *Americanization in Puerto Rico and the Public School System 1900–1930* (Río Piedras, 1971).
79. One of the New England teachers who came later wrote a novel that vividly shares her experience of teaching in Carolina in 1910. See Marion Webster, *Jangled Bells: A Story of Puerto Rico* (Boston, 1950).

Chapter 14

1. See John Kenneth Galbraith, *The New Industrial State* (New York, 1986).
2. See Luis Muñoz Marín, *La historia del Partido Popular Democrático* (San Juan, 1984).
3. See Norberto Barreto Velázquez, *Rexford G. Tugwell: El último de los tutores* (San Juan, 2004).
4. See Rexford Tugwell, *The Stricken Land: The Story of Puerto Rico* (Garden City, 1947); Charles T. Goodsell, *Administration of a Revolution: Executive Reform in Puerto Rico under Governor Tugwell, 1941–1946* (Cambridge, Mass., 1965).

5. Tugwell, op. cit., 296, 336–37, 360–61.

6. Bothwell, vol. 1, part 1, 6661–66, and vol. 3, 419–27, 456–76, 496–505.

7. See Kal Wagenheim, *A Survey of Puerto Ricans in the United States Mainland in the 1970s* (New York, 1975); Centro de Estudios Puertorriqueños de Nueva York, History Task Force, *Labor Migration Under Capitalism: The Puerto Rican Experience* (New York, 1979), 117–264; Luis Nieves Falcón, *El emigrante puertorriqueño* (Río Piedras, 1975); Manuel Maldonado Denis, *Puerto Rico y Estados Unidos: Emigración y colonialismo* (3rd ed.; Mexico City, 1982); Joseph Fitzpatrick, *Puerto Rican Americans: The Meaning of Migration to the Mainland* (2nd ed.; Englewood Cliffs, 1987).

8. See Virginia Sánchez Korrol, *From Colonia to Community: A History of the Puerto Ricans in New York City* (Berkeley, 1994).

9. See Carmen Teresa Whalen, *From Puerto Rico to Philadelphia: Puerto Rican Workers and Postwar Economics* (Philadelphia, 2001).

10. See Clara E. Rodríguez and Virginia Sánchez Korrol, eds., *Historical Perspectives on Puerto Rican Survival in the United States* (Princeton: Markus Wiener Publishers, 1996).

11. See José Figueroa, *Survival on the Margin: A Documentary Story of the Underground Economy in a Puerto Rican Ghetto* (New York, 1989).

12. See Richard Jacoby, *Conversations with the Capeman: The Untold Story of Salvador Agrón* (Madison, 2004).

13. Ruth M. Reynolds, *Campus in Bondage: A 1948 Microcosm of Puerto Rico in Bondage*, edited by Carlos Rodríguez Fraticelli and Blanca Vázuez Erazo (New York, 1989). On the first decades of the student movements at the University of Puerto Rico, see Isabel Picó de Hernández, "Los estudiantes universitarios y el proceso político puertorriqueño, 1903–1948" (Ph.D. thesis, Harvard University, 1974).

14. Miñi Seijo Bruno, *Historia de la Insurrección Nacionalista de 1950* (San Juan, 1989).

15. Bothwell, vol. 1, part 1, 702–6; vol. 1, part 2, 774–95, 796–800; vol. 4, 209–12, 273–75, 401.

16. See Ivonne Acosta, *La mordaza: Puerto Rico 1948–1957* (Río Piedras, 1989).

17. Luis Muñoz Marín, *Memorias: Autobiografía pública, 1898–1940* (San Juan, 1982).

18. See Félix Ojeda Reyes, ed., *Vito Marcantonio y Puerto Rico: Por los trabajadores y por la nación* (Río Piedras, 1978).

19. José Trías Monge, *Historia Constitucional de Puerto Rico*, vol. 3 (Río Piedras, 1982), 274–307.

20. Ibid., 300, 309; Constitution of the Commonwealth of Puerto Rico, article 7, section 3.

21. See Pedro Malavet Vega, *La vellonera está directa: Felipe Rodríguez (La voz) y los años 50* (San Juan, 1984).

22. There were 5.4 homicides per hundred thousand persons in 1957 (see Vales and others, op. cit., 52–54).

23. See Luis Figueroa Martínez, "Las actividades organizativas de las uniones internacionales norteamericanas en Puerto Rico, 1949–1963," *Anales de Investigación Histórica* 8 (1981): 1–89.

24. On the problems and dynamics of schooling in such areas see Iris Rivera, "Estudio etnográfico de una escuela rural aislada en el distrito escolar de Yauco," Ph.D. thesis in education at the Interamerican University.

25. See Tarsicio Ocampo, ed., *Puerto Rico: Partido Acción Cristiana 1960–62: Documentos y reacciones de prensa*, CIDOC 11 (Cuernavaca, 1967); María Mercedes Alonso, *Muñoz Marín vs. the Bishops: An Approach to Church and State* (Hato Rey, 1998).

26. See Edna Belén Acosta, ed., *La mujer en la sociedad puertorriqueña* (Río Piedras, 1980); *Indicadores socioeconómicos de la situación de las mujeres en Puerto Rico, 1970–1989* (San Juan: Junta de Planificación, n.d.).

27. See Junta de Planificación de Puerto Rico, *Indicadores socioeconómicos de la situación de las mujeres en Puerto Rico, 1970–1989* (San Juan, n.d.).

28. See Himilce Esteve, *El exilio cubano en Puerto Rico: su impacto socio-político, 1959–1983* (San Juan, 1984).

29. See Norma Tapia, *La crisis del PIP* (Río Piedras, 1980); Rubén Berríos, *Hacia el social-*

ismo puertorriqueño (San Juan, n.d.) and *La independencia de Puerto Rico: razón y lucha* (Mexico City, 1983).

30. Trías Monge, *Historia*, 4:435–42; Antonio Fernós Isern, *Estado Libre Asociado de Puerto Rico: Antecedentes, creación y desarrollo hasta la época presente* (Río Piedras, 1974), part 3.

31. Bothwell, 4:406–16; 418–29. See Luis Martínez Fernández, *El Partido Nuevo Progresista: Su trayectoria hacia el poder y los orígenes sociales de sus fundadores (1967–68)* (Río Piedras, 1986).

32. See Junta Estatal de Elecciones, *Informe oficial sobre la votación del Plebiscito de 1967 relacionado con el status político de Puerto Rico 23 de julio de 1967* (San Juan, 1967); Eduardo Luis Cruz Hernández, *El plebiscito de 1967: Orígen, desarrollo y consecuencias en la política puertorriqueña* (Río Piedras, 1993).

33. On these years see Antonio Quiñones Calderón, *La obra de Luis A. Ferré en la Fortaleza* (Santurce, 1976).

34. See Marcia Rivera, *Elecciones de 1968 en Puerto Rico: Análisis estadístico por grupos socio-económicos* (San Juan, 1972).

35. See Junta de Planificación de Puerto Rico, *Informe económico al Gobernador 1981* (San Juan, 1982); Eliezer Curet Cuevas, *Economía política de Puerto Rico, 1950 a 2000* (San Juan, 2003).

36. See Manny Suárez, *Two Lynchings on Cerro Maravilla: The Police Murders in Puerto Rico and the Federal Government Cover Up* (San Juan, 2003).

37. See *Informe al Gobernador del Comité para el estudio de las finanzas de Puerto Rico (Informe Tobin)* (Río Piedras, 1976).

38. Curet Cuevas, op. cit., 357.

Chapter 15

1. See Tom Wolfe, *The Kandy-Kolored Tangerine-Flake Streamline Baby* (New York, 1966), 33–34.

2. See Alvin Toffler, *Future Shock* (New York, 1972), 268–69; André Gorz, *Ecología y política*, translated by Miguel Gil (2nd ed.; Barcelona, 1982), 26–28.

3. See Joe McGinnis, *The Selling of the President 1968* (New York, 1969).

4. See Joan Didion, *Slouching Towards Bethlehem* (6th impression; New York, 1968), 84–128.

5. Junta de Planificación de Puerto Rico, *Informe económico al Gobernador* (San Juan, 1981), 37.

6. On life in this community in the 1960s see Oscar Lewis, *La Vida: A Puerto Rican Family in the Culture of Poverty—San Juan and New York* (New York, 1966).

7. Junta de Planificación de Puerto Rico, op. cit.

8. See Gerardo Navas Dávila, "Indicadores de calidad para los municipios de Puerto Rico," *Plerus* 11, nos. 1–2 (1977): 138.

9. Luis Muñoz Marín, "Discurso pronunciado en Barranquitas el día de Luis Muñoz Rivera, 17 de julio de 1973," in Departamento de Instrucción Pública, *Celebración del 88vo. aniversario del natalicio de Don Luis Muñoz Rivera* (San Juan, 1986), 51–56.

10. See Richard Weisskoff, *Factories and Food Stamps: The Puerto Rico Model of Development* (Baltimore, 1985).

11. See Pedro Santaliz, "Diversiones y condiciones del teatro popular de los barrios de Puerto Rico: Acercamiento de 'El Nuevo Teatro Pobre de América'," in Asela Rodríguez de Laguna, ed., *Imágenes e identidades*, 173–78.

Chapter 16

1. See Carlos Pabón, *Nación Postmorten: Ensayos sobre los tiempos de insoportable ambigüedad* (San Juan, 2002).

2. See Rafael Bernabe, *La maldición de Pedreira (Aspectos de la crítica romántico-cultural de la modernidad en Puerto Rico)* (Río Piedras, 2002).

Selected Bibliography

1. Bibliographical and Methodological Guides and Collections of Documents

Caro Costas, Aidra R. *Antología de lecturas de historia de Puerto Rico, siglos xv–xviii.* Río Piedras: Editorial Universitaria, 1977.

Castro, María de los Angeles, María Dolores Luque, and Gervasio Luis García. *Los primeros pasos: Una bibliografía para empezar a investigar la historia de Puerto Rico.* Río Piedras: Centro de Investigaciones Históricas, Universidad de Puerto Rico, 1984.

De la Rosa, Luis. *Lexicon histórico-documental de Puerto Rico (1812–1899).* San Juan: Centro de Estudios Avanzados de Puerto Rico y el Caribe, 1986.

Fernández Méndez, Eugenio. *Crónicas de Puerto Rico desde la conquista hasta nuestros días (1493–1953).* 2nd ed. Río Piedras: Editorial Universitaria, 1955.

Picó, Rafael, et al. *Nueva geografía de Puerto Rico: Física, económica, y social.* Río Piedras: Editorial Universitaria, 1969.

2. The Amerindians of Boriquén

Alegría, Ricardo E. *History of the Indians of Puerto Rico.* Translated by C. Virginia Matters. San Juan: Colección de Estudios Puertorriqueños, 1983.

Chanlatte Baik, Luis. *La hueca y sorcé (Vieques, Puerto Rico): Primeras migraciones agroalfareras antillanas: Nuevo esquema para los procesos culturales de la arqueología antillana.* Santo Domingo: 1981.

Chanlatte Baik, Luis. "Cultura ostionoide: Un desarrollo agroalfarero antillano," *Homines* 10, no. 1 (1986).

Chanlatte Baik, Luis. *La cultura saladoide en Puerto Rico: su rostro multicolor.* Río Piedras: Museo de Historia, Antropología y Arte, 2002.

Moscoso, Francisco. "Tributo y formación de clases en la sociedad de los taínos de las Antillas." *Revista Dominicana de Antropología e Historia* 9 (1977–79): 89–118.

Rouse, Irving. *The Tainos: Rise & Decline of the People Who Greeted Columbus.* New Haven: Yale University Press, 1992.

Sued Badillo, Jalil. *Los caribes: realidad o fábula.* Río Piedras: Editorial Antillana, 1978.

3. From the Sixteenth to the Eighteenth Centuries

Abbad y Lasierra, Fray Agustín Iñigo. *Historia geográfica, civil y natural de la isla de San Juan Bautista de Puerto Rico.* Estudio preliminar de Isabel Gutierrez del Arroyo. 3rd printing. Río Piedras: Editorial Universitaria, 1970.

Alegría, Ricardo E., ed. *El pleito por indios de encomienda entre el ex-contador Antonio Sedeño y el contador Miguel de Castellanos, Puerto Rico, 1527.* San Juan: Centro de Estudios Avanzados de Puerto Rico y el Caribe, 1993.

Ballesteros Gaibrois, Manuel. *La idea colonial de Ponce de León: Un ensayo de interpretación.* San Juan: Instituto de Cultura Puertorriqueña, 1960.

Brau, Salvador. *La colonización de Puerto Rico: Desde el descubrimiento de la isla hasta la reversión a la corona española de los privilegios de Colón.* 4th ed. San Juan: Instituto de Cultura Puertorriqueña, 1969.

Caro, Aida R. *El cabildo o régimen municipal puertorriqueño en el siglo xviii.* 2 vols. San Juan: Municipio de San Juan e Instituto de Cultura Puertorriqueña, 1965–74.

Caro, Aida R. *Villa de San Germán: Sus derechos y privilegios durante los siglos xvi, xvii y xviii.* San Juan: Instituto de Cultura Puertorriqueña, 1963.

Damiani Cósimi, Julio. *Estratificación social, esclavos y naborías en el Puerto Rico minero del siglo XVI: La información de Francisco Manuel de Lando: Ensayo de cuantificación y transcripción paleográfica.* Cuadernos de Investigación Histórica, no. 1. Río Piedras: Centro de Investigaciones Historicas, 1994.

Gelpí Baíz, Elsa. *Siglo en Blanco: Estudio de la economía azucarera en el Puerto Rico del siglo XVI (1540–1612).* Río Piedras: Editorial de la Universidad de Puerto Rico, 2000.

López Cantos, Angel. *Historia de Puerto Rico (1650–1700).* Sevilla: Escuela de Estudios Hispanoamericanos de Sevilla, 1975.

Lluch Mora, Francisco. *La rebelión de San Germán.* Mayaguez: Editorial Isla, 1981.

Morales Carrión, Arturo. *Albores históricos del capitalismo en Puerto Rico.* Río Piedras: Editorial Universitaria, 1972.

Morales Carrión, Arturo. *Puerto Rico and the Non-Hispanic Caribbean: A Study in the Decline of Spanish Exclusivism.* 2nd ed. Río Piedras: Universidad de Puerto Rico, 1971.

Moscoso, Francisco. *Agricultura y sociedad en Puerto Rico, siglos 16 al 18: Un acercamiento desde la historia.* San Juan: Instituto de Cultura Puertorriqueña y Colegio de Agrónomos de Puerto Rico, 1999.

Moscoso, Francisco. *Lucha agraria en Puerto Rico 1541–1545: Un ensayo de historia.* San Juan: Ediciones Puerto; Instituto de Cultura Puertorriqueña, 1997.

Murga Sanz, Vicente. *Juan Ponce de León: Fundador y primer gobernador del pueblo puertorriqueño descubridor de la Florida y del Estrecho de las Bahamas.* Río Piedras: Editorial Universitaria, 1971.

Ortíz, Altagracia. *Eighteenth-Century Reforms in the Caribbean: Miguel de Muesas, Governor of Puerto Rico, 1769–1776.* Rutherford, N.J.: Farleigh Dickinson University Press, 1983.

Stark, David M. "Discovering the Invisible Puerto Rican Slave Family. Demographic Evidence from the Eighteenth Century." *Journal of Family History* 21, no. 4 (October 1996): 395–418.

Torres Ramírez, Bibiano. *La Compañía Gaditana de Negros.* Sevilla: Escuela de Estudios Hispano-Americanos de Sevilla, 1973.

Sued Badillo, Jalil. *El Dorado borincano: La economía de la Conquista 1510–1550.* San Juan: Ediciones Puerto, 2001.

Vilá Vilar, Enriqueta. *Historia de Puerto Rico (1600–1650).* Sevilla: Escuela de Estudios Hispano-Americanos de Sevilla, 1974.

Zapatero, Juan Manuel. *La guerra del Caribe en el siglo xviii.* San Juan: Instituto de Cultura Puertorriqueña, 1964.

4. The Nineteenth Century

Alvarez Curbelo, Silvia. *Un país del porvenir. El afán de modernidad en Puerto Rico (siglo xix).* San Juan: Ediciones Callejón, 2001.

Baralt, Guillermo. *Esclavos rebeldes: Conspiraciones y sublevaciones en Puerto Rico (1795–1873).* Río Piedras: Ediciones Huracán, 1982.

Bergad, Laird W. *Coffee and the Growth of Agrarian Capitalism in Nineteenth-Century Puerto Rico.* Princeton: Princeton University Press, 1983.

Camuñas, Ricardo. *Hacendados y comerciantes en Puerto Rico en torno a la década revolucionaria de 1860.* Mayaguez: Comisión Puertorriqueña para la Celebración del Descubrimiento de América y Puerto Rico, 1993.

Caro, Aida R. *Ramón Power y Giralt. Diputado puertorriqueño a las Cortes Generales y Extraordinarias de España 1810-1812 (Compilación de documentos).* San Juan: Instituto de Cultura Puertorriqueña, 1969.

Córdova, Pedro Tomás de. *Memorias geográficas, históricas, económicas y estadísticas de la isla de Puerto Rico.* 2nd facsimile edition. San Juan: Instituto de Cultura Puertorriqueña, 1968. 6 vols.

Cruz Monclova, Lidio. *Historia de Puerto Rico (siglo XIX).* 6th ed. Río Piedras: Editorial Universitaria, 1970. 3 vols.

Cubano Iguina, Astrid. "Legal Constructions of Gender and Violence Against Women in Puerto Rico under Spanish Rule, 1860–1895." Offprint from *Law and History Review* 22, no. 3 (Fall 2004): 531–64.

Dávila Cox, Emma A. *Este Inmenso Comercio: Las relaciones mercantiles entre Puerto Rico y Gran Bretaña 1844–1898.* San Juan: Universidad de Puerto Rico and Instituto de Cultura Puertorriqueña, 1996.

Delgado Pasapera, Germán. *Puerto Rico: Sus luchas emancipadoras (1850–1898)*. Río Piedras: Editorial Cultural, 1984.

Díaz Soler, Luis M. *Historia de la esclavitud negra en Puerto Rico*. 3rd ed. Río Piedras: Editorial Universitaria, 1970.

González Vales, Luis. *Alejandro Ramírez y su tiempo: Ensayos de historia económica e institucional*. Río Piedras: Editorial Universitaria, 1978.

Jiménez de Wagenheim, Olga. *El grito de Lares: sus causas y sus hombres*. Río Piedras: Ediciones Huracán, 1984.

Morales Carrión, Arturo. *Auge y decadencia de la trata negrera en Puerto Rico (1820–1860)*. San Juan: Centro de Estudios Avanzados de Puerto Rico y el Caribe e Instituto de Cultura Puertorriqueña, 1978.

Moreno Fraginals, Manuel, Frank Moya Pons, and Stanley I. Engerman. *Between Slavery and Free Labor: The Spanish-Speaking Caribbean in the Nineteenth Century*. Baltimore: Johns Hopkins University Press, 1985.

Ramos Mattei, Andrés, ed. *Azúcar y esclavitud*. Río Piedras: Oficina de Publicaciones de la Facultad de Humanidades, 1982.

Ramos Mattei, Andrés. *La hacienda azucarera: Su crecimiento y crisis en Puerto Rico (siglo xix)*. San Juan: CEREP, 1981.

Ramos Mattei, Andrés. *La sociedad del azúcar en Puerto Rico: 1870–1910*. Río Piedras: Universidad de Puerto Rico, 1988.

Rivero, Angel. *Crónica de la Guerra Hispanoamericana en Puerto Rico*. San Juan: Instituto de Cultura Puertorriqueña, 1972.

Rosario Natal, Carmelo. *Puerto Rico y la Crisis de la Guerra Hispanoamericana (1895–1898)*. Hato Rey, 1975.

Scarano, Francisco A. *Sugar and Slavery in Puerto Rico: The Plantation Economy of Ponce, 1800–1850*. Madison, Wis.: University of Wisconsin Press, 1984.

Schmidt-Nowara, Christopher. *Empire and Antislavery: Spain, Cuba and Puerto Rico, 1833–1874*. Pittsburgh: University of Pittsburgh Press, 1999.

Sonesson, Birgit. *La Real Hacienda en Puerto Rico: Administración, Política y Grupos de Presión, 1815–1868*. Madrid: Instituto de Estudios Fiscales, 1990.

5. The 20th Century

Baralt, Guillermo A. *Historia del Tribunal Federal en Puerto Rico, 1899–1999*. Hato Rey: Publicaciones Puertorriqueñas, 2004.

Barreto Velázquez, Norberto. *Rexford G. Tugwell: El último de los tutores*. Río Piedras: Ediciones Huracán, 2004.

Bird Carmona, Arturo. *A lima y machete: La huelga cañera de 1915 y la fundación del Partido Socialista*. Río Piedras: Ediciones Huracán, 2001.

Bothwell González, Reece B. *Puerto Rico: Cien Años de lucha política*. Río Piedras: Editorial Universitaria, 1979. 5 vols.

Clark, Victor S., et al. *Porto Rico and Its Problems*. Washington, D.C.: The

Brookings Institution, 1930.

Curet Cuevas, Eliezer. *Economía Política de Puerto Rico: 1950 a 2000.* San Juan, 2003.

García, Gervasio L., and Angel G. Quintero Rivera. *Desafío y solidaridad: Breve historia del movimiento obrero puertorriqueño.* Río Piedras: Ediciones Huracán, 1982.

Lewis, Gordon K. *Puerto Rico: Freedom and Power in the Caribbean.* New York: Harper and Row, 1963.

Llanes Ramos, Juan. *Desafiando al poder: Las invasiones de terrenos en Puerto Rico.* Río Piedras: Ediciones Huracán, 2001.

Mathews, Thomas L. *La política puertorriqueña y el Nuevo Trato.* Río Piedras: Editorial Universitaria, 1970.

Mintz, Sidney W. *Worker in the Cane: A Puerto Rican Life History.* New Haven: Yale University Press, 1960.

Moraza Ortíz, Manuel E. *La masacre de Ponce.* Hato Rey: Publicaciones Puertorriqueñas, 2001.

Pabón, Carlos. *Nación Postmortem: Ensayos sobre los tiempos de insoportable ambiguedad.* San Juan: Ediciones Callejón 2002.

Quintero Rivera, Angel G. *Patricios y plebeyos.* Río Piedras: Ediciones Huracán, 1988.

Quintero Rivera, Angel G. *Salsa, sabor y control!: Sociología de la música "tropical".* 2nd ed. Mexico City: Siglo XXI, 1999.

Silvestrini, Blanca. *Los trabajadores puertorriqueños y el Partido Socialista (1932-1940).* Río Piedras: Editorial Universitaria, 1979.

Silvestrini, Blanca. *Violencia y criminalidad en Puerto Rico 1898-1973: Apuntes para un estudio de historia social.* Río Piedras: Editorial Universitaria, 1980.

Steward, Julian H., and others. *The People of Puerto Rico; A Study in Social Anthropology.* 2nd printing. Urbana: University of Illinois Press, 1956.

Trías Monge, José. *Historia constitucional de Puerto Rico.* Río Piedras: Editorial Universitaria, 1980-83. 4 vols.

Vázquez Calzada, José L. *La población de Puerto Rico y su trayectoria histórica.* San Juan: Centro Multidisciplinario de Estudios Poblacionales, 1978.

Villaronga, Gabriel. *Toward a Discourse of Consent: Mass Mobilization and Colonial Politics in Puerto Rico, 1932-1948.* Westport, Conn.: Praeger, 2004.

CPSIA information can be obtained at www.ICGtesting.com
Printed in the USA
BVOW070420120112

280222BV00001B/3/P